1

A SHORT HISTORY OF SOCIALISM

A Short History of Socialism

George Lichtheim

LIBRARY
SOUTHERN SEMINARY

PRAEGER PUBLISHERS
New York • Washington

14186

BOOKS THAT MATTER

Published in the United States of America in 1970
by Praeger Publishers, Inc.,
111 Fourth Avenue, New York, N.Y. 10003

© 1970 by Praeger Publishers, Inc.

All rights reserved

Library of Congress Catalog Card Number: 69–15750

Printed in the United States of America

For Francis
and Ruth,
in token of friendship

Contents

Preface

The title of this work should not mislead anyone into supposing that I have aimed at a condensation of the immense literature on the history of socialism—an impossible task in any case. The purpose has been more modest: to set up a number of signposts for the benefit of readers who may wish at a later stage to inquire into the details of a particular period or set of problems. What is needed, I believe, is a certain amount of background for the study of those texts to which undergraduates are exposed by the normal operation of the academic treadmill. The brief reading list appended to this volume serves the same end: it purposely omits a number of standard works which would normally find their place in any proper bibliography, the aim being to stimulate interest, not to provide answers to every conceivable question.

If a guiding thought runs through this book, it is that the upheaval of the industrial revolution needs to be distinguished from the particular form it assumed, under historically unique and unrepeatable circumstances, in Western Europe and North America. A new mode of production, and a new way of life, came to birth in an environment already transformed by the rise of the market economy and the slow growth of bourgeois civilization. Elsewhere, industrialism made its impact upon societies which had not passed through this preparatory stage and consequently evoked a different response. This approach will, it is hoped, help to bridge the still considerable gap between the historical and the sociological perspectives. Both are necessary, as is some knowledge of the philosophical concepts underlying the new science of economics (itself a response to the phenomenon of a market-centered society). When what was originally called Political Economy is seen in relation to the ends it served, one realizes that conservatives, liberals, and socialists were not merely defending different interests; they were carrying on a debate over fundamentals. Conservative traditionalism, liberal individualism, and socialist collectivism stood—and stand—for different forms of social organization. They embody alternative ways of looking at the world. At the same time, they obviously reflect differing and conflicting material forces. But the term "reflection" is not to be understood as signifying something like a mirror image or the simple translation of economic interest into what is popularly styled "ideology." The individuals and groups in question discover their separate identities, and their conflicting interests, in the very act of seeking common ground.

The term "socialism" can be employed in a very general manner, denoting currents of thought hostile to the theory and practice of bourgeois individualism. In the strict or narrow sense, it is only relevant to ideas and movements compatible with the outlook of the new intelligentsia and the industrial working class. It therefore excludes agrarian romanticism, on the one hand, and fascist elitism on the other—the former because it repudiates the modern world, the latter because it rejects the principle that all men are equal and seeks the permanent rule of a privileged caste holding uncontrolled sway over a disenfranchised mass of industrial helots. In contrast, the cleavages separating communists from democratic socialists, and both from anarchists or anarchosyndicalists, occur within what may broadly be termed the socialist movement. The reason is that these parties or sects, however bitter and at times even murderous their internecine conflicts, share certain basic assumptions about the nature of man and society—assumptions traceable to the Enlightenment, which transformed the outlook of significant minorities in Western Europe and North America between the middle of the eighteenth and the middle of the nineteenth century. Socialism in this sense is not a party label, but the designation of a historically conditioned response to a particular challenge. Other reactions were and are possible. They do not come within the purview of this study.

So as not to burden the reader, I have dispensed with the usual apparatus and in particular have renounced the practice of backing every citation with a source reference, save where it has been found convenient to quote from a work included in the short reading list. In such cases the quotation is followed by a page reference to the book or author. Thus, to take an example, "(Baron, 358)" refers the reader to page 358 of S. Baron's work listed at the back of the book. This procedure is not ideal, but I cannot think of a better one, and at least it has the virtue of simplicity.

I must once more record my gratitude to Elisabeth Sifton for her editorial tact and fortitude, already unfairly tested by the antecedent task of seeing my *Origins of Socialism* (1969) through the press, and to Mrs. Esther Howell for her unflagging secretarial assistance.

G.L.

London
September, 1969

A SHORT HISTORY OF SOCIALISM

1 The Foundations

Histories of socialism traditionally begin with an account of collectivist doctrines from Plato to Thomas More which can be linked to movements in Western thought since the American and French revolutions. This approach has the advantage of establishing a perspective in which the ideas of modern thinkers can be measured and, if necessary, found wanting. There is some obvious justification for this procedure. Philosophy was born in Greece and almost from the start was concerned with the enduring problems of citizenship. When joined to the social ethics of the Old Testament centuries later, this kind of theorizing gave birth to what is conventionally known as Christian morality, until recent times accepted as the ethical code of Western society. It thus has seemed reasonable to look for the Hellenic or Judaic origins of socialist morality. If one did not wish to carry the investigation so far back, one might still contrast modern and medieval thought—a convention favored by writers in the Christian socialist tradition. There have been distinguished representatives of this school down to our own day, and with the global spread of socialist doctrines they have latterly found an echo among adherents of other religious faiths.

The drawback is that this procedure entails a certain cultural provincialism, and at the same time detracts from specific problems raised by the industrial revolution in its European birthplace. It is easy and tempting to rehearse the moral precepts of one's favorite philosophy or religion, thereby providing oneself with a distinguished ancestry. In a primitive community, religion is the principal source of social morality; hence religious faith can be invoked as the legitimation of demands for "justice"–meaning equal or at least equitable treatment. This has frequently been done, but it has always run into the same obstacle: conservatives no less than radicals can cite these religious precepts, for it is their peculiar nature to lay down principles so vague and general that all members of the community are able to accept them. Religion has thus traditionally served to sanctify the existing state of affairs, while furnishing a respectable form of protest for the oppressed by legitimizing their complaints against inequality and injustice. Philosophy, for its part, has commonly tended to transfigure the real world of servitude, conflict, and irreconcilable aims into an imaginary realm where all disputes are settled by reasonable debate among equals. The fact that such a state of affairs has rarely existed anywhere–at any rate in recorded history–is either ignored or blamed on the failure of those concerned to follow the sage advice they are offered. It is this cleavage between the real world of scarcity, inequality, and conflicting interests and the Eden of theology or of philosophic discourse that has prejudiced ordinary people against the kind of elevated talk they have come to expect from their betters.

Nonetheless, there is a sense in which socialism, like democracy (from which it stems), is rooted in sentiments as ancient and permanent as human society itself. To put the matter simply, men have always lived in communities and experienced the need to cooperate. Individualism is a comparatively recent faith, an outgrowth of a particular type of social organization. This is not contradicted by the functional division of labor, which has always existed, beginning with the most primitive of all–that between the sexes. In a traditional community, agrarian or urban, a division of functions is quite compatible with cooperation or association for common purposes. Indeed, the one cannot exist without the other. Adam Smith's calculating savage, with his inborn or acquired "propensity to truck, barter, and exchange one thing for another," never had any real existence, any more than did Robinson Crusoe on his island (providentially supplied with a colored helper who did much of the real work). These fantasies–worthy forerunners of Bentham's Economic Man and the philosophy of utilitarianism–were born in the heads of eighteenth-century writers who had recently discovered the charms of the market economy. The latter being propelled along by a self-regulating mechanism, they naively supposed that men had always lived in an environment that clearly distinguished economic relationships from family, social, tribal, and political ties. In reality, this had never been the case until an exchange economy arose. Even then, economic activity for most people remained subordinate to the social life within their villages or townships, until these small communities were disrupted. This transformation occurred not because an inborn "propensity" had at last found a suitable outlet in the exchange of saleable commodities, but because a social earthquake had drastically altered what for most people had until then been their customary way of life.

It is necessary to grasp that this revolution entailed a radical change in the prevailing mode of existence and the moral values that went with it. Economists are generally in the habit of treating the industrial revolution as a beneficial, albeit painful, short-cut to a better life for all. Even those among them who concede that the transition period was uncomfortable take it for granted that people really wanted what in the end they got: a functioning market economy which, in the literal sense, "delivered the goods." But this is nonsense. Most people in the areas where the original transformation occurred wanted nothing of the kind. Rather, they desired the continuation, and if possible the improvement, of their customary way of life–one based upon the economic independence of small farmers and urban craftsmen. These strata were virtually wiped out by the sudden introduction of the new technology and the emergence of a market economy. In strict logic, there was no inherent link between these two aspects of industrial capitalism, for after all machines might have been introduced into an economy where production was carried on for use rather than for profit. But it so happened that the industrial revolution was accompanied by a social one, and production of goods for use became production of commodities for a distant market. Moreover, once the logic of the new system had been grasped, it was generally seen to involve the subordination of all other considerations to a single overriding aim: that of keeping the wheels going at all cost, on pain of condemning the newly created urban proletariat to starvation and the remainder of society to volcanic eruptions from below.

The novelty of all this emerges most clearly when one asks what the term "economics" had come to signify in the early years of the nineteenth century. Traditionally, it had been identified with production for use and only incidentally with commodity exchange in a market. The ancient term *oikonomia* pertained to household management and was so employed by Aristotle in his *Politics*. Aristotle knew well that there was such a thing as production for gain, but he treated it as marginal. Similarly, the medieval schoolmen made do with a doctrine that subordinated exchange value (trade) to use value (householding). Everyone knew that markets existed for wares to be exchanged, and there was some debate over the proper fixing of the "just price" which a trader might legitimately demand for the commodity he brought to market; but it did not occur to anyone to suppose that production and exchange had any purpose other than the satisfaction of material wants. Markets had to be regulated by the public authorities to perform their proper role—as to this there was general agreement. Money was a necessary evil, and the taking of interest was generally regarded as immoral, though it might be unavoidable. Private property was legitimate, inasmuch as it was normally owned by small-scale producers working on a plot of land or manufacturing consumer goods with the help of a few assistants who might thereafter become independent craftsmen. On the whole one may say that the normative *principles* of the schoolmen were not significantly at variance with the causal *theories* they elaborated to explain how things actually worked. Of course, nothing was perfect, but the imperfections were themselves normal, representing departures from rules which everyone understood and approved (in principle, anyhow): production was for use, and trade existed for the purpose of facilitating the exchange of technical skills. Difficulties or conflicts were of a practical kind, and it was the duty of the authorities to settle them in a manner conducive to the public good.

Fundamentally, this was still Locke's standpoint in the *Two Treatises of Government*, published in 1690 with the avowed aim of justifying the Whig Revolution of 1688. John Locke (1632-1704) is among the ancestors of what socialists were later to call "bourgeois liberalism," and indeed he places a great deal of emphasis upon the civil power's duty to safeguard private property. But his basic approach is that of a philosopher with his roots in the Bible and in Aristotle. Property is personal ownership acquired by individual labor. Production is for use. To what property is a man entitled? To that which his labor has created. Some men possessed more than others, and Locke's doctrine made room for a primitive form of capital accumulation: a man's natural right was only to such property as his own labor created, but with the income he derived from it he might acquire "servants" who would toil for him. Locke knew that as a matter of fact the majority of people in the England of his day possessed very little property, or even none at all. This made it impossible for him to advocate political democracy (which would have been dangerous for the wealthy minority), but it did not shake his belief in the principles he had stated. Life, labor, property, and liberty were all interconnected. They were rooted in a state of nature in which men were free and equal. Had such a state of nature ever actually existed? "In the beginning all the world was America, and more so than it is now; for no such thing as money was anywhere known" (*Second Treatise*, Chap. V).

Before going further with this topic, we may note that Locke was both an absentee landlord and a stockholder in the slave-trading Royal Africa Company (Dunn, 211). We may also note that the chapter on "Slavery" in the *Second Treatise* attempts a discreet justification of involuntary servitude, by defining it as "the state of war continued between a lawful conqueror and a captive." The latter, "whenever he finds the hardship of his slavery outweigh the value of his life, 'tis in his power, by resisting the will of his master, to draw on himself the death he desires." This sounds cynical but was not so intended. It is just as well to remember that Locke had scriptural justification for his attitude. His morality was that of the age and the class to which he belonged. A century later the more enlightened members of that class felt uncomfortable with the notion that a human being might be the property of another, but in Locke's day this arrangement was still accepted by men who in other respects had come to value personal freedom. "Gross social inequality was compatible with equality of religious opportunity" (Dunn, 250), this last being what really mattered. In this sense Locke is a transitional figure–an early liberal who still had one leg planted in medieval soil.

It is characteristic of him that, without repudiating the Thomist doctrine of the "just price," he amended it so as to make the market the regulator of what "justice" signified in practice. At the same time, he conserved a residue of medieval morality by insisting that labor "puts the difference of value on everything . . . of the products of the earth useful to the life of man, nine-tenths are the effects of labour" (*Second Treatise*, para. 40). Yet it is obvious that the labor he had in mind was primarily that of the early entrepreneur. In other words, he drew no clear distinction between "labor" and "capital." If all this sounds muddled, the explanation is that Locke was not a very acute thinker, but in part his confusion stemmed from a circumstance that does him credit: he did not wish to dissociate economics altogether from morals. There were some conventional values that took precedence over profit-and-loss calculation, at any rate within the society to which he belonged. Wealth creation was important and beneficial, but the stability of the social order came first.

This attitude was still shared in all essentials by Adam Smith almost a century later, notwithstanding his far greater sophistication in economic matters. "Political economy" had meanwhile acquired the status of a specialized discipline, but it was still subordinated to broader social or moral considerations. Its "laws" might be strictly causal, but it was tacitly understood that the creation of wealth was merely one aspect of communal life, its purpose being to serve the material welfare of "the great body of the people." If this was an illusion, it was one to which Smith adhered as a moralist. Needless to say, he was aware that social equality (if it had ever existed) was no more. Chapter VIII of *The Wealth of Nations* opens with a reference to "that original state of things which precedes both the appropriation of land and the accumulation of stock" and where consequently "the whole produce of labor belongs to the laborer. He has neither landlord nor master to share with him." This primitive or idyllic state having passed away, wealth could be accumulated by those who did not perform physical toil. The laborer raised the crop and the landlord demanded a share of it. The manufacturer likewise made a deduction from the "produce of labor," for "the greater part of the workmen stand in need of a master to advance them the materials of their work, and their wages and maintenance till it be compleated. He shares in the produce of their labor, or in the value which it adds to the materials upon which it is bestowed; and in this share consists his profit." This clearly echoes Locke; equally clearly it is compatible with Rousseauist notions about equality. Whether it is useful as a tool of economic analysis need not concern us here. The relevant point is that, for Smith as for Locke before him and for Robert Owen after him, wealth creation was part of a social process to which Natural Law principles were applicable. The autonomy of "economics" was relative, not absolute. It described a particular kind of activity in which men engaged for purposes subordinate to the broader aims of the commonwealth.

Now this way of looking at the world did not simply fade out because it was unduly simple. It was overtaken by a cataclysmic change in the actual state of things: at first in England, later on the European Continent too, and ultimately in the world as a whole. Between 1760 and 1840, Britain was transformed by the industrial revolution, while social morality was simultaneously transformed by the impact of the new economics. The watershed lay somewhere around 1800, *after* Adam Smith had summed up the traditional wisdom of the eighteenth century. *The Wealth of Nations* was published in 1776—also the date of another fundamental document in the history of early liberalism: the Declaration of Independence. Smith and Jefferson represent the two poles of the Enlightenment, at any rate so far as the English-speaking world is concerned. On the eve of the industrial revolution, early liberalism was still identified with private property in the original sense of the term: that of the farmer, the craftsman, the small businessman. At this stage the distinction between "capital" and "labor" did not have the meaning it later possessed for the hordes of propertyless laborers cast adrift by the industrial revolution. Nor had the "laws" of the self-regulating market economy acquired the terrifying mechanical effectiveness they were to develop in the early nineteenth century. Lastly, there was not as yet that clear-cut distinction between social and economic aims which by 1840 had become a commonplace. Even the commercial and entrepreneurial middle class which propagated the new creed had only the dimmest notion of what its triumph portended.

In all these respects, the change brought about by the sudden impact of the new mode of production was revolutionary and had a traumatic effect upon millions of people whose accustomed mode of life was thereby transformed. At first, the cataclysm was limited to England, while Continental and American thinkers tended to believe their own societies might be able to escape the awful blight the British Isles had recently undergone. The onset of the industrial revolution had catastrophic results in Britain because it occurred before any counterforces had been mobilized and because it was superimposed upon an already successful capitalization of agriculture, which had gone further than elsewhere and had virtually eliminated the class of small peasant-proprietors. Resistance to industrialization was weak, and the ruling stratum was virtually unanimous in imposing the new way of life. Moreover, blind faith in the operation of a market economy was encouraged by an upsurge of technical innovation which promised to make everyone richer, though the immediate effect was to make millions poorer. The results have often been described:

> Before the process had advanced very far, the laboring people had been crowded together in new places of desolation, the so-called industrial towns of England; the country folk had been dehumanized into slum dwellers; the family was on the road to perdition; and large parts of the country were rapidly disappearing under the slack and scrap heaps vomited forth from the "satanic mills." Writers of all views and parties, conservatives and liberals, capitalists and socialists, invariably referred to social conditions under the Industrial Revolution as a veritable abyss of human degradation. (Polanyi, 39)

This social upheaval, however, was only half the story. The factory towns, the slums, the long working hours of men, women, and children, the fall in real wages, the disappearance of the independent artisan—the entire disaster of the early industrial revolution occurred in response to the operation of an economy which had escaped from social control and acquired a kind of automatism resembling that of a machine. No one had consciously willed these results. Everyone, or almost everyone, deplored them or at least affected to deplore them. Statesmen, clergymen, scholars, and philanthropists were at one in describing "pauperism" as the greatest of evils. It was, they said, a terrible misfortune. The government, it appeared, could do nothing. On the contrary, state interference would only make matters worse. It was the price that had to be paid for a new kind of rationality which did not trouble itself over moral or social considerations. The laws of economics must be allowed to take their course. Poverty should be relieved by public assistance (this notion was very narrowly defined after 1830, when the newly triumphant Whigs turned *laissez-faire* into the official creed of society), but the only real remedy lay in expanding production as fast as possible, so as to absorb the new urban proletariat and provide it with a steady income from regular wages. By 1850 this aim had actually been achieved, and thereafter wages even began to rise. Victory had been won at last. Industrialism had triumphed. Free trade had brought down the price of imported food. Even the famine of the 1840's, which littered Ireland with corpses and swept millions of survivors across the ocean to America, did not undermine the fanatical faith of that generation of *laissez-faire* liberals. If anything, it strengthened them in their conviction that "economic laws" were all-powerful and brooked no interference. Ireland had been overpopulated–the proof was that millions had died of starvation! At least one eminent economist, the worthy Nassau Senior, affirmed (in private, anyway) that the Irish famine had not done its job properly: it had killed only one million people (this was an underestimate), and that, he said, was not enough to put the country on its feet!

Now this way of looking at the world was quite novel. It had been pioneered by Robert Malthus (1766-1834), whose *Essay on the Principle of Population* (1798) introduced a new manner of reasoning about social phenomena such as poverty in terms of "laws" as unalterable as the laws of gravity. But Malthus still had the excuse of being a clergyman and, as such, a professional pessimist about life in this vale of tears. By the time Senior improved on his performance, another half-century had passed, the industrial revolution was in full swing, and over most of the British Isles it could be said to have triumphed. It was beginning to pay off–even to the extent of permitting a slight but perceptible improvement in the living standards of the working class. By the 1850's it was possible to take an optimistic view of progress, at any rate in England. By contrast, Ireland had the misfortune of being a colony and the added misfortune of depending on an inefficient agriculture. In both respects it resembled India, except that the Indian problem was on a larger scale. From the standpoint of the new liberal economics which had come into being alongside the self-regulating market economy, a catastrophe such as the Irish famine was a disaster due to circumstances over which the state had no control. It was certainly to be regretted, but there was no help for it. The most one could hope for was that in due course these wretched countries would learn to manage their affairs properly by getting rid of their surplus population and raising their levels of productivity.

This kind of reasoning was an extrapolation from a very special set of circumstances which had come together in Britain during the first half of the nineteenth century. But it also described the operation of a new kind of society that had never before existed in history but was now coming into being in all those industrialized countries which copied the British pattern. The principles of the new creed could be stated as follows: first, the "laws" of the market economy were analogous to physical laws, in that they were objectively valid, whatever anyone might think of the consequences; second, the operation of the economy ought not to be judged by success or failure in serving social or moral ends; third, it was nonetheless the case that the new mechanism, if not ignorantly interfered with, would automatically make everyone richer and therefore happier; and fourth, the self-interest of millions of private individuals was the best guarantee of the general welfare, since competition was bound to bring down costs of production and thus cheapen the price of goods. Consequently no public regulation was called for. On the contrary, the institutional distinction between state and society must be turned into an effective separation at all levels. Only if the state did not interfere–only if the private entrepreneur was left free to pursue his short-range economic goals–would the welfare of the nation be adequately safeguarded. Everyone was the best judge of his own interest, and in particular the owners of private wealth were the best judges of where and how to invest it. If they were left alone, they could not fail to better themselves, and in the long run everyone would profit.

Whether or not this system of beliefs ever made sense, it was firmly, indeed fanatically, defended by the theorists who worked out the basic doctrines of the faith around 1830. In saying this one must not, of course, overlook either their eighteenth-century Scottish predecessors or the founder of utilitarianism, Jeremy Bentham (1748-1832), who furnished the philosophical basis for what was then known as liberalism and what socialists later came to describe as "bourgeois ideology." It is perhaps worth stressing that this judgment did not comport a wholesale condemnation of eighteenth-century rationalism. Socialists and liberals alike occupied the ground recently cleared by the democratic revolution and its intellectual counterpart, the philosophy of the Enlightenment. Marxism too is an outgrowth of what its founder termed the "bourgeois revolution." What appealed to Marx was the heroic side of early individualism–the Promethean revolt against authority, divine or terrestrial, as reflected in the pre-romantic *Sturm und Drang* poetry of the youthful Goethe on the eve of the French Revolution. But the Enlightenment had another and more prosaic side to it, of which utilitarianism was the typical expression. Its spirit was reflected in Bentham's serene conviction that the principle of utility was as reliable as arithmetic, provided all nonarithmetical considerations were left out. As he put it in a letter to the Reverend John Forster in 1778, utility provided "an oracle which if properly consulted would afford the only true solution that could be given to every question of right and wrong." He himself never failed to consult the oracle: witness his ready acceptance of his father's suggestion that he try to find himself a rich wife; happiness being compounded of pleasure and pain and both being measurable, it was only sensible to apply the monetary yardstick to the object of one's affections. And thus one finds the youthful Bentham reporting dutifully to his father in these terms on his pursuit of the wealthy Miss Stratton:

> I like her much better now . . . provided always that the fortune be a large one: less than £30,000 in possession or expectancy it must not be. . . . She appears good-natured, affable and unaffected: and upon the whole her countenance, especially when she smiles, is far from being unpleasing. . . .

Apply the same calculus to society, and everyone would be better off. We are very far here from the Tory romanticism of Coleridge and Carlyle, or from its metaphysical German source in the pantheism of Goethe, Schelling, and Feuerbach. None of them had any use for Bentham's way of looking at the world, and one need only consult *Capital* to see what Marx thought of "that insipid, pedantic, leather-tongued oracle of the ordinary bourgeois intelligence. . . . Bentham is among philosophers what Martin Tupper is among poets. Both could only have been manufactured in England." (Not many years later the youthful Nietzsche gave vent to similar utterances.)

Trivial as this may appear, it is in fact central to the understanding of what it was that Tories and socialists alike found intolerable about the middle-class consciousness of the age. It was not simply that Bentham happened to be a philistine: that might have been forgiven him, in view of the undoubted good he and his followers did in many fields of legal and administrative reform–notably in clearing up the impenetrable jungle of English law and civilizing the atrocious penal code. And, in all fairness, Bentham had some sensible notions about education, e.g., that children learn best by actually seeing and touching some object. Unfortunately, what mattered most was the blight he cast upon the administration of the Poor Law, a set of regulations designed to confront the laborer with the grim choice between the factory and the workhouse. This legislation was promptly put into effect by the victorious liberals, whereas Bentham's speculative notions about full employment had to wait for another century, when his Fabian descendants at last obtained a share of power. In the long run, and when reinterpreted by socialists like Robert Owen, utilitarianism in practice did some good, even though it never made much sense as a philosophy. In the short term, it was just one more disaster inflicted upon the British working class.

It has often been noted that the new creed was assailed from two different directions. The early socialists between 1829 and 1834 turned themselves into spokesmen of a spontaneous working-class upsurge that led to the formation of the first effective trade-union movement in Britain. At the same time, a number of romantic conservatives–later described as "Tory Chartists" because they aimed at an alliance between the aristocracy and the workers–were likewise in revolt against the Benthamite legislation adopted by the reformed Parliament after 1832. The core of this legislation was the New Poor Law of 1834, which did away with the general category of "the poor." In its place it introduced a distinction between useless paupers, whose place was in the workhouse, and unemployed workers, temporarily excluded from the factory but normally dependent on it for their wages.

> While the pauper, for the sake of humanity, should be relieved, the unemployed, for the sake of industry, should *not* be relieved. That the unemployed worker was innocent of his fate did not matter. . . . The perversion of cruelty consisted precisely in emancipating the laborer for the avowed purpose of making the threat of destruction through hunger effective. This procedure makes intelligible that dismal feeling of desolation which speaks to us from the works of the classical economists. (Polanyi, 224)

What matters in our present context is the doctrine's logical coherence. It was both an economic and a social theory. It stated the ground rules of the new market economy and at the same time offered a rationalization for the changeover from an agrarian to an industrial order. Much of its success, indeed, rested upon the fact that it conflated these two quite different phenomena. For historical reasons, the introduction of the new industrial technology and the emergence of a market-centered society had occurred at roughly the same time. It was therefore asserted with considerable plausibility that they were *logically* connected. You could not, it was said, have one without the other. If people wanted the new industrial technology, they had to take the market mechanism as well. Industrialism only worked if the market was allowed to operate. Conversely, if the market economy was given the necessary freedom, it was bound in due course to sprout the new industrial technology which would make everyone richer. There were indeed some perverse people who asserted that one could have machinery without submitting to the self-regulating market, but they had no influence and were regarded as eccentrics. The laws of economics, as interpreted by the dominant liberal school, rested on the assumption that industrialism and individualism went together. "Individualism" was the creed of the private entrepreneur–the man who happened to have investment capital at his disposal. (How he had acquired it was nobody's business, and investigations into this topic were discouraged.)

Among present-day liberals, it has become the fashion to dismiss this whole system of ideas as primitive and outdated. And, indeed, since about 1930 the liberal creed has been remodeled so as to make room for intervention by public authorities to guarantee full employment and the maximization of welfare. It is therefore all the more necessary to emphasize that liberalism in its heroic age made no such concessions to human frailty. It insisted upon the full rigor of the new economic logic, and it did so with the backing of the utilitarian school headed by Bentham and James Mill. It was a doctrinaire system of thought–far more doctrinaire than socialism, which from the start embodied a strong "historical" element. Classical liberalism emphasized the absolute and universal truth of its dogmas, and it included among them a number of wholly arbitrary notions about what it was pleased to call "human nature," which in practice meant the nature of the representative British manufacturer. It asserted, among other allegedly unquestionable truths, that private individuals are anterior to society and that states are founded on contract; that human needs are measurable, as are the felicities available to consumers by purchasing material goods in the market; that good and evil are synonymous with pleasure and pain; that individuals are invariably animated by self-regard and that the pursuit of self-interest is the surest road to happiness; that human nature is unalterable and the same throughout all historical epochs; that the private enterpriser's activity is essential for the public good and that no other system is workable. These principles had already been suggested in a more general form by Thomas Hobbes in the seventeenth century, and by John Locke and David Hume in the eighteenth, before Bentham converted them into the doctrine of utilitarianism. They made up the philosophical substance of early liberalism and underlay the reasoning of the new economics.

By the time industrial capitalism burst upon the scene, the new outlook was already predominant among the entrepreneurial middle class which had gradually emerged from the Nonconformist Protestant sects left over from the abortive English Revolution of 1640-60. It was equally prevalent among the gentlemen farmers who spearheaded the independence movement in America, with the important difference that the availability of free soil there made it possible for large numbers of people to elude the full rigors of the market. This circumstance, and the introduction of representative democracy following the American Revolution, took the edge off the social protest and thus for a time effectively prevented the rise of a socialist movement on American soil. What anticapitalist sentiment there was in the United States after 1830 commonly took the form of agrarian populism. In Britain this option was precluded by the disappearance of the self-supporting farmer and by the rapid growth of an urban proletariat whose living standards until 1850 were either stationary or declining. Hence the socialist protest emerged in Britain (and, for different reasons, in France) earlier than it did elsewhere, and when it was formulated, it immediately focussed on the centerpiece of the new institutional arrangement—the transformation of labor into a commodity.

A self-regulating capitalist economy is one in which labor is bought and sold in the market. Now it is plain that under any conceivable social system, material production is dependent upon such factors as land, labor, machinery, and technical skill. But it is by no means self-evident that land and labor are commodities to be bought and sold with no regard to any considerations other than strictly economic ones.

Land and labor had indeed always been bought and sold, and in so far as the pre-industrial stage of European and American merchant capitalism embraced the "peculiar institution" of slavery, the principle even extended to unfree labor. But the affirmation that land and labor were simply commodities was something quite new. And it was patently absurd.

> Labor is only another name for a human activity which goes with life itself, which in its turn is not produced for sale, but for entirely different reasons, nor can that activity be detached from the rest of life, be stored or mobilized; land is only another name for nature, which is not produced by man. . . . Money, finally, is merely a token of purchasing power. . . . The commodity description of labor, land, and money is entirely fictitious. (Polanyi, 72)

The fiction, however, served its purpose in making the market economy operative. It supplied an organizing principle that took no account of noneconomic ends, and this principle was translated into legislation by the entrepreneurial class which from 1830 onward held effective political control in Western Europe. In the United States, as remarked before, the social consequences were blurred by the existence of free soil, which made it possible for millions of farmers to evade the logic of the system. In France and England its meaning was immediately and painfully evident–in a mild form to the landed aristocracy which lost power around 1830, in an infinitely more drastic manner to the urban proletariat. The landowners, after all, remained socially privileged even when they had lost control of the state. For the workers there was no escape; they were subjected to the full rigor of capitalism. In disposing of their labor power, the system also disposed of their physical and moral traits. On paper, "labor" and "capital" might rank as "factors of production" along with "land" and "machinery." In actual practice, labor–and hence the laborer–was controlled by the owners of capital.

The social system therefore entailed a plain disharmony between its ideology and the material circumstances. But it also came up against a more general objection. There was now a market in labor, just as there was a market in everything else. But labor was not an ordinary commodity; it was an attribute of life–life lived by millions of individuals whose ancestors had been independent farmers or artisans, but who now found themselves reduced to the role of two-legged commodities in a market controlled by a small number of people who owned the new means of production. Labor was supposedly free, and it was indeed legally free. The abolition of slavery was the last great triumph of democratic liberalism and the termination of its heroic age. It provided a fitting climax for the era of revolution that had opened almost a century earlier. It also gave the adherents of liberal democracy a justifiable cause to feel proud: in the United States, they had followed out the logic of their creed even to the ultimate test of civil war. But the abolition of slavery likewise signalized the depth of the gulf separating the most radical of liberals from the most moderate of socialists. All liberals without exception held that private ownership in the means of production was justified and would ultimately be beneficial, while socialists maintained that any system which treated labor as a commodity was inherently absurd and immoral. Under capitalism, they argued, the function of work was subordinated to the automatism of a process whereby capital reproduced itself and, in so doing, reproduced the servile condition of the real producer. So far from being recognized as the most basic of human activities and the true foundation of the new industrial order, labor had become synonymous with a condition into which free men were forced when they were employed by others. The emancipation of labor thus demanded the abolition of capitalism—the latter term signifying the appropriation of salaried labor by owners of capital.

This was to become the fundamental aim of the emerging socialist movement, and in Britain anyway this movement took shape against the background of the bleak factory towns described by Engels in his *Condition of the Working Class* (1845). The British proletariat of those days, had it been lettered, might with justice have cited the words St. Joan addressed to her captors:

> Then lead me hence; with whom I leave my curse:
> May never glorious sun reflex his beams
> Upon the country where you make abode;
> But darkness and the gloomy shade of death
> Environ you, till mischief and despair
> Drive you to break your necks or hang yourselves!

(Shakespeare, *King Henry VI*, Part One, Act V, scene 4)

2 Man and Society

What has been said so far relates in the main to the industrial revolution and to the basic innovation at the core of the new economic system: a free market in labor. But the same period also witnessed a series of democratic uprisings against absolutist regimes, the political emancipation of what was vaguely known as the "third estate," and a number of minor convulsions stemming from the American and French revolutions. It did not escape the more acute thinkers that in a certain fundamental sense these phenomena were somehow connected, and in the 1840's the various analytical and critical strands were pulled together by the early socialists in a more or less coherent doctrine. There is no harm in bearing Marx's theoretical construct in mind—we shall examine it more closely later on—but one must not suppose that it was generally accepted around 1848. If one inquires what radical democrats and utopian socialists actually thought they were doing at this time, one had better consider the legacy of an earlier thinker, namely Rousseau. The theory, and to some extent the practice, of the French Revolution in its Jacobin phase was Rousseauist, and Jacobinism for almost a century became the model of radical democratic movements in Continental Europe and Latin America. (It is arguable that Rousseau's thinking was never very relevant to the Anglo-American world, but we are concerned with the roots of *European* socialism, and Rousseau's importance cannot be overlooked in this context.)

We have seen that between 1750 and 1850 the industrial revolution was virtually confined to one country, Britain. During the same period, the democratic movement in Europe was almost coterminous with the history of Britain's chief rival, France. This is not to say that other nations were not affected by it, but the original breakthrough occurred in France alone. In Rousseau we thus confront the theorist of a democratic movement which was to overstep its own limitations. At the peak of the revolutionary transformation in France, the Republic was governed by men who regarded themselves (and were regarded by others) as followers of Rousseau, and when their power had waned, their spiritual heirs became the organizers of an egalitarian conspiracy which merged with the earliest beginnings of a primitive communist movement. Communism, no less than socialism, was born in France, and it came to life under circumstances in which plebeian leaders felt obliged to ask why the Revolution had failed to establish social equality. This alone is sufficient to justify some interest in the thinker who blazed the trail for the first European experiment in radical democracy.

Jean-Jacques Rousseau (1712-78) is commonly described as the originator of the romantic movement, as the inventor of a new style in autobiography, and as the inspirer of Robespierre. What matters for our theme is that he developed a theory of democracy which was not liberal and individualist in the Lockean sense. This is not to say that he urged the abolition of private property: he did nothing of the kind, although on occasion, like other writers of his time, he toyed with the notion of common ownership. What he did was to enable his followers to think of themselves as democrats without having to accept the set of values held by rival theorists who figure in intellectual history as the ancestors of liberalism. In France these writers included Montesquieu, Voltaire, and most of the learned contributors to the joint enterprise known as the *Encyclopédie,* of which Denis Diderot (1713-84) was the prime mover. Although associated with this multi-volumed Bible of the Enlightenment, Rousseau inaugurated a line of thought which in later years enabled the early socialists to differentiate themselves from the liberals. He was not himself a socialist–nor could he be one, socialism being a reaction to an industrial capitalism which had not yet emerged in Rousseau's lifetime. But his theory of society served as a bridge across which radical democrats were able to move into new and unexplored territory. These pioneers included François-Noël Babeuf, who was guillotined by Robespierre's successors and who may be said to have inaugurated the tradition of primitive egalitarian communism in France and Europe. Our problem is to define what made Rousseau important for later generations of men who shared neither his personal eccentricities nor the illusions of his immediate followers.

The precise relationship of democracy to socialism will be considered later. For the moment let us simply note that in the nineteenth century it was possible for a democrat to be either a liberal or a socialist, depending on whether or not he accepted the institution of private property in the means of production, the establishment of a self-regulating market economy, and the transformation of labor into a commodity. Liberals approved these principles; conservatives were critical of them, but could only advocate a return to a pre-industrial and pre-capitalist age; socialists accepted the industrial revolution, but not the unrestrained rule of capital or the introduction of a self-regulating market economy. Rousseau's political thought antedated these divisions and was thus irrelevant to the specific problems of industrial society. Among the French socialists of the following age, only Proudhon can in any serious sense be called a Rousseauist, and this circumstance was no help to him in understanding the modern world. On the other hand, it gave him a firm hold upon the affections of those among his countrymen who shared his dislike of urban civilization. It also supplied him with a ready-made set of moral principles, for Rousseau had been something of a philosopher, though of an unsystematic kind.

Rousseau's social philosophy, albeit attuned to the circumstances of a pre-industrial age, on some points anticipates the subsequent socialist critique of bourgeois society, for the simple but sufficient reason that he took democracy seriously. The liberals–Montesquieu and Voltaire above all–had followed Locke in extolling the Whig Revolution of 1688, which instituted parliamentary government and made freedom a reality for the aristocracy and for intellectuals like themselves. For what Voltaire called "the rabble"–that is to say, the mass of ordinary people–freedom became a reality, or at any rate a concrete aim, only with the French Revolution a century later. Because Rousseau was a democrat, he stated the political question in a manner offensive to the liberals of his age, who were anything but democrats, and it is for this reason that we can consider him a precursor of utopian socialism.

The difficulty with Rousseau as a thinker is that he put forward a doctrine of social morality in the form of a highly personal, and quite unscientific, philosophy of history. In the *Discourse on the Origin of Inequality* (1755), and in some of his later writings, he presented an imaginative reconstruction of human history, the purpose of which was to explain in nontheological terms what Christianity described as the Fall of Man. According to the Stoic philosophers of antiquity, there had once been a golden age without property, slavery, and war. This belief went well with the account of Eden in Genesis, in which the human condition was ascribed to a prehistoric catastrophe due to the inscrutable workings of Providence. Rousseau accepted the notion of a Fall, but not its theological explanation. Christianity had tended to regard human nature as ineradicably evil. Rousseau believed it was fundamentally good. But if this was so, why was the history of mankind such a wretched affair? For pessimists like Machiavelli and Hobbes this had been no problem: human nature (as they saw it) could only manifest itself in perpetual warfare, and this was as true in the original "state of nature" as in all civilized arrangements. But for Rousseau the "state of nature" was not what it had been for Hobbes; rather, it signified an age of primitive harmony and contentment, antedating property, inequality, and crime. It was pre-social in the sense that men had no need for legal institutions, but this did not rule out interpersonal relations founded on mutual sympathy and cooperation. In principle at least, it was conceivable that society might once more be so arranged as to recover at least a modicum of reasonableness. The criterion of such an arrangement was nature itself. "The simple, central, powerful concept in Rousseau is that of a human nature which is overlaid and distorted by existing political and social institutions, but whose authentic wants and needs provide us with a basis for morals and a measure of the corruption of social institutions" (MacIntyre, 183-84).

Clearly this was not a scientific analysis of what had actually happened in history, but then Rousseau did not think it was. His purpose was to contrast the currently prevailing state of affairs with what he supposed primitive life might have been like. In the same spirit, Proudhon a century later asserted that "Property is Theft." Neither Rousseau nor Proudhon intended to make a factual statement. Each thought he knew what sort of existence ordinary men would want to live if they were free to follow their natural bent, and each also thought that society had departed from a primitive equilibrium that satisfied men's basic needs. Rousseau held that political institutions owed their existence to a social contract, and that the public good was best served by consulting the general will (as distinct from the sum of individual wills). These were not meant to be descriptions of empirical reality, for neither the social contract nor the general will could ever be encountered in ordinary experience. To Rousseau these concepts suggested how history *might* actually have worked or be made to work in future. To invoke the general will was to assert that all citizens of the community were at bottom united in recognizing the existence of a common good. Because such a recognition was possible, democracy was possible. The social order might be corrupt–Rousseau thought it was–but under favorable circumstances it could be put right by appealing to the community's uncorrupted sense of what it *really* wanted and needed. This was a possible theory of democracy, though there were others. The important thing is that it provided a starting point for men of a later age who believed that the common good demanded the abolition of private property.

Let us pause here for a moment and consider the relevance of Natural Law to the notion of a social contract. The two doctrines do not appear to be very closely correlated, and indeed Natural Law is a good deal older than contractual theorizing. Historically, it goes back to the Stoics, who were the first thinkers to derive principles of human sociability from what they supposed to be the order of nature. This was a departure from the Aristotelian concept of citizenship, which defined human rights and duties solely in the context of the state–concretely, the Greek *polis*. For Aristotle, there was no conflict between the authority of the *polis* and the individual rights of its citizens; neither did he recognize a distinction between state and society. On his assumption, men had rights and obligations only in so far as they were citizens of the *polis*. Stoicism introduced the notion of a pre-social age and thus laid the foundation for what in medieval and post-medieval European philosophy became the doctrine of Natural Law. This doctrine necessarily begins by asserting the existence of a state of nature and then deduces the character of civil society from *man's* nature. Natural Law thus assumes the presence of isolated individuals prior to the emergence of a social order. It is compatible with a contractual theory of how civil society and the state have come into being, but it also permits the conclusion that laws and the state have been instituted by coercion, or by the will of the deity. Natural Law does not necessarily lead to a doctrine of the social contract type, but the latter, if it is to make any sense at all, must be grounded in Natural Law. "Every social contract reduces the will of the state to the wills of the individuals and must thus have a definite view of man's character prior to the conclusion of the social contract" (Neumann, 76).

Natural Law philosophy and contractual theorizing thus come into contact if and when it is assumed that the state has arisen from the free consent of the citizens composing it. This assumption is required for any thinker who believes that the order of society has been created by a deliberate act of will guided by reason. It does not by any means follow from the thesis that there are moral rules of conduct appropriate to an unchanging human nature. Nonetheless, social contract theorists have commonly tended to derive their specific political arguments from general statements about the nature of man. If the philosopher happens to take an optimistic view of human nature, he may (but need not) find reasons for supposing that men might have continued indefinitely in an uncorrupted pre-social existence, had they not been expelled from it by some historic misfortune. This conclusion, however, does not impose itself with logical necessity. In eighteenth-century theorizing prior to the revolution introduced by Rousseau, pre-social forms of existence were commonly identified with barbarism, whereas the emergence from this stage was celebrated as the blossoming of civilization. This was the liberal variant of the Enlightenment, but in the second half of the century there emerged an egalitarian current, prominently represented by Rousseau and his contemporary Mably (1709-85). If one started from egalitarian ideals, civilization ceased to be an unmixed blessing, primitive people were credited with hitherto unsuspected virtues, and in particular it was asserted that they were happier than the civilized because social inequality and the resulting injustice had not yet corrupted their way of life. On these assumptions, what was natural was equated with what was primitive and, therefore, just and uncorrupted by civilized artifice. If the natural is most clearly seen under primitive conditions, it follows that civilization–any civilization–is likely to be tainted with injustice, for the simple reason that it is no longer natural.

That, more or less, is what Rousseau asserted, and down to our own age there have been great figures in literature—Tolstoy is the most famous—who have made this belief the centerpiece of their social teaching.

At first sight Natural Law in the sense of moral rules of conduct seems quite unrelated to the vision of a primitive social life antedating civilized society and its corruptions. There may in fact be no logical connection, but there is certainly a historical one. Let us see how it arose and why it has remained influential down to our own day. The crucial idea is that of equality. In Western culture, this had both classical and religious roots. The Stoic doctrine that all men are created equal is not to be found in the Bible—Jewish and Christian affirmations to the contrary notwithstanding. It is a purely philosophical notion, and even within the Greek tradition it was opposed to the teaching of Aristotle (not to mention Plato, whose elitist utopia is the ultimate source of all authoritarian theorizing). What the ancient Hebrews and the primitive Christian community—which of course was largely Jewish in membership—contributed was something else: a fervent belief in social justice and the vision of a coming age when injustice would vanish or be rooted out. For practical purposes, the concept of equal justice signified mainly that everyone had a right to live in the station to which Providence had called him. This was not much, but when one considers that economic liberalism took no account whatever of non-marketable human needs and wants, it was something. At the very least, it suggested that allowing people to starve was immoral.

These traditions—considerably watered down in medieval Christianity and even more so in the Calvinist variant of Protestantism, which sanctioned almost any degree of social inequality—survived in a form that made it possible for eighteenth-century writers like Rousseau and Mably to preach a doctrine bordering on communism. I say "bordering," because Rousseau did not in fact dispute the practical necessity of private ownership: he merely asserted that it had not existed in the golden age. There is a well-known passage in his writings to the effect that the first man who enclosed a plot of land with a fence thereby became the author of all the evils plaguing mankind. This sort of thinking lends the weight of a moral judgment to any proposition which affirms that social inequality is "unnatural," in the sense that there once existed a "natural" order when men were equal because they held their goods in common. An assertion of this kind could always be put forward by people in revolt against what they regarded as injustice. It was in fact constantly invoked during the Middle Ages by rebellious peasants and artisans, and thus furnished an undercurrent of egalitarian sentiment long before the modern democratic movement came on the scene.

There are two points to be made about this kind of thinking. In the first place, it is irrelevant to what degree it is mythical or to what extent it is grounded in actual recollection of an archaic state of affairs before the dawn of what Marxists call "class society" and liberals prefer to describe as "civilization." Very likely the Stoics were mistaken when they postulated the historical existence of a primitive golden age, but the legend expressed an acute awareness of the actual change that had come over Greek society with the passing of the ancient tribal order, where every man knew his place and his duties. (This was also substantially the Old Testament view of the matter.) Secondly, belief in a universal order to which man is "naturally" subject carries normative implications. If the universe is harmonious and governed by immutable law, it follows that the terrestrial order ought to exhibit the same features. If it fails to do so, there must have been a falling away from an earlier state of perfection. In this sense "natural" signifies both "right" and "ancient." This reasoning inevitably raises the question whether the social order is in tune with the divine, or universal, order. Conservatives will generally assert that by and large it is; radicals, that it is not.

This kind of theorizing about the origins of society, and the ethical norms proper to it, is not peculiar to any one civilization. It was to be found in ancient Egypt as well as in ancient Greece, and it accounts for the fact that a number of non-Western contemporary movements such as Chinese Communism tend to be expressed in a moralistic rhetoric concerning the overriding importance of social harmony. Indeed, one may say that in Chinese theorizing, whether Confucian or Communist, the notion of a common interest is taken for granted. Some of the mental confusion apparent in recent Chinese history has been due to a failure to perceive that this notion is not so simple or unambiguous as it seems at first sight. The idea of a common interest was of course also taken for granted by Plato and Aristotle, but they identified it with the existing structure of the Greek city-state. And it was certainly taken for granted by Rousseau and his followers.

But what was the immediate political relevance of these rather abstract speculations? Why should men like Robespierre, who after all had to govern under extremely difficult circumstances, have based themselves on Rousseau's theory of democracy? The answer is that, in a society still overwhelmingly composed of peasants and craftsmen, his doctrine up to a point made sense. In so far as most citizens still had certain basic interests in common, it was not wholly absurd to postulate a political order responsive to their will. France had not yet undergone the industrial development which across the Channel was creating an entirely different kind of society. In Britain, where the small farmer had been swept away and the artisan was being transformed into a wage laborer, democracy signified the rule of the propertyless majority and hence terrified the new entrepreneurial middle class, which had staked its all on the success of the industrial revolution. In France, "bourgeois democracy" was still possible because the bourgeoisie had the mass of the peasantry on its side and could, if necessary, play it off against the nascent proletariat. This, in brief, is the reason why there was a democratic revolution in France but not in Britain.

To sum up: the Jacobin experiment was possible because Frenchmen of that age were briefly persuaded that the common interest of the body politic could be identified by consulting the general will of the whole body of citizens. Bourgeois society having emancipated itself from the state, it then turned out that it was not in fact possible to impose an egalitarian order by legislative fiat. In this sense it may be argued that Rousseau's notions about the social contract and the general will had their share in promoting the catastrophe of the Jacobin regime. The reign of terror resulting from the vain attempt to make everyone conform to the moral notions entertained by Robespierre and his colleagues has sometimes been described by conservative writers as an essay in "totalitarian democracy." The term is not very happily chosen, since totalitarianism presupposes a degree of state control over civil society which in the eighteenth century was simply not practicable. It also ignores the fact that a temporary dictatorship of the "consular" or Roman type is quite compatible with republican democracy. Like so much else instituted by the Jacobins during their brief reign of less than two years (1793-95), it was in fact a Roman invention. What destroyed the first French Republic was not "totalitarianism" but the military rule of Napoleon, following a confused period between 1795 and 1799 when the successors of the Jacobins lost their popular following: principally because they failed to institute a minimum of social equality while giving free reign to the appetites of a flourishing caste of profiteers. What followed is best described as an orgy of individualism, which found its expression at the ideological level once Napoleon had left the scene. From 1815 on, and increasingly after the July revolution of 1830 which placed the liberals in power, the French middle class was converted to doctrines imported from England. These doctrines assumed not merely the new industrial technology, but capitalism—the rule of the private entrepreneur and the transformation of the artisan into a salaried worker. Once the logic of this arrangement was grasped, it became evident that democracy in the Jacobin sense was no longer possible. There had come into being a new sort of class conflict: no longer between "the rich" and "the poor" but between those who controlled the new industrial wealth and those who worked for wages. The *aim* of the industrial system—maximal development of all the productive forces of society—was accepted by liberals and socialists alike, although the former approved of capitalism and the latter did not. But unlimited wealth creation was irrelevant from the traditional democratic standpoint and, indeed, subversive of equality. Democracy therefore could no longer be Rousseauist. Yet the gospel of equality was retained—by the communists.

Once this is grasped, one can see more clearly why France, and not Britain, was the birthplace of communism, just as a generation earlier it had been the testing ground of Jacobinism. The term "communism" here signifies a revolutionary creed that specifically aims at the overthrow of "bourgeois" institutions and the transfer of political power to the industrial proletariat. The ancestors of this faith are François-Noël Babeuf (1760-97) and Filippo Buonarroti (1761-1837), men who had emerged from the extreme wing of the democratic movement at the peak of the French Revolution. Its theoretical formulation is linked with the name of Étienne Cabet (1788-1856), who can also be classed among the utopians, while its first effective political organization occurred in the *Société des Saisons*, founded by Louis-Auguste Blanqui (1805-81). This early communism was a purely French phenomenon, having no counterpart elsewhere, although after 1830 "communist" doctrines began to spread among German and other working men domiciled in Paris.

A distinction needs to be drawn between "communism" as a particular revolutionary movement stemming from French experience in the 1790's and "socialism" as a general critique of the new economic order. What distinguished "communism" from "socialism" at this stage was its proletarian character and its radical egalitarianism, both inherited from the Babouvist tradition, which also comported another French trait: the emphasis on the need for a revolutionary dictatorship during the transition period. When the term "socialism" came into general use in France and England around 1830, it was evident that what was intended was an indictment of liberalism, specifically as an economic doctrine. In this sense the "communists" too were socialists. But the obverse was not necessarily true, for not all socialists accepted the principle of radical equality, which at this stage entailed a demand for the levelling of civilized institutions and a return to an egalitarian (and therefore natural) state. The early socialists, by and large, accepted civilization in general and the industrial revolution in particular. What they rejected was the particular historical form it had taken: capitalism and the liberal-individualist creed that went with it. Later socialists might agree that the industrial revolution *could not* have taken any other form, coming as it did and when it did, since in early nineteenth-century Britain, the class of private entrepreneurs was the only significant group which had a vital interest in sponsoring the new technology. But this philosophical acceptance of past horrors was too sophisticated for the first generation of socialist intellectuals, and it certainly made no sense to communist proletarians. *Their* immediate reaction, when confronted with the appalling spectacle of the new industrial capitalism, was either to denounce it as immoral or to aim at its violent overthrow. When the latter proved impossible, the next step consisted in discriminating between the technical progress inherent in the new mode of production, and the system of economic exploitation and privilege associated with it. This distinction made it possible for men like Robert Owen in England and Henri de Saint-Simon in France to demand that the new technology be subordinated to the general interest of society.

But all this took time, and meanwhile democratic writers brought up on the philosophy of the Enlightenment had to introduce some logical order into the connection between Natural Law and the Rights of Man, as proclaimed by the American and French revolutions. These rights had been asserted for the benefit of a generation which believed profoundly that every citizen was entitled to the produce of his own labor. Even Adam Smith, as we have seen, paid lip-service to this doctrine, although he was careful to specify that it was enforceable only in an "early and rude state of society." This was just the trouble with Natural Law: for those who took it seriously the golden age lay in the past. The best that could be hoped for, if access to private property was thought desirable, was the kind of arrangement to which Rousseau and his followers had given their consent: a society of independent citizens. Ideally these would be peasant farmers and artisans living in rural communities or in small, easily governable countries. This particular vision of democracy was respectable enough, whether its spokesmen drew their inspiration from the Bible or from the Greco-Roman classics. There was only one thing wrong with it: the industrial revolution had rendered it illusory.

This is not to deny that the appeal to moral principles was immensely effective. For thinking people in Europe and America, the Rights of Man plainly included the laborer's natural right to the produce of his labor. Moreover, in religious tradition–which the churches and lawgivers in a nominally Christian community could not formally repudiate even when it had become inconvenient–moral principle was considered the only legitimate source for general rules about particular rights and duties. This was as true in Britain as in France and the United States, where the framers of the revolutionary constitutions had specifically claimed to be drawing on the command of reason, *rationis ordinatio* in the traditional scholastic meaning of the term. Socialist critics of the new economic order could thus take their stand on principles they held in common with conservatives who retained their allegiance to Natural Law. This common ground explains why the professional economists increasingly fought shy of traditional moral philosophy, and why consistent individualists like Bentham wanted no part of Natural Law. For Bentham any doctrine of natural rights was "nonsense on stilts." He was content to base his own morality on "the greatest happiness of the greatest number," at a time when the "greatest number" were carrying the burden of the new social policy devised by Bentham's friends. Considered as a philosophy, utilitarianism was shallow and its practical consequences were horrendous, but it served its purpose: those who adopted it preserved a good conscience while they traversed the Iron Age of early industrial capitalism. They even converted a substantial section of the British working class to their creed, an achievement much envied by contemporary liberals in France, where the industrial revolution encountered a less friendly ideological climate.

Yet we shall see that socialism emerged simultaneously in Britain among an elite of craftsmen who had preserved their ancient skills, or acquired new ones, throughout the turmoil of the technological upheaval briefly described in our first chapter. This circumstance needs to be emphasized as a corrective to the notion that socialism, unlike communism, was a philanthropic affair sprung from the minds of middle-class reformers. Socialist and communist theoreticians alike stemmed from the middle class and had a following among the workers. What distinguished them was their outlook rather than their upbringing. Nor is it possible to define socialism as a movement of the intelligentsia; for while it is true that every intellectual carries his capital in his head and may therefore be described as a mental laborer, those writers who gave birth to the early socialist creed did not, with rare exceptions, see themselves as spokesmen of a stratum destined to manage the new industrial technology. Such notions were never entirely absent, but they were not typical of the early socialists, nor was communism as a faith confined to authentic members of the proletariat. What divided these nascent sects were political issues stemming from the French Revolution.

3 *Capital and Labor*

A simplified account of the birth of socialism might begin with the statement that the industrial revolution furnished the thesis and the French Revolution the antithesis, while socialism brought about a synthesis of these two parallel but unconnected phenomena. Setting aside the fact that this kind of logic is always fallacious, there is another good reason for not indulging in it: it would be factually wrong. The two currents were not independent of each other. Indeed they intermingled because they had a common source: the general transformation of West European society by what Marx was to describe as the "bourgeois revolution." This process had been going on since the sixteenth century, and in England at least it had already gone very far *before* the sudden upsurge of the new industrial technology in the 1760's. Britain could not have become the laboratory of the new industrialism if it had not already possessed an older, and very successful, agrarian and merchant capitalism. Inversely, the Revolution in France cleared the ground by turning political power over to the bourgeoisie. In one respect the short-term effect of the Revolution was indeed unfavorable to capitalism: it entrenched peasant proprietorship, thereby rendering more difficult the modernization of agriculture which in England had preceded the investment of capital in mining, industry, and transport.

But in other spheres, the Revolution facilitated the accumulation of capital by sweeping away a mass of restrictive customs and writing economic liberalism into the constitution (or rather, into the several constitutions rapidly enacted after 1789). At the same time, it dramatized the issue of social conflict, thereby encouraging a surge of feeling which evolved into utopian socialism.

The decisive economic breakthough, as we have seen, occurred in Britain and was then exported: first to Belgium, then to France, Germany, Austria, and other European countries. The problem for the historian of socialism is this: industrial capitalism was born in Britain, but the socialist protest against it found its most coherent intellectual expression in France, a country that was slow to absorb the impact of the new mode of production. And the doctrine which pulled all these strands together namely Marxism—was worked out in the 1840's by a theorist who obtained his philosophical training in his native Germany, his political education in France and Belgium, and his understanding of economics in England. For the moment we are obliged to neglect these complications. Let us then focus upon the epicenter of the great technological earthquake: early nineteenth-century Britain.

Here we encounter another paradox. Britain was economically far ahead of its rivals and, by 1850, had transformed itself into what was then proudly called "the workshop of the world." For some decades, indeed, it was the only country in the world which had fully absorbed *both* the new industrial technology *and* the intellectual innovations that went with it. At the same time, the country remained in some ways remarkably old-fashioned by comparison with the Continent (not to mention the United States, then the only important nation to be governed more or less democratically). Not only did the monarchy and the Whig Constitution of 1689 remain in force: public life—even after the partially successful Benthamite overhaul of the 1820's and 1830's—continued to present a curiously archaic picture. The economy was being transformed, but the social and political structures retained many features belonging to an earlier age. Modernization in these spheres proceeded in a rather shaky fashion, even after the Tories had been driven from office in 1830 and the urban middle class admitted to the parliamentary franchise by the Reform Bill of 1832. The prevailing atmosphere is well illustrated by the grotesque incident which in 1834 resulted in the Houses of Parliament being burned down, not by a rioting mob, but by Treasury officials trying to get rid of office waste. Ever since the original Exchequer accounts were begun by William the Conqueror, they had been kept on wooden tally sticks in which notches were cut when a tax had been paid. This system survived for seven hundred years, until about 1780, when it occurred to an unusually enterprising official that one could keep written accounts instead. The tally sticks were, however, not disposed of until the 1830's, when the death of the then Head of the Treasury gave the bolder reformers their opportunity. Unfortunately they decided to burn the accumulated mass of rubbish in the Palace yard of Westminster, with the result that the House of Lords caught fire and the entire Parliament building was burned to the ground. It was London's biggest conflagration since the Great Fire of 1666, and the Guards had to be called out to control the populace. Far from being untypical, this kind of casual disaster was quite characteristic of an age also distinguished by a mania for railway building, a mass of factory legislation, and the novels of Charles Dickens. It was just this bizarre intermingling of the old and the new, the survival of ancient institutions in the midst of a volcanic technological upheaval, that struck contemporaries as peculiarly British.

There is some justification for saying that the beginnings of socialism in England were marked by a similar quality. They had their emotional and intellectual background in a conservative reaction against the disruption of established ways of life. And when this Tory romanticism had passed away, the new socialism at first presented itself in the guise of a defensive movement to safeguard the existence of the independent artisan. In the words of a well-known economic historian:

> In a very real sense the bulk of British workers had adjusted itself to a changing, industrializing, though not yet revolutionized society. . . . An important group had even accepted, indeed welcomed, industry, science and progress (though not capitalism). These were the "artisans" or "mechanics," the men of skill, expertise, independence, and education, who saw no great distinction between themselves and those of similar social standing who chose to become entrepreneurs. . . . The "artisans" were the natural leaders of ideology and organization among the labouring poor, the pioneers of Radicalism (and later the early, Owenite, versions of Socialism), of discussion and popular higher education . . . the nucleus of trade

> unions, Jacobin, Chartist, or any other progressive movements. . . . Hostile to capitalism, they were unique in elaborating ideologies which did not simply seek to return to an idealized tradition, but envisaged a just society which would also be technically progressive. Above all, they represented the ideal of freedom and independence in an age when everything conspired to degrade labour. (Hobsbawm, *Industry and Empire*, 70-71)

These "artisans" were not the independent craftsmen whom the industrial revolution had swept away, though by convention they bore the same title. They worked for wages–though not necessarily in large-scale factories–and were thus pitted against the new stratum of middle-class manufacturers. At the same time they represented the elite of the industrial working class. In modern parlance, they formed an "aristocracy of labor." As such they conserved habits of mind inherited from the independent yeomen and craftsmen of the eighteenth century who had provided the broad base of the democratic movement in the age of the American and French revolutions. Such men were not downtrodden proletarians but skilled workers, conscious of their importance in the new scheme of things and unwilling to put up with a state of affairs where "capital" monopolized the economic surplus created by "labor." It was to this "labor aristocracy" that the early socialists made their appeal. This crucial circumstance has been obscured by the prominence of a protest literature which made poverty the central theme of what was coming to be known as the "social problem." It was easy for well-meaning Tory romantics or religious philanthropists to condemn the spread of pauperism or the inhuman hours worked by women and children in the new factories, while staying silent on the central issue: the line of division between capital and labor. In consequence it came to be widely believed that socialism was primarily a protest against poverty, whereas the real issue had to do with equality. The new factory proletariat was too downtrodden to do more than seek an improvement in living conditions, and to this sort of appeal the more philanthropic conservatives lent a ready ear. Hence the spread of what in the 1840's was called Tory Chartism or Christian socialism. Poverty was indeed a very real issue, and so was factory legislation to limit the exploitation of labor. But socialism from the start stood for something else: not merely an improvement in the conditions of the working class, but a new social order.

If there was some confusion on this issue, the reason is plain enough: until about 1850, when real wages began to rise, industrialization went hand in hand with an abnormal pressure upon working-class living standards. That this pressure *was* abnormal became evident when the abolition of the Corn Laws (1846) and the Ten Hours Bill (1847) initiated a gradual improvement in the material conditions of most workers. Even then pauperism remained the lot of a mass of casual laborers at the bottom of the social heap (many of them Irish immigrants fleeing from the famine). But this depressed stratum did not respond to socialist slogans any more than it took an interest in the liberal-radical ideology which after the collapse of Chartism in 1848 replaced the older democratic faith. It was the elite of labor which since the 1820's furnished an audience for the spread of socialist ideas.

The term "socialist" is found for the first time in the *Co-operative Magazine* of November, 1827. In the same year, Robert Owen (1771-1858)–then temporarily in the United States, where he was trying to organize cooperative settlements on the land–published in the *New Harmony Gazette* a series of articles under the title "Social System," the burden of which was that "social" signified "cooperation." He was thinking in terms of small communities. But what was the significance of cooperation when applied to the new industrial order? This question had been debated for some years in the London Cooperative Society founded in 1824, and by 1827 the editor of its magazine thought he knew the answer. The value of a commodity, he wrote, consisted of both present and past labor (capital or stock), and the great issue was "whether it is more beneficial that this capital should be individual or common." Those who held that it should be commonly owned were "the Communionists and Socialists," and the chief of them was Robert Owen.

In considering the early beginnings of a movement, there is always a temptation to dwell too much upon the personality of the founder. If he is a notable eccentric, his private idiosyncrasies will loom unduly large, at the expense of more important considerations. Owen, during the earlier stages of his career, was remarkably level-headed, but he seemed eccentric to his contemporaries for two quite unrelated reasons. In the first place, he was a successful manufacturer–a pioneer of the new cotton industry, which was at the very heart of the Industrial Revolution–who yet condemned a social order based upon private enterprise and the unrestrained search for profit. Secondly, he had no use for religion and said so publicly, thereby shocking a good many people who might otherwise have approved of him and alarming a ruling oligarchy that had recently emerged, victorious but exhausted, from the war against revolutionary and Napoleonic France. Most of his fellow manufacturers stemmed from the lower middle class and adhered to various forms of Nonconformist Protestantism, as did those Tory supporters among the workers who had been enrolled by John Wesley's successors in the Methodist movement. Owen's rational secularism was not to their taste, and his criticism of religion—first publicly voiced in 1817, when he was briefly popular with the Establishment as a wealthy philanthropist who could do no harm—ended his career as an adviser to statesmen and churchmen. In the light of his subsequent involvement in the theory and practice of the labor movement, all this may seem accidental and irrelevant, but to Owen it was a matter of great importance. The idea of social regeneration was closely connected in his mind with the rejection of what he termed "individualization," by which he meant the fixing of responsibility for crime and other social evils upon the inborn nature of the individuals concerned. It was an axiom with him that human nature was malleable and that the formative influence of society was the decisive factor in conditioning people's behavior for good or ill. He objected to religion, as it was taught in a predominantly Protestant country, because it was indifferent to society. He did not reject Christian ethics but rather the notion that men could better themselves by their own efforts. As he put it, "individualized men, and all that is truly valuable in Christianity, are so separated as to be utterly incapable of union through all eternity." His rationalist psychology was somewhat naive (it did not in essentials depart from Bentham's "greatest happiness" principle), but he was realistic enough in noting the effect the new mode of production was having on the laboring poor: it degraded them. He made the point in one of his early writings, the *Observations on the Effect of the Manufacturing System* (1815):

> The general diffusion of manufactures throughout a country generates a new character in its inhabitants; and as this character is formed upon a principle quite unfavourable to individual or general happiness, it will produce the most lamentable and permanent evils, unless the tendency be counteracted by legislative interference and direction.

It is important to grasp that Owen condemned not industry as such, but capitalism; not the new technology, but the unrestrained spread of competition. Yet he also dabbled in communitarian experiments on the land (notably the luckless New Harmony venture in the United States between 1824 and 1829) which cost him most of his personal fortune. These and other aspects of his career are not, however, central to Owenism as a doctrine and the role it played in the British labor movement.

Owen's long career as a social reformer falls into several distinct stages. In the first, which began in 1813 with his *New View of Society* and terminated in 1821 with his *Report to the County of Lanark*, he was primarily concerned with what he regarded as the avoidable evils of pauperism, unemployment, and excessively long hours worked in factories. In this phase he told his fellow manufacturers (who were not greatly impressed) that "the pillar of the political greatness of the country is a manufacture which, as it is now carried on, is destructive of the health, morals, and social comforts of the mass of the people engaged in it." This argument was to become a *leitmotiv* of later laborist and welfare-state propaganda and was not in principle incompatible with what the more intelligent conservatives thought of the matter. During those years Owen also dabbled with Benthamite reform schemes for settling unemployed laborers on the land in specially constructed villages: "Mr Owen's Parallelograms of Paupers," as the Tory democrat William Cobbett called them—a trifle unfairly perhaps, but fairness was never Cobbett's strong suit, and anyhow Owen had laid himself open to ridicule by drafting a plan which resembled Bentham's notorious Industry-Houses for setting unemployed paupers to work. Unlike Bentham, who had no use for democracy and wanted his Industry-Houses to be run by a centralized authority, Owen made some provision for self-government in his projected Villages of Unity and Cooperation. Nothing came of the scheme, which was offered as a cure for unemployment and as such had the support of the celebrated economist David Ricardo and other luminaries. Having broken with official Britain, Owen in 1824 departed for America, where he was equally unlucky with communitarian settlements on the land. In the meantime, however, Owenism had been turned into an elementary form of socialism by his working-class followers in England, and it is this circumstance which relates Robert Owen to our topic.

Between 1820 and 1840, Owenite ideas gradually fused with anticapitalist notions which had been deduced from the writings of Ricardo by the so-called "Ricardian socialists": principally William Thompson (1775-1833), Thomas Hodgskin (1783-1869), John Gray (1799-1883), and John Francis Bray (1809-97). Whether one thinks that they deserved the label conventionally attached to them depends on whether or not one believes that they understood Ricardo's writings. On the whole it seems doubtful. They did, however, make effective use of one aspect of Ricardo's thinking, as developed in his great work *On the Principles of Political Economy and Taxation* (1817): his labor theory of value, the general notion of which he had inherited from Adam Smith. The labor theory of value does not follow logically from a distinction between value and market price. The belief that there is an "inherent value" in material goods, as distinct from their commercial or exchange value, can be held to signify that the usefulness of things, their "virtue" or inherent quality, renders them valuable. In this sense, the notion was familiar to Aristotle, the medieval schoolmen, and Locke, who held "intrisick value" to mean use value (*Second Treatise*, Chap. V). But Locke, as we have seen, also maintained that "labor" (by which in general he meant entrepreneurial labor) gave a title to "property." How could these ideas be squared under an industrial system that turned the owners of capital into controllers of labor? The answer is that they could not be squared. This was just what the "Ricardian socialists" were eager to point out.

The central paradox about the labor theory of value is that it was put forward in the seventeenth century by writers like William Petty and John Locke to justify private property—the property of the private entrepreneur or pioneer capitalist—while two centuries later socialist spokesmen of the workers' movement turned it against the industrial manufacturers. In itself this does not make the theory either right or wrong. One may hold that it never had any analytical value and still recognize that it was of great importance socially. What matters in our context is that the doctrine was originally meant to apply to the "labor" of the proprietor. From Petty to Ricardo, no economist ever thought of wage-labor as the creator of "value"—hence the alarm when the early socialists began to use it in this way. It then became necessary for the liberal economists to specify that "capital" also created "value." (The more extreme among them even maintained that wage-labor created no "value" at all.) As for the notion that salaried labor gave its owners (the workers) a title to the capitalist's profit, this could certainly not be deduced from Locke, for whom the laborer's share was merely a subsistence wage. There was a passage in Adam Smith to the effect that in common equity "they who feed, cloath and lodge the whole body of the people, should have such a share of the produce of their own labour as to be themselves tolerably well fed, cloathed and lodged" (*Wealth of Nations*, Book I, Chap. VIII). But this kind of sentiment, while agreeable enough to Christian opinion, had no socialist–or even egalitarian–implications. It simply laid down a reasonable moral precept. Socialist conclusions could be read into the labor theory of value only after capital itself had been defined as past labor. Now Ricardo had not been altogether clear as to whether "labor" was the actual *source*, or merely the *measure*, of "value," but the "Ricardian socialists" read him to mean that the expenditure of physical energy (labor) was the ultimate source of wealth or value. This was quite enough for them. It gave a kind of theoretical underpinning to Owen's moral condemnation of capitalism, and for the moment this was all that mattered.

British socialism, we may then say, developed on the two-fold foundation of a moralistic critique of the market economy and a laborist literature that implied something like a primitive doctrine of class conflict. What was the relation of this nascent socialism to the parallel stirrings in France, where a socialist movement had silently grown up since 1815 and suddenly burst upon the scene in 1830? Owen's socialism belonged to the pre-democratic age, in the sense that its founder did not work consistently for a democratic reformation of society which would institute a new social order. Down to about 1817 he had placed his hopes on enlightened rulers. In this he followed the example of Bentham, but Bentham's liberal pupils could appeal to the manufacturing middle class which gained political power in 1832, whereas Owen remained isolated. When his communitarian experiments in America failed, he could only fall back upon the customary last resort of disappointed reformers: the hope for a "change of heart" or, as he put it, a "revolution of the human mind directed solely by truth, by charity, and by kindness." Yet by the 1830's a genuine labor movement had grown up which to some extent adopted Owen's doctrines. The years 1830-34 witnessed a great wave of union organization, culminating in the temporary enrollment of half a million members in what was proudly styled the Grand National Consolidated Trades Union. This enterprise sprang from a drive to establish a nationwide union movement, centrally directed and under socialist control. A number of labor leaders during this period turned to Owen, and he responded with a utopian scheme for Home Colonization, which inevitably failed. The upshot was that Owen withdrew from politics, while the union leaders from 1836 onward turned in the direction of Chartism: essentially an attempt to make Parliament responsive to the will of the people by introducing universal suffrage. This too failed, and the British labor movement thereupon was taken in tow by the middle-class liberals. It is hardly surprising that in these circumstances Owen lapsed into political quietism. It is less clear why his enduring practical achievement as a founding father of the cooperative movement (1844) should have been succeeded by those sad last years when his remaining energies flowed into mystical channels, including spiritualist sessions in which he held converse with, among others, the shade of Benjamin Franklin. But then Owen had always been one of those men in whom faith needed a supersensible outlet. In the end, socialism was not quite enough. It is easy to make fun of the community at Queenwood he directed as Social Father of the Society of Rational Religionists. But the conversion of religious faith into secular humanism was in fact among his more lasting achievements. It had its counterpart in France, in the Saint-Simonian movement. France, however, was a Catholic country which had recently passed through a great revolution. On both counts it was volcanic soil compared to England, and French socialism from the start was something very different from the pacific and gradualist movement on the other side of the Channel.

This is not to overlook the distinction between socialism and communism, to which reference has been made earlier. Communism in France by the 1840's had become a primitive proletarian class movement, for the most part organized in secret societies or fraternities whose leaders thought in terms of conspiracy and armed insurrection. French socialism, at the start, was the work of men who had no thought of overturning society, but wished to reform it, by enlightened legislation if possible. This is the link between Robert Owen, Charles Fourier, and Henri de Saint-Simon, and the reason why in communist literature all three figure as "utopians." Perhaps they should rather be described as doctrinaires, though doubtless there is a connection. Saint-Simon's schemes were fantastic enough, and Fourier in some phases of his career was just barely on the border line of sanity, if not on the other side altogether. From the historian's viewpoint these personal traits are relevant only because they show that the whole movement was still in a very early stage. It was possible then for private eccentricities to loom large; it does not follow that they were important.

There was a background to this new movement: the Bourbon Restoration (1815-30) following the fall of Napoleon; the rise of the bourgeoisie to social prominence and economic power; its political triumph in the July Revolution of 1830, which in turn invigorated liberalism in England and helped to push the Reform Bill through in 1832; the spread of the industrial revolution to France and Belgium and the consequent emergence of a factory proletariat; the first primitive working-class revolts in Lyon and elsewhere; and the dawning notion that the French Revolution had inaugurated an era of social conflict. Some of these topics will be discussed in the next section. Here we must take account of the two men who, more than any others during this time, turned French socialism from a vague aspiration into a coherent intellectual system.

Henri de Saint-Simon (1760-1825) has many claims to eminence, not the least of them being his parentage of a movement which sought to fuse the Enlightenment with romanticism, the heritage of religion with the impact of rationalism, faith with reason, mysticism with science—one could go on forever. Saint-Simonism became the cradle of feminism, pacifism, philo-semitism, Europeanism, and Christian socialism. It was also the driving force behind such enterprises as the construction of France's first railway system and the building of the Suez Canal. Saint-Simon's personal career included active service under Washington at Yorktown in 1781, participation in the Thermidorian regime after the fall of Robespierre in 1794, incarceration as a lunatic in Charenton together with the Marquis de Sade, and the founding of a new religious creed, set out in his last published work, *Le Nouveau Christianisme* (1825). His extraordinary band of disciples included bankers, mystics, veterans of Napoleon's campaigns, and founders of the Charbonnerie—the French branch of the international secret society better known under its Italian name as the Carbonari. Heinrich Heine was a sympathizer and so for a while was Hector Berlioz. Barthélemy Prosper

Enfantin (1796-1864), on whom Saint-Simon's mantle fell after the master's death, undertook a search for the Female Messiah who was to replace Christ, and ended as a railway director. He also proclaimed free love and the emancipation of women, and made a public issue of sexual repression a century before Freud. It is fair to say that virtually every new political or social idea that convulsed Europe in the wake of the Romantic movement between 1820 and 1850 had its origins in the Saint-Simonian sect. Marx inherited an entire stock of ideas from Saint-Simon, and so did Auguste Comte. In the period between World War I and World War II, there was a Saint-Simonian revival among captains of industry in France and Germany, and after 1945 Saint-Simonism furnished some of the ideological inspiration of the Gaullist movement. When Europe's African and Asian colonies were emancipated, the new rulers–politicians, officers, and technologists–hastened to deck themselves out with a Saint-Simonian ideology behind which they could in good conscience launch a modernization drive. What is known today as "African socialism" or "Asian socialism," prevalent in areas of the world that have not accepted Communism in its Stalinist or Maoist forms, is usually a variant of Saint-Simonism–the ideology of an industrial revolution which can *but need not* be socialist in the conventional sense of the word. It can also be run by private entrepreneurs in collaboration with the state apparatus. What matters to the political elites of a society undergoing this kind of modernization is that a new industrial technology should be implanted in an archaic society. Whether the outcome is a socialist order or not depends upon political circumstances. By itself Saint-Simonism is indeterminate. It can help to launch a socialist movement. It can also become the ideology of the industrial bourgeoisie, and in its authoritarian Comteist form it has occasionally played this role.

But this is the wisdom of hindsight. Today one can see some of the reasons for the movement's immense success and the almost unbelievable rapidity with which it spread across France and Europe. It was both a reaction against individualism and a glorification of the Industrial Revolution. It had come into being as a response to the new society born from the political upheaval of 1789. This society was bourgeois, and the Saint-Simonians inaugurated the critique of liberalism, which was then just coming into its own. Saint-Simon himself had briefly toyed with liberalism around 1815, but his writings after that date opened up a cleavage between his more radical followers and the bankers and economists who at first supported him because they wanted what he wanted: Anglo-French reconciliation after the Napoleonic wars; enlightened government (but not democracy); and industrial modernization. What frightened the liberals about Saint-Simon had been in the first place his attacks on organized religion, as with Owen, but in the end the issue was more clearly defined. Saint-Simon had begun by extolling captains of industry as the organizers of a new mode of production, and he looked forward to a world order supervised by a committee of bankers (another interesting anticipation of the future). But although hostile to Jacobin democracy (hardly surprising, since he had narrowly escaped the guillotine during the Terror), he was temperamentally out of tune with liberalism. The ideal society of his imaginings centered upon the scientific organization of industrial production, and the "producers" were not to be hampered by bourgeois notions about the sacredness of private property. This is the message of his later writings, some of which were composed with the help of his then secretary, Auguste Comte: notably *L'Industrie* (1816-18) and *Du système industriel* (1821-22). These works, as well as the famous *Catéchisme des industriels* (1823-24) to which Comte contributed an entire section, somehow crossed the invisible border line between liberalism and socialism. They also led to a breach between Saint-Simon and Comte, who in later years made a career by converting socialism into sociology. *Le Nouveau Christianisme* (1825) did the rest. It inaugurated a tradition of Christian socialism which became politically influential in the 1830's and 1840's. Saint-Simon may not have been quite conscious of what he was doing when he drew up his various blueprints for an industrial society which would be centrally planned. It was his followers who turned Saint-Simonism into the ideology of the technical intelligentsia. It was they too who placed the new romantic sensibility in the service of the socialist faith. The movement ran its course between 1830 and 1848, after which it lost its revolutionary coloration and became the private hobby of successful bankers and industrialists who still yearned for socialism but had cut their connection with the labor movement. As such it endured down to 1870.

By comparison with Saint-Simon, Charles Fourier (1772-1837) cuts a lesser figure, though not for want of originality. He was the great eccentric of the early socialist movement, the inventor of a fantastic cosmology; he was also the descendant of Rousseau, in that his criticism was directed against modern civilization as such, not merely against the middle class (from which he stemmed and whose mental traits he shared to a remarkable degree). Today he is best known as the originator of a communitarian scheme of mixed industrial-agricultural settlements similar to Owen's: the "phalanstery." Experiments in setting up groups along these lines were undertaken (mainly in the United States) by his followers, and after his death the school experienced a new upsurge under the direction of Victor Considérant, who ranks among the more important figures of the movement culminating in the 1848 revolution. Considérant's *Principe du socialisme* (1847) foreshadows some of Marx's ideas and probably influenced the author of the *Communist Manifesto*. But Considérant was no communist (Fourier had admitted private property, at least in principle); the journal he edited in the 1840's bore the title *La Démocratie pacifique*, and this was no camouflage. Considérant regarded the industrial proletariat as an exploited class, and he was fully convinced that France and Europe were drifting toward revolution–as indeed they did in 1848–but he was no advocate of violence. In principle, he (like other socialists of the period) did not exclude the possibility of a reconciliation between the classes: specifically, between the industrial bourgeoisie and the proletariat. This was just what set them off from the early communists, for whom such a notion had ceased to possess any reality. We shall see in the following chapter why and how this issue came to a head in 1848 and what its significance was for the socialist and communist movements of the post-1850 age.

Saint-Simonism has been described as "the religion of the engineers," partly because it found its original disciples mainly among the students of the École Polytechnique, which to this day has remained a great center of French industrial management (and of a "technocratic" version of centralized economic planning). Fourierism and Owenism are more difficult to place in sociological terms. They were private visions spun by thinkers reflecting upon material circumstances which they themselves did not share. All three schools were "utopian." Their principal achievement was to anticipate social and moral issues still lying in the future: the conversion of religious faith into humanism; feminine emancipation; sexual liberation; the abolition of war, social oppression, and racial intolerance. Some of these aims were also shared by the more radical liberals of the period, and there was constant coming and going between the two camps; but the social issue continued to divide them. The liberals accepted individualism and "free enterprise" as the only possible motivations of a modern and progressive society. The socialists saw conflict and disaster looming where the liberals saw harmony and contentment. Both movements were animated by the common stock of ideas inherited from the Enlightenment and the Revolution; neither can simply be explained in class terms. In the last resort the cleavage was philosophical: it arose from conflicting and incompatible visions of man's role in the world.

4 Socialism and the Workers' Movement

The title of this chapter may seem rather oddly chosen: socialism *and* the workers' movement–are they not the same? We shall see that this question has recurred frequently in socialist and labor history, at any rate since 1848, when the French working class for the first time assembled under the red banner. Before that crucial episode few observers would have argued that socialism (as distinct from communism) represented labor's aims. After 1848 this notion became common in France but not in England, where with the disintegration of Chartism the unions lost their interest in politics and Owenism became a mere sect. Between 1830 and 1850 there was an immature labor movement whose leaders were socialists. When in 1867 the bulk of the urban working class obtained the vote something quite different emerged: a union movement increasingly won over to liberalism, although a sizable minority, then and later, supported the Conservatives, either from dislike of Irish immigrants and other foreigners (always a safe Tory attitude) or because Britain's "imperial" role was beginning to have an effect on working-class voters who identified with the ruling oligarchy of their own country. Whatever the cause, socialism in Britain went to sleep for a generation, rising to the surface once more in the 1880's in the wake of unemployment and general disillusionment with Gladstonian *laissez-faire* liberalism. Meanwhile, Germany–having botched its first democratic revolution in 1848–from 1863 onward witnessed the growth of a social-democratic movement and the spread of a watered-down form of state socialism: the Lassallean agitation. About the same time, the First International assembled in London in 1864, with mainly Anglo-French participation and a program (drafted by Marx) of the type that would later be called social democratic. There was thus in the 1860's a partial emancipation of the labor movement from liberalism, but one must not suppose that this process was uniform or that the participants were conscious of what was happening. Some were–Marx and Engels above all. But they were virtually isolated until the founding of the International in 1864 provided them with a ready-made audience. Even then, they had to accommodate themselves to a mental climate radically different from that of the 1840's, when "socialism" (as we have seen) was sharply distinguished from "communism."

The crucial watershed is June, 1848, when the Paris proletariat manned the barricades and was duly massacred by an army obeying the instructions of a newly elected republican government. A year later, in June, 1849, a coalition of repentant democrats and reformist socialists–the embryonic social-democratic movement–tried its hand at a different form of protest–peaceful mass demonstrations in Paris against an unpopular government–failed miserably, and dispersed. These events entailed an enduring loss of faith in democracy on the part of a working class which until then had naively identified the Republic with the notion of popular sovereignty. Until 1848 democracy had been a revolutionary cause. After that date it became safely bourgeois, at any rate in Western and Central Europe, where the authorities could rely on the peasantry and the lower middle class to keep "communism" in check. But what was communism? This was another puzzle. To the radical Parisian workers in the 1840's it had meant something like an equal distribution of property, but this slogan became meaningless once the industrial revolution had been absorbed: "property" now took the shape of huge factories which could not be "equally distributed" in the way that land had been divided among part of the French peasantry in 1793. Then what was the meaning of communism as distinct from socialism? Nobody knew.

One can also look at the matter from a different angle, in the economic perspective of our opening chapter. Between 1776 and 1848, the liberal democratic movement ran its course in North America and Western Europe, and by the mid-century it had run out of steam. These dates are not chosen at random. The year 1776 witnessed both the publication of *The Wealth of Nations* and the start of the American war of independence. The year 1848 witnessed an abortive national democratic movement in Germany, the final disappearance of peasant serfdom in Europe outside Russia, a proletarian insurrection in France, the failure of Chartism in England, and the publication of the *Communist Manifesto*. The long-run effect of these events was momentous, but some of the more important signposts to the future were only very dimly perceived even by Marx and Engels. Both men had counted upon a successful national democratic uprising in Germany, which in turn would link up with Chartism in Britain and "communism" in France. Not only was the German revolution defeated, but communism disappeared, while British socialism went into eclipse for a generation. The *Manifesto* went unread for years: it had summarized the faith of a radical vanguard in the 1840's, but this elite was dispersed and disillusioned by the events of 1848-1851. By the time its survivors reassembled in the 1860's, "communism" in the sense of the *Manifesto* had ceased to have any political meaning. Paradoxically, the only people who still believed in it were a group of Russian emigrants in Geneva. But they were followers of Bakunin and consequently had no use for those who came to be known as "Marxists"—originally a term of abuse coined by Bakunin's adherents to designate a handful of German socialists who took their line from Marx.

The principal event of the 1860's undoubtedly was the reconstitution of the old democratic movement on a new social basis. In the 1840's there had been a democratic coalition, but it had little to do with socialism, even though during this decade socialist doctrines entered labor's mentality. There was also a primitive workers' movement which for the most part equated "democracy" with "communism." By the 1860's a new phenomenon had arisen: the First International. But alongside it there was a potent liberal-radical current among both the lower middle class and the workers. In Britain and the United States the unions on the whole accepted liberalism. On the Continent of Europe during the same period they turned toward social democracy. At no stage was the entire labor movement unequivocally committed to socialism as the term is currently understood. It would be truer to say that the early socialists had to convert the working class to their own faith. In some areas they succeeded; in others they failed or lost ground. Their most spectacular failure occurred in Britain. Their most solid and enduring success was scored in Germany, where they captured the democratic inheritance and the workers' movement along with it. France provided the scene for a series of bloody disasters, from the "June days" of 1848 to the Paris Commune of 1871, but it lagged behind industrially. The world outside Europe was not as yet affected by these issues, although the American Civil War of 1861-65 did become an issue in the formation of the First International, as we shall see later on. Marx, in the preface to the first German edition of *Capital*, hailed it as a turning-point: "As in the 18th century the American war of independence sounded the tocsin for the European middle class, so in the 19th century the American civil war sounded it for the European working class."

Let us return to the starting point and try to imagine what the situation looked like in France and Britain around 1840. Let us also try to settle, once and for all, what was the difference between "socialism" and "communism" during this period—that is, what was the *real* distinction, and what did the participants think it amounted to? There is, after all, a difference between what men do and what they imagine themselves to be doing. If one takes the Marxian view, one may even hold that there is a logic of social development which has an existence of its own, and to that extent is quite indifferent to the psychological motivations of the individuals concerned. On this assumption, what socialists and communists *thought* they were doing in the 1840's matters a good deal less than what they were actually accomplishing. The same applies to learned bystanders, such as the German sociologist Lorenz von Stein, who in 1842 published a celebrated work entitled *Der Socialismus und Communismus des heutigen Frankreich*. Stein (who in his spare time operated as a secret agent for the Prussian government among the German refugees in Paris) clearly thought there was a distinction to be drawn between the two terms, and so did his contemporaries. But what was it? According to Stein, "socialism" signified the writings of Saint-Simon and Fourier, while "communism" was identified with the doctrines of Babeuf and his successors, notably Etienne Cabet. Socialism was philanthropic and had for its aim a peaceful reorganization of society, while communism was revolutionary and "immediately practical": a circumstance that impressed this learned conservative as dangerous, and which he did not fail to stress in his confidential reports to his employers.

But Stein had also noticed something else: communism (he wrote) was a proletarian movement and indeed possible only among men who owned nothing, since it amounted to a radical rejection of the existing social order. He likewise saw the connection between industry and the modern working class: only France and England possessed a genuine proletariat. Russia and China might have many poor people, but these did not form a separate "estate." Germany had not yet acquired a proletariat (in 1842, when Stein published his work, this statement was ceasing to be true), and North America was too rich in resources to have to bother about it. France was the danger zone, for there the proletariat was politically conscious: it had inherited the revolutionary doctrines of the plebeian *sans-culottes* who had brought the Jacobins to power in 1793. Stein's book was duly noticed by Moses Hess (1812-75), who was doing his best to implant socialism in Germany, and it was probably read by Marx. But neither Hess nor Marx had need of Stein to tell them that there existed a revolutionary movement in France which descended from Babeuf's *Conspiracy of the Equals* in 1796 and his death on the scaffold in 1797: the topic was thoroughly familiar to French writers of the period. They could hardly fail to notice the numerous proletarian insurrections in Paris, Lyon, and other cities after 1832, and the share taken in them by Buonarroti's disciples: notably the youthful Louis-Auguste Blanqui, who had graduated from left-wing Jacobinism to "communism." They also knew that socialists (unlike communists) by and large disapproved of violence, although they were beginning to address themselves to the workers. What then did "communism" signify? First, it was a French movement; next, it was descended from the traditions of the extreme wing of the Great Revolution; third, it was based on the new industrial proletariat. Beyond this point everything became rather vague. In particular it was not easy to tell the difference between socialist and communist utopian literature–save that the utopian communists (for practical purposes this meant Cabet) were more authoritarian and proposed to ban private property altogether, whereas Fourier and the socialists were willing to tolerate it.

Fourierism made converts in the United States and to a lesser degree in Russia and Poland, where it was taken up by philanthropic aristocrats such as the youthful Alexander Herzen (1812-70) and the Polish philosopher August von Cieszkowski (1814-94), who combined Hegelian idealism with Catholic mysticism and utopian socialism. For the Germans Fourier was too eccentric and not systematic enough. They assimilated utopian socialism in its Saint-Simonian version. The Hegelian philosopher Eduard Gans, whose lectures Marx attended at Berlin in the late 1830's, had come across Saint-Simon's doctrines in 1825 and thought well of them. Another prominent Hegelian, K. L. Michelet, discovered Saint-Simonism during a visit to Paris in 1828 and apparently informed Hegel about it. The general public in Germany learned of socialism from Heinrich Heine, whose reports from Paris were widely circulated. The aged Goethe regularly read one of the Saint-Simonian journals, and Marx's future father-in-law, Ludwig von Westphalen, on occasion expressed Saint-Simonian views, as did other members of the social elite in Trier, where Marx was born in 1818. In short, socialism in its Saint-Simonian form was at first considered both respectable and harmless. This situation changed in the 1840's, when Moses Hess, in his far from respectable manner, began to preach a democratic revolution leading to socialism. From then on, the distinction between socialism and communism narrowed, and in the end Hess himself became a member of the Communist League (originally founded by German "democrats," i.e., radical intellectuals and working men, in Paris in 1836). Yet influential leaders of French "socialism" in the 1840's, such as Louis Blanc, still refused to associate with "communists" like Marx (in Blanc's case because he disapproved of their atheism). The controversy went on, coming to a provisional climax in 1850, when the Communist League itself split (and when Marx for all practical purposes ceased to be a communist).

It is worth remarking that in the formative period between 1830 and 1850, when all these ideas and movements took shape, London and Paris were the only cities that counted. Germany still lagged behind, and the remainder of Europe had barely reached the stage of debating the merits of political and economic liberalism, although in Russia at least a few advanced spirits began to toy with the notion that the liberal phase might be skipped altogether.

What, then, was the central issue? Above all the continuing relevance of the French Revolution for the theory and practice of the workers' movement. Here two radically different viewpoints were possible and were indeed maintained: (1) that the Revolution–more particularly the rule of the "Mountain" in 1793-94–was the proper model for the inevitable phase of "proletarian dictatorship" which would precede the classless society: this became the "communist" faith; (2) that Jacobinism was irrelevant to the "organization of labor" and had best be abandoned altogether: this had been the opinion of Saint-Simon and Fourier, although it was qualified by their successors. There were also some intermediate positions, and by the 1840's there had emerged something like a "republican socialist" ideology which combined republican democracy (but not Jacobin dictatorship) with the aims of labor. Its outstanding representative until 1848 was Louis Blanc. Alongside these democrats, the secret societies founded by Buonarroti and Blanqui, with their following of communist workers and radicalized students from the middle class, continued the Babouvist tradition of minority dictatorship.

But was the proletariat actually a minority? It depended on one's definition of the term. In 1836, when asked by a court to describe himself, Blanqui replied "proletarian," and when the judge objected that this was no proper occupation, Blanqui exclaimed: "What, no occupation? It is the occupation of thirty million Frenchmen who live by their labor and are robbed of their political rights!" Babeuf might have said the same thing forty years earlier (and substantially did). But to later socialists this kind of talk was meaningless. Blanqui equated all the "toilers," including peasant-owners and craftsmen. The ruling class he visualized as a handful of landowners, bankers, and industrialists who monopolized political power. Given the fact that under the Bourgeois Monarchy of Louis Philippe (which collapsed in the February revolution of 1848), only some 240,000 Frenchmen out of 36 million had the vote, this was a plausible notion, but it signified that radical democracy must be equated with communism. For if all Frenchmen except for a small wealthy stratum were by definition "proletarians," then the "dictatorship of the proletariat" was synonymous with the rule of the great majority. This simple faith was destined to have a great career in pre-industrial societies at a later date, notably in China after 1949, when under the name of Maoism it became the official creed. But it was already too primitive for France in the 1840's, and in the end even the Blanquists ceased to hold it. What took its place was the

Marxian view that capitalism had created an industrial proletariat which might—or would—become a majority of the population.

But this was a later development. In the 1840's and for some decades thereafter it was clearly evident that outside Britain the industrial working class formed a minority of the citizenry. This was just why democratic socialism did not seem a very hopeful prospect—unless allies could be found. Socialism in *this* sense could signify one of two things: (1) that labor must form an alliance with the lower middle class and the peasantry, so as to obtain an electoral majority and then legislate for socialist reforms; (2) that the labor movement must count solely upon its own strength, develop its organizations, above all the unions (*syndicats*), and pay no attention to parliamentary politics, which were bourgeois by definition. The reformist position became identified with Louis Blanc (1811-82), the syndicalist (not then so described) with Proudhon (1809-65). Both were plausible and obtained wide support. Neither promised early victory. Meanwhile the notion of an insurrectionary *coup d'état* went on being cherished by the Blanquists. They were able to retain it because they held the ancient faith that a basic identity of interests bound workers and peasants together. The perspective of armed revolt did not frighten them—why should the people not rise against its oppressors? This was sound Jacobin logic. The flaw in the reasoning lay in the fact that most French peasants had become conservative and could be enrolled in the armed forces for the purpose of crushing urban insurrections. In the Blanquist view this danger was to be met by setting up an energetic dictatorship in Paris and then appealing to the peasant masses over the heads of the conservative forces—the church above all. On this point Blanqui anticipated both Bakunin and Lenin. For a while—between 1847 and 1850 to be precise—he also persuaded Marx that it was possible to short-circuit the democratic process. Then their ways parted: a circumstance not often noted in later Communist literature.

Let us disregard these quarrels for a moment and look at the social circumstances of the age. Such influential writings as Louis Blanc's *Organisation du travail* (1839), Cabet's *Voyage en Icarie* (1840), and Proudhon's *Qu'est-ce que la propriété?* (1840) made their appearance against a background of acute social misery. They also revived a few archaisms. Thus when Proudhon posed the question "What is Property?" and gave the famous reply, "Property is Theft," he merely repeated a slogan already employed in 1780 by the Rousseauist Jacques-Pierre Brissot, later prominent among the Girondists. It was standard doctrine among Rousseau's followers that there had once been a golden age without inequality and private property, but Proudhon was as inconsistent on this topic as on most others. For practical purposes he disapproved only of large-scale capitalist property, while defending and indeed extolling the economic independence of the small farmer or craftsman. In brief, he was not a "communist," for even in relation to industry he preached "mutualism" (a form of cooperative association) rather than socialization in the modern sense. At bottom he never renounced the vision of a society in which the producers would own their tools, individually rather than collectively, and it was just this which set his later followers apart from the "collectivism" of the Marxists. Here was another difference between "socialism" and "communism": one that had nothing to do with the issue of dictatorship, but rather with the organization of industrial society. Proudhon's doctrine appealed to craftsmen who still owned their tools (just as his archaic notions about women and family life appealed to the peasantry from which he sprang). He was in this sense a transitional figure, and his death in 1865 symbolically occurred a few months after the First International–the International Workingmen's Association–had got under way.

But this once more is to anticipate. Something more must still be said about the year 1848, when democracy and socialism separated–for in that year universal suffrage in France produced a bourgeois majority which relied upon the army and the peasantry against the urban working class. The resulting conflict was uniquely French, in that the participants re-enacted some of the events of 1793-95. Yet France was becoming an industrial country, although rather more slowly than Britain and Belgium. In neither of the two latter countries did the 1848 turmoil lead to an armed confrontation between the state and the proletariat. In France it did, thereby confirming the Blanquists in their belief that nothing was to be expected from parliamentary democracy, while deepening Proudhon's conviction that the labor movement must stay out of politics: the first tentative formulation of what later became the syndicalist faith. One is thus driven to the conclusion that the opposing forces in the France of 1848 saw the actual situation through the distorting lense of memories inherited from the great revolution fought out by their ancestors. To employ a phrase later made famous by Marx and Engels, they were equipped with a "false consciousness." The democratic republicans of 1848, self-styled *Montagnards*, were a mere caricature of the real "Mountain" of 1793-95: the radical wing of the Convention which had pushed the revolution through to a conclusion. Louis Bonaparte, elected to the presidency of the Republic by the peasantry in December, 1848, and self-proclaimed Emperor of the French in 1852, caricatured Napoleon. And the Blanquists? If they did not exactly parody the movement led by Babeuf in 1796, they certainly were no more successful than their ill-starred ancestors.

For the time being, the defeat of June, 1848, brought the revolutionary movement to a halt. In 1871, with the repeat performance of the Paris Commune, the disaster was on such a scale that even the surviving Blanquists began to question the entire Jacobin tradition of Parisian insurrection, whereas in 1848 even bourgeois republicans had still thought it quite normal: one seized power in Paris and the rest would follow. Those who no longer put their faith in this practice might be either democratic socialists like Louis Blanc or anarchists like Proudhon. In either case they had one thing in common: they did not greatly care for the spiritual legacy of Robespierre and St. Just. To the majority of French republicans this was still heresy. Babeuf in 1796 had proclaimed "Robespierrism is democracy, and both these words are absolutely identical." This was not what either Blanc or Proudhon thought: they had begun to work their way through to a different conception of democracy.

If Blanqui stood for the residual Babouvist tradition and Blanc for democratic socialism ("to prepare for the future without breaking violently with the past," as he put it), P.-J. Proudhon is usually described as one of the two fathers of anarchism (Bakunin being the other). There is considerable justification for this view, but it is well to bear in mind that for every "anarchist" statement in Proudhon's voluminous writings one can find an "authoritarian" utterance: just as one can find him simultaneously on the side of revolutionary workers, conservative peasants, Louis Bonaparte (whose military dictatorship in 1851 he greeted with applause), and the slaveholders of the American South, whose vile cause he espoused in 1861 because they were fighting against "centralization." Perhaps the only consistent thing about Proudhon was his attachment to what he called "justice"–(a principle he was never able to define, although what he probably meant was the exchange of equivalents)–and his dislike of religion: "*Dieu c'est le mal*" ("God is the principle of evil"). On the issue of centralized authority he was a Rousseauist, even though he characteristically described Rousseau as "the Genevan charlatan" (it is not recorded that he ever expressed a favorable opinion of another writer). That is to say, he was against the state in principle and against state socialism in particular. This attitude separated him from utopian communists like Cabet and from moderate socialists like Blanc, both of whom he tirelessly abused. It also led him, by a rather circuitous route, to defend private property (in his posthumously published *Théorie de la Propriété*) as a counterweight to the menace of state power. An earlier treatise, the *Système des Contradictions Économiques, ou Philosophie de la Misère* (1846), provoked a celebrated rejoinder from Marx but is otherwise insignificant. Proudhon was self-taught both as an economist and as a philosopher, and while endowed by nature with a better mind than Bakunin, he does not rank high as a theorist. His importance is historical: he somehow bridged the gap between agrarian populism and urban syndicalism, and in his posthumously published writings he threw out some hints about labor unionism and politics on which men of a later age could build. In this sense, he is one of the ancestors of anarchosyndicalism–a considerable achievement, whatever one may think of the man and his writings.

If all these issues were brought to the test in 1848, the reason is that this stormy year witnessed Louis Blanc's spectacular failure as a member of the Provisional Government hastily set up after Louis Philippe's flight, and the subsequent slaughter of the proletariat in the streets of Paris. By 1849 both the nascent social-democratic movement represented by Blanc and the tradition of armed insurrection kept alive by Blanqui had suffered shipwreck. These opponents having been discredited, Proudhon had some cause for satisfaction. His earlier doctrinal quarrel with Marx was of small importance to him and did not at the time attract much attention. What mattered was that Blanc had failed to win effective public support for abolishing unemployment by what he called the "organization of labor," while Blanqui's cause had been drowned in blood during the "June days." As for utopian or "Icarian" communism, Cabet left for America in 1849 with a group of disciples and after an unsuccessful experiment in Texas duly founded a communist "Icaria" on the territory of the former Mormon center at Nauvoo,

Illinois. Like the Owenite settlements in the New World which preceded it, Icaria lingered on for a while and then quietly gave up the ghost in 1895. Cabet had dreamed of a self-sufficient commonwealth with something like a million inhabitants, organized on communist lines and including industry as well as farming. The real Icaria never got beyond 1,500 members. It was the end of the communitarian dream. It was also–or so it seemed at the time–the end of democratic socialism (Blanc) and Jacobin communism (Blanqui). What then was left? Triumphant bourgeois society on the one hand, military rule on the other. For in December, 1851, parliament was got rid of by Louis Bonaparte who was thereupon confirmed in power, for the second time in three years, by millions of peasant voters who preferred him to the liberals. Proudhon took this as final proof that popular sovereignty was a myth, since the electorate could be fooled by any demagogue. "I shall belabor the people" (he wrote), "until I have made the dogma of its alleged sovereignty fly to pieces. It is not enough that we should not see the incapable leaders of 1848 again; what matters is that we should not reconstruct their idol" (Hampden Jackson, 104).

Very well, but what was the alternative? Proudhon's first move, grotesquely enough, was to call upon Louis Bonaparte to fulfill his "mission" by introducing Proudhon's cherished "mutualism": a utopian project for supplying millions of small producers with unlimited and gratuitous bank credit. This led to the ban on his recent writings being cancelled by a grateful dictator who stood in need of socialist champions, but it had no further practical consequences. In so far as the self-styled Napoleon III had ever entertained socialist inclinations, they were of the Saint-Simonian variety, and his twenty-year reign consequently witnessed an unparalleled upsurge of capitalist industrialization. Much of this was pioneered by former Saint-Simonians who had turned Bonapartist, somewhat in the spirit in which a century later numerous disillusioned champions of "workers' rule" transformed themselves into ardent Stalinists: if industrialization was not socialism, it was the next best thing. Proudhon, needless to say, had no more use for Saint-Simonism than for Blanquism, and much of his energy was spent denouncing the orgy of financial speculation in the 1850's. During the 1860's political life revived, the labor movement began to reorganize, the unions obtained some degree of legal recognition, and their leaders turned to Proudhon. He advised them to abstain from politics. At the same time he put forward a political idea of his own–federalism: the break-up of France into self-governing units on the Swiss model. In the economic sphere, industry should be carried on in workshops which would "federate" for common purposes. This at least was an advance upon his earlier schemes for extending interest-free loans to all and sundry through a national bank. "Federalism" became an element of the syndicalist creed in France, although qualified by a growing awareness that large-scale industry had outgrown the dimensions of the workshop.

Proudhon's other writings were mainly directed against the authority of state and church and thus helped to promote the anarchist cause. However, this statement (like every other generalization about Proudhon) needs to be qualified. In the first place he was no pacifist, as any reader of his 800-page treatise *La Guerre et la Paix* can discover (if indeed one can imagine anyone reading 800 pages of Proudhon). So far from condemning war, he regarded it–in principle anyhow–as the ultimate revelation of justice. Secondly, he had no use for feminine emancipation, although it would be unfair to say that he disliked women. He liked them well enough, but only as housekeepers and domestic servants. A woman's place was in the home (he was greatly devoted to the memory of his mother, a hardworking peasant woman). Outside the home she could only disgrace herself by losing her morals. On this issue Proudhon stood quite alone among the early socialists, all the others being champions of women's rights–a tradition established by the Saint-Simonians and Fourier. Consistent with his puritanical and conservative outlook, Proudhon regarded the family as the basic unit of society. This archaic side of his personality connects him with the agrarian roots of French Catholicism, and it explains why the political right in France has always had a certain fondness for him. Anti-urban, anti-liberal, anti-foreign and (needless to say) anti-Jewish, he stood for traditional rural values. Some of these themes were later revived by the best known of his spiritual heirs, Georges Sorel. Still later, in the 1940's, slogans of this kind became the inspiration of that section of the right which supported Pétain and the Vichy regime. And yet it is undeniable that in his own queer fashion Proudhon was a genuine socialist. Janus-faced, he pointed simultaneously to the past and to the future, to rural populism and to urban syndicalism, to the peasant and to the worker. The founder of anarchism was also the defender of a traditional society which the industrial revolution had disintegrated.

For if these were the years when socialism made contact with the working class, it was also the age when capitalism uprooted the peasantry on the Continent of Europe. These were two sides of the same coin, for the peasant who left his customary way of life behind to seek work in the city was likely to encounter socialist ideas if he joined a labor union. In France, one aspect of rural life was the peasant's more or less active attachment to the Catholic Church, and the same was true in Austria, Belgium, Italy, Spain, and parts of Germany, Holland, and Switzerland. Hence in all these areas the industrial revolution not only separated the peasant producer from his plot of earth, it also disrupted a culture of which the Church was the spiritual center. As time went on, urban Catholicism gave birth to a labor movement (though not one that cared to describe itself as socialist), but for millions of workers whose ancestors had been peasants or craftsmen, the social and cultural catastrophe of the industrial revolution swept away their inherited religious faith along with established modes of life. Socialism stepped into the breach. In Protestant regions such as Scandinavia, northern Germany, and England, Socialism normally coalesced with a union movement which had already created something of an autonomous working-class culture. In Catholic Europe, where industrialization generally came later (Belgium was the exception) and encountered stiffer resistance, socialism and anarchism not only ran ahead of the labor movement: they also showed a tendency to substitute themselves for religion to a higher degree than in the Protestant north, where liberalism was more influential and had a following among the workers. For the working classes of France, Italy, Spain, and other predominantly Roman Catholic areas, socialism thus acquired the character of a *faith*. The bitterness of anti-clericalism in these countries was a measure of the mutual hostility with which believers and atheists regarded each other, and they did so because the Catholic Church claimed an allegiance which an increasingly rebellious proletariat was no longer willing to accord it.

Proudhon was not alone in preaching militant atheism. Moreover, some aspects of his thinking retained a traditionalist character; it was his great rival Blanqui who popularized the slogan "*Ni Dieu ni maître"*–"neither God nor master." Yet it was left for the anarchists–notably in Spain, the most fanatically Catholic of all European countries–to place the struggle against the Church in the forefront. The search for a new morality that would supersede religion while retaining some of its egalitarian features had been initiated earlier, by the Saint-Simonians and the Fourierists. But it became a practical problem for millions of men after the culture of a predominantly agrarian order of society had been uprooted. It may be worth adding that the traditional cleavage between Protestant northern Europe and the predominantly Catholic south had always been more marked in politics and culture than in economics (fashionable sociological notions to the contrary notwithstanding). It is true that the industrial revolution came first in Britain and that the religious climate there clearly favored its progress. But once the new mode of production was established, it spread–admittedly with varying speed–in Protestant and Catholic areas alike. This is not to deny that liberalism encountered a more hospitable climate in Britain and the United States than in Spain or Latin America. Indeed, Spanish liberalism was a failure (even economically from the standpoint of the middle class), and Italian liberalism was no great success. One can perhaps ascribe these crucial differences to the religious background, just as one might attribute to the influence of the Catholic tradition the astonishing passivity with which the Irish peasantry endured the disaster of the 1845-47 famine. But then how is one to account for the revolutionary temper of the Spanish peasants and workers who in the 1870's reacted to the behavior of the Church by going over *en masse* to the anarchist faith? National as well as religious traditions must be taken into account, as may be seen from the curious parallel between the Lutheran inheritance of northern Germany, Holland, and Scandinavia, and the Social Democratic form of Marxism (or pseudo-Marxism) which struck root in these areas.

Such topics properly form the subject of a history of culture in the nineteenth century, whereas here we are concerned with the theoretical aspect of the socialist movement. Still, it does no harm to bear in mind that socialism became the *faith* of the working class, which it helped to civilize by making available to it the heritage of the Enlightenment. In the same manner, liberalism may be said to have had a civilizing effect on the middle class, with which the labor movement now entered into political conflict. Liberalism and socialism were rivals. They also had something in common: both movements demonstrated a capacity for raising men above themselves. And, needless to say, both were mediated by intellectuals, although not every country witnessed the emergence of an intelligentsia in the Russian sense: a stratum with a corporate consciousness and a sense of mission. In the most advanced industrial countries, where radical liberalism in the later nineteenth century became the creed of the masses–Britain and the United States are the chief examples–the intellectuals were fairly well integrated and hardly felt the need to differentiate themselves from the ruling stratum and its culture. Tsarist Russia stood at the other extreme, most of Continental Europe somewhere in the middle. In some areas of Eastern and Central Europe, the radical oppositional intelligentsia was largely Jewish, thus adding an extra dimension to an already ancient problem which in the end proved insoluble. Whatever its background, the intellectual stratum produced and mediated the body of ideas–conservative, liberal, or socialist–in terms of which the whole society experienced and debated its internal problems and tensions. The labor movement was not exempt from this general rule. Its spontaneous drive toward a different, egalitarian order of society had to be raised to the level of generality by theorists reflecting on material conditions which they themselves did not share. It is, then, a mere truism to say that socialism was bound to be the creation of intellectuals of bourgeois origin. Nor does this statement comport any judgment upon the validity of socialist theorizing. General concepts, though of particular origin, are universally valid irrespective of their social background and the psychological motivations of their inventors. Were it otherwise, social science could never have been distinguished from class-bound ideology.

5 *Marx: Social Theory*

Karl Marx (1818-83) is the central figure in the history of socialism. That much is conceded even by his critics. It is less easy to establish a consensus as to the reasons for his obvious pre-eminence, and it is notoriously impossible to obtain agreement even among Marxists as to the significance of all he said and did. There is a further difficulty: as a man of his age Marx stood in a particular relationship to the philosophical legacy of what is known as German idealism, notably the philosophy of Hegel (1770-1831). In a historical sketch of nineteenth-century thought, or in a study of European intellectual history from the French to the Russian Revolution, this theme would have to figure prominently, if only because the Russian intelligentsia discovered French socialism and German philosophy at roughly the same time: in the 1830's. We shall have to say something on this topic when we come to the immediate ancestors of Russian Marxism, the Populists of the 1860's and 1870's. But for the moment we are still concerned with the western half of the European Continent and with that phase of socialist history which ran its troubled course between 1848 and 1871. We therefore start off not by considering what effect Marx had on the generation that came after him but by asking what it was that enabled him to create the intellectual system to which his name has been attached.

There exists a popular and plausible reply to this question, first suggested by Marx's life-long friend and comrade Friedrich Engels (1820-95) and later given additional prominence by Lenin and his followers. Marx, they said, had synthesized the basic elements of three national traditions: German philosophy, French socialism, and British economics. In a sense this is obvious, but it leaves unexplained the secret of the operation. How could one man, even if endowed with extraordinary intellectual powers, take hold of these disparate elements and turn them into a coherent theoretical structure? But after what has been said earlier, the answer should be evident: Marx was able to bring German idealist philosophy, French socialist politics, and British classical economics together because they had all grown from a common root–the combined impact of liberalism and democracy. German philosophy, French socialism, and British economics were three different reactions to this revolution. In fusing them, Marx disclosed their common ancestry and provided the socialist movement with a doctrine that encompassed philosophy, history, sociology, and economics. On its theoretical side, Marxism was at once an explanation and a critique of bourgeois society.

Stated in this manner, the answer to our question–what was it that Marx did and how was he able to do it?–has another implication: namely, that Marxism had (and has) a built-in reference to the official liberal ideology of the new society. What Marx did was to take the basic assumptions of the liberal creed and subject them to systematic critical analysis. Earlier socialists had tried their hand at this operation, but they had never advanced very far, because for one reason or another they remained content with moralistic censure or fragmentary attempts at theorizing. Thus Owen, as we have seen, repudiated liberal economics and took some steps on the road to providing the British labor movement with a socialist orientation at a time when that movement was activated by the Chartist struggle for a democratic reconstruction of society; but even before the unions turned away from Chartism, Owen had abandoned politics. In France, the utopian socialism of Saint-Simon and Fourier was succeeded by the political propaganda of Blanqui and Louis Blanc, and by Proudhon's theoretical system; but Blanqui and Blanc suffered shipwreck in 1848, and Proudhon thereafter maintained contact with the still rather primitive French workers' movement only because his own thinking did not seriously challenge its traditional prejudices.

Proudhon's system resembled Marxism in that he too aimed at a synthesis of philosophy, economics, and politics. But self-taught and muddled as he was, he never rose markedly above the level of what might be called applied Rousseauism. His basic position amounted to this: the French Revolution had promised equality but had not achieved it because bourgeois privilege stood in the way. Equality demanded justice (the exchange of equivalents), but capitalism as an economic system worked to the disadvantage of the immediate producer. Its effective operation rested upon the exchange of nonequivalents: labor on the one hand, property on the other. The property-owner was privileged because he was able to live on rent, interest, or dividends, whereas the worker had only his labor, which he was obliged to sell in the market to the highest (or lowest) bidder. As a critique of bourgeois society this was too simple, although it satisfied the first generation of anarchosyndicalists (especially since Proudhon also denounced the state). It was only after Marx had intervened that socialists began to understand how capitalism actually worked. They could get no such understanding out of Proudhon. For proof one need only consider his major work, the *Système des contradictions économiques ou philosophie de la misère* (1846) where he tried his hand at economics.

The doctrine that emerged on this occasion went something like this: what people really needed were use values, whereas they were actually being offered exchange values by the market economy. These represented thesis and antithesis; Proudhon (having on this point misunderstood Hegel) looked for a synthesis which he termed "constituted value." This amounted to saying that goods should be exchanged in proportion to the amount of labor embodied in them—an arrangement that would do away with market fluctuations and at the same time satisfy the requirement of "justice." Proudhon was extremely proud of this discovery, in some respects already anticipated in England by Owen and J. F. Bray. The solution of the social problem, as all these writers saw it, lay in establishing labor exchanges where workingmen's cooperatives and independent craftsmen could exchange their products according to prices based on labor-units, thus at one blow circumventing the market and realizing the ideal of social equality. To facilitate this procedure, Proudhon advocated the establishment of a national bank that would extend interest-free loans to qualified candidates, so that everyone might have access to means of production and become an independent proprietor. Implicit in all this was a desire to retain bourgeois society while purging it of its "negative" aspect. But the "negative" was just what kept it going.

Bourgeois society of course was older than modern industrial capitalism, and this must be kept in mind if we are to see where Marx's reasoning diverges from that of his predecessors, the Enlightenment theorists. For as a thinker Marx was in a tradition: that of the French Encyclopedists and their British, Dutch, Swiss, Italian, and German contemporaries. We have seen that both nineteenth-century liberals and their socialist critics could invoke Rousseau, but they could likewise appeal either to French materialism or to the heritage of German idealist philosophy. Marxism is a critique of liberalism, but one that shares with it the legacy of the Enlightenment. What this legacy was we may take for granted: it was spelled out in the American and French revolutions, whose basic documents are familiar to anyone able to read, and this early liberalism also found an echo in classical German philosophy, from Kant and Fichte to Hegel (although there were influential German thinkers, notably Schelling, who repudiated it). In taking German philosophy for his point of departure, Marx took off from a line of thought that ran parallel to the Anglo-French Enlightenment. This parallelism is particularly noticeable in Kant, less so in Fichte and Hegel. The reason is that these two latter thinkers had begun to come up against some of the problems raised by the new social order: politically in the experience of the French Revolution, philosophically in the form of Rousseauism and later of the Romantic movement. Hegel stands at the point where all these currents intermingle, which is why he has been claimed by liberals (as a rationalist) and by conservatives (as a historicist). What does this mean?

Hegel–in this respect resembling Goethe and other contemporary German poets and philosophers–started out by asking why European culture was inferior to the classical *polis* of Greek antiquity, and the reply he gave was that modern society had been fragmented into selfish individuals who cared for nothing but their own interest. This notion (already suggested by Schiller in 1794-95, in his "Letters on the Aesthetic Education of Man") was in part inspired by Rousseau's view of culture as in some sense contrary to nature, but the German thinkers were also struck by the baleful effects of the division of labor. This line of thought is an obvious ancestor of the youthful Marx's concern with human alienation. Hegel and Schiller idealized the Greeks in a manner hardly compatible with Marx's more realistic outlook, yet in a certain fundamental sense Marx always adhered to the credo of classical German philosophy, in so far as it signified that man is a "universal being"–one capable of unlimited development–who has been spiritually mutilated by the conditions of the modern world. While the romantics (and the conservatives generally) looked back to the lost harmony of the Middle Ages, Rousseau, Diderot, Kant, Schiller, Goethe, Fichte, Hegel, Feuerbach, and Marx, consciously or not, sought a model in classical antiquity. This is the hidden link between Marxism and the tradition of Western rationalism, and it accounts for the fact that a philosophical critique of *civilization* could be turned into a sociological indictment of *capitalism*. This, however, is not to say that Marx was ever a Rousseauist. As we have seen, Rousseau believed that the "general will" could operate in a society of independent property-holders, though on occasion he also toyed with the notion of socialization. Almost a century later Proudhon landed himself in an intellectual tangle by trying to make Rousseau's philosophy work under the conditions of industrial society. Marx avoided these pitfalls because–like Hegel and unlike Rousseau or Kant–he took history seriously. That is to say, he realized that the historical process had a logic of its own which could not be ignored.

This approach, too, stemmed from the Enlightenment tradition. Its originator was Giambattista Vico (1668-1744), who first introduced the notion that history is made by man and that the historical process can be understood because society–unlike nature–is the work of man. From Vico the road goes via Montesquieu and the Scottish historians (Hume and Ferguson above all) to the Saint-Simonians on the one hand, Hegel and Marx on the other. The philosophy of history they held in common was rooted in a more ancient tradition: that of the Stoics and Epicureans and their modern successors, e.g., Spinoza. This tradition was "naturalist" in the sense that it recognized only natural causes and quietly ignored the belief in divine intervention; it was "determinist" in that it looked for a chain of causal explanation; but it was not fatalist, for if man can understand himself and his creation, he can also become the creator of his own destiny. The general formula is summed up in the statement that true freedom is insight into necessity. This notion, which goes back to Spinoza and was revived by Hegel before being popularized by Engels, is not to be understood as signifying that there are historical determinants in the sense of physical or natural causation which men can do nothing about. The historical process is not something that goes on regardless of human wishes (although Hegel sometimes talked as though he believed it did). Men's aspirations are themselves part of the process, and human insight may be critical as well as contemplative. Man makes himself and is the creator of what is called "universal history." His insight into the material preconditions of the process serves to guard him against the folly of supposing that anything is possible at any moment. What can be achieved in practice depends upon the material potentialities of the particular stage of development which has been reached. This is the meaning, or one meaning, of what Engels later called the "historical materialism" of Marx. It is not a fatalist doctrine, but it does impose limitations upon the doctrinaire voluntarism of the true utopians. What these limitations are can only be discovered in practice and in theoretical analysis of the material conditions underlying and conditioning this practice.

Now this mode of thought was common to thinkers who stood in the tradition of the French Enlightenment, so that it is not obvious at first sight in what way Marx introduced an intellectual revolution. He was of course a socialist, but so were others, and indeed he had originally come to socialism by way of the Saint-Simonians and their German followers, notably Moses Hess. He rejected the capitalist form of industrialization and the standard definition of "property" in the liberal or Lockean sense of ownership of means of production belonging to private entrepreneurs, but he had been anticipated on this point by Owen and by the Ricardian socialists. As for the doctrine of class conflict, which is frequently associated with his name, we have seen that it was a commonplace among the early French communists. For that matter, French historians like Guizot (1787-1874) and Saint-Simonians like Thierry (1795-1856) were familiar with it, although they differed from each other, and from the communists, in the conclusions they drew from it. That the French Revolution had dethroned the aristocracy and in some sense inaugurated the reign of the bourgeoisie was a notion with which hardly anyone in the France of the 1830's and 1840's would have quarrelled, though there were different opinions as to the beneficial aspects of this change. Likewise, the British middle class was quite conscious of itself as a class and indeed gloried in its role as the "backbone of the nation." Even in Germany, where lawyers and statesmen were still in the habit of invoking the different rights and interests of the "estates" (*Stände*), the concept of class was beginning to make headway. What, then, was the novelty Marx introduced? Or did he simply fuse all these notions? But in that case why did the fusion have the effect of an earthquake?

We shall get nowhere if we try to answer this question with reference to the political upheaval of 1848-49, for Marx's personal intervention during this stormy period, though important, did not become decisive, and the organization he led, the German Communist League, fell apart after 1850. Nor did the *Communist Manifesto* (which was published just before the February, 1848, rising in Paris) have much of an effect upon that generation of revolutionaries: in fact it was hardly noticed in the general excitement, and a second edition had to wait until 1872, by which time Marx had achieved public notoriety in the wake of an explosion over which he had no control whatever—the Paris Commune of 1871. Until then he was less well known to the general public, or even to the workers' movement outside Germany, than Proudhon, Blanqui, Mazzini, or Bakunin. Yet ever since the 1840's there had been a number of people—mainly German socialists, but also a few radicals from other countries—who realized that Marx was somehow unique and incomparable. In the spring of 1850, after the failure of the general democratic uprising, his former friend and teacher Moses Hess, who differed quite sharply from him on a number of issues, still testified to this conviction in a letter to Alexander Herzen. What you and I have been writing about the recent European upheaval (he said in substance) resembles a neat sketch drawn on paper, whereas Marx's judgment upon these events is, as it were, engraved with iron force in the rock of time. Coming from an older man who was also an old associate (and who in the same letter complained bitterly about Marx's intolerable dictatorial manner), this was high praise; nor was it unmerited. No one who compares Marx's series of articles published later as *The Class Struggles in France* (1850) with Herzen's highly personal and emotional outpourings, or even with Proudhon's eloquent diatribes, can fail to realize that as a thinker Marx was in a class by himself.

Setting aside the incalculable factor known as "genius" and the tediously familiar variations on the theme of Marx's German-Jewish background (which he shared with the amiable but not very effective Hess plus a crop of lesser personalities), there is at least one clearly definable circumstance which no one has ever questioned. If liberalism represented a vision of the social whole encompassing philosophy, history, politics, and economics, then Marx's formulation of socialism was the only alternative doctrine that was both coherent and universal. For Marx challenged liberalism not in this or that respect, but all over the field. Moreover, being the product of a single mind–and an extremely powerful one at that–his theorizing necessarily had a systematic character. However empirical a thinker may be by inclination, if he is a theorist of the first order he is bound to impose some kind of unity upon the composition of his brain, so that the finished system will be a totality, not a mere casual aggregate of disparate thoughts. Normally this effect is achieved by specialization: the theorist settles down in one particular corner of the field and makes it his business to analyze its structural principle. But Marx was a "generalist" before he became a specialist, and moreover he lived in an age when a single mind could still encompass the entire domain subsequently broken up into the competing fields of history, political philosophy, sociology, and economics. Auguste Comte (1798-1857)–a writer much inferior to Marx in general ability and almost entirely ignorant of anything that went on beyond the borders of France–had yet achieved an impressive synthesis of contemporary knowledge simply by refusing to accept the crippling limitations of specialization. Now Marx was a genuine European in the fullest sense. It is more than just a biographical circumstance that after leaving Germany in 1843 he spent five years in France and Belgium and in 1849 settled down for the remainder of his life in London, then the capital of the world's greatest power and in a very real sense the center of the Western world. Marxism was a fusion of three different national traditions; it was a synthesis of philosophy, politics, and economics; and it was socialism's answer to liberalism. A fourth characterization must be added: it outlined *a theory of the bourgeois revolution.*

What Marx meant by this frequently misunderstood term is best made clear by citing the opening passage of his pamphlet on the Bonapartist *coup d'état* of 1851, *The Eighteenth Brumaire of Louis Bonaparte* (1852):

> Hegel remarks somewhere that all great world-historical events and personalities occur, as it were, twice. He forgot to add: the first time

as tragedy, the second time as farce. Caussidière for Danton, Louis Blanc for Robespierre, the *Montagne* of 1848 to 1851 for the *Montagne* of 1793 to 1795, the Nephew for the Uncle. And the same caricature occurs in the circumstances attending the second edition of the eighteenth Brumaire!

Men make their own history, but they do not make it just as they please, under circumstances chosen by themselves, but (rather) under conditions immediately encountered, given and transmitted from the past. The tradition of all the dead generations weighs like a nightmare on the brains of the living. And just when they seem engaged in transforming themselves and their surroundings, creating something unprecedented, precisely in such periods of revolutionary crisis do they anxiously conjure up the spirits of the past in their service, deriving from them names, battle cries, and costumes, so as to enact the new world-historical drama in time-honored disguise and borrowed language. Thus Luther donned the mask of the Apostle Paul; the Revolution of 1789 to 1814 draped itself alternately as the Roman Republic and the Roman Empire; and the Revolution of 1848 could think of nothing better than to parody either 1789 or the revolutionary tradition of 1793 to 1795. . . .

Camille Desmoulins, Danton, Robespierre, Saint-Just, Napoleon, the heroes as well as the parties and the masses of the old French Revolution, performed in Roman costume and with Roman phrases the task of their age: that of unchaining and establishing modern bourgeois society. . . . Once the new social formation had been brought into being, the antediluvian colossi disappeared and with them the resurrected Romans–all those Brutuses, Gracchi, Publicolas, Tribunes, Senators, and Caesar himself. Bourgeois society in its prosaic reality had brought forth its true interpreters and spokesmen in the Says, Cousins, Royer-Collards, Benjamin Constants, and Guizots; its authentic field marshals sat behind the office desk, and the hogheaded Louis XVIII served as its political chief. Wholly absorbed in the production of wealth and the peaceful rivalry of competition, this society no longer realized that its cradle had been surrounded by the departed spirits of Roman antiquity. And yet, for all its unheroic nature, it nonetheless required heroism, sacrifice, terror, civil war, and national slaughter to bring bourgeois society to birth. And in the classically austere traditions of the Roman Repub-

> lic its gladiators found the ideals and the art forms, the self-deceptions they needed in order to conceal from themselves the bourgeois limitations of their struggles, and to maintain their passion at the level of historic tragedy. Thus too at another stage of development, a century earlier, Cromwell and the English people borrowed from the Old Testament the language, the passions, and the illusions [they needed] for their bourgeois revolution. When the real aim had been achieved, when the bourgeois transformation of English society had been accomplished, Locke supplanted Habakkuk. (*Selected Works*, 97-98; tr. in part revised after the German original)

What this signified was (1) that modern society had arisen from a series of political convulsions dating back at least to the seventeenth century and (2) that the "bourgeois revolution" had given birth to a social reality quite unlike anything its creators had actually intended. That is to say, the actual transformation had been accomplished through the instrumentality of what Marx and Engels came to describe as "false consciousness" or "ideology." It followed that, for socialists to avoid a similar outcome, they must above all guard themselves from the temptation to relapse into the "ideological" thought-forms proper to the bourgeois revolution. Their own theorizing had to be "scientific" and historical at once: they must not merely perceive empirical reality as it presented itself, but *see through it.*

In principle it was open to mid-Victorian liberals to adopt a similarly disillusioned view of their ancestors. The revolution having been accomplished, it was possible to look back and draw up a balance-sheet (to employ the language of the age). But those who felt inclined to systematize liberalism—John Stuart Mill is the greatest name in this tradition—were handicapped by their commitment to the culture of their age. Mill to some extent outgrew the utilitarian creed in which he had been brought up by his father, James Mill; nor was he indifferent to the claims of socialism—in a fashion he even sympathized with them—but he never saw either capitalism or bourgeois society as a whole. He was inside the system, and if he disliked some aspects of it, he did not question its assumptions. Marx was both an insider and an outsider. So, in his own queer way, was Comte, who had started his career as secretary to Saint-Simon. But Comte (in this respect resembling Proudhon, with whom otherwise he had little in common) was limited, and, for good measure, he was more than a little mad. Socialism and sociology both came to birth in France, while theoretical economics reached its ultimate perfection in England. But it was Marx who fused all these intellectual creations, and he did so against the background of Germany's recent revolution in philosophy.

In a later chapter, something will have to be said about the part played by Bentham, Mill, and Comte in preparing the ground for the Fabian school of British socialism. In a different context, more attention ought perhaps to be paid to Comte's role in formulating an authoritarian creed which a century after his death could still be invoked by Latin American military dictatorships officially committed to the Comtean slogan "Order and Progress." There is food for thought here, especially when one considers that Comte had broken with the Saint-Simonians on the issue of socialism versus private entrepreneurship. Comte's doctrine was from the first distinguished by its determinist character, its emphasis upon "science," and its tendency to turn "society" into an entity different from, and superior to, the individuals composing it. Even so, a considerable distance separates his early writings from his celebrated *Cours de philosophie positive* (1830-42) and the latter (which had some influence upon John Stuart Mill but none upon Marx) from the full-fledged Comtean doctrine outlined in the *Système de politique positive* (1851-54). It was this work that supplied the authoritarians of a later age with a philosophy of sorts, but it also provoked a split among Comte's followers—a subject we shall briefly examine when we approach the ancestry of Fabianism. Here it is sufficient to say that Comte represented the side of Saint-Simonism which did *not* appeal to Marx. In consequence Marx tended to ignore him, while going back to Saint-Simon and reinterpreting him in the light of Hegel's philosophy.

This rather difficult topic is only indirectly relevant to our main theme, but the preceding extract from Marx's celebrated pamphlet of 1852 can serve as a guide to what was principally at stake between Hegelians and adherents of the empiricist school, of which J. S. Mill was then the outstanding representative in England, while Comte may be said to have founded its French branch. Anyone who takes the trouble to follow Marx's argument will see that he is operating with an essentially Hegelian concept: the "cunning of history." For a theist, this notion might signify something very closely related to the inscrutable design of Providence. To an atheist like Marx it signified that history had a logic of its own which could be deciphered, on condition that no serious account was taken of the "ideological" fantasies spun by the actors of the drama. In this sense, the "historical materialism" of Marx was still indebted to the idealist philosophy of Hegel. It was also at variance with empiricism. Since German philosophy after Kant was largely animated by a romantic distaste for Anglo-French rationalism, and since this bias carried over into politics (inasmuch as the Romantics came to distrust liberalism as being Western and therefore "mechanistic"), one can argue that both topics are relevant to Marxism, but one must not make the mistake of identifying the historical materialism of Marx with the "dialectical materialism" later put forward by Engels. Unlike his friend, Marx never proposed a theory of the universe. And secondly, even if he had done so, it would not necessarily affect one's judgment of the contribution he made to the understanding of history. This must be the excuse for saying nothing about dialectical materialism: a doctrine elaborated by Engels and others after the death of Marx. Anyone is free to believe that historical materialism (so described by Engels in his polemic against Dühring in 1876-78) is rooted in a more general theory of how the material world operates. But in point of fact it was the other way around: Marx's followers transformed his theory of history into what the Germans call a *Weltanschauung*, and Lenin's successors eventually turned it into something even more grandiose, namely a state religion. Although extremely important in its own way, this development is quite extraneous to our theme. Socialists do not necessarily have to be Marxists, and Marxists are not obliged to adopt "dialectical materialism"–in fact they are better off without it.

Now clearly this does not apply to those of Marx's own writings which were either published by Engels after his death, e.g., the *Theses on Feuerbach*, originally jotted down in 1845, but made public only in 1888; or neglected until the 1930's, e.g., the celebrated Paris Manuscripts of 1844, which made their first appearance in 1932, were largely ignored at the time and came to be read by the general public only in the 1950's, when they were republished in the original German and in a number of other languages. By now these early works are so well known that neither exposition nor comment is necessary. Anyone who is at all interested in Marx or in socialism has read or will read them–to say nothing of the quite astonishing amount of nonsense that has been written about them. Their significance within the corpus of Marx's work has become the theme of impassioned debates in East and West—debates which (in the Soviet sphere anyhow) tend to acquire both political and emotional overtones. The humanist creed they embody has been endorsed by democratic Socialists, "revisionist" Communists, philosophical existentialists, and practicing anarchists. They have also made an impact upon left-wing Catholics and liberal Protestants and, for that reason, have been treated with suspicion by old-fashioned atheists, whether Social Democrats or Communists. In short, the topic has entered the general consciousness. But it is by no means evident that it ought to figure prominently in an account of socialist theory, for the specifically socialist content of the *Economic and Philosophical Manuscripts* is not easy to disentangle from Marx's general indictment of modern civilization—which of course is why these writings have become popular with people who happen to dislike not just capitalism but industrialism generally. Take the following passage:

> Just as alienated labour transforms free and self-directed activity into a means, so it transforms the species-life of man into a means of physical existence. Consciousness, which man has from his species, is transformed through alienation so that species-life becomes only a means for him. Thus alienated labour turns the species-life of man, and also nature as his mental species-property, into an alien being and into a means for his individual existence. It alienates from man his own body, external nature, his mental life and his human life. A direct consequence of the alienation of man from the product of his labour, from his life activity and from his species-life, is that man is alienated from other men. (Bottomore, ed., *Early Writings*, 128-29)

Now it is true that Marx combines this analysis of what the division of labor does to *man* with an indictment of what capitalism does to the *worker*. There is thus an implication that the whole disaster is due to the particular historical form taken by the Industrial Revolution in its transitory bourgeois phase, from which it follows that communism will abolish not only the bourgeois property relationship, but the division of labor itself, including the antithesis between mental and physical labor. Since Marx made a statement to this effect over thirty years later, in the *Critique of the Gotha Program* (1875), one cannot dismiss the philosophy of the Manuscripts as a piece of youthful romanticism. But even though it be agreed that the humanist vision held out in these early writings was never quite abandoned, and indeed was concretized in *Capital*, one has to face the fact that in 1844 Marx had not yet gone very far in disentangling the critique of capitalism from the familiar habit of deploring the atomization of modern society, a theme he shared with classicist admirers of antiquity and romantic adherents of medievalism alike. The Paris Manuscripts are important just because they are *not*, strictly speaking, a finished piece of social analysis. They are philosophical in that they disclose the unspoken assumptions with which Marx approached his task. And of course they are "utopian" in that they anticipate a distant future and a complete "transvaluation of values" (to employ the language of a very different school of philosophy). But Marx, unlike Bakunin and his anarchist progeny, did not place his trust in mere agitation. He was enough of a Hegelian to believe that history had its own logic and that this logic pointed obscurely in the direction of communism.

At this point one inevitably comes up against the difficulty of having to decide how much of Hegel's philosophy Marx retained in his later years, when he had absorbed Comte, Darwin, and the climate of positivism generally. There is no problem about his early writings. His starting-point was Hegel (or Hegel plus J. G. Fichte [1762-1814], who was then rather popular with the Young Hegelians because of the stress he laid upon purposeful activity). Like Hegel, Marx envisaged freedom concretely, as the overcoming of obstacles to the fulfillment of man's historic destiny; unlike Hegel, he thought in terms of going beyond bourgeois society (not to mention the Prussian state, whose official apologist Hegel became in his later years). Having begun with the philosophy of the Enlightenment, then, he turned the table on the liberals by taking the promise of human emancipation seriously and contrasting it with the miserable reality of bourgeois society. In doing so, he was not merely, like so many other radicals of his age (e.g., the materialist philosopher Ludwig Feuerbach [1804-72]), measuring reality against a humanist ideal. He was asserting the superior realism of his own viewpoint. Bourgeois society had "alienated" the worker from the instruments of his toil. It had thereby opened up a gulf between the classes, but at the same time it furnished the means for transcending its own contradictions. The industrial proletariat—reduced to servitude by the operation of the economy–was the predestined instrument of human emancipation. Existing society was a veiled form of class rule, although its official ideology denied this. A radical critique of this ideology was thus at the same time a precondition of actual change. For what kept the system going was an economic mechanism that subordinated the elementary needs of human beings–specifically, the material needs of the exploited class–to the interests of capital. The class conflict inherent in this situation would eventually reflect itself in a political revolution whereby the bourgeois limitations of freedom and equality would be overcome. This revolution would in principle serve the needs of all men, but only the working class could bring it about. Hence mere appeals to freedom and justice were futile, for each class interpreted these ideals in its own specific terms. Hence too the ineffectiveness of old-style Rousseauist democrats. Proudhon, for example, being the more or less conscious spokesman of the peasant or the craftsman, interpreted "justice" to mean "exchange of equivalents." But an exchange of equivalents was impossible under capitalism, as Marx sought to demonstrate in his polemic against Proudhon. What was possible and necessary was the transfer of the means of production to the collectivity. This, however, was only a means to an end. The end was the "classless society."

It is as well to be clear about the fact that this was a *communist* slogan, not merely a *socialist* one. The idea of an egalitarian community without private property, and thus without class distinctions, was very ancient, but in its modern form it had been developed by the followers of Babeuf and Buonarroti, that is, by the French communists we encountered earlier. We have also seen that the realization of this aim could be conceived in two different ways: the "Icarian" utopia of withdrawal from the world of capitalism, and the revolutionary overthrow of the existing society by a (transitional) dictatorship. As envisaged by Bakunin's heirs (and later by Lenin's), the political form of a communist society would differ from liberal (bourgeois) democracy in that there would be no need for parliamentary government or indeed for any separation of power between executive and legislative. All these institutions would be replaced by the unitary and consensual self-administration of the people: that is to say, the people in its entirety would be legislator, administrator, and judge. This anarchist ideal was implicit in early French "communism," but the true anarchists did not think it could be made to work on a large scale–not only must the state disappear, but society must be broken up into small self-governing units–whereas the communists held that the classless society would be nationwide and inherit modern industry and everything that went with it. Marx developed this theme in the *Communist Manifesto* and more briefly in his pamphlet on the Paris Commune, *The Civil War in France*. He also hinted at it in his *Critique of the Gotha Program*, although by then (1875) he had come to reserve communism–as distinct from socialism–for a distant future, so distant as to have virtually no political meaning for the first generation of Marxists. In practice, his German and French followers were concerned with socialism: public ownership of the means of production and exchange.

A philosophy of history is not, of course, the same as a theory of society, and while it was certainly Marx's intention to analyze the actual logic of the historical process, one may legitimately inquire to what extent he was helped or hindered by his philosophical inheritance. It is arguable that this heritage was in a sense irrelevant: a provisional structure to be taken down after the building (a theory of society) had been put up. This later became the standpoint of the more positivist among Marx's followers. To cite an eminent representative of this school: "Marx's materialistic science, being a strictly empirical investigation into definite historical forms of society, does not need a philosophical support" (Korsch, 169). But the same author also had this to say:

> Just as positivism could not move with freedom in the new field of social science, but remained tied to the specific concepts and methods of natural science, so Marx's historical materialism has not entirely freed itself from the spell of Hegel's philosophical method, which in its day overshadowed all contemporary thought. This was not a materialistic science of society which had developed on its own basis. Rather it was a materialistic theory that had just emerged from idealistic philosophy; a theory, therefore, which still showed in its contents, its methods, and its terminology the birth-marks of the old Hegelian philosophy from whose womb it sprang. (Korsch, 231)

Since the author of these lines was at the time of writing (1938) still a Communist, it is significant that in substance he was repeating what the arch-revisionist Eduard Bernstein (1850-1932) had suggested forty years earlier, when he first scandalized Engels' followers among the German Social Democrats by questioning the value of Hegel's philosophy. Evidently, then, this is not a party matter.

There is a further difficulty. Suppose we agree to treat Marx as a theorist of society who had emancipated himself (though perhaps never completely) from Hegel's outlook. We are then faced with a different kind of problem: to what extent did Marx, in the act of criticizing the liberal philosophy of his time, nonetheless retain some elements of it? We have seen that his theory of the bourgeois revolution and his critique of capitalist economics were taken over by the socialist movement and made to serve labor's struggle for emancipation. As such, Marxism proved enormously effective—far more so than any rival socialist doctrine. The question is how far the theory served its long-run purpose. Marx's aim had been to formulate a socialist critique of bourgeois society, and no one can deny that he succeeded where his predecessors had failed. He penetrated to the heart of the system—the logic of the market economy. Whatever may be thought of his theoretical economics (we shall come to that presently), there is no questioning the acuteness of his insight. His critique of liberalism struck at the system's inmost nerve: the way in which its philosophy had drawn a veil over the process that converted live human substance (labor) into material wealth (capital). There is a celebrated passage in *Capital* where Marx appends an ironic gloss to the then customary description of a social order in which self-interest supposedly serves the general good:

> This sphere that we are deserting, within whose boundaries the sale and purchase of labour-power goes on, is in fact a very Eden of the innate rights of man. There alone rule Freedom, Equality, Property and Bentham. Freedom, because both buyer and seller of a commodity, say of labour-power, are constrained only by their own free will. They contract as free agents, and the agreement they come to is but the form in which they give legal expression to their common will. Equality, because each enters into relation with the other, as with a simple owner of commodities, and they exchange equivalent for equivalent. Property, because each disposes only of what is his own. And Bentham, because each looks only to himself. The only force that brings them together and puts them in relation with each other is the selfishness, the gain, and the private interests of each.

> Each looks to himself only, and no one troubles himself about the rest, and just because they do so, do they all, in accordance with the pre-established harmony of things, or under the auspices of an all-shrewd providence, work together to their mutual advantage, for the common weal and in the interest of all. (Marx, *Capital*, I, 155)

The point Marx is making is that whereas this *appears* to be the case to those concerned, the true outcome is quite different. The purpose of his analysis is to tear the ideological veil off. As he puts it in the same context: "Here we shall see, not only how capital produces, but how capital is produced. We shall at last force the secret of profit making."

Still, it is important to see that while Marx held up the mirror to a social order whose economic mechanism "produced capital" out of living labor, he followed the economists (Ricardo above all) in describing the process and employed their logic in defining class interest in economic terms. Classes had arisen on the basis of market relations; what distinguished them from the "estates" of an earlier age was precisely that they were defined not in legal but in economic terms. On paper, all individuals had equal rights, once the ancient privileges of "rank" had been abolished. In actual fact, the property-owners constituted a new privileged stratum, even where they had extended the parliamentary franchise to the workers. (By 1867, when *Capital* was first published in the German original, this was substantially the case in England.) Class was rooted in property, and property automatically conferred political power. The question was whether this would always be the case. By the same token, one might ask whether the distinction between "state" and "society" would always be as clear-cut as it appeared to Marx—and to the liberals.

Let us see what this distinction implied. To the ancients and their modern successors, down to and including Machiavelli, there was no theoretical problem about the difference between civic status and political power. How could there be if all citizens took part in public affairs? The first modern thinkers to distinguish the political authority (the state) from society were Hobbes and Locke—not accidentally both English, since England was further along the road of bourgeois development than the other European countries and a clear-cut division between state and society was possible only after the typical feudal amalgam of social-economic and legal-political "rights" had been replaced by the new institutional arrangements that grew up alongside the market-centered economy. Politics was now perceived as something distinct from the sphere of ordinary social life. The latter was rooted in market relations—that is to say, in relations between propertied individuals. In the eighteenth century this state of affairs was taken for granted by the Scottish economists and historians and by their French contemporaries: notably the physiocrats, of whom François Quesnay (1694-1774) is the best known. These writers, aided by constitutional theorists like Montesquieu (1689-1755), built up the body of doctrine later known disparagingly as *laissez-faire* liberalism, although the physiocrats are perhaps more celebrated for their peculiar doctrine that farming is the only truly productive economic activity. (They had in mind, however, the capitalist landlord, not the peasant or the agricultural laborer.) Rousseau had no adequate theory of the modern state and thus got his Jacobin pupils into trouble, since they could never understand why eighteenth-century Frenchmen did not behave like ancient Romans. After the Revolution had run its course, Saint-Simon and Comte found the explanation: bourgeois society had emancipated itself from the state. From then on French and British historians and sociologists made a sharp distinction between the political and social spheres. So did the Germans, although they tended to think more highly of the state than did the French and English liberals. Hegel, indeed, in his *Philosophy of Right* (1821), made a final and not very successful attempt to represent civil society as an inferior domain. He saw that it existed, disliked its autonomy, and demanded that it be regulated in accordance with the overriding aims of the supreme political authority. His doctrine, which is closer to Hobbes than to Locke, rests on the notion of an antagonism between selfish individual and group interests (civil society) and the superior claims of the community (or the nation) as embodied in the state. In this respect he had been preceded by Fichte and was to find a distinguished pupil in Ferdinand Lassalle (1825-64), of whom little more need be said than that he differed from Marx principally in that he remained an orthodox Hegelian (and for this reason always had admirers among German professors and civil servants who could not stand Marx). For Lassalle, socialism represented the interest of the entire community because it placed the common good above the selfish claims of the individual or the group. Not that Lassalle was a "national socialist" in the pejorative sense this term later acquired. He was too civilized for that, quite apart from the fact that as a Jew he could not well function as the herald of a rabidly Teutonic and racialist movement. The fact remains that Marx stood out among the early German socialists—though not among the French who were already "materialists" in his sense of the term—just because he did *not* share the traditional idealist veneration for the state. Indeed, his first real break with the Hegelian legacy occurred in 1842-43 in the form of an (unpublished) critical essay on Hegel's *Philosophy of Right*, specifically on those passages where Hegel had tried to represent the state as an ethical construction superior to civil society (see Avineri, 17 ff.).

If the state did not transcend society—as Hegel, in common with the entire German idealist tradition, had held—then what did it do? The customary liberal-democratic reply to this question was simple enough: politics served the welfare of the citizenry. To this the socialists in general, and Marx in particular, objected that society was not homogenous. Neither was it a mere aggregate of private individuals. Rather, it was split into conflicting classes that differed on fundamentals. The state, on this assumption, might attempt to mediate between the classes, but it would do so primarily in the interest of safeguarding ruling-class interests defined as "order," which in turn signified that there would be no basic political change that could be represented as "disorder." If radical liberals argued that under democracy there was no "ruling class," because all citizens had equal rights and (approximately) equal chances, the answer was that such a condition of things presupposed a society of free and equal citizens who were owners of private property, which was just what modern capitalism tended to eliminate. The theory of liberal democracy was no longer relevant to a state of affairs under which organized capital and organized labor confronted one another. But what would happen if the working class acquired political power within the system? In the *Communist Manifesto* (1848) this possibility had barely begun to appear on the horizon. Marx was here concerned to oppose "proletarian dictatorship" to "bourgeois dictatorship." By the time of the First International (1864-76), he and Engels had modified their standpoint sufficiently to allow for the democratic conquest of power, and eventually this became the conventional outlook of Marxist Social Democracy. But in the 1840's, Marx's newly adopted "materialist" standpoint permitted only one conclusion: if the state in some sense expressed or reflected the class structure of society, then the existing state must be the political guardian of bourgeois society—as indeed it was.

So far as nineteenth-century politics went, the Marxian analysis was realistic, but we must inquire what were its built-in limitations. In retrospect it is clear that in the *Manifesto* Marx read a particular notion of class conflict back into earlier situations to which it was not really applicable. He corrected this mistake in his later writings, but his mature analysis was too subtle for his followers. As a result they never quite grasped that the phenomenon of class—as well as the sharp distinction between state and society—was closely linked to the market economy and its social counterpart: bourgeois society. The *Manifesto* made far too sweeping a claim when it asserted that "the history of all hitherto existing society is the history of class struggles," and Engels did not help matters when (in a footnote added in 1888) he introduced an exception for primitive tribal society. For the real issue was not the existence of communal ownership of land among the ancient Celts or Slavs, but the mechanism of social strife under conditions where "class" could no longer be defined in strictly economic terms. Later Marxists eventually came around to the view that class analysis in economic terms was applicable only to bourgeois society, but by then a good deal of energy had been wasted. Moreover, it took them some further time (plus the experience of the Russian Revolution and the Communist movement) before they realized that the particular form of class conflict described in the *Manifesto* was a by-product of the bourgeois revolution. A Jacobin-Blanquist theory modeled on French experience might suit the Russian Marxists (or some of them), but it could not provide a model for the Western labor movement, even though that movement had inherited the democratic tradition once associated with the emancipation of the "third estate."

But Marx's approach also had a more general theoretical horizon. Having rid himself of Hegel's political philosophy and accepted the Anglo-French view of society as autonomous, he likewise adopted the conclusion that society was in some sense more "real" than the state. This belief was inherent in his familiar distinction between "economic base" and "political superstructure," a notion which would have done little harm if Engels had not later generalized it into his own private version of the doctrine miscalled "historical materialism." As formulated by Marx in the Preface to his *Critique of Political Economy*

(1859), the contrast between "structure" and "superstructure" has genuine analytical value as a way of saying something about the process of societal evolution. By the time Engels had begun to popularize Marx's thought for the benefit of the German labor movement in his *Anti-Dühring* (1878), the "materialist" standpoint was understood to signify that "the final causes of all social changes and political revolutions are to be sought . . . not in the *philosophy*, but in the *economics* of each particular epoch." Now clearly a great deal depends on how "final" the "final cause" is thought to be. It may be so remote as to be invisible. It may also be confused with what goes on in the market place. Marx intended neither of these silly meanings. What he had in mind was the relationship of a particular technological upheaval (the industrial revolution) to a particular society (the bourgeois one). Beyond that, he simply took for granted—as Smith and Ricardo had done before him—that "society" was both logically and historically anterior to the "state."

This depreciation of the political realm is one aspect of what later became known as the "materialist conception of history." As outlined by Marx and then popularized by his followers, this doctrine lent itself to a kind of technological determinism: new "forces of production" somehow generated new "relations of production" (corresponding more or less to what Comte meant by "society"), and upon this "material base" there arose the "superstructure" of politial institutions and ideas. There are some notorious errors to be avoided in trying to picture this process. First, it is not a matter of technology by itself causing a social revolution. It was Napoleon, not Marx, who said "Cannon killed feudalism." Cannon did nothing of the sort. It merely speeded the demise of the typically feudal form of military combat, which is not the same thing. Napoleon's own career was to show that artillery (the French artillery was already the best in Europe before he employed it to smash enemy armies, but he certainly made more efficient use of it than his opponents) was powerless to alter the relation of social forces or to overcome the handicaps of geography. The kind of technological enthusiasm typified by Napoleon's dictum about cannon became an article of faith in the École Polytechnique, where his officers were trained and where the Saint-Simonians later got their first foothold. But it is not "Marxist," and if on rare occasions Marx employed similar language, he later qualified it. Second, the kind of "economic determinism" to which Marx's theory of history has sometimes been reduced fails to do justice to its complexity. And third, this sort of determinism must on no account be confused with the question of economic motive. The notion that individuals and classes have throughout history been uniformly "motivated" by the hope of economic gain was an article of faith with the disciples of Smith and Bentham; it was also what Marx most disliked about them. So far from regarding it as true, he invariably treated this belief as an instance of what in his impolite fashion he termed "bourgeois asininity." If this is kept in mind, a great deal of vacuous talk about "the economic interpretation of history" can be (and should have been) avoided.

Nonetheless, liberalism and Marxism had more in common than was visible during the years of the epic contest between them—a contest that began in real earnest about 1870 and reached its peak around 1930, when both classical liberalism and classical Marxism began to disintegrate, politically and theoretically. For our immediate purpose it is enough to say that Marx set out his critique of Hegel's authoritarian doctrine of the state before he had himself become a socialist. Once having turned from liberalism to socialism—a process set in motion by his encounter with the French socialists and communists in Paris between 1843 and 1845—he developed the critique of classical economics for which he was to become famous. But he never worked out a consistent theory of the state, although this was part of his original intention in drafting the general plan of *Capital*. We are thus obliged to register the fact that the only great thinker the socialist movement produced—for none of the others are within a hundred miles of him—did not try to forecast the transition from the existing social order to another. *Capital* was not meant to be a blueprint for socialism. This did not begin to trouble his followers for another generation, but the lack of an adequate political theory then made itself felt.

6 Marx: Economics

Enough has already been said to make it clear that Marx the economist cannot be separated from Marx the sociologist or historian. Nonetheless, even Marx's followers, not to mention his critics, have been seriously divided over the relevance of his philosophy to his economics. Matters are not eased by the fact that some of his most important writings came to light after the more technical controversies over his economic doctrine had spent themselves. It was bad enough that the second and third volumes of *Capital* were left unfinished and had to be edited and published by Engels (in 1885 and 1894 respectively) after Marx had died. An immense treatise on the history of economic doctrine, composed in 1861-63, was made public by Karl Kautsky in 1905-10 in three volumes under the title *Theories of Surplus Value* (subsequently re-edited and re-published in the East German edition of Marx's collected *Works*). And in 1939-41 the Marx-Engels Institute in Moscow brought to light for the first time the full text of Marx's 1857-58 draft of *Capital*: a thousand-page work entitled *Grundrisse der Kritik der Politischen Ökonomie*. These circumstances may seem important only to specialists, but in fact they concern anyone interested in the theory of socialism, for the only genuine link between Marx's sociology and his economics is to be found in the *Grundrisse*, a work whose gradual dissemination has obliged Marxists and non-Marxists alike to revise a number of previously accepted notions concerning the Marxian approach. Acquaintance with the *Grundrisse* makes it plain, for example, that Marx's economic and social theorizing in the 1840's, down to and including the *Manifesto*, does not carry the full authority of his subsequent utterances.

Since it is quite impossible in the space at our disposal to give an account, however brief, of Marx's economic doctrines, we shall have to content ourselves with a sketch of his intellectual development, plus a few general observations on the relevance of his work to socialist economics at the present day. The student in search of enlightenment on technical points may consult the works listed in the short bibliography, which should satisfy his or her appetite, as long as it is understood that we are dealing with Marx, not with his followers, and that the purpose of this chapter is to bring out the internal logic of his argument. Our aim is restricted to clarifying (1) what he actually said and (2) in what way his work on economics was related to his theory of society.

If the matter is put in this way, there appears at first sight to be a fairly simple conclusion. As an economist, Marx inherited a certain body of doctrines from his predecessors, notably Ricardo, subjected them to systematic investigation, and developed a theory of his own which was both an analysis of capitalism and a critique of classical "political economy." This is the conventional view of the matter; it is also perhaps the only aspect of this whole topic on which both Marx's followers and his critics are agreed. In itself this approach is not wrong, but it is deficient in that it fails to make clear precisely what distinguished Marx from writers like Proudhon on the one hand, and from the Ricardian socialists on the other. The latter included the German economist Johann Karl Rodbertus (1805-1875), who was both a conservative in politics (being a landowning Prussian monarchist) and a socialist in economics, in that he derived a theory of exploitation from his reading of Ricardo. Contrary to a legend put about by some German academics, Marx and Engels derived no inspiration whatever from Rodbertus, whereas Lassalle did.

Since Lassalle's brief and stormy political career was largely determined by a tactical attempt to strike a bargain with Bismarck (after having first created a socialist labor movement led by himself), there was every reason why he should go to Rodbertus rather than to Marx for his economic theorizing, and in fact Lassalle's observations in the 1860's on what he called the "iron law" of wages were an echo of doctrines put forward earlier by Rodbertus. Both men held that under capitalism real wages cannot rise above a mere subsistence level; both agreed that proof of this contention was to be found in Ricardo; and both demanded that the state should do something about it. Here their paths diverged. Rodbertus placed his faith in the benevolence of the ruling bureaucracy and was skeptical of Lassalle's campaign for universal suffrage. Lassalle, a political adventurer with a career to make (and a Jewish intellectual to boot, hence ineligible for entry into the Prussian ruling caste, although his personal ties were with the aristocracy), looked to the labor movement to put pressure on the government and for the rest sought to draw it away from the liberals. At the same time he had no faith in the effectiveness of trade unions or in consumer cooperatives on the Owenite model. His long-term remedy, which seems to have been suggested by Louis Blanc's unsuccessful experiments in 1848, was strikingly simple: the workers must become their own employers. Industry should be reorganized on the basis of producer cooperatives, with ownership and control vested in the workers. But who was to effect this transformation? Lassalle's reply testified to his intellectual descent from Fichte and Hegel: it was to be done by the state—not some future socialist regime, but the existing Prussian one! This, however, could only be done if the workers gained political control of the government by means of universal suffrage.

In this way Lassalle constructed a plausible link between his socialist economics and the drive for a broader electoral franchise: two quite distinct issues held together only by his personality. And his branch of the nascent Social Democratic movement inherited this legacy after his sudden death in a duel in 1864. In a certain fundamental sense the German socialist movement remained true to his spirit even after it had become superficially reconciled to Marxism (largely through the instrumentality of Engels and his two distinguished pupils, Liebknecht and Bebel, in the 1870's and 1880's). Lassalle was emphatically a German patriot. And even more emphatically he was an authoritarian who looked to the state to refashion society. All this was in the best (or worst) German tradition, arising from an outlook born in the so-called "war of liberation" against Napoleon in 1813 and pointing straight to the patriotic attitude adopted by German Social Democracy in 1914.

No one familiar with this tradition could have had the slightest doubt how the movement would react to the challenge of war, especially since the Lassalleans had already struck a patriotic note on the occasion of the Franco-German conflict in 1870.

This is the place to introduce a few remarks about German socialism and the early German labor movement. The industrial revolution having reached the Continent about half a century after its first disastrous impact on the British Isles, socialist ideas were already in existence when the nascent labor movement in Central Europe began to look for political leadership. One consequence of this was the relatively early maturation of a Social Democratic party, which then took the lead in organizing the working class. With only a slight degree of exaggeration it may be said that on the Continent, more especially in Germany, trade unions were created by the political party, whereas in Britain the party was created (after 1900) by the unions. One may also say that in Germany the unions became socialist at a relatively early date–in part due to Lassalle's very effective oratorical campaign in 1862-64–whereas British unionism for another generation trailed in the wake of political liberalism. Both the British and the German movements reflected a deep-rooted hostility to the operation of an uncontrolled market economy and a determination to assert labor's rights against the power of capital. But the German unions looked to the state, the British to collective self-help. On the Continent, the authoritarian state was hostile to democracy–more so than in Britain–but ready enough to pass legislation which rendered the impact of the market economy upon the worker's welfare somewhat less disastrous. This had long-term implications for the political outlook of the German labor movement. Marxism and Lassalleanism articulated a rudimentary form of class consciousness, but they also taught the workers to identify socialism with the passage of welfare legislation extracted from the state.

Rodbertus and Lassalle left their mark on German public life, but neither of them exercised any influence abroad. Friedrich Engels (1820-95) did so as Marx's lifelong associate from 1844 onward, when he was twenty-four and just about to publish his famous indictment of British capitalism and the Manchester school: his book on the condition of the British working class (1845). What drew the two young men together in the first place was an essay Engels contributed in 1844 to the *Deutsch-Französische Jahrbücher*, then briefly edited by Arnold

Ruge and Marx. In this sketch, of which Marx evidently thought highly, Engels put forward a socialist critique of British capitalism in essentially moralistic terms derived from Owen and from Carlyle, whose *Past and Present* (1843) Engels had liked, although he deplored Carlyle's Tory romanticism. The edge of Engels' polemic was turned against the market economy, whose ruthless logic (as he saw it) threatened to dissolve the bonds of family life, of social solidarity, and of human morality itself. Private property and free competition, those twin poles of liberalism, had begun to animate a feverish struggle in which the weak went to the wall. Capital and labor, originally one and the same thing, had been torn asunder, thus giving birth to a class antagonism which threatened society with dissolution. On top of this, economists such as Malthus were preaching the inhuman doctrine that the poor should not be encouraged to propagate children, there being already too many of them. This "infamous, abominable doctrine" was but the logical consequence of the system excogitated by the liberal economists. Birth and death subordinated to the demands of the market—there was capitalism in practice! Unbridled competition was the law of the system. It must be replaced by a rational organization of production if mankind was to be preserved from catastrophe.

There is evidently a connection between the appearance of this essay and Marx's 1844 Paris Manuscripts, but Marx, while elaborating on Engels' rather vague hints about the destructive side of the market economy, introduced a different line of reasoning: what was wrong with bourgeois society was not that it relegated moral considerations to the attic in favor of cold calculation, but that it turned labor into a commodity, thereby causing the alienation of the producer from his human essence. Still, Marx's early writings on economics did emphasize the importance of competition and the market for the functioning of the system. The *Communist Manifesto* likewise had a rather moralistic passage on the all-pervasive rule of economic motivation leaving "no other nexus between man and man than naked self-interest." On the theoretical side, Marx's *Poverty of Philosophy* (1847) demolished Proudhon's fantasies about equal exchange among individual producers, while in a lecture series delivered in 1847 (later published under the title *Wage Labor and Capital* in 1849), he affirmed that competition tended to hold wages down to a subsistence level. This was then standard socialist doctrine and was confirmed by experience. But Marx introduced an interesting dialectical argument: profits rise in proportion as labor's share of the total product declines, and yet "the rapid growth of capital is the most favorable condition for wage labor." This observation anticipates the striking remark in the preface to the first German edition of *Capital* (1867): "We . . . suffer not only from the development of capitalist production, but also from the incompleteness of that development." With a side-glance at his native Germany, Marx adds, "Alongside of modern evils, a whole series of inherited evils oppress us, arising from the passive survival of antiquated modes of production, with their inevitable train of social and political anachronisms. We suffer not only from the living but from the dead." It may be noteworthy that a generation later, Lenin, in a polemic with the Russian Populists, made the same point: for Russia the only thing worse than capitalist exploitation was the relative backwardness of capitalist development. Such an approach is quite in accordance with Marx. Unlike most writers of his time, who never saw more than one side of any question, he realized that capitalism, for all its horrors, was a way of developing society's latent wealth: the forces of production. What he detested about the liberal hosannas was their unqualified jubilation over "progress" and their refusal to acknowledge that the whole process was taking place at the expense of the producer. The accumulation of capital was only possible because wage labor had been turned into a commodity subject to the mechanism of demand and supply. From this it followed that wages would normally tend toward a minimum, although it did *not* follow that they must sink below the subsistence level, thus turning the worker into a pauper. Contrary to a popular misconception, pauperization or "immiseration" figures in Marx's mature writings not as an absolute necessity, but as a "tendency"—the obvious implication being that there may also be countervailing tendencies.

What keeps capitalism going is the operation of an impersonal "law." The worker has to sell his labor—or rather, his labor-power (Marx introduced this distinction in *Capital* and Engels incorporated it in the revised text of Marx's earlier writings)—in order to live. He would not do so if labor had not been turned into a commodity. In *Wage Labor and Capital* the social consequences of this state of affairs are spelled out in language reminiscent of the 1844 Manuscripts. This fact, by the way, undercuts the notion that Marx had by then abandoned his earlier standpoint in favor of a "class" approach. He never did anything of the kind, even though after 1846 he gradually abandoned the term "alienation" because it had been discredited by sentimentalists among the so-called "true socialists." Marx's attitude in 1847-49 remained substantially the standpoint he adopted in *Capital*:

> Labor [power] is . . . a commodity which its possessor, the wage-worker, sells to capital. Why does he sell it? In order to live. But the exercise of . . . labor is the worker's own life-activity, the manifestation of his own life. And this life-activity he sells to another person in order to secure the necessary means of subsistence. Thus his life-activity is for him only a means to enable him to exist. He works in order to live. He does not even reckon labor as part of his life, it is rather a sacrifice of his life. It is a commodity which he has made over to another.

The dehumanizing aspect of this transaction always remained Marx's basic objection to capitalism, even though he recognized that wage labor was "free labor" by comparison with the work performed by slaves or serfs. He did not regard this as sufficient reason for enthusing over the institution of a labor market in which the worker was "free" to sell himself on pain of starving to death. Capitalism was "progressive" indeed, but it was progress bought at the price of turning the living worker into an appendage of his own alienated labor. This labor had the unique faculty of producing material value over and above what the worker needed to maintain himself and his family, and this surplus wealth (or value) went to the owner of the means of production: the capitalist.

This may be the place to utter a warning against a rather common misconception. A writer who holds that labor is in some ultimate sense the only source of value is not necessarily committed to the further belief that the prices of all commodities can be reckoned in terms of labor units. There are sound practical reasons for not trying to calculate commodity prices by counting up labor-hours: for example, the difficulty of measuring different kinds or skills of labor, not to mention the awkward problem introduced by the growing importance of scientific technology—a "force of production" clearly dependent upon the input of intellectual labor (including education). Technology blurs the distinction between physical and mental work. How then does one measure "value," if the term is not simply taken to mean the incorporation of physical labor?

One eminent contemporary socialist economist has argued that "there never will be a unit for measuring national income that has the same meaning for everyone, still less a unit that means the same thing at different dates or in the setting of different economic systems" (Robinson, *Economic Philosophy*, 34). Marxists committed to the labor theory of value could agree with this and still maintain that the theory tells one something about the difference between capitalist and pre-capitalist social formations. But what this really means is that it tells one something about the social arrangements characteristic of bourgeois society; it is not a very helpful tool for economists who have to get on with the job of trying to measure the national income. Nor does it indicate where precisely to draw the line between productive and unproductive labor: a distinction Marx had inherited from Smith. In practice this resolved itself into a discrimination between output of physical goods and the performance of noneconomic (albeit socially important) services. This was quite a useful approach, since physical goods are more easily measurable than services, but the sort of measuring-rod it introduced was not designed to analyze the factors entering into the formation of prices. Nor does this particular distinction satisfy those present-day theorists who are concerned to establish rules for measuring skills by transforming physical into intellectual labor, or vice versa. In Marx's day, "labor" could still be equated, by and large, with unskilled manual labor.

Even on this latter assumption, the labor theory of value in Volume I of *Capital* does not work as a theory of prices. But then Marx never supposed it did (Henry Smith, 58 ff.). Its purpose was to set forth the distribution of income between social classes. When Marx got down to price formation (in the concluding volume of *Capital*), he set out a theory which was logically independent of his propositions about the role of labor in value formation. The labor theory is an exploitation theory. (Incidentally, Marx did not hold that labor is the only source of material wealth, as is sometimes suggested. On the contrary, he condemned this popular notion as pernicious nonsense [see his *Critique of the Gotha Program*] because it tended to make people forget that nature was just as much the source of use-values [riches]. It was just because the worker possessed nothing but his naked labor power, the instruments of production having been taken away from him, that he was in practice dependent upon others: those who owned the *natural* sources of wealth.) The entire concept of "exploitation"—in the Marxian sense, not in the popular meaning of the term—stands and falls with the thesis that under capitalism the worker *necessarily* produces a surplus for the benefit of those who own or control the material means of production: including those resources which nature places at the disposal of man. "Exploitation" signifies just this and nothing else. It has nothing whatever to do with the upward or downward movement of wages, and it is not a matter of anyone's good or bad intentions.

Until 1850, then, Marx was a "Ricardian socialist" so far as the analysis of capitalism went. He was a "communist" inasmuch as he envisaged a type of society in which private property in the means of production would be abolished, not merely controlled or regulated in the interest of social harmony, which was what the "socialists" were after. What the mature Marx after 1850 put forward was an analysis of capitalism as a system of commodity production destined to develop the "forces of production" up to a certain point and to decline from that point onward, and he spelled out the reasons for this necessary failure at great length in *Capital*.

Now it is plain that between 1850 and 1880, when Marx virtually stopped working on *Capital*, he not merely heaped up a mountain of unpublished drafts, but also revised some of his earlier notions. One such revision has already been noted. Whereas in his writings of the 1840's he followed the convention of treating "labor" as a commodity like any other, in *Capital* he explained that what the worker sold was rather his "labor power," a unique human attribute in that it denoted a capacity for producing surplus value over and above the value consumed in the process of production. Those classical economists who argued that "labor" was remunerated at its "value" had been unable to explain the phenomenon of profit, while their socialist critics could explain it only by suggesting either that the consumer was being overcharged or that the worker was somehow being cheated or underpaid. The point Marx makes in *Capital* is that, on the contrary, the worker gets the full "value" of his "labor"—that is to say, the "value" of what it costs to keep him and his family going. It merely so happens that his labor *power* (or *potential*) adds "surplus value" to the product, which surplus value accrues to the owner of capital. This obviously has nothing to do with how much the worker is paid or whether real wages tend to rise or fall. The point at issue concerned the source of profit. That the product of "labor" was normally worth more than the reproduction costs of the laborer (his minimum wage or subsistence wage) was obvious, and Marx took it for granted in his early writings. But it is only in *Capital* that "surplus value" becomes the explanation of profit. Of course, if one believes that the concept of value is itself inherently faulty—because value cannot be measured or because it refers to a social relationship rather than an economic magnitude—one need not bother about it. But for Marx, having inherited the notion that "labor" was the measure of "value," there was no logical objection to the further step of arguing that "surplus value" was the source of profit. The typical form of labor (or labor power) in his day was unskilled, hence more or less uniform, and thus measurable. The difficulties his followers encountered when they tried to apply this "value" concept to market prices do not concern us here; with the wisdom of hindsight we can now see that they would have done better to treat "value" as a social category signifying a relationship between people—namely, the producers of commodities; instead, both they and their critics became involved in the pseudo-problem of relating "values" to market prices. This was an inheritance from the classics. Ultimately the idea of measuring commodity prices by making use of a unit of labor-time went back to Ricardo. His immediate followers had deduced from his use of units of labor-time to measure commodity prices the "law" that commodities normally exchange at prices proportional to their *value* (in the sense of labor-time), and were then baffled when they discovered that in actual fact this was not so. But they did not think of "surplus value": this refinement belongs to Marx.

Let us see what the theory of surplus value involved for Marx's sociology of capitalism as a system of production. This analysis took shape in the *Grundrisse* of 1857-58 and was only briefly spelled out in the published text of *Capital*, which is why its importance has frequently been overlooked. Marx had before him a social division of labor still nebulous to Adam Smith but already clear to Ricardo and Malthus: with production carried on under circumstances where the only bond holding the producers together was the exchange value their products fetched in distant markets. On top of this there was the antagonism between capital and labor, concretely manifested in the rise of a workers' movement whose ultimate aim could be summed up in one phrase—recovery of control over the means of production, now monopolized by the capitalist class. What was the connection between these phenomena? Exchange value was associated with commodity production for markets, while surplus value arose in the exchange between capital and labor. On the surface, it appeared that the worker gave his labor and received wages in exchange. In actual fact, the capitalist obtained temporary control over a unique source of energy which possessed the faculty of creating material riches. This was what Marx called exploitation. It was a social arrangement whereby the capitalist class collectively appropriated the creative power of the working class and then used it for purposes of its own. The chief of these purposes was the accumulation of capital. Satisfaction of material wants was incidental to the system, for although use values had to be produced for sale, what the capitalist really needed was *exchange value*. The secret of the operation lay in the fact that he obtained the source of this exchange value by entering into what looked like an equal exchange with the worker. The latter was legally free and could withdraw his labor—especially after he had learned to organize for that purpose. Thus, in the exchange between both parties, capital and labor were mutually dependent on each other and appeared to be on an equal footing. Yet this equal exchange produced social inequality. As Marx put it in the *Grundrisse*, the worker necessarily impoverishes himself "because the creative power of his labor establishes itself in opposition to him, as the power of capital, as an alien power. . . . The separation of labor from possession of the product of labor, the divorce of labor and wealth, is already posited in this act of exchange."

Stored-up labor (capital) enters into an exchange with living labor. The relationship between capital and labor, although juridically an equal one, is in fact weighted in favor of capital because the law assigns to the capitalist the right to dispose over society's productive apparatus, which latter in turn is the creation of past labor, appropriated by earlier generations of capital owners and inherited or bought by new owners. For historical reasons, then, the crystallization of past labor has taken the form of privately owned means of production, controlled by a class of private entrepreneurs (and in a later age by their successors, the banks and the great corporations). These owners constitute a class and confront the laborers collectively, even if the individuals composing the class are not aware of this circumstance. Operating as they do in a market economy, they are obliged to extract a profit from their transactions, and the ultimate source of this profit is living labor—the labor belonging to the individuals under their control.

Now clearly this vision of the capitalist production process is not affected by practical considerations having to do with the increasing or declining share taken by labor in the total product. What Marx is saying, quite simply, is that under capitalism the worker is engaged in building a world which does not belong to him. This "world" includes the entire legal and cultural "superstructure" of bourgeois civilization, a civilization controlled by the possessing class. The notion of "superstructure" is employed in the *Preface* to the 1859 *Critique of Political Economy* (itself an extract from the *Grundrisse*). It is a way of stating the basic principle inherent in the "materialist conception of history." Marx holds that under given conditions the existing property relations (or "relations of production") will correspond to the "material forces of production." This must not be misunderstood as a kind of technological determinism. When Marx speaks of "relations of production" he has in mind the social mechanisms that keep the economy going. The extraction of surplus value from labor power (to use his vocabulary) is such a mechanism. It determines the relationship of the ruling class to those under its control. Bourgeois "relations of production"—supporting the edifice of law, government, politics, and culture: the "superstructure"—have come into being historically and are thus subject to change. But what are we to understand by the "material productive forces of society"? These "productive forces" clearly include technology and science, but equally clearly they also comprise the creative force of labor, itself raised to the highest pitch of effectiveness by the capitalist mode of production. Marx leaves the reader in no doubt on this point. In the *Grundrisse* there is a striking passage on how capitalism creates the preconditions for its own disappearance by developing the productivity of labor:

> What appears as surplus value on the side of capital, appears on the worker's side as surplus labor . . . beyond the immediate requirement for the maintenance of his existence. The great historic side of capital is to *create* this surplus labor, superfluous labor from the standpoint of mere use value, mere subsistence; and its historic destiny is

> fulfilled as soon as, on the one hand, needs [wants] have been so far developed that surplus labor beyond necessity [subsistence] has itself become a general need [want] . . . on the other hand, the general disposition to work [industriousness] has, through the severe discipline of capital . . . been developed into the general property [possession] of the new breed of men [*des neuen Geschlechts*]—finally, when the development of labor's productive forces . . . has reached the point where the possession and maintenance of societal wealth requires a diminishing quantity of labor-time, and where the laboring society takes up a scientific attitude to the process of its progressive reproduction . . . where consequently the kind of work man does, instead of letting it be done by things on his behalf, has come to an end.

A passage such as this tells one a great deal about how Marx's thinking developed in the interval between the writing of the *Communist Manifesto* and the drafting of the first volume of *Capital*. In the first place, there is no longer any romantic or anarchist utopianism about a sudden rising ushering in a new kind of society. In other words, he had by then realized what some of his nominal followers only began to grasp a century later—that the political perspective sketched out in the *Communist Manifesto* was applicable only under fairly primitive conditions. Secondly, we have in this passage a fusion of the historical, sociological, and economic aspects of his theorizing. Thirdly, the attainment of socialism is placed at the end of a lengthy process in the course of which capitalism becomes *superfluous*. Lastly, the humanist philosophy of the 1844 Manuscripts has not by any means been abandoned. On the contrary, it has been concretized into a perspective which is both analytical and normative. From the standpoint of the mature Marx, capitalism appears as a historically conditioned mechanism for developing society's productive powers to the point where the subordination of labor to capital, of living people to dead matter, will become unnecessary. It will be looked upon by later generations as a barbarous relic of the past, in the same way that the liberals of his age had come to regard slavery and serfdom.

But why should capitalism—that is, private property in the means of production—not go on forever, making use of scientific technology, constantly expanding production, improving the conditions of work, and thus rendering itself invulnerable? Marx believed the system was inherently self-destructive, having come into being under conditions where the "material productive forces of society" could only be developed by accumulating riches and poverty at the two opposite poles of society. He clearly underestimated the extent to which real wages could rise under capitalism. (So, for that matter, did the liberal economists of his age.) This is strictly an empirical issue. If "capital" is reckoned in terms of labor-units or wage-units, it is evident that real wages must rise if technical development leads to a cheapening of wage goods or to greater output per man-hour (provided the labor force does not grow faster than the gross social product). In this respect there is no difference between capitalist and socialist economics, as may be seen by comparing the respective developments in Eastern and Western Europe since 1945: on both sides of the political divide, real wages have generally kept pace with technological progress, and where they have not done so this has been due to an insufficient rate of growth, in other words to an inadequate rate of capital formation, whether public or private. The public authorities may use their power to keep labor's share of a growing national product artificially low. (They did this very effectively under both Stalinism and Fascism, the two rival systems having in this respect precisely the same economic function.) But given a normal degree of political freedom, organized labor cannot be prevented from obtaining a more or less constant, or even rising, share of society's output.

Why then is it still possible to employ Marx's analysis to demonstrate the economic superiority of socialism? Because this analysis does not depend on a doctrine of "increasing misery." Capitalism does entail the creation of an urban proletariat during the transition from an agrarian to an industrial order, and where it does so under conditions of political instability it gives its opponents a chance: which is why Communist movements have been notably successful in backward countries suffering the birth-pangs of industrialism. But a mature capitalism does *not* entail "increasing misery," if the public authorities possess the minimum of competence needed to maintain full employment and to keep booms and slumps under control. What it leads to is a state of affairs where it becomes plain that modern industry operates more effectively if it is not loaded down by a body of parasites: the heirs of the original entrepreneurs.

This conclusion is usually associated with Fabianism, and we shall see that the Fabian socialists were indeed among the first to suggest something like it. But it can also be deduced from Marx's argument in the *Grundrisse* and in *Capital*. In the earlier work he looked forward to a state of affairs where, as he put it, "Labor no longer appears as an integral element of the productive process; rather man acts as supervisor and regulator of the productive process itself." In *Capital* he specified the particular reasons why the bourgeois mode of production was self-contradictory and ultimately self-defeating: (1) cyclical crises of over-production and (2) a concentration of ownership whereby production is in the end so centralized that it is no longer compatible with the legal institution of private property. The second point is no longer in dispute. It has been tacitly accepted by modern economists (whose intellectual ancestors would have been horrified by the use currently made of their heritage). As to cyclical crises, the debate between liberal and socialist economists became rather pointless after the Keynesian revolution of the 1930's and 1940's had done away with faith in the self-regulating market economy. Once it was admitted that the public authorities could ensure full employment if private capital investment failed, socialists could start quoting Keynes as well as Marx.

The later development of Marxian economics is chiefly associated with two controversies: over the nature of capitalist crises and over the economic roots of imperialism. The second of these topics became prominent in socialist literature after 1900 and eventually reached a global audience by way of Lenin's theorizing. Marx himself had no theory of imperialism, and neither did Engels, while Karl Kautsky (1854-1938) suggested only the bare rudiments of one, and Rudolf Hilferding (1877-1941) concentrated on the role of finance capital to the exclusion of other factors. What Marx did have was a theory of capital accumulation leading to cyclical crises: that is, periodic convulsions arising from the nature of the production process. This became very topical in the 1930's when capitalism behaved exactly as the more pessimistic Marxists had always said it would. Instead of going over this well-trodden ground, let us briefly look at the connection between Marx's basic assumptions and his account of how the system actually works under ordinary empirical circumstances.

From the economist's standpoint, capitalism is simply a particular way of solving a problem every society must wrestle with: the allocation of resources among the various branches of production. Under ideal conditions (from the liberal viewpoint), the market allocates resources without any central planning by the political authority (the state). Under less ideal conditions, the state makes the basic decisions and leaves the rest to the private entrepreneurs. Either way, the system functions through competition among individual units, whether private firms or publicly controlled enterprises. Competition maximizes technical progress and at the same time eliminates the less efficient units. A competitive market economy normally expands because it has a built-in dynamic principle: capital must be accumulated and production techniques improved in order to keep up with or surpass rivals. Since productivity is not evenly spread throughout the economy, some units will be ahead of others (the same is evidently true of competition among nations, at any rate as long as there is no central world authority). Although progress is uneven and may become catastrophically unbalanced, the system taken as a whole is dynamic, in that growth is a condition of its very existence. All this is familiar stuff, but it took the founders of classical "political economy" quite some time to work out the logic of the argument. The question for us is where Marx stands on this issue. And the answer (which can no longer surprise the reader) is that he regarded the system as inherently unstable and ultimately self-contradictory. It was unstable because there was no over-all planning. It was self-contradictory because it steadily undermined its own foundations. Capitalism's built-in motor–competition–functioned only as long as the economy was atomized into independent units, each trying to price its output above production costs. The mechanism for achieving this aim was technological innovation which raised the productivity of labor, i.e., altered the "organic composition of capital" (the ratio of capital to labor) so as to replace labor by machinery. But the operation of this mechanism tended to bring about a concentration of capital such that in the end the competitive motor ceased to function. This paradoxical result arose because each individual capitalist must try to evade the logic of the system by expanding his own sphere of control. The "anarchy of production" inherent in the system was tolerable in its early stages; it would become socially intolerable once the competing units had become large enough to permit conscious planning. Marx wrote before the era of cartels, monopolies, and other forms of conscious organization, themselves the forerunners of today's nationally planned state capitalism. But the outcome would not have surprised him. It is consistent with his argument in the *Grundrisse* and in the later volumes of *Capital*. It is also consistent with his value theory (although not necessarily dependent on it–on this latter point even Marxist economists have to this day been unable to reach complete agreement).

Marx remains relevant as an economist, then, because he was *more* than an economist. This has indeed long been recognized, but it is only in recent years that the precise link between his sociology and his economics has been clarified by the belated excavation of the massive drafts preceding the only major work of economic theory made public in his own life-time: the first volume of *Capital*. Yet even before these drafts came to light, the logic of his argument had been perceived by economists who for the rest were wholly out of sympathy both with his methods and his aims. Let us conclude by citing the greatest of them all, Joseph Schumpeter, in his *History of Economic Analysis*, a work whose monumental scale would in itself be sufficient to dwarf the efforts of lesser men, even were it not the product of a mind unequalled among modern economists for breadth of vision and depth of penetration:

> Marxist analysis is the only genuinely evolutionary economic theory that the period produced. Neither its assumptions nor its techniques are above serious objections–though, partly, because it has been left unfinished. But the grand vision of an immanent evolution of the economic process–that, working somehow through accumulation, somehow destroys the economy as well as the society of competitive capitalism, and somehow produces an untenable social situation that will somehow give birth to another type of social organization–remains after the most vigorous criticism has done its worst. It is this fact, and this fact alone, that constitutes Marx's claim to greatness as an economic analyst. (Schumpeter, *History of Economic Analysis*, 441)

7 Russian Socialism: 1840-80

1. From Panslavism to Anarchism

A historical study arranged in proper chronological order would at this stage move to the First International–to give it its proper name, the Working Men's International Association–founded in London with the active participation of Marx in 1864, a year that also witnessed the death of Lassalle, and Proudhon disappeared from the scene a few months later. The subsequent conflict between Marx and Bakunin within the International leads on logically to the next stage: the rift between socialism and anarchism. This is how historians of the European labor movement have usually seen it. Bakunin was after all Proudhon's successor, and the motley army he led was for the most part composed of Frenchmen, Belgians, Italians, and Spaniards, although after 1871 Marx too had the support of an influential French faction: the Blanquists. If one is content to describe what occurred in Western and Central Europe during and after the 1870's, the picture is simple enough: social democracy on the one hand, anarchism on the other. The adventitious circumstance that one of the rival camps was headed by a Russian is easily explained in terms of Bakunin's earlier involvement with the 1848 insurrection.

Unfortunately, none of this helps one to understand the peculiar character of the Russian revolutionary movement. Neither does it help if one inquires how it came about that in the 1880's some of the Russian Populists transformed themselves into Marxists while others became liberals. There must have been something in the ideology of the movement that permitted its leaders to box the compass in this manner. What that something was can be discovered by going back to its origins. One then sees that both before and after Bakunin's death in 1876 there were rival currents within Populism, one of which corresponded to the West European anarchist movement, while the other mingled with the Marxist stream. One also understands why it was possible for one and the same man–N. G. Chernyshevsky–to become the patron saint of Populism and the teacher of the first generation of Russian Marxists. And finally one sees that these Marxists, albeit in their own estimation orthodox social democrats, retained some of the characteristic traits of their ancestors. For the moment, however, we must ignore Chernyshevsky and turn our attention to the rival school: that conventionally associated with Alexander Herzen and Michael Bakunin. This procedure is justified on biographical grounds, inasmuch as both men were Marx's contemporaries. But it also has the advantage of establishing that what we are concerned with here is related to the history of socialism. Our theme is the inner logic of the Russian socialist movement during the generational span marked at one end by disillusionment after the failure of the 1848 risings in Europe, and at the other by the crisis of pre-Marxist, "agrarian" radicalism of the Populist variety, in the 1880's.

Now clearly the term "socialism" is here applied in a very broad sense. We have already seen, in dealing with the revolutionary current in Western Europe between 1830 and 1870, that one must discriminate between "socialism" properly so called and "communism": the latter really signifying a subdivision within the French movement. We have also seen that the *Communist Manifesto* could be so described by its authors only because at the time of writing they adhered to the "communist" wing of a West European movement which in a generic sense was later described as "socialist" by historians no longer concerned with these pre-1848 disputations. After 1871 and the split in the First International, a similar problem arises in regard to the distinction between "socialism" and "anarchism" (or, as the anarchists preferred to call it, "libertarian socialism," to distinguish it from the "authoritarian"

Marxist brand). If one is so minded, one may retain the term "socialism" only for those who did not follow Bakunin; but until the founding of the Second International in 1889, this does not leave one with a great deal to talk about outside Germany, where a Social Democratic Party had established itself in the 1870's under the nominal patronage of Marx. In a wider sense, the loosely controlled organizations that adopted the anarchist program formed part of the general socialist movement, if only because they looked back to Proudhon.

With the Russian Populists we are in a different world. *Their* spiritual ancestors included the more liberal Slavophils of the 1840's, and it is not always entirely obvious in what respect they can be described as "socialists." The nature of the problem becomes a little clearer when we inquire into the faith and works of the man who has been called the "father of Russian socialism": Alexander Herzen.

Alexander Herzen (1812-70) was the illegitimate son of a wealthy Moscow nobleman and until his departure from Russia in 1847 a member of the brilliant circle which grouped the pro-Western, liberal, and oppositional leaders of thought in Petersburg and Moscow: Stankevich, Turgenev, Granovsky, Belinsky, Ogaryov, and Bakunin being the best known among them. The group had come into being in consequence of a dispute dividing radical modernizers from conservative nationalists, but both factions shared certain notions about Russia's past and future which may broadly be described as "Slavophil." (In saying this one does an injustice to those genuine "Westernizers," Pushkin among them, who rightly sensed that Russia's lack of political freedom had something to do with the absence of a genuine feudal tradition; but let us stick to biography.) As a student, Herzen, like his friends, duly underwent the influence of Hegel and the Left Hegelians, became involved with mildly conspiratorial activities in the spirit of aristocratic liberalism and tyrannicide, spent a few years in fairly comfortable exile not far from Moscow, and in 1847 was able to transfer his family and most of his considerable fortune to Western Europe. Unlike Marx or Proudhon he did not play a prominent part in 1848-49; unlike Bakunin, who had gone to Germany and then to Paris some years earlier, he did not even play a minor part. Whether resident in Italy, France, or Switzerland, his attitude during these stormy years was that of a critical spectator, a role which suited his contemplative bent and his grandseigneurial style. Thereafter, personal problems occupied much of his time and energy, his wife having fallen in love with a minor German poet called Herwegh, a misfortune that deepened Herzen's already confirmed dislike of all things German. The year 1851 witnessed the death of his mother and his second son in a storm at sea, and this disaster was followed by an even more crushing blow: the collapse of his marriage and the death, shortly thereafter, of his unfaithful Natalie. Coming at the ebb of revolutionary fortunes all over Europe, these personal tragedies plunged Herzen into a state of despondency from which he never really recovered. Paradoxically, however, the most notable stage in his career as a publicist dates from this unhappy period, for it was only after he had settled in London in 1852 that he found both the means and the energy to launch those journals of opinion which enabled him to reach a select public in Russia. Previously he had come to the attention of French and German readers with disillusioned reflections on recent European history, and he had also engaged in a public controversy with the French historian Jules Michelet, which prompted him to acquaint the public with his views on Russia's probable future. But it was his establishment (with the help of the Polish underground organization) of what he proudly called the Free Russian Press that made him an important figure: the first Russian publicist to address himself to his own countrymen in uncensored language. That an early enterprise of his private press should have been the publication of parts of his celebrated autobiography, *My Past and Thoughts*, is doubtless understandable in the circumstances, the more so since it gave him an opportunity to unburden himself on topics of general importance, in addition to producing what his biographer has described as an *apologia pro vita sua* (Malia, 394).

It is with Herzen the ancestor of Russian utopian socialism, however, rather than with Herzen the diarist and man of letters, that we are here concerned. *My Past and Thoughts* is a minor literary classic, but the reader who looks for enlightenment on its author's philosophical and political affiliations must be prepared to tackle (in addition to Professor Carr's and Professor Malia's critical studies) the thirty volumes of the complete *Works* in the orginal language gradually made available by the Soviet Academy of Sciences. Even if he is content to dip into the one-volume English-language selection published in Moscow in 1956, he will discover that Herzen raises awkward problems not only for present-day Leninists, but for Western liberals too. It is perhaps safe to classify him as a democrat, but the term has always had a very special connotation on Russian soil. It can hardly be an accident that the Soviet editors of the 1956 selection found it possible to introduce the volume with a laudatory essay Lenin wrote in 1912 on the centenary of Herzen's birth. It is true that Bolshevism was in 1912 no more than a faction within the Russian social-democratic movement, and that Lenin was at pains to claim Herzen for the democratic cause, while deploring his failure to understand Marx. But it is worth bearing in mind that by 1869 Herzen had given some evidence of having become tired not only of liberalism, but of Bakunin's anarchism too. The possibility cannot be excluded that, had he lived a few years longer, he might have ended his days as a kind of social democrat.

Be that as it may, we are under an obligation to ask what it was that originally separated Alexander Herzen from the aristocratic liberals among whom he grew up and whose Voltairean outlook he shared before he experienced the combined attraction of German idealist philosophy and French utopian socialism. This topic leads back to a consideration of the Russian intelligentsia's radicalism. Readers of Herzen's autobiography may easily derive the impression that he and his friends, being "Westernizers" and rationalists, had nothing in common with their conservative opponents, generally described as "Slavophils" by Herzen himself. This is to simplify a complex situation. The conservatives worshipped Muscovy's despotic tradition which was semi-Asiatic and lacked the characteristic elements of West European feudalism: personal freedom at least for the nobility, and some constraints upon the ruler. Liberals and radicals detested just this lack of personal liberty. On the other hand, both sides to the controversy had certain attitudes in common: above all an invincible distaste for the bureaucratic regime that Peter the Great and his successors had clamped upon Russian society. They likewise agreed in regarding the village community as the true foundation of all that was healthy in the national life. The difference was that the conservatives were prepared, with whatever qualifications, to put up with serfdom and the autocracy, while the radicals dreamed of a democratic revolution in the Jacobin manner. Lastly, both parties held that Russia's future development was bound to be quite different from that of Western Europe or Germany. But what was it to be? The conservative Slavophils naturally thought in terms of national greatness, but Herzen and his friends were patriots too, even to the point of sharing the traditional view that Russia had a claim to possession of Constantinople.

What, then, divided them? In *My Past and Thoughts* Herzen gave a sort of answer, and it is worth quoting. After disputing the conventional Slavophil doctrine that Russia's golden age lay in the ancient past, before Peter imposed his "German" reforms upon the country and moved the capital from Moscow to the artificial new city on the Baltic, he had this to say about the village community and its collectivism:

> The immediate foundations of our way of life are insufficient. In India there has existed for ages and exists to this day a village commune very like our own and based on the partition of fields; yet the people of India have not gone very far with it.
>
> Only the mighty thought of the West, with which all its long history is united, is able to fertilise the seeds slumbering in the patriarchal mode of life of the Slavs. The workmen's guild and the village commune, the sharing of profits and the partition of fields, the meeting of the *mir* and the union of villages into self-govering *volosts*, are all the corner-stones on which the mansion of our future, freely communal existence will be built. But these corner-stones are only stones . . . and without the thought of the West our future cathedral would not rise above its foundations. (II, 528)

This was not exactly to the taste of the conservatives, for whom "the West" was the enemy, but neither was it what the liberals wanted to hear. For the latter, if they adhered to the enlightened wing of the aristocracy (Herzen's own class), an "English Constitution" on the Whig model was the dream to be pursued. Behind this lay a dim apprehension of the fact that what differentiated Russia from Europe was the absence of a genuine feudal tradition. Muscovy had been despotic, not feudal. Thereafter, when Peter's "German" reforms had sunk in, the ruling bureaucracy had taken Prussia for a model, and the "conservative liberals" within that bureaucracy fancied themselves the equals, if not the superiors, of the Prussian reformers of 1807-19 who had somehow managed to modernize their country while preserving the autocratic power of the ruler. It was precisely because Hegel had after 1820 accommodated himself to the Prussian state that his more conservative German disciples possessed a following in Moscow and that Hegelianism itself was regarded as respectable. Indeed, some of the rebels of the 1840's (Belinsky and Bakunin among them) began their intellectual careers as right-wing Hegelians and defenders of the *status quo*, and remained so until this position became morally impossible. They then discovered to their relief that Hegel could also be interpreted quite differently–by the atheist and democrat Ludwig Feuerbach, but also by the mystical Polish philosopher A. von Cieszkowski, who combined Hegelianism with Roman Catholicism and utopian socialism. What in later years became the creed of the first Russian Populists emerged from this intellectual turmoil of the 1840's, when a group of young men in Petersburg and Moscow moved from the extreme right to the extreme left wing of the Hegelian school. There were others who contented themselves with plainer fare–Bentham, Mill, and English liberalism in general. And, needless to say, the bureaucracy to the end clung to its faith in the Prussian model, especially after Bismarck had shown them in the 1860's how to harness nationalism in support of Throne and Altar. Herzen and his friends opted for a different solution: the village commune as the basis of Russia's coming social regeneration. One may say that they had synthesized the Slavophil enthusiasm for the common people, the *narod*, with the socialist doctrines pouring in from France. One then begins to see how and why some of these Populists a generation later turned to Marx, once it dawned on them that a fusion of Hegelian logic with the revolutionary will to "change the world" had been accomplished by the author of *Capital*.

But in the 1840's and 1850's all this still lay in the future. So far as Herzen was concerned, socialism was then identified with France–specifically with Louis Blanc and/or Proudhon–and after 1850 it became clear that France was in no mood for a further revolutionary effort. The Germans clearly were philistines in politics, whatever the profundity of their philosophers. As for the British, Herzen admired and envied the political liberty he encountered during his stay in England, and the liberal *grandseigneur* in him had some affinities with the Whig aristocracy. But in the last analysis he agreed with the Slavophils in holding that Western institutions could not be acclimatized in Russia. Even in 1852, at the lowest depth of his private fortunes and of the revolutionary cause, he had sounded a defiant note in the celebrated pamphlet (a sort of Open Letter to Michelet) commonly cited under the title "The Russian People and Socialism":

> Russia will never be a Protestant country.
>
> Russia will never be *juste-milieu*.
>
> Russia will never make a revolution with the object of getting rid of Tsar Nicholas and replacing him by other tsars—parliamentary representatives, judges, and police officials. We perhaps ask for too much and shall get nothing. That may be so, but yet we do not despair. Before the year 1848 Russia could not, and should not, have entered the arena of revolution: she had to learn her lesson. Now she has learnt it. . . .
>
> We should have no blind faith in the future: every seed has its claim to growth, but not every one actually grows up. The future of Russia does not depend on her alone, it is bound up with the future of Europe. Who can foretell the fate of the Slav world if reaction and absolutism finally suppress the revolution in Europe?
>
> Perhaps it will perish.
>
> But in that case Europe too will perish.
>
> And history will pass over to continue in America. (*Selected Philosophical Works*, 497)

Now it may be said that this kind of talk was not uncommon among disillusioned democrats after the failure of 1848. Many of them actually felt that Europe *had* perished, and they drew the logical conclusion by emigrating to the New World; others, Marx and Engels among them, retired temporarily into their private shells while awaiting the next turn of the wheel. What makes Herzen's case peculiar is that for him "the fate of the Slav world" was inextricably involved with the prospects of what he called "the revolution." To that extent one may safely describe him as a Slavophil, though he would have repudiated the label, Panslavism being in bad odor among European democrats, who still remembered Russia's armed intervention in Hungary in 1849 and the pseudo-revolutionary antics of the minor Slav nationalities (the Poles always excepted), whose behavior in 1848-49 had on balance only benefited the Habsburg Monarchy. Herzen was certainly no Panslavist in the vulgar sense, although Marx on occasion suspected him (and Bakunin) of being just that. But he did believe that the cause of socialism was in some fashion bound up with the national development of the Slav peoples, above all the Russians. One has only to read "The Russian People and Socialism" to perceive that this faith was grounded in a piece of socio-historical exegesis which he and Bakunin shared with their conservative opponents. This creed had its patriotic aspect: it was now the turn of the Slavs. There was even a Great Russian undertone (although diluted by sympathy for Poland): "There is . . . no future for the Slav world apart from Russia. Without Russia it will not develop, it will fall to pieces and be absorbed by the German element. . . . But that in our opinion is not what it is destined for." There was likewise the vision of a democratic revolution which, starting from the basis of the village commune, would carry over into socialism. At times Herzen sounds remarkably modern, even though his economics were extremely shaky and even his knowledge of the Russian village had for the most part been acquired by reading what a German traveler, the Baron von Haxthausen, had to say about it. Consider the following:

> The commune has saved the Russian people from Mongol barbarism and imperial civilization, from the Europeanized landlords and the German bureaucracy. The communal system, though shattered, has withstood the interference of the authorities; it has successfully survived *to see the development of socialism in Europe.* This circumstance is of infinite importance to Russia. . . .
>
> From all this you can appreciate how fortunate it is for Russia that the village commune has not perished and personal ownership has not split up the property of the commune; how fortunate it is for the Russian people to have remained outside all political movements, outside European civilization, which would undoubtedly have undermined the commune, and which today has reached in socialism the negation of itself. (*Ibid*., 486, 489)

Before hastening to describe the author of these lines as a precursor of Lenin—which of course is how Soviet historians prefer to view him—one had better face the paradox that a few years later, after the accession to the throne of the "liberal" Alexander II in 1855, Herzen began to sound like a Whig grandee, to the point of publicly congratulating Alexander on his projected abolition of serfdom, on terms of maximum economic disadvantage to the wretched peasants. It is true that Herzen eventually got over his enthusiasm for the Tsar. It is also true that in 1863 he very properly sided with the Polish insurgents when they claimed their freedom from Russian imperial domination. (Bakunin's arrival in London about this time may have had the effect of replenishing Herzen's dwindling stock of radicalism.) Nonetheless it will not do to make a proto-Bolshevik out of Herzen on the strength of a few passages about the socialist potentialities of the village commune. Lenin had no illusions on this topic. In his anniversary article of 1912, Herzen is expressly blamed for his failure to understand "the bourgeois nature of the Russian revolution." The emancipation of the peasants in the form proposed by Herzen (he observed on that occasion) would simply have resulted in the more rapid spread of capitalism!

Herzen's inconsistencies have never bothered his admirers or damaged his considerable reputation with liberals and socialists alike. Essentially a literary man, endowed by nature with a fine artistic sensibility and generous emotions, he was a medium through whom other men's ideas passed, rather than an original thinker in the proper meaning of the term. Although he prided himself on his youthful immersion in German philosophy, there is no evidence of any systematic concern on his part for what might be called the serious business of theorizing. In this respect he differed from the radicals of the following generation, the "men of the sixties," whom he intensely disliked for their plebeian manners and who in turn regarded him as an aristocratic dilettante. *Their* hero was the radical democrat Chernyshevsky, for whom Herzen had no use. Setting aside the personal element in these animosities, one cannot altogether disregard the evident connection between Herzen's lack of system and his disdain for the dull but essential grind of mental labor that must precede the completion of any major theoretical construction. Professor Carr's description of Herzen as "a distinguished minor figure—one of the select company of diarists and memoir writers who continue to be read long after their own time" hits the nail on the head. It also helps to explain Herzen's reputation with the public: literary and academic critics generally prefer diarists to theorists. In his lifetime Herzen made few enemies, and after his death the translation of his memoirs into the principal Western languages continued to win him friends. Like Turgenev, he was the sort of Russian whom foreigners could understand: a cultivated aristocrat whose heart was in the right (that is to say, the left) place. With Herzen one was on familiar ground: he represented what the Russian nobility and gentry *might* have become if Muscovy had not systematically destroyed the feeble beginnings of a genuine feudalism (and every element of personal liberty, at least among the privileged, along with it.)

And yet this assessment is not altogether fair. There was another side to Herzen's thought, but it is unlikely to disclose itself to readers immersed in the complex story of his personal and political entanglements. The romantic *mise-en-scène* never fails to enthrall a public that could not care less about *narodnichestvo*. Yet the only reason for including Alexander Herzen in a history of socialism lies in the fact that he did have something to say that was relevant to the orientation of the Russian socialist movement: he drew the attention of the radical non-gentry intelligentsia to the importance of the village commune. Perhaps one had to be an eccentric Russian *grandseigneur* to toy with such dangerous thoughts, while staying on amiable personal terms with liberal aristocrats who went on hoping for something like the English constitution. And there was something else: in his *Letters to an Old Comrade*, addressed in 1869 to Bakunin, Herzen showed some awareness of the European workers' movement which was then taking its first halting steps. The *Letters* culminated in an appeal to his old friend to take the labor movement more seriously. This may seem odd, for Bakunin was furiously active within the First International, whereas Herzen as usual adopted the role of philosophic bystander. But Bakunin's frenzied conspiracy-mongering was in the tradition of Mazzini (another old acquaintance of both men), while Herzen had been impressed by the practical and unrhetorical spirit of the labor movement:

> The International Congresses of Workers are becoming sessions at which one social question after another is discussed; they assume an ever-increasing organizational nature; their members are experts and lawyers. They call strikes and allow the cessation of work only as a dire necessity, as a *pis aller*, as a way of testing their strength. . . . In forming a sort of "state within a state" which establishes its own system and its rights without capitalists and proprietors, the workers will constitute the first . . . germ of the economic organization of the future. (*Selected Philosophical Works*, 582)

Although probably derived from Proudhon, whom Herzen liked and admired, these sentiments were in accordance with what Marx was thinking and doing at the time, and they were incompatible with Bakunin's chiliastic vision of an armed rising that would smash state and society. But then, as Herzen observed on the same occasion, "The term 'gradual progress' holds no terrors for me, discredited though it is by the vacillations and mistakes of diverse reformers."

The fact is that by 1869 Herzen had lost some of his sovereign contempt for the Western way of life. Not merely was he now more deeply aware of the strength of rural conservatism ("All throughout Europe the peasant population will rise to a man in defense of the old order"), he believed these enfranchised citizens of Western Europe had a claim to being taken seriously:

> The denial of private property as such is nonsense. . . . Love of his land is as deeply rooted in the peasant of the West as is the idea of communal possession in the Russian peasant. There is nothing absurd in this. Property, particularly the ownership of land, has represented to the man of the West his emancipation, his independence, his dignity, and constituted an element of the highest civic importance. It may happen that one day he will realize that the continuous parcelling of his dwindling land is detrimental and see his account in the free economy of the common cultivation of the fields; but in the meantime how can one make him suddenly and of his own accord renounce a dream he has been fostering for centuries, which has been his life and joy, which really did put him on his feet and attached the land to him; the land to which until then he had been attached. (*Ibid.*, 585-86)

And what of Bakunin's pet notion, the destruction of the state as the first step to social regeneration? Herzen, without renouncing his old libertarianism, had come around to the view that the state might after all be a necessary evil. "Lassalle wished to utilize state power in order to introduce his social system. Why destroy the mill, thought he, when its millstones are capable of grinding our flour as well? For this same reason I see no sense in refusing to make judicious use of it" (*Ibid.*, 592). What of the systematic employment of violence?

> I do not believe that people who prefer destruction and brute force to evolution and to amicable agreements are really serious. . . . An outburst of unbridled savagery provoked by obstinacy will spare nothing. . . . Along with the capital amassed by the usurer will be wiped out that which has been transmitted from generation to gener-

> ation and from nation to nation, a capital which bears the imprint of the personality and creativeness of different ages and which is itself an annal of human life and a crystallization of history. The unbridled forces of destruction will wipe out, along with the fences, those extreme mileposts of human power which mankind has attained . . . since the dawn of civilization. (*Ibid*., 594)

So much for Bakunin's vision of a day of judgment when a cleansing storm would blow away not merely bourgeois society but urban civilization as a whole. Herzen even had an inkling of what might some day be let loose upon a startled universe, if radicals went on toying with violence. "Christianity and Islam have demolished enough of the ancient world; the French Revolution has destroyed enough statues, pictures and monuments for us to be able to dispense with playing at iconoclasm." It would be unjust to the Parisian Communards of 1871 to say that their brief revolt a year after his death lent point to this warning, for the destruction wreaked upon Paris in the final days of the Commune was the work of men driven frantic by the coldblooded savagery of the "forces of order." Still, one may say that Herzen was guided by a sound instinct when he warned his old friend not to play at revolution. The warning fell on deaf ears. For if Alexander Herzen represented the civilized side of Populism, the destructive forces barely contained within that complex movement found their embodiment in the person of Bakunin.

To turn from Herzen to Michael Bakunin (1814-76) is to enter a different zone of the same mental universe. The two men were contemporaries and for a while belonged to the Moscow literary circle which in the late 1830's discovered German literature and philosophy. But then so did Turgenev, whom no one would ever suspect of being anything but a very moderate liberal. For that matter Michael Katkov, in later years an arch-reactionary, made his debut there too. If these philosophical and literary influences do not account for the peculiarity of Bakunin's later political outlook, neither does his social origin. As a descendant of the landowning nobility, destined for a military career but unwilling to pursue it, he naturally sympathized with the Decembrists: that gallant band of aristocratic rebels in uniform who in December, 1825, vainly tried to launch an armed insurrection against the new Tsar and paid for it with their lives or with exile to Siberia. By temperament Bakunin was no doubt closer to the Decembrists than were the other members of the Moscow circle. He remained, one may fairly say, all his life a man of action rather than a thinker. It is, however, possible to be both. Measured by the standards of someone like Saint-Amand Bazard—veteran of Napoleon's campaigns, co-founder of the Charbonnerie, and prominent exponent of Saint-Simon's thought after the Master's death—Bakunin does not strike a particularly heroic figure, although he never missed a chance to rush to the nearest barricade, and, after the defeat of the revolution in 1849, he spent some years in Saxon, Austrian, and Russian prisons. Yet this does not explain how and why he came to found the anarchist movement. He might, after all, have simply remained faithful to the model already established by the Charbonnerie, as indeed in a certain sense he did, for the secret societies he founded in the 1860's, while committed to anarchism in principle, were centralist and dictatorial in practice. Or he might have devoted his entire energy to the Slav cause, to which he had become an early convert. But although Slav unity, and especially the destruction of the Austrian Empire, remained among his aims, he was not satisfied with Panslavism. In 1861, after making a spectacular escape from Siberia, he informed Herzen (in a letter mailed from San Francisco) that he was still wholly committed to the cause of "the glorious free Slav federation," but by 1864 or thereabouts he had widened his aim: the federation of peoples was to encompass the entire world, even though Russia was destined to play a privileged part within it. One may say that Bakunin anticipated that element in the naive Bolshevism of the 1920's which saw Russia marching at the head of the world revolution. In the 1860's, this sort of rhetoric struck no spark even among Poles, let alone West Europeans.

For Bakunin, as for Herzen and the men of the next generation whom they inspired, Russia had a very special part to play: that of leader of the Slav nations in the long march toward self-determination and socialism. But how could that be while the Tsarist autocracy caused the other Slavs (notably the Poles) to view all Russians with hatred? Only by destroying the Tsardom and showing the world that Russia had been purged of its ancient stains. The theme is well and eloquently put in a joint letter Bakunin and Ogaryov addressed late in 1862 to a group of Russian officers in Poland who had decided to throw in their lot with the Polish insurgents.

> We understand that you cannot but join the Polish rebellion whatever form it may take; you give yourselves as atonement for the sins of the Russian Tsardom [this Christian formulation occurs in the part of the letter composed by Ogaryov] ; moreover, to leave Poland to be slaughtered without any protest from the Russian army would possess the fatal aspect of Russia's taking a humbly submissive, immoral part in Petersburg's butchery. Nevertheless, your position is hopeless and tragic. We see no chance of success. Even if Warsaw were free for one month, it would only mean that you had paid a debt by your share in the movement of *national independence*, but to raise the Russian socialist banner of "Land and Freedom" is not vouchsafed to Poland; and you are too few.

To which Bakunin added the characteristic rider:

> It must be owned that in the present temper of Russia and of all Europe there is too little hope of success for such a rebellion. . . . But on the other hand the condition of the Poles is so insufferable that they will hardly be patient for long. . . . And when, driven beyond the utmost limit of possible patience, our unhappy Polish brothers arise, do you rise too, not against them but for them; rise up in the name of Russian honour, in the name of Slav duty, in the name of the Russian people, with the cry, "Land and Freedom"; and if you are doomed to perish, your death will serve the common cause. (Herzen, *My Past and Thoughts*, 1371-73)

The handful of Russian officers belonging to the secret revolutionary society then known as Zemlya i Volya were indeed doomed, as were their Polish associates. Within months, the rising had been crushed and its leaders hanged by the Tsarist authorities, whereupon concessions were made to the peasants, so as to draw them away from the nobility which had spearheaded the rebellion. Bakunin's reaction was to proclaim that "only the bloody prologue called *the heroic collapse of the nobles' democracy* is over. Now it is the turn of the Polish serfs whom the Russian government will never be able to break or to satisfy." The surviving Polish revolutionaries–all of them drawn from the landed gentry, like Bakunin himself—would come to understand that "the future of Poland, like that of all the Slavs, depends on the peasants, and there is only one way of salvation for all—the 'red' social, geological revolution" (Venturi, 127). In actual fact, the peasants were bought off for half a century with land confiscated from the rebellious nobles, and Polish nationalism remained as before the exclusive affair of the gentry and the intelligentsia. The peasant *jacquerie* to which Bakunin looked forward never materialized—at any rate not in Poland, although it is arguable that he contributed something to the subsequent explosion in Russia.

What needs to be understood here is that "libertarian socialism" was a West European issue. In Russia, Bakunin had sown dragons' teeth of quite a different sort. In the 1860's and 1870's there was not even the beginning of a labor movement, and the more radical Populists wavered between terrorism and faith in a peasant revolt. In either case a conspiratorial leadership was necessary, and they did their best to provide one. Sergey Nechaev (1847-82) and P. N. Tkachev (1844-86), who around 1868 constituted the nucleus of a little group of student revolutionaries, saw themselves as adherents of Bakunin, but they were far from being libertarians in the Western sense. What they aimed at was a popular uprising, secretly directed from the two capital cities by a self-appointed group of what would later be called "professional revolutionaries" drawn from the intelligentsia. For this enterprise they won the sanction of Bakunin, who befriended Nechaev during the young man's stay in Switzerland in 1869 and helped with the composition of the *Revolutionary Catechism.* This curious document, which was made public at the trial of Nechaev's followers, defined "the revolutionary" as one who "despises public opinion" and is "without pity for the state and for the privileged and educated world in general." His sole aim is a revolution "that destroys every established object root and branch, that annihilates all state traditions, orders, and classes in Russia." Paragraph 25 adds as an afterthought, "To do this we must draw close to the people. . . . We must ally ourselves with the doughty world of brigands, who in Russia are the only real revolutionaries," and Paragraph 26 adds ominously: "All our organization, all our conspiracy, all our purpose consists in this: to regroup this world of brigands into an invincible and omni-destructive force." Attempts have been made to ascribe all this to

Nechaev, but Bakunin placed his own gloss on their joint program when he wrote: "Brigandage is one of the most honored aspects of the people's life in Russia. . . . The brigand in Russia is the true and only revolutionary. . . . Popular revolution is born from the merging of the brigand's revolt with that of the peasant." The reverse side of the coin was extreme secrecy and conspiracy. But no prearranged political forms or authorities! "New forms of life can spring only from complete amorphism" (Venturi, 365-69).

This was a purely Russian development. How then was it that Bakunin inherited the mantle of Proudhon when the latter's death in 1865 left his French followers orphaned? The answer would appear to be that he was temperamentally suited to the role because he had already made up his mind on quite different grounds that Western bourgeois society must be uprooted. What his later followers in France, Italy, and Spain called his "libertarianism" was a philosophy, or *Weltanschauung*, he had acquired between 1836 and 1842 by reading Fichte, Hegel, and Feuerbach. Much of his subsequent career is foreshadowed in the letter he addressed to his sister in February, 1836, after reading Fichte: "I have no other aim than to be a man, and I shall smash everything that blocks my path to this goal. A curse on all the institutions created by the abasement of mankind. . . . All that is false must be destroyed, without exception and without pity, so that the truth may triumph—and it will triumph!" It is idle to dismiss this as youthful Byronic romanticism. Bakunin meant it when he said that the old world must be "smashed." What is more, he did not allow Hegel to deflect him from this aim, although during his years as a member of the Stankevich circle he went through the then customary phase of trying to justify the Russian autocracy and serfdom on the grounds that they were "real," hence rational. The discovery that he had misunderstood Hegel dawned upon Bakunin when he moved to Berlin in 1840 and took up German philosophy in earnest. Characteristically, he thereupon moved from the extreme right to the extreme left of the political spectrum. The article he published in 1842 under the pseudonym Jules Elysard in Arnold Ruge's *Deutsche Jahrbücher* had for its title *The Reaction in Germany*, and the peroration with which it closed summed up Bakunin's philosophy for the remainder of his life: "Let us then put our trust in the eternal spirit which destroys and annihilates only because it is the unfathomable and eternally creative source of all life. The lust of destruction is also a creative lust."*

This was a promising start, but it still lacked something to become politically relevant. That something Bakunin discovered when in 1843-44 he removed from Germany to Paris (by way of Zürich, where he encountered the German apostle of primitive utopian communism, Wilhelm Weitling). In Paris he naturally became acquainted with Marx and his friends; with George Sand and Pierre Leroux; with Cabet and Lamennais; and above all with Proudhon. With the latter Bakunin struck up a true and enduring friendship, and it was from Proudhon that, during night-long discussions over countless glasses of tea, he obtained some insight into the emerging workers' movement. "Proudhon is the master of us all," he declared long afterward, though his own anarcho-communism was not easily squared with Proudhon's worship of the artisan and the family. At any rate both men were in agreement that the state must be destroyed. They also shared an unshakable confidence in the truth of their respective doctrines. Proudhon in 1848 confided to his diary the rather undemocratic thought "The representative of the people–that am I. For I alone am right" (Woodcock, 98). Bakunin might have said the same and in later years was to display the kind of certitude that goes with a conviction of having a privileged insight into the nature of reality. The trait was not uncommon in that age of system-building, and it may be said in Proudhon's and Bakunin's defense that (unlike their great contemporary Auguste Comte) neither of them was ever clinically insane, even for a brief period. Their oddities–which included a belief in the existence of a Jewish conspiracy encompassing Marx, Heine, and the Rothschilds–were not particularly startling by the standards of their age, which after all was the era of decomposing romanticism. Secret societies pullullated–even Marx for a brief period became involved with the Blanquists in an enterprise of this kind, though he quickly abandoned it when its absurdity became evident–and nervousness about occult forces and underground machinations was not confined to "The Pope and the Tsar, Metternich and Guizot, French Radicals and German policemen," to cite the pillars of

*This is sometimes tactfully mistranslated to read "urge to destroy," but Bakunin was writing in German, of which he had a fair command, and the words he used were: *"Die Lust der Zerstörung ist eine zugleich schaffende Lust."*

society apostrophized in the opening passage of the *Communist Manifesto*. Proudhon had an *idée fixe* about Saint-Simonian bankers running the government of Napoleon III from behind the scenes, and Bakunin was convinced in the 1870's that all the trouble in the First International stemmed from Marx's Jewish entourage. (One might add the equally unfounded belief held by Wilhelm Liebknecht and other German Social Democrats that Bakunin was not merely a Panslavist but also an agent of the Russian government.)

What is rather more important than these mutual suspicions and animosities–though they took up a great deal of space in private correspondence and wasted everyone's time and energy–is that Bakunin inherited both Proudhon's doctrine (or as much of it as he could assimilate) and his hostility to Marx. This last was qualified by Bakunin's reluctant recognition that Marx (with whom he had a friendly reunion in London in 1864 before they started their quarrel) had to be taken seriously–something Proudhon, who read no German and anyway died before the first volume of *Capital* appeared, had failed to grasp, if only because he was wholly immersed in French affairs and incapable, as even Herzen complained, of taking the least interest in anything or anyone beyond the borders of his native country. Bakunin saw the importance of Marx clearly enough, but reacted with a mixture of admiration, envy, and hostility that did not help Marx to overcome his own distrust of Russian revolutionaries: an attitude he abandoned only during his closing years, when the Russian emigrants in Geneva turned to him for advice. Thus the stage was set for an epic conflict which has furnished material for countless biographers. Its significance, when all is said and done, was historical rather than intellectual. Proudhon had been a theorist, though a self-made one. Bakunin was a propagandist, and his muddled thinking never rose above the level of the professional agitator with a few fixed ideas and a stock of ready-made phrases. Even a sympathetic historian of the anarchist movement has been obliged to note his deficiency in this respect: "Though he scribbled copiously, he did not leave a single completed book to transmit his ideas to posterity" (Woodcock, 135).

Bakunin did, however, have one great central theme: all authority was dangerous. Hence no reliance could be placed on radical movements which shirked the issue of political power. This was reasonable enough and quite compatible with the doctrine enunciated by Marx in the 1864 Inaugural Address of the International: the working class must accomplish its own emancipation. But the gloss Bakunin placed on this text was quite different from the interpretation given to it by the German Social Democrats and the British trade unionists who made up the "Marxist" majority on the International's General Council. For Bakunin it was a matter not of "conquering political power" (as the Address put it), but of *destroying* it! The state must go at once and completely, otherwise the movement would revert to all the old illusions of bourgeois democracy: belief in popular sovereignty, in the Republic, even in that deadliest of all myths, universal suffrage, which Proudhon after the disappointment of 1848 had indefatigably denounced as a pernicious Jacobinical invention. The only democracy tolerable to Bakunin was the self-government of the producers, plus "federalism" in the Proudhonist sense, i.e., the break-up of the nation-state into autonomous regions. How these self-governing units were to federate without at least a minimum of central administration, neither Proudhon nor Bakunin ever managed to explain to the satisfaction of their critics, who could only conclude that the "libertarians" failed to understand what the political process was about.

All this may seem academic and hardly worth the passions it aroused. But Proudhon had already involved himself in the major controversies of his time—e.g., by denouncing Italian nationalism, to the fury of Mazzini, Garibaldi, and their foreign liberal sympathizers, including Herzen. Now Bakunin duly followed suit, although he chose a different and more promising terrain. The International Brotherhood he founded in Naples in 1865-66 was as conspiratorial and dictatorial as he could make it, for Bakunin's libertarianism stopped short of the notion of permitting anyone to contradict him. The Brotherhood was conceived on the Masonic model, with elaborate rituals, a hierarchy, and a self-appointed directory consisting of Bakunin and a few associates who were let into the secret. This society duly spawned a more public body, the Alliance of Social Democracy, for which Bakunin in 1868 formally sought admission to the International in a letter to Marx mixing flattery with insincere assurances of conversion to the democratic faith. Marx was not taken in, and the General Council backed him in demanding that the Alliance be dissolved before its branches were admitted to the International (Nicolaevsky, 286 ff.). In fact, though not in form, the Alliance continued to operate underground, and after the Geneva Congress of the International in September, 1872, when Marx, with the help of the Blanquists plus his own German followers and most of the British, had Bakunin and his adherents formally expelled, it became the nucleus of the later Anarchist movement in France, Belgium, Italy, French Switzerland, and the Iberian peninsula: in short, all over Latin and Catholic Europe. The cleavage between Social Democracy and Anarchism, which dated from this era, was also a geographic and a cultural affair, although there were small anarchist groups in Germany and Austria, and larger socialist ones in the Romance countries. It was only in 1889, when French, German, British, Belgian, Italian, Russian, and other socialists came together in Paris to found the Second International (symbolically on the centenary of the French Revolution), that this particular division was more or less overcome.

When one turns to the substance of Bakunin's doctrine, so far as it was not simply a matter of denouncing the state and all its works, one comes up against the problem that while Bakunin was regarded, by himself and others, as the heir of Proudhon, he differed from his old teacher in that he was willing to make room for a certain amount of collectivism in the running of industry. Proudhon to the end had remained attached to the ideal of the individual artisan cooperating with others. Bakunin—perhaps helped by the Slavophil worship of the village commune which he shared with Herzen—recognized that the collectivity also had its rights. In consequence his collectivism differed from Proudhon's mutualism in that he made provision for the aims of workers' organizations, then emerging in France and elsewhere, whose leaders had lost faith in Proudhon's "mutualist" doctrine. For this reason former Proudhonists like the Parisian bookbinder and labor leader Eugène Varlin, who played a major role during the Paris Commune of 1871, felt able to join Bakunin's organization while also adhering to the International. By the end of 1869, "mutualism" (which in practice meant retention of private ownership and worship of the independent peasant or craftsman) was virtually a dead issue so far as the congresses of the International were concerned, and "collectivism" had triumphed. From Marx's standpoint this was an advance, but he now had to put up with Bakunin's faction, which had inherited Proudhon's old following and grafted a new character onto it by substituting for its outdated individualist legacy an "anti-authoritarian collectivism." This, however, was only meant for France and other West European countries. For his native Russia, where no labor movement as yet existed, Bakunin relied as before upon secret societies, peasant rebellions, and individual terrorism, the latter propagated by fanatics like Nechaev and documents like the *Revolutionary Catechism* (the discovery of which furnished an ample topic for moral indignation on the part of Dostoyevsky and other conservative Slavophils, not to mention the Tsarist authorities, who naturally made the most of it).

The organizational issue was connected—in Bakunin's mind anyway—with another grievance against Marx and his followers: their commitment to the goal of conquering political power. In principle, he maintained, they were agreed on the ultimate aims:

> Both parties equally seek the creation of a new social order founded wholly on the organization of collective labor . . . founded on economic conditions equal for all, and on the collective ownership of the instruments of labor. But the communists imagine that they will be able to achieve this by means of the development and organization of the political power of the working classes and especially of the urban proletariat, with the assistance of bourgeois radicalism; while the revolutionary socialists . . . believe on the contrary that they can attain this goal only by the development and organization not of the political, but of the social (and consequently anti-political) power of the working masses both urban and rural, as well as of those men of good will in the upper classes who . . . would be willing openly to side with them. . . . Whence two different methods. The communists think they must organize . . . to seize political power . . . The revolutionary socialists organize for the destruction of states. (*The Paris Commune and the Idea of the State*, translated from the French edition of 1899)

Wisdom resided in *the people,* which for Bakunin meant "the working masses both urban and rural," whereas Marx and Engels by 1871 had come to base their political strategy upon the organized labor movement. Not that they ignored the power latent in the peasant masses, but agrarian populism figured in their mature theorizing as an element of the *bourgeois* revolution: however radical in intention, a movement of this kind could only promote bourgeois democracy.

What, then, was the quarrel with Marx about, so far as it was not a matter of personal incompatibility or of Bakunin's conspiratorial designs, which furnished the occasion for expelling him and his followers from the International? Perhaps the simplest answer is to be found in the pamphlet from which the passage just quoted comes–a sort of rejoinder to Marx's deservedly better-known production, *The Civil War in France* (1871). Marx on that occasion had virtually adopted the sensible part of the Proudhonist legacy, notably by stressing the need to break up the bureaucratic apparatus of the French state. But Bakunin was not satisfied. After affirming that "revolutionary socialism has just attempted a first brilliant and practical appearance in the *Paris Commune*" (an odd statement to make on the morrow of the bloodiest disaster ever suffered by the French working class), he went on:

> Contrary to authoritarian communist belief–in my opinion wholly erroneous–that a social revolution can be decreed and organized, either by a dictatorship or by a constituent assembly sprung from political revolution, our friends, the socialists of Paris, believed that it could be effected and fully developed only by means of the spontaneous and incessant action of the popular masses, groups and associations.
>
> Our Paris friends were a thousand times right. In fact, what mind, however brilliant, or–if we want to consider a collective dictatorship, even one consisting of several hundred individuals endowed with superior faculties–what intellects are powerful enough . . . to embrace the infinite multiplicity and diversity of real interests, aspirations, wills, needs whose sum constitutes the collective will of a people? What intellects are powerful and broad enough to invent a social organization capable of satisfying everyone? Such an organization would only be a bed of Procrustes on which violence more or less sanctioned by the State would compel the unfortunate society to lie. (*Ibid.*)

To which every Communist since Lenin has replied that without a centralized organization there can be no hope of victory. So far as Marx is concerned, this topic is irrelevant, since all he asked for was the minimum of effective leadership without which even the most powerful spontaneous movement must run into the sands.

In Bakunin's mind the issues raised by the Paris Commune, and by his private quarrel with Marx and the German socialists generally, were still in some fashion linked with his ancient notions about Russia's coming role in the social revolution. In one of his last pieces of writing, *Statehood and Anarchy* (1873), which today is worth reading principally for the sake of Marx's critical notes and excerpts from the Russian original, Bakunin expounds the familiar argument that the Slavs are predestined to take the lead in a libertarian reorganization of European life, Italy and Spain being among the other countries ripe for agrarian revolution and Proudhonist "federalism." The Russian people "can boast of its extraordinary poverty and also of its exemplary enslavement. Its sufferings are countless and it bears them not patiently but with a profound and passionate despair which has already been expressed twice in history by two fearful outbreaks: the rebellion of Stenka Razin and the Pugachov rebellion." Unlike Herzen, Bakunin looked forward to another "fearful outbreak" that would make an end not only of the Tsarist autocracy, but of the Russian Empire, while at the same time leading to, or being set off by, a military confrontation with Germany. In this respect, however, the old Panslavist was merely repeating what almost everyone in Europe thought after Bismarck in 1871 unified Germany under Prussian leadership.

For Bakunin, the last years of his life were anticlimactic. Ever since his unsuccessful attempt to aid the Polish insurrection of 1863 by shipping armed Polish legionaries from Sweden to Lithuania on board a British freighter, he had interspersed his subterranean intrigues in the International with brief military excursions which invariably terminated in a ludicrous fiasco. Unlike Garibaldi, whose successful Sicilian campaign of 1860 provided the model for all such enterprises, he possessed no organizational talent, although plenty of personal courage. Unlike Mazzini, whose Italian followers he tried to attract into his own organization, he had no patience and gave no attention to detail. The secret societies in whose name he despatched emissaries abroad existed for the most part only in his own imagination, or else they were plainly intended to bluff the authorities: the most celebrated of all being the nonexistent World Revolutionary Alliance into which Nechaev was solemnly introduced as Agent No. 2771, before being sent back to Russia, where he distinguished himself by murdering a harmless student. All this makes a wearisome tale, occasionally enlivened by comic escapades, such as Bakunin's brief attempt to seize power at Lyon in September, 1870, in the wake of the French military defeat: an enterprise that lasted exactly twenty-four hours. By 1873 he was getting weary of these fruitless activities and thought of retiring to a villa in the Ticino bought as a hideout for persecuted anarchists with money provided by Italian sympathizers, with whom he soon managed to quarrel. To salve his conscience (he had been accused by his own followers of spending political funds for his personal use), he made his way from Switzerland in 1874 to Bologna, where an anarchist rising was due to take place, but had to escape in a hurry (disguised as a priest and carrying a basket of eggs) after the failure of the usual comic-opera plot laid by his Italian disciples. His death in Berne on July 1, 1876, after a prolonged illness removed a tired man whose last years were saddened by the failure of his hopes, and only a few old friends attended the funeral. To all appearances, anarchism was at an end. In fact, as a movement it was only beginning.

If one is to make sense of Bakunin's heritage, one must bear in mind that it meant different things to different people. In Russia, Bakunin helped to launch an elitist and terrorist movement almost exclusively composed of *déclassé* intellectuals and committed to doctrines in part at least derived from the Slavophilism of his own student years. In France, Belgium, and French Switzerland (where his Fédération Jurassienne was led by the young schoolmaster James Guillaume and composed of poor watchmakers and other craftsmen), he appeared as the heir of Proudhon. In Italy he enrolled radical intellectuals who were dissatisfied with Mazzini's old-fashioned republicanism, and landless peasants looking for a way out. In Spain his emissaries paved the way for the later growth of an anarchosyndicalist movement which sought to bridge the gulf between town and country, the worker and the peasant. All this somehow sailed under the black flag of anarchism or the black-and-red banner of syndicalism, after the latter movement had got under way in France during the 1890's. It entered into competition with Marxist, or pseudo-Marxist, socialism—then universally committed to the red flag—but the two movements also overlapped. In the case of syndicalism it would have been impossible to say where the Marxist influence began and where it ended. There were also geographical variants. It is plain that from 1871 to 1881 the Italian anarchists had a virtual monopoly of what was then vaguely called "socialism"—in practice meaning anyone who sympathized with the Paris Commune. It is equally plain that after 1881 they lost their hold on the Italian labor movement, which then became "socialist" in quite a different sense—

one more in tune with what Marx and Engels meant by the term. But this (like the Neapolitan origin of some of Bakunin's own notions about decentralization and federalism) belongs to the history of the various national branches of the socialist, or anarchist, movements. The topic cannot be pursued here, any more than we can plunge into the tangled history of Spanish anarchism (not to mention the question why Spanish liberalism proved such a complete failure).

There remains the philosophical aspect, for Bakunin of course had to have a philosophy–as a former Hegelian he could hardly afford to be without one. But what was it? We have seen that he surreptitiously introduced a certain amount of "communism" into his interpretation of the anticapitalist doctrine associated with the name of Proudhon: a circumstance facilitated by his acquaintance with *Capital* (which at one moment he even undertook to translate into Russian). But this was more in the nature of an accommodation, and it did not touch upon what were to him the essentials of his faith. These essentials were grouped around a theme he shared with Proudhon: rebellion against authority–any authority, divine or terrestrial. Anarchism to him was an extension of atheism. Belief in a deity was not merely absurd but degrading, since it implied subordination to an arbitrary despot (and a nonexistent one at that). So far we are on familiar ground, for Proudhon had already yoked God and the state together. This was common coin in the romantic age, however shocking it might be to Mazzini, a heretical Catholic for whom *Dio* and *Popolo* went together, though he had no use for the Catholic Church. There would seem to be no inherent reason why Bakunin could not have adopted the Mazzinian view (itself in some fashion derived from Rousseau) that although traditional Christianity might be dying, a different faith would succeed it. But whereas Mazzini during his impressionable years had read Lamennais, Bakunin at the same time had made the acquaintance of Fichte, and Fichte plus the Left Hegelians had taught him to regard the idea of God as an abomination. This, by the way, shows how foolish it is to settle such questions by appealing to psychology, for Bakunin could with the greatest of ease have counterposed the virtuous Russian People (or even the Earth Mother) to the Divine Autocrat and his mundane representative, the Tsar. That he chose atheism rather than some form of cosmic dualism was evidently due to his intellectual environment; it is not explicable in terms of the quite normal urge to break the yoke of a despotic authority. "What moves Bakunin is tyranny, and by tyranny he means any infringement of liberty" (Gray, 354). But this hardly accounts for the peculiar form his revolt assumed, nor does it establish a link between his atheism and his anarchism. One must go back to his credo of 1842: "The lust of destruction is a creative lust."

In an earlier age the author of such sentiments would have been reckoned a member of the Devil's party, and there is no denying that a streak of primitive antinomianism runs through Bakunin's utterances, as when he asserts that Church and state both owe their existence to the same tyrannical desire to enslave many for the benefit of the few. In his pamphlet *God and the State*, this theme is spelled out at some length. More relevantly, Bakunin thoroughly approved of "revolutionary" manifestations such as the burning of the Tuileries and other public buildings by the Communards at the close of their struggle in May, 1871, when hope was gone and only despair remained. Marx, impassioned in his defense of the Commune against the Versailles government, put the blame for the resulting destruction where it belonged: on a government that had launched a civil war against the defenders of Paris and left them no hope even of being treated as prisoners, since they knew they were going to be butchered. Bakunin saw the matter differently. If the Communards in their rage and despair at last burned down entire sections of the city, that was nothing to lament. The flames they had lit illumined the future he envisaged for the "old world." We have seen what Herzen—who did not live to witness the event—thought of this kind of reasoning.

And yet it has to be said in justice to Bakunin that his passion for destruction went with a thoroughly benevolent disposition and an unshakable faith in the essential goodness of man. He was after all a Romantic. Unlike Nietzsche and his progeny, Bakunin felt neither hatred nor contempt for the mass of mankind. Having been converted in his youth to the philosophy of Feuerbach, he remained faithful to the humanist creed as he understood it: man is the highest being for man, hence it is incumbent upon those who have grasped this truth to rid the earth of man's oppressors. But where his contemporaries—notably Herzen and Belinsky—spoke of transcending a social order in which men were debased by their own creation, Bakunin could not rid himself of the urge to witness the actual destruction not merely of "the state" as an abstraction, but of concrete things and institutions: buildings, cities, the heritage of civilization. Without such a conflagration, how could the revolution become the great liberating experience to which he looked forward? Certainly he agreed that society was destined to endure, but so that society might become free and self-governing, the state must crumble into dust. The social community is essentially harmonious, for man is essentially good. It is the state that blocks the way to freedom, or rather state and Church combined. Both must be swept away–not to let chaos and old night come back, but so that mankind may at last settle down in a world freed from oppression.

All of which perhaps is no more than to say that Bakunin had translated into words what the Russian peasant–or the landless Italian and Spanish laborer–dimly felt about the civilization erected at his expense. Anarchism was destined for a career in these lands, although even in Bakunin's native Russia the succession was, in part at least, taken up by men whose outlook had been shaped by Tolstoy and for whom freedom did not spell destruction. The most important of them, Peter Kropotkin (1842-1921), falls outside our survey, for he belongs to the later history of anarchism. He is mentioned here only for the sake of establishing that anarchism as a doctrine did not necessarily signify either barbarism or the cult of violence for its own sake. Not that Kropotkin shrank from the thought of revolution, but in his benevolent manner he hoped that when the great upheaval came it would entail "the smallest number of victims and a minimum of embitterment" (Avrich, 27). Neither he nor his followers are to be blamed for the fact that Russia proved unsuitable soil for the kind of decentralized anarcho-communism in which they had put their faith.

And something else is noteworthy too: for all Bakunin's efforts to mobilize the *Lumpenproletariat* of the Russian slums, and even the underworld, the only real success he ever had was with students and emigrants. The latter for the most part congregated in Switzerland, where they collaborated with him in publishing short-lived journals. The student Populists who "went to the people" in 1874 had been vaguely affected by his doctrines, which also spread to some clandestine groups of factory workers. "Nevertheless, no genuine Bakuninist organization was founded on Russian soil during his lifetime" (Avrich, 37). When one considers the long legacy of religious sectarianism, peasant rebellion, and intelligentsia conspiracy, this must seem odd. The explanation perhaps lies with Bakunin's inability to establish a plausible connection between the two extreme poles of his *Weltanschauung*: liberty on the one hand, conspiracy on the other. No secret society could operate unless it was willing to subordinate itself to a self-appointed directorate invested with powers of life and death over its own followers. But when Nechaev and Tkachev spelled out the logic of this approach, Bakunin shrank back and broke off contact with them. To the end his mind remained a muddle, and his organizational principle typically took the form of demanding the impossible: a spontaneous countrywide rebellion based on the people of the "lower depths," under the control of a secret society which was somehow *not* to be the kind of organization that consistent "Jacobins" like Tkachev favored. In the end his followers went their separate ways. If, like Kropotkin, they took the libertarian creed seriously, they dropped the dictatorial approach–not to mention Bakunin's anti-Semitism, his Panslavism, or his childish fondness for armed banditry and the cult of violence and destruction that went with it. Those who clung to the conspiratorial model, plus faith in the peasantry and the village commune, eventually blossomed out as founders of the Social Revolutionary Party in the early years of the twentieth century. Bakunin's personal legacy was retained only at the level of symbolism, e.g., in the proud motto "The lust to destroy is a creative lust," which Kropotkin's followers in Geneva around 1903 chose to adorn the masthead of their journal: with the consent, be it noted, of Kropotkin, a descendant of the princely clan that had ruled Russia before the Romanovs and himself one of the Emperor's pages before he decided to renounce his noble heritage. Russian anarchism to the end retained something of the eccentric flavor Bakunin had brought to it, and this circumstance perhaps accounts for its inability to come to terms with the modern world. A better scholar than Bakunin and certainly a more amiable man, Kropotkin embodied the Rousseauist faith that lay at the back of so much populist and anarchist theorizing. The movement he led was destined to be a political failure, but it may be said to have left an enduring monument in literature. For in that sphere the internal dialectic of Russian populism was preserved by Tolstoy and Gorki: the former a "repentant nobleman," the latter a vagrant arisen from those lower depths set astir by the spiritual unrest of a revolutionary century.

It may be objected that this brief summation takes no account of the phenomenon of Russian gentry culture as a whole, a culture originally rooted in the classicism of the Enlightenment (as the reader of Pushkin's magnificent poetry cannot fail to realize). But then we are not trying to write literary history or to assess what may be called the enduring legacy of the Russian gentry: that tragic class whose one dramatic moment, the Decembrist rising of 1825, was foredoomed by the absence of a genuine feudal spirit linking nobles and peasants in a common alliance against the autocracy. Had Russia possessed a tradition of this sort, the soldiers might have followed the noblemen in uniform who were trying to win constitutional freedom, and then perhaps the stream of history would have taken another course. But it was not to be. Aristocratic liberalism died on the scaffold, and with it perished the only chance of removing the Tsardom and the despotic tradition it embodied by anything short of a revolution rooted in the exploited peasantry. For nobles and serfs to make common cause, it would have been necessary for the landowners—or at least a section of them—to repudiate the despotic legacy of old Muscovy. But only an elite of the gentry followed the call in 1825, and they were abandoned by the serfs in uniform who trusted the Tsar—until the day came when the peasant was ready to slay Tsar, official, and landlord alike. Then indeed the revolution would triumph, but it would do so under circumstances that involved the destruction of the gentry, along with the downfall of the autocracy which for so long had incarnated all that was worst in the semi-Asiatic heritage of old Russia.

2. From Populism to Marxism

"[In his mind] he already saw the red flag of 'Land and Freedom' waving on the Urals and the Volga, in the Ukraine and the Caucasus, possibly on the Winter Palace and the Peter-Paul fortress," Herzen wrote, with a touch of exasperation, describing Bakunin's feverish activity on the eve of the doomed Polish insurrection in 1863. The red flag of peasant insurrection (which had no great appeal for Polish nationalists) did indeed occupy an important place in Bakunin's mind before he launched out on his new career as the inspirer of "black flag" anarchism in the 1870's. Even then he did not abandon his old vision, and it was this circumstance that enabled a faction, or fraction, of the Russian revolutionary movement in the 1880's to make the transition from radical populism to something perhaps best described as anarcho-communism. At the back of it all there remained the belief—first publicly voiced by Herzen in the 1850's—that the village commune, the *obshchina,* could and would one day become the germ of a specifically Russian form of collectivism. This aspect of the Slavophil legacy is to be borne in mind when one inquires into the credentials of the group of radicals conventionally known as "the men of the sixties." They too formed part of the general stream of Russian populism, but while on amicable terms with Bakunin, they no longer looked to Herzen, whom they had written off as a liberal constitutionalist. Contemptuous of philosophical idealism, austere in manner, and resolved to act on their beliefs, these "nihilists" (as their opponents called them) represented a new type, and their patron saint was a radical materialist who devoted his life solely to the cause of revolution: N. G. Chernyshevsky.

In their own fashion the authorities were not wrong in thinking that something had changed since those idyllic days when Herzen, Bakunin, and other advanced spirits debated Hegelian philosophy with their Slavophil opponents in the salons of Moscow. In the 1840's only Belinsky had represented the new type that rose to prominence in the 1860's: the uprooted radical of lower-class origin, and Belinsky's mind had been shaped by the gentry culture of an earlier age—a circumstance that lends a special flavor to his writings. In the 1860's there were still a few representatives of the older breed around—aristocratic rebels with a following among disaffected officers and civil servants who tried to preserve something of the Decembrist inheritance—but they tended to be absorbed by the *raznochintsy* ("commoners") pouring from the new schools and universities: *déclassé* intellectuals of plebeian origin for whom "the revolution" was a way of life. Belinsky, Herzen, and Bakunin—albeit still in the tradition of the aristocratic conspirators of 1825—had equipped them with a philosophy. Nicholas Gavrilovich Chernyshevsky (1828-89) provided a faith. As a thinker he was unoriginal, as a writer undistinguished to the point of tedium. What he did possess was an approach to politics that was radically democratic. And there was something else: his moral austerity had a touch of grandeur about it that invested even his most commonplace utterances with a kind of prophetic authority. He was capable of expounding even the dreariest aspects of scientific materialism in the manner of one who had found the truth and was willing to lay down his life for it. One cannot even for a moment imagine him capable of doing what Bakunin had done when he was imprisoned in the Peter-Paul fortress ten years earlier: try to win the good graces of the Tsar by casting himself in the role of a true Russian patriot. Chernyshevsky was above that sort of thing, and he paid for it. As usual in such cases, the saintliness of his character, plus the savage treatment he got from the authorities, inspired a violent reaction among younger men who venerated his memory. The terrorist Ishutin, who gave the name of Hell to his own secret organization in the 1860's, maintained that "there have been three great men in world history: Jesus Christ, Paul the Apostle, and Chernyshevsky." It is improbable that Chernyshevsky (by then in Siberian exile) would have relished the comparison, but prophets are not responsible for all the utterances of their followers. This also applies to the "nihilism" of those intellectuals–Chernyshevsky's former pupil D. I. Pisarev (1840-68) among them–who reacted to his arrest in 1862, on trumped-up charges of moral responsibility for terrorism, by developing a kind of elitism. From the standpoint of the authorities, intellectual nihilism and revolutionary terrorism were both a good deal more dangerous than the humanist doctrine preached in the St. Petersburg literary journal *Sovremennik (The Contemporary)* during Chernyshevsky's editorship between 1859 and 1862, and if they had possessed any sense they would have left him alone. But the autocracy was doomed by its own imbecility even more than by the class interest of the landowners whom it felt obliged to protect, and it duly committed suicide by driving all the more intelligent and energetic representatives of the intelligentsia into prison, exile, or conspiracy.

What made Chernyshevsky important to the *raznochintsy* was that he spoke a new language. This was partly a matter of style, or rather lack of style. A certain provincialism (he was born in Saratov on the lower Volga, the son of an Orthodox priest) may have been responsible for the fact that for all his very considerable erudition he could never work up any real interest in aesthetic problems. In the chief editor of what was after all supposed to be a literary journal this was undoubtedly a defect, and when added to his lowly origin it evoked expressions of lordly disdain not only from Turgenev but also from Tolstoy, who on other grounds might have been expected to sympathize with the defender of the peasantry: Chernyshevsky's principal role during this period. Unfortunately Tolstoy, then at the beginning of his great career, disliked Chernyshevsky, complained about his provincial manners, and asserted that he smelt of bugs–an odd affectation of superiority on the part of a man who liked to pose as a friend of the people. Chernyshevsky for his part seems to have felt only a kind of weary distaste for all these literary celebrities. When at the end of his life he was asked to write his memoirs of the 1860's, he replied: "My memories of Turgenev and the others are incapable of arousing in me any other feeling than a longing to sleep. . . These people had no interest for me. . . . I was a man crushed by work. They lived the usual life of the educated classes, and I had no inclination for that" (Venturi, 157). He also differed from most of them on political grounds, since they were either reactionary Slavophils who idealized the Muscovite past or–if liberals and Westernizers–naive supporters of enlightened absolutism who expected the Tsar to turn the peasant-serfs into freeholders "with land." Chernyshevsky did not share these illusions, and his pessimism was amply confirmed by the facts.

What, then, was his political platform? Here one comes up against the difficulty of defining the meaning of the term "Populism." The word is a literal translation of the Russian *narodnichestvo*, itself derived from *narod* (people), and it was first employed around 1870. It is thus arguable that in the strict sense there were no Populists (*narodniki*) until they made their appearance as an organized group in the summer of 1874, when thousands of them poured into the villages to "awaken" the peasants from their lethargy–an attempt whose failure drove some of them into terrorism, others into elitism of the Jacobin-Blanquist type imported from France. Yet in a broader sense the entire Russian socialist movement from 1848 to 1881 may be described as Populist. Even after March 1, 1881–when Alexander II was assassinated by the Executive Committee of the Narodnaya Volya, or People's Will, a select band of terrorists who thought the autocracy could be destroyed at one blow by killing the Tsar–Populism remained in being, but some of its former adherents now turned to Marx while others sought consolation in Comte's positivism. Yet all remained faithful to Chernyshevsky, who for good measure enjoyed the personal esteem of Marx: a commodity in such rare supply that when Marx, in the Preface to the second edition (1873) of *Capital*, approvingly cited "the great Russian scholar and critic," the circumstance was noted with pride by the growing number of his Russian followers.

In 1873, however, Chernyshevsky had been reduced to silence for a decade and was in solitary confinement at Vilyuisk, a small Siberian town whose Yakut inhabitants could not even speak Russian. Moreover, the work that drew praise from Marx (an annotated Russian translation of J. S. Mill's *Principles of Political Economy* with a critical commentary on his doctrines) had been composed as early as 1860 and had not then attracted much attention. What mattered to Chernyshevsky's public were his contributions to *The Contemporary*: notably "The Anthropological Principle in Philosophy" (1860), a rambling essay setting out a humanist doctrine for the most part derived from Feuerbach. What this piece of writing chiefly disclosed was Chernyshevsky's lack of interest in anything that could properly be called metaphysics. But that was just the point: he and the younger men for whom he spoke–Nicholas Dobrolyubov (1836-61) and Pisarev being the best known–were converts to scientific materialism and had no time for subtleties not immediately related to practical human needs. If there was anything they disliked more than Herzen's aristocratic dilettantism it was the aestheticism of Turgenev, the famous novelist with whom they had a celebrated quarrel and who revenged himself on them by drawing an unflattering portrait of the "nihilist" Bazarov in *Fathers and Sons*. Chernyshevsky's own standpoint may be inferred from his novel *What Is To Be Done?* composed in 1863, while he was in prison awaiting trial. No one has ever claimed literary merit for it, but its impact was enormous. It is not too much to say that this solemn piece of writing furnished an entire generation of Russian radicals with a moral foundation for their beliefs. Almost forty years later, Lenin deliberately chose its title for the caption of the pamphlet that was to become the organizational bible of Bolshevism.

Yet when viewed in this light, the subsequent line-up appears simpler than it really was. Herzen's personal dispute with Chernyshevsky had originally been provoked by a quarrel over tactics, but what was subsequently at stake in the conflict between the two men (briefly composed after Chernyshevsky traveled to London for this purpose in 1859) was something quite different: both considered themselves socialists, but Chernyshevsky rejected the notion that Russia had a "mission" to rejuvenate Europe. This was a fantasy Herzen had inherited from the Slavophils together with his belief in the virtues of the village commune. Chernyshevsky too saw the *obshchina* as a possible germ of socialism, but he had no use for Herzen's and Bakunin's faith in a Russian national destiny. Europe, he thought, was by no means decadent, and anyway the Russians had nothing to teach their Western neighbors:

> We are far from praising the present social conditions in Europe, but we do say that they have nothing to learn from us. It may be true that Russia has retained, since patriarchal times, a principle which corresponds to one of the solutions at which progressives are aiming; it is none the less true that Western Europe is moving towards the realization of this principle quite independently of us. (Venturi, 160)

The *obshchina* might, under favorable circumstances, be transformed into a socialist community, but only if Western Europe showed the way. In 1882 Marx and Engels incorporated this perspective in their joint Preface to the second Russian edition of the *Communist Manifesto.* A few months later the first Russian Marxist group came together in Geneva: Chernyshevsky's work had borne fruit.

A final point may be worth mentioning. Although respectful of Mill, Chernyshevsky *mirabile dictu* was not a positivist. He had no faith in the gospel of progress, thought Comte ridiculous (an opinion shared by Marx), and perceived the Malthusian element in Darwin's theorizing. The writer he detested most of all was Herbert Spencer (though in later years he was obliged to translate him for a living, after he had been released and allowed to live in Astrakhan, in European Russia), while his favorite philosopher, next to Feuerbach, was Spinoza. All in all, for a provincial man of letters who spent the greater part of his life in Siberia, Chernyshevsky comes through as a man of quite astounding intellectual standing. He was not an original thinker, but his judgments were seldom wrong. The man who on reading Darwin at once perceived that the boneheaded application of his doctrine to social history could only produce "bestial inhumanity" was unlikely to be taken in by the fashionable belief in progress through mutual slaughter and the extinction of the weaker races. When it is borne in mind that some of the leading Fabians fell for this rubbish, one feels like congratulating Chernyshevsky on having read Spinoza and Feuerbach early enough in life to avoid becoming a worshipper of "progress." There was after all some advantage in having come to intellectual maturity in a milieu where philosophy had not been driven out by scientism. As he said of

Comte in 1876, "The poor fellow . . . knew nothing of Hegel or even of Kant." Chernyshevsky knew enough of both to see at a glance that Comte's celebrated doctrine of three evolutionary stages of thought (theological, metaphysical, and positive) was–as he unkindly put it–"completely idiotic." It is no great wonder that Marx liked the man, or that Chernyshevsky's pupils in the 1880's found no difficulty in adding historical materialism to the legacy they had inherited.

Although Chernyshevsky can in a sense be called a pre-Marxist, it does not follow that he was a precursor of Bolshevism, though Lenin greatly admired him. So far as political tactics were concerned, the student rebel P. G. Zaichnevsky and the other self-styled "Jacobins" of Young Russia in the 1860's (whose terroristic utterances the authorities attributed to the influence of Chernyshevsky) were close to the later Bolshevik model of the "professional revolutionary," and their heritage was preserved in the 1870's by the chief propagator of Jacobin-Blanquist ideas among that generation, Peter Nikitich Tkachev (1844-86) who threw in his lot with the French Blanquists after emigrating to Switzerland in 1874 (Venturi, 389 ff.). However, there was another current within the Populist stream: the evolutionary socialism of Peter Lavrov (1823-1900), who was on friendly terms with Marx and Engels but did not altogether share either their philosophy or their political outlook. Significantly, it was Tkachev who later furnished Lenin with his organizational model, whereas the Marxist group that came together in Geneva in 1883 was headed by Lavrov's former disciple G. V. Plekhanov, who had become a convert to the Social Democratic version of Marxism. All these men counted themselves followers of Chernyshevsky. This was as true of the "Jacobin" Tkachev who advocated a political dictatorship issuing from a *coup d'état*, as it was of Lavrov who put his faith in peaceful propaganda and education.

What then did they all have in common? Faith in the *obshchina* and in socialism, of course, and, increasingly, respect for Marx as an economist. But beyond this the cleavage between them became increasingly obvious, as Lavrov in the 1870's expounded his version of socialism while the future terrorists of the conspiratorial Narodnaya Volya moved in another direction. It was possible for revolutionaries drawn from the intelligentsia to describe themselves as socialists without being altogether sure in their own minds whether or not they believed Russia was in danger of passing through a lengthy phase of capitalist development. Depending on how they saw the matter, they would put their faith in the peasantry and the village community or seek to abort the threatened bourgeois takeover by a timely stroke at the autocracy. Even if they all held to the creed of Chernyshevsky, they still had a choice between the "Jacobinism" of Tkachev, Bakunin's anarchism, or Lavrov's faith in the intelligentsia as the stratum that would gradually educate the masses and spread socialist ideas among them, until the moment came for—well, for what?

Lavrov had no time for Jacobinism. "Revolutionary Socialists must give up their old ideas of being able to replace the State—after they have succeeded by a lucky stroke in destroying it. . . . We do not want a new constraining authority to take the place of that which already exists" (Venturi, 458). This was the heritage of Bakunin, or possibly of Varlin, with whom Lavrov had made friends before and during the Paris Commune. The latter, Lavrov wrote after having experienced it and talked it over with Marx in London, represented "a new kind of State. It had been put into practice for a short time, but it had shown that a workers' government was possible." At the same time he was critical of the Commune's leadership (as was Marx). "Lack of an economic program allowed the true Socialist elements of the Commune to be dominated by traditional forces, mainly the routiniers of the Jacobinism of 1793."

Here then was yet another version of the Populist faith. The common basis was still the creed of Herzen and Bakunin: an agrarian revolution led or supported by "that fraction of the intelligentsia which was capable of defending the interests and traditions of the peasants and voluntarily fusing with them" (Venturi, 62). To this original vision Chernyshevsky had added a concrete economic thesis: the former serfs ought to pay nothing for the land they had tilled before the 1861 Emancipation Decree. From this it followed that the landowners must be dispossessed, peacefully or otherwise. So far, so good (or not so good, from the standpoint of the liberal wing of the nobility and gentry who still hoped for a parliamentary regime but had no desire to install a democratic republic based on peasant votes). Strictly speaking it was possible to envisage a "Jacobin" solution of the agrarian problem without being a socialist in the Western sense, and indeed the subsequent quarrel between Populists and Marxists in the 1890's turned largely on the question whether radical democracy automatically spelled socialism (as the *narodniki* affirmed) or whether it would not on the contrary promote the rapid growth of capitalism (this being the position of Plekhanov and his friends after they had assimilated Marx's analysis). In retrospect it seems difficult to understand how the Populists could ever have believed that the agrarian democracy of their dreams was synonymous with socialism, but in the 1860's they (or their predecessors) felt able to cite Proudhon: it was only necessary to supply the self-governing village communities of the future with credit facilities, while blocking the path to capitalist development which would naturally be chosen by the landlords. Proudhon's "mutualism" and his "federalism" answered the prime need of all the toilers, or so it seemed to his Russian followers. These men became active after Chernyshevsky's enforced departure from the scene, and eventually they laid the basis of what came to be known as "legal Populism." It is not without interest that their chief competitors in the later 1860's, the "nihilists" around Pisarev, while Jacobinical in their political views, were coldly utilitarian when it came to economics. Pisarev was all for enlightened leadership by a scientifically trained elite of managers, and his colleague on the journal *Russkoe Slovo,* Varfolomey Zaytsev, on one occasion provoked a minor storm by asserting that the colored races were congenitally inferior (Venturi, 327). Not surprisingly, such men were enthusiasts for the Malthusian aspect of Darwinism, with its emphasis on the "struggle for existence" which would eliminate the lesser breeds. As Zaytsev's own career was to show, it was possible to hold such views and then become an adherent to Bakunin's brand of anarchism, but then a certain ruthlessness necessarily went with their intellectual extremism.

What makes Lavrov significant is that he developed in the opposite direction. Having made his debut in the (first) Zemlya i Volya under Chernyshevsky's patronage, the former mathematician and artillery officer then went abroad, made contact with the Paris members of the International, established friendly relations with Marx, broke with Bakunin's adherents, and gradually developed his own doctrine. As he saw it, socialist intellectuals in Russia had only one duty: to prepare themselves intellectually and then to "go to the people." On the theoretical side, his *History of Social Doctrines* was partly inspired by positivism, though unlike Comte he asserted that "true sociology is

Socialism." Among the Populists he was the most "Western" and the one who came closest to Marx, although he never relinquished the hope that the revolution would start in Russia. What marked him out from the beginning of his career in the 1860's was his opposition to "nihilism," his stress on moral principles, and in general his emphasis on the ethical meaning of socialism: members of the privileged class, the intellectuals had incurred an obligation they must repay by making themselves useful to the people. Some of his followers in the 1870's appear to have taken the view that capitalism was inevitable and must be given its head before a workers' movement could be expected to develop, but even so it was their duty to serve the popular cause as best they could. There was a certain ambiguity about this position: it could lead in the direction of either liberalism or Marxism. In any case those who held it had surrendered the central tenet of the original Populist creed: faith in the village commune and its durability. And, needless to say, they had no time for Tkachev and his Jacobin-Blanquist notion that the growth of capitalism in Russia could be aborted by a purely political coup. In this sense they may be said to have prepared the ground for the emergence of a social democratic attitude among the intelligentsia, or that part of it which followed Lavrov. They were in this sense reformists. Plekhanov–not perhaps the most impartial of witnesses–many years later summed up their attitude in the phrase: "We must leave it to the liberals to win political freedom, and only then on the basis of this freedom must we begin to organize the proletariat."

For such an attitude to win support, there had first to be a transfer of emphasis from the rural to the urban areas. The summer of 1874 witnessed the celebrated "going to the people" movement, when thousands of students descended on the villages to preach the gospel to the peasants. Some four thousand were arrested for what in any civilized country would have been regarded as a harmless exercise in propaganda. By the time the "mad summer" was over, the movement had been crushed, and the Populists had gained some valuable experience. The authorities, with their customary obtuseness, held Bakunin and Lavrov –especially the latter–responsible for the student crusade. In fact it had been spontaneous, although Lavrov's ideas may be said to have in part inspired it.

To appreciate what came next one must grasp the peculiar dialectic of the Populist creed. Its intellectual formulation in the 1860's and

1870's revolved around the twin themes of faith in a mysterious entity called "the people" and faith in themselves. "Go to the people" had been Herzen's advice to the new generation in 1862. By the end of that decade, Lavrov was arguing that the task of the intellectuals was primarily educational, while Bakunin insisted that it was political: all they had to do was to detonate the explosive mass of peasant rage which centuries of oppression had heaped up beneath the shaky throne of the Tsarist autocracy. The "going to the people" movement in 1874–itself spurred by famine conditions in the Volga region–put these conflicting ideas to the test. The young men and women who went out into the villages did so in a spirit of humility and with a genuine desire to be accepted by the peasants. Even the Lavrists insisted that it was their task not to bring strange ideas to the village but rather to enlighten the peasants about their own half-conscious aims. The reception they got disillusioned them: so far from being either revolutionary or even willing to listen, the peasants turned out to be sullenly hostile. Whether viewing themselves as Lavrov's "conscious minority" or as Pisarev's elite the young revolutionaries encountered ridicule, enmity, or simple stupor. To this experience there could be two different reactions. It was possible to assert that the Populists must adapt themselves to the primitive consciousness of the masses, and this was the conclusion hesitantly drawn by the (second) Zemlya i Volya organization which came together in 1876. But those who despaired of the masses, and of the Lavrist faith in education, now turned to Tkachev, then in Geneva and editing his own journal, *Nabat.* From 1874 onward the theorist of Russian Blanquism began to preach a message that struck home because it had behind it the first faint glimmer of an understanding of Marxian economics. Capitalism (Tkachev told his readers) was not an impossibility in Russia, as Herzen and Bakunin had affirmed. It was a real and present danger. Unless something was done immediately, the village community would be destroyed. Indeed, it was already beginning to crumble, and a stratum of conservative peasants was coming into existence:

> This is why we cannot wait. This is why we insist that a revolution in Russia is really indispensable, and indispensable right at the present time. We will not stand for any pause, for any temporization. It is now or very far in the future, maybe never! Now conditions are for us; in ten, twenty years they will be against us. (Haimson, 16)

Engels did not approve of this approach and had a lively argument with Tkachev about it, but to the Populist vanguard Engels had not yet become an authority. Tkachev's message alarmed them, while the indifference of the peasant masses disillusioned them. The result was another wave of internal disputation which split Zemlya i Volya into rival factions: the elitists of Narodnaya Volya who decided to act on Tkachev's recommendations; and the gradualists of Cherny Peredel (Black Repartition–of the land, that is), who opposed terrorism and stuck to propaganda among the workers. Narodnaya Volya spent the next three years in a campaign of terror which culminated in the assassination of Alexander II. Cherny Peredel went on defending the Populist faith, although by now its leaders no longer knew whether they were Bakuninists or Lavrists. The men and women of Narodnaya Volya fell in the armed struggle against the autocracy. Their rivals were arrested, dispersed, or went abroad. There the ablest of them read the *Communist Manifesto,* and a new chapter in the history of Russian socialism had begun.

Georgii Valentinovich Plekhanov (1856-1918), often described as the "father of Russian Marxism," was born in Tambov Province, the son of a conservative landed gentleman of Tartar origin whose estate was halved by the emancipation of the serfs. His mother, a distant relative of Belinsky, the famous critic and friend of Herzen, taught school to support her twelve children after her husband's death in 1873. Georgii Plekhanov, like his three half-brothers, was destined for an army career, was graduated from Voronezh military academy, and in 1873 enrolled as a student in a Petersburg military school. After 1874, having meantime transferred to the Mining Institute, he became a Populist, joined the (second) Zemlya i Volya, and in 1876 organized an illegal protest demonstration in front of Kazan Cathedral, in consequence of which he had to flee abroad. Returning on forged papers a year later, he joined Cherny Peredel. Abroad once more in 1880 after the arrest of most of his friends, he settled in Geneva, whence he observed the destruction of the rival People's Will group after the assassination of the Tsar in 1881, engaged in polemics with the surviving Bakuninists and with Tkachev, translated the *Communist Manifesto* into Russian, and, in 1883, with P. B. Axelrod (1850-1928) and Vera Zasulich (1852-1919), founded the first Russian Marxist organization, the Emancipation of Labor group.

Plekhanov had briefly worked with Lavrov and Kropotkin, but his increasing disenchantment with the Populist creed made cooperation with them impossible in the long run. Although he retained his faith in the socialist potentialities of the *obshchina*—so for that matter did Marx and Engels, who contributed a joint preface to his translation of the *Manifesto*—Plekhanov now envisaged Russian socialism in Marxist terms as a movement based on the growing factory proletariat. At the same time, he rejected the Herzen-Bakunin legacy of national "exceptionalism" and hostility or indifference to Germany and Western Europe. The revolution, he held, would be a European affair, and Russia's place in it would be determined by the growth of its own labor movement, not by peasant risings directed by secret conclaves of terrorists. In short, he had become a Social Democrat of the Marxist variety: the sort who believed that the strategy outlined in the *Manifesto* for Germany in 1847 was still applicable to Russia, though evidently not to Western Europe, where bourgeois democracy was now a reality. His translation of the *Manifesto* marked, as he said, "an epoch in my life." Until then he had adhered to the school of Populism inspired by Chernyshevsky. His discovery that it was possible to adopt Marx without renouncing this heritage altered the course of his life and made it possible for him to construct a theoretical bridge across which growing numbers of disillusioned Populists moved into the illegal Russian Social Democratic movement (Baron, 59 ff.).

The decisive importance of Plekhanov's conversion to Marxism must be seen against the background of the crisis the radical intelligentsia was then passing through. Contrary to expectation, the assassination of the Tsar had resulted not in the fall of the autocracy, but in its hardening. The People's Will organization was wrecked by the arrest or execution of its leaders—Zhelyabov, Mikhailov, Kibalchich, and Sofya Perovskaya being the most celebrated—and its followers dispersed or went into hiding, if they were not shipped off to Siberia. This might have given Cherny Peredel its chance, had not its Bakuninist inheritance rendered it useless as an instrument of political combat. The rift between the two factions in the late 1870's was in its origins a continuation of the already ancient quarrel between "anarchists" and "centralists," with

Plekhanov provisionally enrolled on the Anarchist side. When Cherny Peredel failed to strike root, Plekhanov reluctantly concluded that "federalism," the *obshchina*, and talk about Cossack revolts and Stenka Razin were not enough. Bakunin clearly was out of date. On the other hand, Narodnaya Volya–faithful to Alexander Mikhailov's slogan "fire at the center," i.e., strike at the Tsar–had tried and failed. What was to be done? In Geneva, reading the *Manifesto* before translating it into Russian, Plekhanov finally realized the futility of the whole quarrel between "Jacobins" and "libertarians." Tkachev and Bakunin, he now saw, had both been wrong, or rather, each of them had got hold of only one end of the stick. They had divorced politics from economics, the struggle for power from the analysis of the social process. Not surprisingly, their followers had got nowhere. It was necessary to transcend these factional disputes, and this could only be done with the help of Marx.

From Plekhanov's standpoint, this conversion to Marxism did not in any way represent a change so far as the ultimate aims of the revolution were concerned. At the celebrated demonstration in front of Kazan Cathedral on December 6, 1876, with which he had inaugurated his career, the orators had addressed an astonished crowd on the subject of Chernyshevsky's banishment to Siberia "because he wished the people well," whereupon a young working man unfurled a red banner on which were inscribed the words "Land and Liberty." Thus the continuity of the revolutionary tradition was unbroken. The edifice connecting Populism and Marxism was constructed out of material both schools held in common. Moreover, those who continued to adhere to the central Populist tradition (after having read Marx) did so with arguments they had culled from his writings. The first volume of *Capital* had appeared in Hamburg in 1867. Even before there was a Russian translation (in 1872), well-known sociologists and economists such as N. K. Mikhailovsky, N. I. Ziber, and N. F. Danielson found support in Marx for their thesis that Russia could and should skip the capitalist stage. Danielson indeed completed G. A. Lopatin's Russian translation of the first volume of *Capital*–legally, since the censor passed it, on the grounds that the book was too dull to stir up trouble. This may well rank among the outstanding critical misjudgments in literary history. And yet it can be held that in the short run *Capital* made life easier for the harassed Tsarist bureaucracy, since the effect of reading it was to inspire doubt as to the correctness of the Populist analysis. If "economic laws" were all-powerful, then what was the point of trying to rescue the *obshchina,* since it was doomed to disappear anyhow? Marx himself had to intervene repeatedly in order to clarify his meaning on this crucially important topic. In the postscript to the second (1873) edition of *Capital*, he quoted Ziber approvingly as one who in 1871 had fully understood his theoretical position. He also found much to praise in a review of *Capital* published in May, 1872, in the Petersburg *Vestnik Evropi.* Yet he could not ignore the awkward fact that he was being cited in support of the thesis that Russian society must passively accommodate itself to the inevitable spread of capitalism and liberal constitutionalism. This was not at all what he had meant, as he took pains to make clear to the editors of the Petersburg *Otechestvenniye Zapiski* in a letter composed in November, 1877, but not mailed and made public only after his death (by Engels, who sent a copy to Vera Zasulich in Geneva). The letter–in substance directed against Mikhailovsky, soon to become the acknowledged theorist of "legal" Narodism–made a point which Marx later developed at greater length in drafting a reply to an inquiry Zasulich addressed to him on behalf of the Russian exiles in Geneva: namely, that there was no "law" which condemned Russia to a mechanical repetition of the Western experience. "If Russia continues to pursue the path she has followed since 1861, she will lose the finest chance ever offered to a people and undergo all the fatal vicissitudes of the capitalist regime."

Here then was a poser. The author of *Capital*, so far from being committed to what in 1877 he described as "an historico-philosophic theory of the general path every people is fated to tread" (in other words, a positivist doctrine in the spirit of Comte, whom he loathed), insisted on the contrary that his own work was merely a "historical sketch of the genesis of capitalism in Western Europe." Naturally if Russia chose to industrialize along capitalist lines she would not succeed without having first transformed most peasants into proletarians, and after that, once taken to the bosom of capitalism, she would experience its pitiless laws like other profane countries. But there was no historical necessity about it! The first step counted, but the irrevocable choice had not (yet) been made. Thus Marx in November, 1877. Exactly forty years later Lenin was to draw the appropriate conclusion: Russia need *not* copy the Western experience. In support of this contention he could have cited Marx's preface to Plekhanov's translation of the *Manifesto*: "If the Russian Revolution becomes the signal for a proletarian revolution in the West, so that both complement each other, the present Russian common ownership of land may serve as the starting-point for a communist development." As ill luck would have it, Plekhanov by 1917 had arrived at the opposite standpoint. Having gradually become a Menshevik in the factional struggle set in motion by Lenin in 1903, he had worked around to the reluctant conclusion that it was too late to halt Russia's Westernization. By the time he returned to Petersburg in 1917, after thirty-seven years of exile, he had become a democrat in the Western sense and was ready to back the Provisional Government against Lenin. The Bolshevik seizure of power later that year struck him as an act of madness. By 1918 the dying man even began to feel that he had incurred some responsibility for what Lenin had done. "Did we not begin the propaganda of Marxism too early in backward, semi-Asiatic Russia?" he asked an old comrade who spent his last hours with him (Baron, 358).

But all that lay in the distant future. In the 1880's and for many years thereafter, Plekhanov–ably seconded by P. B. Axelrod and Vera Zasulich–represented the central core of the growing Russian Marxist school. His learned pamphlets against the Populists–notably *Socialism and the Political Struggle* (1883) and *Our Differences* (1884)–put the case against them with unsurpassed clarity and with a wealth of citations from the works of Marx and Engels, notably their polemics against Bakunin and Tkachev. During the crucial three years 1881-84, Plekhanov effected a fusion of the Populist creed with Marxist sociology. So as to render it comprehensible, Marxism had to be translated into the Populist language created by Chernyshevsky, and the task was performed by a man who in his own person had once incarnated the tradition associated with Bakunin. For of course the doctrine bore the unmistakable stamp of its origins. *Socialism and the Political Struggle* is full of passages that testify to their author's awareness of the importance of maintaining the continuity of the movement, e.g.: "our revolutionary movement . . . will gain a lot if the Russian *narodniks* and the Russian *Narodnaya Volya* at last become Russian Marxists" (*Selected Philosophical Works, 104*).

Where, then, lay the novelty? Certainly not in an abandonment of faith in the village community. On the contrary, Plekhanov quoted approvingly from Marx's and Engels' relevant remarks in their introduction to his translation of the *Manifesto*. Nor did he oppose the idea of seizing and holding power by revolutionary means. "Having gained political domination, a revolutionary class will retain that domination and be relatively secure against the blows of reaction only when it uses against reaction the mighty weapon of state power." Shades of Bakunin! And yet Plekhanov had not become a "Jacobin." He was a Social Democrat and proud of it:

> But there is no more difference between heaven and earth than between the dictatorship of a class and that of a group of revolutionary *raznochintsi.* This applies in particular to the dictatorship of the working class, whose present task is not only to overthrow the political domination of the unproductive classes in society, but also to do away with the anarchy now existing in production and consciously to organize all functions of social and economic life. The mere *understanding* of this task calls for an advanced working class with political experience and education, a working class free from bourgeois prejudices and able to discuss its situation by itself. In addition to this, its *solution* presupposes that socialist ideas are spread among the proletariat and that the proletariat is conscious of its own strength and confident in victory. But *such* a proletariat *will not allow* even the sincerest of its well-wishers to seize power. It will not allow it for the simple reason that it has been to the school of political education with the firm intention of finishing it at some time and coming forward as an independent figure in the arena of historical life, not to pass eternally from one guardianship to another. . . . Such a guardianship would be harmful, for the conscious participation of the producers in organizing production cannot be replaced by any conspiratorial skill, any daring or self-sacrifice on the part of the conspirators. (*Ibid.*, 110)

Plekhanov knew to whom he was addressing this caution. In *Our Differences*, he tackled the subject head-on:

> There was a feature that can be considered common to all our revolutionary trends. This feature common to them all was faith in the possibility of our revolutionary intelligentsia having a powerful and decisive influence on the people. In our revolutionary calculations

> the intelligentsia played the role of a beneficent providence of the Russian people, a providence upon whose will it depended whether the wheel of history would turn one way or the other. . . . This self-assurance of the intelligentsia went along with utter idealization of the people and the conviction—at least so far as the majority of our revolutionaries were concerned—that "the emancipation of the working people has to be the affair of the working people themselves." This formula, it was assumed, would be applied in a perfectly correct manner once our intelligentsia took the people as an object of its revolutionary influence. The fact that this basic principle of the Statute of the International Working Men's Association had another, so to speak philosophico-historical meaning, that the emancipation of a definite [given] class can be its own affair only when an independent emancipation movement arises within that class—all this . . . did not occur at all to our intelligentsia. (*Ibid.*, 166-67)

The author of these lines had learned his Marxist lesson well (probably in the first place from Axelrod, who had preceded him as a convert to Marx and who later became the most consistent exponent of Menshevism, Plekhanov after the split of 1903 having wavered for some time between the Mensheviks and Lenin's faction.) In retrospect, one may wonder whether Plekhanov had not learned his lesson *too* well. After all, it is arguable that orthodox Marxism was not applicable to the Russian situation, for the simple reason (instinctively discerned by Lenin) that if the party wanted to seize power, it could not afford to ask the workers what *they* wanted.

But in the 1880's, when Plekhanov formulated his standpoint, Lenin was still a schoolboy. By the time he had come to the forefront, there was a workers' movement and a revival of revolutionary activity among the Populist and Marxist intellectuals alike. In the reactionary 1880's, a Russian socialist needed a good deal of faith in "history" if he was to implant a Marxist consciousness in others. In the end Plekhanov succeeded in persuading himself that Marx had demonstrated the *objective* necessity of socialism. There were laws of social development which could not be flouted, but fortunately they worked in the right direction. A bourgeois revolution in Russia was inevitable, now that the capitalist process had got under way, and the working class would know how to take advantage of it. In his heart of hearts Plekhanov believed that a revolutionary need only understand the logic of history in order to insert his own activity into it. For him there was no doubt that "the Social Democrat [was] swimming along the current of history" (Haimson, 46). Two decades later Lenin revived the basic faith of the *Narodovoltsy*: if they wanted to make a revolution they had to swim *against* the current!

And yet Plekhanov effected that enduring fusion of Populism and Marxism which was to be the secret of Lenin's "national" appeal. And it was on the strength of his later philosophical essays, which in the 1890's were influential in expounding Marx's historical materialism and, rather less fortunately, Engels' dialectical materialism (so described by Plekhanov himself, who is the inventor of the term), that Lenin regarded Plekhanov as his teacher and stressed the importance of his work, even after they had parted company politically. Soviet Marxism on its philosophical side represents the legacy of Plekhanov: a circumstance duly stressed in all official pronouncements down to the present day. But the Western reader is not obliged to treat this topic with the solemnity accorded to it in the Soviet Union and its dependencies. No one who has slept through Plekhanov's *Defense of Materialism* (pseudonymously, but legally, published in Russia in 1894-95 under the long-winded title *On the Question of the Development of the Monist View of History*) is likely to share the opinion of the Soviet editors of his collected works, viz., that the author of this treatise was "one of the world's greatest thinkers."

Plekhanov was nothing of the kind, though he comes off fairly well in comparison with Chernyshevsky, and he certainly had a better mind than either Herzen or Bakunin. This is not perhaps saying a very great deal, for Herzen was fundamentally an egocentric belletrist, and Bakunin a born confusionist who only had to take up a theoretical or practical problem to render it insoluble. With Plekhanov one is back in the mental universe of Chernyshevsky. At the same time he points forward to Lenin. But in saying this one must bear in mind that the moral which Lenin extracted from Chernyshevsky was primarily the need for action by a self-constituted elite of professional revolutionaries. After all, Zaichnevsky's revolutionary manifesto of 1862, *Young Russia* (which indirectly landed Chernyshevsky in Siberia), did bear some marks of the older man's influence, even though his rebellious disciple meant it literally when he talked of "taking up the axe." There is evidence to show that Lenin was converted to "Jacobinism," in the style of Tkachev and Zaichnevsky, before he had come across Marx. A long tradition of gentry radicalism launched him on the path of revolution "in the Jacobin manner," that is to say, with the emphasis on the need for an armed confrontation with the Tsarist autocracy. Today one can say with a fair degree of certainty that by the time the youthful Lenin had come across Plekhanov's pamphlet *Our Differences* in 1889, thus beginning his own education in Marxism, he was already committed to the Jacobin-Blanquist standpoint. What is remarkable is that he never wavered in affirming the central tenet of his faith: without "Jacobin" violence, the "dictatorship of the proletariat" was an empty phrase. Conversely, it can scarcely be thought an accident that all the surviving members of Zaichnevsky's circle eventually joined Lenin's faction after 1903. Zaichnevsky himself died in 1896, and "with his death," wrote one of his followers in 1923, "Russian Jacobinism died . . . to rise again . . . in the revolutionary wing of Russian Social Democracy, in Bolshevism" (Valentinov, 75).

8 Western Socialism: 1864 - 1914

1. The First International

Historians of socialism generally date the birth of the First International from a meeting of English and Continental labor leaders in London on September 28, 1864. But, as we have seen, the International Working Men's Association was the inheritor of an older tradition which had climaxed and failed in 1848. We have already encountered most of the leading figures associated with those dim beginnings, from the Owenites and the Chartists in England to Proudhon and his followers in France. We may also remind ourselves that London after 1848 became a place of refuge for Continental personalities as widely different in their outlook as Marx, Herzen, and Mazzini. As the capital city of an empire and of what was then the only fully industrialized country in Europe (if one excepts Belgium, which for geographical and other reasons could not play a decisive role), London was the natural headquarters of the newly formed International. For the same reason, there was always a danger that the movement would be taken over by men or groups stemming from the earlier epoch of democratic radicalism. Let us illustrate this situation by citing a few apparently unrelated circumstances.

In February, 1840, there had been founded in London an offshoot of the Paris-based League of the Just, itself the forerunner of the German Communist League. The organizers–Karl Schapper (a printer), Heinrich Bauer (a shoemaker), and Joseph Moll (a watchmaker)–set up a respectable front organization, appropriately named the German Workers' Educational Society. In due course they got rid of the tailor Wilhelm Weitling (1808-71), a half-mad apostle of Christian communism who aspired to the leadership, and co-opted Marx and Engels instead. The association changed its name to the Communist Workers' Educational Society, acquired an international character by admitting Dutchmen, Scandinavians, Hungarians, Czechs, and a few Russians, issued membership cards in twelve languages carrying the slogan "All men are brothers," and in November, 1847, commissioned the drafting of the *Communist Manifesto*. When this document first appeared in English (in George Julian Harney's short-lived *Red Republican* in November, 1850) its appearance passed unnoticed, but almost a year later a *Times* editorial drew attention to what it called "cheap publications containing the wildest and most anarchical doctrines," quoting a few passages by way of making its readers' flesh creep. These excerpts from what *The Times* called "Literature for the Poor" were reprinted in the *Quarterly Review* of November, 1851, as specimens of what its editor described as "Revolutionary Literature" (*Collins and Abramsky*, 9-10). By that time, the Chartist movement (in which Harney had been an important figure) was on its last legs, although Marx and Engels continued to keep in touch with the Chartist journalist and poet Ernest Jones. The German Workers' Educational Society, curiously enough, stayed in existence until 1917, when it was dissolved by the British government: not because its founders had been communists, but because Britain was at war with Germany and all German citizens were being interned (Braunthal, I, 47).

Now let us take another aspect of this very complicated story. From 1855 until 1859, Ernest Jones, previously active as a Chartist leader and an associate of Harney, moved within a shadowy organization called the International Association, which both Marx and Mazzini boycotted: Mazzini because he wanted nothing to do with socialism, Marx because he wanted nothing to do with Herzen, who addressed the first public meeting of the Association and seized the opportunity to preach his gospel about decadent Europe having to be "rejuvenated through Russian blood," as Marx put it in a letter to Engels. (The matter could also be put more prosaically by saying that Herzen acquainted his audience with his pet notion, namely that the salvation of mankind would come from the Russian peasant commune.) The International Association was, in one of its aspects, a successor to the Fraternal Democrats, a body established in March, 1846, on Harney's initiative to make contact with Continental democrats and "red republicans," as they were then known. Young Italy (Mazzini's creation) did not respond, but the Democratic Association in Belgium (which included Marx among its members) made contact. In the 1850's, Ernest Jones' *People's Paper* reprinted some of Marx's articles from the *New York Tribune*–especially those that were directed against Russia (and against Lord Palmerston, then British Foreign Secretary, whom Marx considered pro-Russian). The Association–which now consisted mostly of surviving Chartists, plus a medley of German, French, and Polish socialists–died an unnoticed death in 1859. Still, certain traditions and habits of mind had been established, and, when in 1862-64 there began a movement among British and French labor leaders in favor of Polish independence, it was quite natural that Marx should be drawn in. What is rather more remarkable is that he should at first have taken a back seat, while the spotlight fell on a small but influential group of London intellectuals with pro-French leanings: the Positivists (Harrison, *passim*).

At first sight it may seem that all this has very little to do with the history of socialism or the founding of the First International. In fact it has everything to do with it. On its industrial side, the origins of the First International have been traced back by historians to a series of lock-outs and strike movements among London construction workers in 1859-62, which brought the London Trades Council into being in 1860. The leading figures of this purely working-class organization became in due course founding members of the International–as a by-product of the pro-Polish campaign they were running jointly with their French colleagues across the Channel. But observe: in October, 1859, Chernyshevsky in *The Contemporary* had begun to inform his readers of the agitation for a nine-hour work day among the London construction workers, described by him as "a grandiose episode in the struggle between capital and labor"; and in May, 1860, the *Russkiy Vestnik* ran a long report on the subject, mentioning some of the London labor leaders by name. There was nothing Chernyshevsky and his friends could do to help, but it is significant that they took note of the British strike movement. On the other hand, when the International was formally constituted in September, 1864, Herzen barely noticed it, while Bakunin at first ignored it and then tried to permeate it with his own secret organization. The first general publicity the I.W.M.A. obtained was due, rather unexpectedly, to Abraham Lincoln, whom it congratulated on his re-relection in November, 1864 (in an address drafted by Marx), and who returned a friendly letter of thanks. "You can imagine how much good this does our people," Marx wrote on February 10, 1865, to Engels, who made no comment and for another year or so continued to hint that Marx ought to get on with *Capital* instead of wasting his time on the International. In short, the decisive event in the history of modern socialism–the founding of an international labor movement on democratic lines–was barely noticed at the time, and some of those who later rose to prominence in it were originally inclined to treat it as a distraction from more important matters.

This was emphatically not Marx's opinion, for he immediately grasped the significance of what had happened. It would be wrong, however, to represent him as the movement's originator, since it had in fact arisen spontaneously from an interchange of opinion among authentic labor leaders, helped and advised by democratic radicals and Continental emigrés. Its founders were groping toward an authentic working-class organization bridging national barriers. This is a notion unfamiliar to Leninists, who have done their best to represent the First International as a small-scale dress rehearsal for the Third: a misreading of history perversely abetted by propagandists of competing sects and schools who fail to understand that all genuine labor movements are necessarily structured on democratic lines. The basic fact about the I.W.M.A. is that none of those concerned with its founding had the least idea how it was going to develop. Even Marx, who drew up its statutes and from the start sat on its General Council, tried to keep as much as possible in the background. Engels at first did not take it seriously at all. The Blanquists disliked it because on the French side it had been brought into being by their Proudhonist rivals. The Lassalleans in Germany took no part in it. The London Trades Council first treated it as an extension of its own activities and later refused to join as a body, although agreeing to cooperate with it. There is evidence that these London union leaders were more interested in Mazzini's ideas than in Marx's socialism, but some of them joined the International's General Council and shared in its work. This is how history really operates–especially labor history, which has always been a very confused and disorderly affair, full of "spontaneity" and quite lacking in that rigid discipline and centralization which present-day Communists so admire. Nor was there anything "Fabian" about this rather formless movement, for it operated in broad daylight, conducted its debates at international congresses, and gloried in its working-class character. In short, it was an early social-democratic organization, albeit this term had only just been invented for the benefit of the renascent German workers' movement (Braunthal, I, *passim*).

If there was not at first an over-all program, there was no lack of conflicting schools and tendencies, all competing for the attention of the British and French labor leaders who made up the core of the International. Three major currents are still dimly visible through the mist of time: Mazzinian nationalism and Freemasonry, Anglo-French positivism, and German socialism, the latter represented at first by Marx alone, though he had some working-class associates (veterans of the German Communist League) whose presence in London enabled him to build up a small "Marxist" faction on the General Council. Eventually, by sheer force of intellect he began to dominate, but this was not foreseeable at the start. Least of all was it foreseen by the British union leaders who gradually became his stoutest supporters. These men had been drawn to the movement by considerations only very distantly connected with what later came to be known as Marxian socialism. Their prime interest, apart from straightforward trade unionism, was the extension of the parliamentary franchise to the workers, a cause in which they cooperated with liberal leaders such as John Bright. In addition, they entertained a somewhat uncritical enthusiasm for the nationalist cause in Poland, Hungary, and Italy. If the British workers had a hero, it was Garibaldi, whose visit to London in April, 1864, led to spontaneous mass demonstrations. Next in order they admired Mazzini, whom the Proudhonists detested because he was opposed to socialism and who returned the compliment because Proudhon had no use for Italian nationalism. Lastly there was Poland: the British and French labor leaders prominent in the I.W.M.A. wanted their governments to take up the Polish cause, and in this they had the backing of a small but influential group of intellectuals, the Positivists.

While historians of the labor movement have devoted a great deal of attention to the secret societies within the First International, from the Freemasons to Bakunin's followers (Drachkovitch, ed., 36 ff.), comparatively little attention has been given to the mental background of the British labor movement during this period. (The standard work on the subject, Royden Harrison's *Before the Socialists: Studies in Labour and Politics 1861-1881*, is virtually unknown outside Britain, with the result that histories of the International tend to get written in terms of a personal struggle between Marx and Bakunin, who did not even attempt to join the organization until it was well under way.) Yet no account of the International is satisfactory if it does not take into account the Anglo-French background. While Mazzini was represented at the foundation meeting and Marx was present in person, the organization was started by French and English labor leaders whose immediate concerns were industrial. Beyond this they shared certain foreign-policy interests in Poland and Italy and a positivist orientation. Neither was destined to last, but both made their contribution at the beginning. The Polish insurrection had already provided the impetus for a public meeting in London on July 22, 1863, which in turn served as the occasion for an exchange of views between the French (mostly followers of Proudhon, with a sprinkling of left-wing Bonapartists) and the British labor leaders. The latter were liberal-radical, with memories of Chartism still in their minds and with a new-found commitment to the anti-slavery cause in the United States. To be precise, they were for Lincoln in the measure in which they were willing to cooperate with liberals like Bright.

The anti-slavery issue has been the theme of a great deal of hagiographic nonsense, mostly produced by Communist authors, who in this as in other respects have proved worthy successors of Church historians. Abolition is supposed to have been the consuming passion of the British working class during the American Civil War: so much so that the ruling classes dared not intervene on the Confederate side, as they would have liked. The prosaic truth is that abolition was primarily a liberal middle-class cause, and the British labor leaders who supported it were decidedly in the minority. Quite a number of union leaders—notably former Chartists who had been won over to Tory democracy (i.e., Disraelian conservatism) through hatred of capitalism and liberalism—favored the South and the secessionist cause. The authoritative account of the subject notes that "it is a problem to find a single influential working-class [news]-paper which consistently favored Lincoln and opposed British intervention. The predominant tendency was decidedly the other way. . . . Famous and respected leaders of the working people sided with the Confederacy" (Harrison, 53). There were, however, exceptions, notably among the union leaders who became prominent in the International. Only—and this is the point that needs to be grasped if one is to make sense of the story—these men were not socialists. On the contrary, they favored the Northern cause precisely because they had become reconciled to liberalism!

To anyone not blinded by propaganda or stupefied by populist worship of the "common people," an explanation of this state of affairs is perfectly simple. Abolition was the cause of liberals like John Bright who spoke for the newly prominent class of industrial manufacturers in the north of England, and there was no group of men whom the average unionist loathed more. During the 1840's Chartists and free-traders had been the bitterest of enemies: not least because the "Manchester Radicals," sound Benthamites and *laissez-fairists* that they were, consistently voted against legislation seeking to limit the inhumanly long work hours in the factories. By the 1860's this issue was dead, but the former Chartists had long memories. Part of the accumulated hatred they had felt for Cobden, Bright, and their liberal friends was transferred to the abolitionists. It was, as they saw it, the same old capitalist crusade: in the 1840's launched by the anti-Corn Law League, now concealed behind hypocritical talk of freeing the slaves. To British union leaders as yet unreconciled to capitalism and liberalism, the cause of the southern Confederacy appeared respectable. This led to paradoxical alignments. The name of Bright being linked with that of Lincoln, it was quite in order for an old-fashioned oligarchic Tory to declare, "If I had my way, I would blow President Lincoln from a mortar with a bombshell, and if there wasn't wadding enough I'd ram John Bright down after him"; but this sort of sentiment had support among the older generation of union leaders too. So far as they were concerned, abolitionism was the slogan of Benthamite "radicals" and Manchester free-traders who for fifty years had kept men, women, and children toiling endless hours in mines and factories.

Chartism and the campaign for factory legislation had gone together, though the Chartists were already on the decline when in 1847 a weird coalition of guilt-stricken Whig aristocrats, evangelical philanthropists, and furious Tory landowners pushed the Ten Hours Bill through in revenge for the abolition of the Corn Laws the year before. As Marx put it twenty years later, when passions had cooled: "They [the Chartists] found allies in the Tories panting for revenge. Despite the fanatical opposition of the army of perjured Freetraders, with Bright and Cobden at their head, the Ten Hours Bill . . . went through Parliament" (*Capital*, 269). Marx wrote this in 1867. In 1863, commenting privately on the meetings then in progress in support of Lincoln and the Northern cause, he took a more tolerant view of Bright, whose anti-slavery campaign had somewhat redeemed him in the eyes of men like Marx and Engels. It was not so easy to make the old Chartists forget what they had suffered from the Manchester economists and their parliamentary representatives. "It was enough for men reared in the hard school of the anti-Poor Law agitation, the factory reform movement and Chartism, that John Bright and his friends identified themselves with the Federal cause for that cause to stand condemned in their eyes. If the North American Republic represented his ideal, it could not be theirs" (Harrison, 56). In domestic matters too, given the choice between the Tories and the sanctimonious Liberals, these Southern sympathizers generally preferred the former. At least the Tories in those days did not wax enthusiastic about *laissez-faire*.

Where, then, did the London Positivists come in? At the strategic point. Being active in the anti-slavery campaign, but also friends of the unions and supporters of welfare legislation, they were able to promote an alliance between radical liberalism and a new generation of labor leaders. During the critical early phase of the First International, they held the limelight, while the key role played by Marx behind the scenes was not at first perceived by press and public. This suited him well enough and indeed made his task a good deal easier. He could count on veteran ex-Chartists like E. Jones, who did not share the Southern sympathies of some former associates, and also on his old circle of German friends from Communist League days, among whom Eccarius came to distinguish himself for a number of years as a prominent member of the General Council. But the immediate problem was to produce a platform that would be acceptable to the British labor leaders and their French friends. Here the Positivists—principally Edward Spencer Beesly and Frederic Harrison—unwittingly blazed the trail for him. Professor Beesly, a prominent disciple of Comte, was acquainted with Bright and at the same time on good terms with the London labor leaders whose ally and spokesman he had become during the 1859 strike. Having induced the London Trades Council to endorse the Northern cause in the American Civil War, he was one of the speakers at a public meeting held at St. James Hall, London, on March 26, 1863, with J. S. Mill on the platform and Bright (a notable orator) as the star attraction. All the other speakers were London union leaders. Marx was present and commented favorably in a letter to Engels on Bright's appearance–"he looked quite like an Independent" (i.e., a follower of Cromwell).

This was the nearest Marx ever came to expressing approval of Bright. When in the following year the organizers of the International turned to him for a suitable program, he duly complied, at the same time making it clear in a private communication to Engels that he had no illusions about the predominantly liberal-radical outlook of the London labor leaders: they were, after all, simultaneously engaged in campaigning for a broader franchise with men like Bright. The occasion for Marx's obliging with a draft of what were to be the statutes of the International arose as a sequel to the famous public meeting held on September 28, 1864, at St. Martin's Hall, Long Acre, when the International Working Men's Association was formally established. Marx and Eccarius were elected to the I.W.M.A.'s first General Council, the only two Germans among thirty-four members: twenty-seven of them English, three French, and two Italian (including Mazzini's secretary Luigi Wolff, who soon dropped out and who may have been a secret agent of the French government). No less than eleven of the British members were associated with the London building trades, the most important of them being George Odger, who had taken the lead in organizing the meeting.

Odger had already come to public attention in December, 1863, when he had drafted a widely circulated *Address to the Workmen of France* on the topic of working-class solidarity and the need for "a gathering together of representatives from France, Italy, Germany, Poland, England, and all countries where there exists a will to cooperate for the good of mankind" (Collins-Abramsky, 26). The French to whom this appeal was addressed and who later joined the General Council of the International, shared these democratic sentiments, but the Proudhonists among them still thought in terms of defending the small farmer and the artisan against the inroads of capitalism, while Odger and his colleagues were already thinking in terms of industrial trade unionism. In the autumn of 1864 Marx had somehow to paper over these cleavages. To add to his problems, Odger was also chairman of a Trades Unionists' Manhood Suffrage Association, which had been constituted in November, 1862, for the purpose of working with Bright and other liberals for a broader franchise (eventually enacted in 1867). The French for their part were soon at loggerheads with the English as well as among themselves. The Proudhonists wanted nothing to do with parliamentary politics, while those labor leaders who took their lead from the middle-class radicals favored the overthrow of Napoleon III and the restoration of republican democracy.

All told, it is surprising that the International ever got under way at all. One incident can stand for many. While Marx sat mutely on the platform, Professor Beesly took the chair at the St. Martin's Hall gathering and delivered an address along the usual Positivist lines. In particular he made a point of calling for an Anglo-French alliance "to secure and maintain the liberties of the world." This sort of thing (like the London Positivists' enthusiasm for warlike intervention in Poland against Russia or their belief that the working classes should have their own organization) was not to the taste of liberals like Bright, who naturally steered clear of the I.W.M.A. and its manifestoes; but it was not altogether to Marx's taste either, since the Positivists were inclined to be tolerant of Napoleon III. On the other hand, he agreed with them in condemning British policy in Ireland, but on this issue they both came up against the traditional dislike of the British working class for the Irish. Thus when Beesly in his address listed Ireland–along with China, India, and Japan–among the countries where British policy was (in his words) "cowardly and unprincipled," the reference to Ireland was not reported in the official organ of the London Trades Council, the *Beehive*. (Its former editor, George Troup, had already distinguished himself by his Confederate sympathies. Its managing director, George Potter, was another Southern sympathizer, but he was also the best known British union organizer of the day: the leader of the London building workers in 1860. This was the human material with which men like Beesly and Marx had to work.) When in 1870 the International finally broke with the *Beehive*, it was partly because the paper systematically suppressed or ignored the General Council's resolutions on Ireland (Collins-Abramsky, 175).

At this stage, then, we have a confluence of half a dozen separate currents, including—most remarkable of all—the beginning of an association between Marx and a group of London labor leaders who were prepared to work with French and German socialists *because they had themselves recently become reconciled to capitalism* and were consequently willing to support the anti-slavery cause in America as well as democratic republicanism in Europe. This is exactly how democratic movements normally get under way. The oddity was not of course apparent to the labor leaders, but it was plain enough to Marx, especially when in October, 1864, he was asked to draft a program for the I.W.M.A. At its inception, the organization had five affiliated national sections—English, French, Italian, German, and Polish—who were in agreement on very little except a few basic democratic principles. Marx squared the circle (after various sub-committees had given up in despair) by producing a document that satisfied everyone: notably the British union leaders—George Odger, W. R. Cremer, George Howell, and Thomas Facey being the most important—who wanted something that made sense to their members, gave expression to the principles of British trade unionism, revived a few Chartist memories, and at the same time voiced their democratic, abolitionist, and pro-Polish sentiments. This was the celebrated *Inaugural Address*, provisionally adopted by the General Council in November, 1864, and subsequently confirmed by the Geneva Congress of the International in 1866 as its definitive statement of aims (Collins-Abramsky, 39 ff.).

Compared to the *Communist Manifesto*, the *Address* is a very moderate document. Indeed, it is questionable whether such a comparison ought to be drawn at all. The *Manifesto* dealt in bold outline with the rise of capitalism, the history of class conflict, and the principles of communism. The *Address* started from a description of economic conditions in mid-Victorian Britain, declared that the great mass of the working class had not shared in the general advance in living standards made possible by technological progress and the industrial boom since 1848, affirmed nonetheless that trade unionism and cooperation were instruments of labor's emancipation, conceded—a trifle reluctantly—that a minority of the working class had bettered its condition on the Continent as well as in Britain, and wound up by declaring that the passage of the Factory Acts, together with the spread of the cooperative movement, represented a "victory of the political economy of labour over the political economy of property." The moral drawn by Marx for the benefit of the British union leaders who commissioned the *Address* was that "these great social experiments" had demonstrated "that production on a large scale, and in accord with the behests of modern science, may be carried on without the existence of a class of masters employing a class of hands." This was an echo of Owen and as such likely to go down well with men who remembered the socialism of their youth. The *Address* indeed referred explicitly to Robert Owen and then went on to affirm that "the working men's experiments tried on the Continent were in fact the practical upshot of the theories not invented but loudly proclaimed in 1848": an oblique reference to Louis Blanc's national workshops which the French delegates could be counted on to appreciate, even if they were skeptical of Blanc. Lastly, there was the conquest of political power—through the democratic process. Existing parliamentary institutions were unrepresentative. Had not Palmerston himself described the House of Commons as a house of landed proprietors? "To conquer political power has therefore become the great duty of the working classes. They seem to have comprehended this, for in England, Germany, Italy and France there have taken place simultaneous revivals, and simultaneous efforts are being made at the political reorganization of the working men's party."

This was a modest enough perspective—in fact a social-democratic one. What is more, it laid down the guide-lines for the future. By the time the fourth Congress of the International five years later, at Basle in September, 1869, had adopted the General Council's report drafted by Marx, it was clear that there existed a steady majority—made up largely of English and German delegates—in favor of what was vaguely known as "collectivism." But what was actually on the agenda at Basle? Land nationalization and the eight-hour day! The former was unwelcome to the Proudhonists, who urged the need for a strong peasantry (as a safeguard against the power of the state) but were outvoted, even Bakunin arguing for common ownership of land—as an enthusiast for the *obshchina* he could hardly do less. The "collectivist" majority then split over Bakunin's proposal that the right of inheritance should be abolished, but this was an academic issue. A proposal which foreshadowed the later emergence of the anarchosyndicalist movement was introduced by a Belgian delegate who maintained that one day the trade unions would overthrow the state and reorganize society along new lines altogether. Bakunin had not thought of that, but then he was more concerned with the *lumpenproletariat* of Naples and its ally, the *lumpenintelligentsia* who formed the social basis of his movement in Italy and elsewhere.

In a history of the labor movement (as distinct from a history of socialism) it would be necessary at this stage to go into some detail about the disputes raging between 1865 and 1870 among "mutualists," "collectivists," and "communists" (the latter meaning German followers of Marx, who were in fact not communists at all, but reformist social democrats); the rivalry between Proudhonists and Blanquists in France; the shattering impact of the 1871 Paris Commune; and the resulting dissensions culminating in the Hague Congress of September, 1872, when socialists of all shades split from anarchists. Fortunately this need not be done here. However, the circumstances attending the death of the I.W.M.A. are worth noting. In September, 1872, a narrow majority of the General Council voted for Marx's proposal to transfer the seat of the Council to New York: ostensibly to remove it from police infiltration and French factional quarrels, in reality to get it away from Bakunin and his followers. The move was opposed by the Blanquists. They had backed Marx to the hilt in his fight against Bakunin but thought it a mistake to shift the seat of the International from what their leader, Édouard Vaillant, prophetically called "the field of battle–France and Germany." When all was over, Marx (who had never before attended a full Congress of the International in person) addressed a public meeting in Amsterdam to sum up what he conceived to be the lesson of the past eight years. His main point, in sharp opposition to the anarchists, was the need for the workers to conquer political power as the sole means whereby they could "establish the new organization of labor." How this was to be done in detail he left to the future. "We know," he said, "that special regard must be had to the institutions, customs, and traditions of the various countries." On the Continent of Europe, political revolution in the French sense would presumably be the rule, but in Britain, the United States, and perhaps Holland, the workers might "hope to secure their ends by peaceful means." This was to become a key element of the Social Democratic credo, setting it off from liberalism and anarchism alike.

The First International thus represents a test case for the understanding of what the European labor movement in the nineteenth century was about. Depending on the historian's angle of vision, he can treat it as the battle-ground of Marxism and Anarchism or as the meeting-place of socialism and democracy or yet again as an attempt to reconstitute the old democratic movement on a new foundation. All these interpretations are legitimate, and we have followed the various signposts in turn. Some of them lead in the direction of the 1872 Hague Congress, which formalized the split dividing Marx's German and British followers (plus the Blanquists) from Bakunin's adherents–mostly former Proudhonists, the rest Italians disillusioned with Mazzini's sterile republicanism–in France, Italy, and Spain. From a different viewpoint one may see the International as an attempt on the part of British and French labor leaders to find a common language: at first in defense of Poland, then over a widening range of political and industrial topics. From yet another angle, the International presents itself as a factor in the deepening cleavage between Lassalle's German followers (who did not join it) and the "Marxist" group around Wilhelm Liebknecht and August Bebel, which formally constituted itself as a separate Social Democratic Party at Eisenach in 1869. Lastly, there is the curious circumstance that the British union leaders who for eight years kept the I.W.M.A. going were personal supporters of Marx without for the most part being socialists, let alone Marxists. Around 1872, most of them allied themselves with Gladstone's Liberal Party, which is why Marx broke with them at the same time that he drove Bakunin out and transferred the seat of the General Council to North America. There a few years later (in 1876) the I.W.M.A. died a painless death at Philadelphia.

All this forms part of the history of the socialist movement, and there is no lack of literature on the topic. But we have not yet considered the topic of Positivism as a rival to Marxism. Since the subsequent development of British socialism was determined by the cleavage between these two schools, something must be said about it. The difficulty with this theme is that it cuts across the approach we have so far adopted. Instead of asking what was done between 1864 and 1872 by labor leaders in Paris and London, we have to inquire what thinkers like Marx, Comte, Mill, and Spencer had to say about society. This appears to be quite a different topic, but it is in fact another aspect of the same story. The difference lies in the shift from what was being done to what was being said, but in the end both came together. We have already seen that Comte's followers were instrumental in encouraging those among the British union leaders who had not become Tory Democrats to adopt an independent line in foreign affairs. They were likewise important in promoting a pro-French orientation (at times even a certain tolerance for Napoleon III, in the interest of Italy or Poland), since they looked upon France as the incarnation of the revolutionary idea: a belief very agreeable to French democrats and socialists of the age, but one that lost a good deal of plausibility after the great debacle of the Paris Commune and the resulting split in the International.

What were the London Positivists doing after 1865? Not being socialists, they lost ground for a time. Marx was on friendly terms with Beesly (though not with Harrison), but both men were admirers of Comte and, for the rest, fairly close in their thinking to John Stuart Mill. Comte had his followers in Paris, but French socialists then were either Proudhonists or Blanquists, while the Italians and Poles affiliated with the I.W.M.A. cared only for their respective national movements. It seems almost unbelievable that Marx should have been able in 1864 to make them accept a document which in due course became the charter of social democracy, but then his political talents were considerable when he cared to exercise them. Moreover, he wisely elected to stay in the background, acting as adviser to the British labor leaders, in recognition of which they gave him a free hand in dealing with the Germans (and later the Russians). The secret of the operation lay in the intellectual ascendancy Marx had established over the British union leaders: all the more remarkable since he was a foreigner. Some of them might have preferred Mill, but Mill was not a socialist. Neither, for that matter, were Beesly and Harrison. They were willing enough to support trade unionism, and their radical orientation made them fervent advocates of the French Republic in 1870 and thereafter of the Commune (Marx and Beesly worked together in support of Communard refugees). But Positivism and Marxism ran along parallel lines that never met. In the end, the Positivists became the ancestors of Fabianism, which duly constituted itself in the 1880's as a rival to the nascent Marxist social-democratic movement.

In what follows, therefore, we shall seek to trace the evolution of positivism into evolutionary socialism as outlined in the original *Fabian*

Essays, published in 1889. The date coincided with the centenary of the French Revolution–perhaps intentionally; certainly the founding of the Second International in Paris that year was deliberately timed to mark the anniversary. The Second International, in contrast to the primarily Anglo-French First International, was largely a German-French creation, German Social Democracy having grown into a mass movement. For the quarter century between 1864 and 1889 witnessed both the evolution of "Marxism" into a coherent doctrine and an eastward shift in the socialist movement's center of gravity, Germany having become the strongest power in Europe and German socialism (now officially identified with Marx and Engels) the dominant influence in the movement. Meantime there had emerged an Anarchist current for the most part confined to southern and southwestern Europe, although Bakunin also had a following in Holland and Belgium, and this forms a separate topic which will have to be pursued independently. Fabian Socialism represented a different option, being the offspring of the Positivist sect which had been instrumental in getting the 1864 movement under way. By 1889, then, there were no longer two socialist movements in existence but three: Continental Social Democracy (now officially Marxist or quasi-Marxist); Anarchism or Anarchosyndicalism; and Fabianism, the last representing the form in which the Benthamite tradition accommodated itself to the socialist movement, to become in due course the intellectual inspiration (if that term is not too high-sounding) of the British Labour Party.

A socialist school could get under way among British intellectuals only after the opponents of Manchester economics had grasped that there was an alternative to Tory romanticism and Carlylean worship of "heroic" attitudes. We have already seen what strange alliances were brought about in the 1860's by the anti-slavery campaign. The growing influence of "Social Darwinism"–meaning the comfortable doctrine that the poor and the weak deserved their fate–presented another challenge, to which different responses were possible:

> The controversy between what might be called "internal" and "external" Social-Darwinism actually antedated the Darwinian hypothesis. Certain mid-Victorian opponents of the "dismal science" of political economy–Thomas Carlyle, Charles Kingsley, and Charles Dickens, for example–had opposed the stern individualism of the Radi-

cals which, they felt, resulted in the brutalization of the British working man, but at the same time these critics of internal *laissez-faire* were unbendingly severe in their attitude toward "inferior" races outside the national pale. Carlyle's racist tract "Essay on the Nigger Question," in which he defended slavery, written ten years before Darwin's *Origin,* can be regarded as "premature" external Social-Darwinism, as can his position in the celebrated Eyre case, during the period between 1865 and 1868. On this occasion, Carlyle and Ruskin, Kingsley, and Dickens all insisted that it was not worth considering the injustices perpetrated against Jamaican "niggers" as long as English working men continued to groan under the oppression of the factory system. On the other hand, the Cobdenite Radicals–including John Stuart Mill, Darwin, Spencer, Huxley and John Bright: good Malthusians and internal Social-Darwinists–took for granted the necessity of the factory system and the internal economic struggle, but protested the brutal suppression of the Jamaican coloured men by the British Governor Eyre. (Semmel, 30-31)

It would be agreeable but misleading to add that the representative British labor leaders of the day stood on a more elevated moral platform. Nothing could be further from the truth. The simple fact is that the labor movement, once it had emancipated itself from liberalism, received its education from socialist intellectuals, and the latter were themselves obliged to shed a few mental blinkers before they could universalize the elements of the new world-view.

2. From Positivism to Socialism: 1864-84

"Positivism (with a small 'p') was the most distinctive intellectual tendency in England between 1860 and 1880," writes Mr. Royden Harrison in his authoritative account of the subject. Among the "advanced thinkers" who, as he puts it, "accepted Comte's view of the scientific method as the only source of knowledge, properly so called," John Stuart Mill and John Morley "owed a direct debt to Comte." To this one may add that T. H. Huxley and Herbert Spencer expressed rather similar views, albeit Spencer in later years made a point of saying he was unaware of Comte when in his *Social Statics* of 1850 he had put forward the concept of the "social organism." Marx, on the other hand, whose correspondence shows that he read Comte for the first time in 1866, promptly conceived a violent aversion for him. Comte and his school, he observed in *Capital*, might have deduced the eternal necessity of feudalism from the principles they applied to the end of demonstrating that industry could only function under the control of capitalists. To Comte's British disciples this kind of criticism–had it come to their notice before the appearance of the first English translation of *Capital* in 1887–would not have been very persuasive. All the same, men like Mill were uneasy with the authoritarian implications of Comte's thought, sometimes apologetically dismissed by later Positivists as the outcrop of Comte's private religiosity, leaving unimpaired the scientific value of his pioneer work in sociology.

Be that as it may, there is little doubt that the Positivists had a larger following among British intellectuals during the mid-Victorian era than the competing sect of Christian socialists, chiefly represented by Frederick Denison Maurice and Charles Kingsley. Both groups were obliged to compete for public attention with popular authors such as Carlyle and Ruskin, but it is arguable that Ruskin at least had himself been affected by positivism, although perhaps without knowing it. To cite Mr. Harrison once more, "it is a measure of the pervasive character of Positivism that Ruskin and Matthew Arnold felt obliged to define their positions in relation to it. The Positivists Frederic Harrison and Patrick Geddes had little difficulty in showing that Ruskin had more in common with Comte than he realised" (*Op. cit.*, 252).

This sort of reasoning allows for a good deal of latitude in attributing unacknowledged influences. It can similarly be argued that since Marx and Comte were both indebted to Saint-Simon, they *must* have had something in common. On the whole this seems more persuasive in relation to Engels than to Marx, who never made a secret of his detestation for Comte and his school. One may add that while both Marx and Spencer were clearly influenced by Darwin, "Social Darwinism" was anathema to Marx's followers, whereas Spencer made a fetish of it, and his Fabian disciples (notably George Bernard Shaw) later employed it in support of British imperialism and the rule of the strong. This shows how dangerous it is to toy with notions such as "influence." Marx, Comte, Mill, Darwin, and Spencer belonged to a generation of thinkers who inevitably had certain traits in common, inasmuch as they all worked with the concept of evolution. But the intellectual cross-currents they set up followed the familiar attraction-repulsion pattern. Spencer, to take only the most obvious example, was an extreme individualist, and those of his former pupils who later turned to Fabianism had to adapt Comte before they could draw socialist conclusions from their dissatisfaction with liberalism. And having done so they promptly decided they had no need of Marx. On the other hand, it can be argued that the philosophy of the later Engels was heavily indebted to Positivism. What all this proves, except that some form of scientism was in the air, it is difficult to see.

Let us then turn to the British group which held the stage between 1860 and 1880. They were Positivists in that they regarded themselves as disciples of Comte. In the words of their biographer, they were "secular religionists" who "sought to exchange the consolations of theology for those of history" (Harrison, 252). Comte had taught a Religion of Humanity grounded in the belief (for which he offered no proof, but for which some latter-day anthropologists have found empirical evidence) that there is a long-run tendency for altruistic feelings to gain strength at the expense of the more self-serving sentiments and appetites. The fundamental law was formulated by him in the following words:

> *Le type fondamental de l'évolution humaine, aussi bien individuelle que collective, y est, en effet, scientifiquement représenté comme consistant toujours dans l'ascendant croissant de notre humanité sur notre animalité, d'après la double suprématie de l'intelligence sur les penchants, et de l'instinct sympathique sur l'instinct personnel.* (*Cours de Philosophie Positive*, 2d ed., 1864, VI, 721)

This doctrine made a deep impression on men like Mill, as well as on the small group of Positivists properly so called: E. S. Beesly, Frederic Harrison, Henry Crompton, and their associates, who from the 1860's to the 1880's acted as intellectual advisers to the British labor movement. Their philosophy had affinities with Benthamism—hardly surprising, since Comte's basic ideas were themselves derived from Condorcet and Turgot. These theorists of the eighteenth-century French Enlightenment believed in a unilinear form of human progress directly attributable to man's intellectual development, which they saw progressing through the celebrated "three stages" of theology, metaphysics, and science, science being the latest and therefore the best. This intellectual progress or development (the terms were never clearly distinguished) was accompanied by moral evolution, the predominance of altruism over egoism being simply another aspect of the same universal process, or progress, from animality to humanity. Now clearly if this was so, there was no need for revealed religion, or rather revealed religion was mistaken in its insistence upon the corruption of human nature. All this was a great comfort to Victorian agnostics like Mill and Morley, especially when it could also be shown that things were actually getting better, instead of deteriorating (as on the Malthusian interpretation of Darwin might easily be thought likely, since the earth was getting more crowded every day with inferior races and lower classes all clamoring to be fed). Comte's Religion of Humanity thus provided the scientific foundation for an ethic of benevolence. It was both a statement of fact (or supposed fact) and a guide to action, inasmuch as those who held the new humanist faith were called upon to make explicit what had hitherto been working itself out unconsciously in the course of natural and human history.

To borrow Comte's terminology (also employed by Herbert Spencer, although he introduced a different emphasis), there was a distinction to be drawn between Social Statics and Social Dynamics. Statics signified for Comte the study of social structures with a view to discovering their organizing principle, or principle of "order," and this notion became a key concept in the school of sociology founded by his disciples. Dynamics, on the other hand, embodied a principle of change and growth. The dynamic principle was secondary and subordinated to statics, but it was real nonetheless. That is to say, social structures have an unchanging character, but they tend to undergo secondary changes which Comte assumes to be progressive. "Dynamics" consequently signifies an investigation into principles of growth and change embedded in the nature of things. This sounds rather like Marxism, and indeed Comte and Marx had both taken off from the common platform of Saint-Simonism—but whereas Marx sought the dynamic principle in the growth of man's productive forces (the French terms *forces productives* or *forces productrices* are not exactly translatable), Comte believed in a self-propelling advance of the human spirit as such, ultimately resulting in the triumph of science and the rule of the industrial *entrepreneur*. So far as he was concerned, the *état positif* of mankind was not the classless society of communism, but the industrial society of capitalism. With classes? Of course. After all, there had to be a ruling elite of scientific organizers! Then where did the Religion of Humanity come in? The answer is that Comte in his later years worked out what T. H. Huxley ironically described as "Catholicism minus Christianity." This is the Comte of the *Système de politique positive* (1851-54) which unlike the *Cours* (1830-42) outlines not a new theory of society but a doctrine of morality. The *System of Positive Polity*, to give it the English title under which it was first published in 1875-77, like its celebrated companion the *Catechism of Positive Religion*, is sometimes labelled Comte II, to distinguish its author from the Comte I who influenced John Stuart Mill and gave a considerable impetus to the development of sociology. Nonetheless the two hang together. In his later writings Comte put forward constructive proposals for organizing the new Positive Society of Humanity which was presently to spread all over the globe: the sort of thing Marx dismissed as "writing recipes for the cookshops of the future." There was a certain consistency about this procedure, for Comte conceived his nontheological Church of Humanity as a spiritual force advising the temporal authorities on how to act so as to ground social progress in moral and educational reform. This notion has often been described as a return to the spiritualist dualism of the Middle Ages, and from Comte's viewpoint certain aspects of the Catholic heritage were indeed worth preserving: he held that a moral reformation was the precondition of social progress, once humanity had taken over from animality.

What did all this have to do with Socialism? Comte was emphatically not a Socialist—on the contrary, he always insisted on the key role of the industrial-capitalist entrepreneur in furthering economic and social progress. This identification of capitalism with industrialism was just what Marx found intolerable, and in *Capital*, vol. I, he cast a scornful side-glance at Comte and his followers for having suggested or implied that industry could not operate without capitalists. As he saw it, the Comtean school was guilty of confusing the function of industrial management with the accidental bourgeois form of ownership. But if Comte's British followers were not socialists, they were nonetheless critical of liberalism. In fact they saw themselves as *both* the theorists of the labor movement *and* the proponents of a doctrine whose ultimate aim it was to reconcile Capital and Labor. How this was to be accomplished they never explained, but in the meantime their republicanism and Francophilia established a bond with Marx and his followers. Over the defense of the Paris Commune in particular they came together—to the surprise of the liberals and the stunned incomprehension of most British union leaders. Beesly and Harrison had by then become republicans (in private, since such sentiments could not be avowed publicly in Victorian Britain). They also supported the Commune, as did Comte's French followers. But in this regard they did not carry working-class opinion with them. "As far as the respectable Labour leaders were concerned, Beesly and Marx, in defending the Commune, might as well have been addressing the inhabitants of another world" (Harrison, 232). These "respectable Labour leaders" were then on the eve of forming the Liberal-Labour coalition which by 1875 had taken definite shape, and the Parisian cataclysm was not to their liking. Its defense was left to a handful of radical intellectuals.

Now it is arguable that in all this the London Positivists were simply following the inherent logic of their creed. After all, Comte himself had written: "It is among the working class that the new philosophers will find their most energetic allies." This certainly does sound as though Positivism and Marxism represented parallel developments, even if Comte was unsound (from Marx's standpoint) on the crucial issue of class conflict and private ownership. Moreover, the Positivist intellectuals in England, on starting their political career, had been pleased to discover that the most important leaders of the London working men (the group hardly tried to operate outside the capital) were generally free from religious prejudice, willing to cooperate with foreigners, and —as we have seen—won over to the anti-slavery cause. On all these counts their association with Marx is easily explained, the more so since Marx was on friendly personal terms with Beesly (though not with Beesly's associates). The Positivists also regarded the International as the keystone in the arch of Anglo-French friendship, which to them took precedence over all other issues. In 1870 they agitated for British military intervention against Germany on the side of the French Republic, established in September of that year after the battle of Sedan and the fall of Napoleon III. In June, 1871, after the Commune and the public outcry against it, one finds Beesly writing to Marx:

You are quite wrong in supposing that my attitude differs in any

> respect from that of my co-religionists. Harrison at bottom agrees with me, though in writing he is inclined to be too diplomatic, in my opinion, and to spare the susceptibilities of the middle class. But Congreve (our director) and Bridges have warmly approved all that I have written.... Our members in Paris, though hostile to Communism, have frankly served it and risked their lives for it. All the English Positivists have been ardent supporters of it from 18th March [the date of the Commune's establishment]. No doubt whenever it becomes a practical question whether private property is to be abolished, you will find us opposed to you firmly. But it is likely that long before then we and you shall have been crushed side by side by our common foe. (Harrison, 275-76)

The "common foe" to the Positivists was what a century later would be called "The Establishment": the British ruling class, then still centered upon the monarchy, the Anglican Church, the landed nobility, and the army and navy. As for the middle class, the Positivists hoped to convert it to their own creed—a watered-down version of what in France was shortly to become the platform of Clemenceau's Radical Party. What in the end this comes down to is that the Positivists thought the working class was the best instrument for a genuine democratic (but nonsocialist) revolution in Britain: a revolution that would break the aristocratic stranglehold and the power of the Anglican Church, give freedom to Ireland, and get rid of the Empire. When this turned out to be impossible they abandoned the field to the Gladstonian Liberals, who in turn promptly relinquished their own principles (an old habit with them, much resented by the Positivists, especially when Gladstone in the 1880's applied coercion to Ireland and sent an army of occupation to Egypt, in the teeth of all his previous affirmations on the subject of overseas conquest). Politically speaking Positivism by then was on its last legs. The trade-union leaders had delivered themselves body and soul to the Liberal Party, and the left-wing radicals among the intelligentsia were drifting toward socialism, where the Positivists could not follow them, since they clung with obstinate persistence to the faith of their master. The Religion of Humanity made few converts, and then only in the middle class and not among the union leaders, even though it clearly had its effect on some former members of the International's General Council (such as Robert

Applegarth, who somehow managed for years to stay on good terms both with Marx and with liberal industrialists like Mundella, one of those enlightened Captains of Industry in whom Comte had seen the predestined ruling elite of the future). Unless one grasps that the British union leaders of the 1860's and 1870's were democratic radicals rather than socialists, one will never understand how after the International's collapse in 1872-76 they could transform themselves into willing allies of Gladstone's Liberal Party. Their defection left the Positivists high and dry. They no longer had a following and by the 1880's had been overtaken by a new breed of radicals: themselves divided between the pupils of Marx and the adherents of the recently founded Fabian Society.

This is not to say that Positivists and Socialists failed to cooperate. While Frederic Harrison became increasingly conservative in his political views, Beesly, as editor of the *Positivist Review*, after 1900 went so far as to advise his readers to vote for the Social Democratic ticket, i.e., for the group headed by the eccentric H. M. Hyndman, who was at least nominally a Marxist. Beesly persisted, however, in believing that socialism would prepare the ground for positivism, whereas in actual fact he and his friends had laid the foundation for the socialist revival of the 1880's. Hyndman's fellow-Marxist, Belfort Bax, typically came to socialism by way of positivism, but in 1881 one finds him writing: "We hear much sometimes from that excellent body of persons, the followers of M. Auguste Comte, of the moralisation of capital in the society of the future. I need scarcely say that to the Socialist this is much as though anyone should talk of the moralisation of brigandage" (Harrison, 337). On the Fabian side, too, there was a current leading from Comte to the reformist socialism of the Society. Both Sidney Webb and Sydney Olivier had been affected by the Religion of Humanity, a circumstance noted by historians of the movement. On joining the Fabians in 1885, Webb read some lectures at a gathering of the newly constituted Society which were distinctly positivist in tone—so much so that he had to defend himself against the charge of actually being a Comteist. Socialism, as he saw it, was a moral issue and to be brought about by a change of opinion (McBriar, 14-15). Mrs. Annie Besant, a militant secularist in the 1870's, had some regard for Comte, but eventually opted for socialism, to the distress of Charles Bradlaugh. And the Reverend Philip Wicksteed, who in 1884 provided the Fabians with something like an economic doctrine, had been one of Beesly's students at University College Hall.

Altogether, one may fairly say that Positivism made a decisive contribution to the socialist rebirth in the 1880's. The principal beneficiaries were the Fabians, but there were others who graduated from Positivism (or secularism—by the 1870's and 1880's these doctrines had come to overlap) to the nascent Anarchist or Marxist movements. They included adventurers like Edward Aveling (later Eleanor Marx's husband and the proximate cause of her misfortunes) as well as reputable scholars. These middle-class socialists were then confronted with the task of carrying the new doctrine to the working-class radicals (the standard term then current to describe left-wing Liberals) who set the tone in the labor movement. For by the 1880's Owenite socialism no longer possessed a following among the workers. The new school had to contend with a labor movement which trailed in the wake of Gladstone's Liberalism, when it did not support those Conservatives who described themselves (or were described by others) as Tory Democrats. The first and most urgent task of the socialist intellectuals was to overcome these barriers and establish contact with the working class.

3. Marxism and Fabianism

A consideration of this topic must from the start renounce any hope of disentangling the complexity of personal, political, and ideological factors that went into the constitution of these two rival schools of socialism on British soil during the three decades separating the political revival of the 1880's from the outbreak of the European war in 1914. The subject has been exhaustively analyzed from the Marxist standpoint by Mr. E. J. Hobsbawm in his studies on the British labor movement and by Dr. Tsuzuki in his scholarly biographies of H. M. Hyndman and Eleanor Marx. For the Fabians there exists a mass of documentary literature in addition to the standard histories by Edward Pease, Margaret Cole, and A. M. McBriar. In what follows we shall perforce have to concentrate upon the intellectual development. Thus the tragic story of Eleanor Marx cannot be retold, although an account of her life tells one more about the spiritual milieu in which British socialism took shape than any amount of theorizing about economics.

Much the same applies to the voluminous *Diaries* of Beatrice Potter, better known as Mrs. Sidney Webb. Anyone who wants to understand what socialism actually meant to that generation of intellectuals will have to study these fascinating documents. From there one may go on to reconsider the contribution made to literature by the best known Fabian of them all: George Bernard Shaw was the friend of both these formidable women, as well as being an enthusiastic Ibsenite and Wagnerite, an expatriate Irishman, and the most gifted dramatist of the age. These are all aspects of the same topic, but it is no use pretending that justice can be done to them. Intellectual history imposes its limitations, the chief of them being a relentless concentration on the theoretical side of any phenomenon it has to deal with. This is regrettable but cannot be helped. Students curious for information about the bizarre career of Henry Mayers Hyndman (1842-1921) or the romantic life and death of Eleanor Marx (1855-98) must be referred to Dr. Tsuzuki. Shavians in search of the Life Force have ample dramatic material at their disposal.

The principal facts can be briefly stated. The 1880's were for Britain a time of economic stagnation and political confusion, consequent upon the disintegration of the Liberal Party in the wake of Gladstone's unsuccessful efforts to solve the Irish problem. At the same time Toryism was reconstituted upon a new social and ideological foundation: no longer merely the bulwark of the landed gentry and the Church, but increasingly the party of Empire and the fountainhead of English (as distinct from British) nationalism. The nationalism, that is to say, of the dominant majority within a multinational society; for the Scots, Welsh, and Irish all had their own forms of national sentiment: not to mention India, the White-settler "Dominions," and the African colonies—all garrisoned by British-officered armies and navies who looked to the Conservative Party to uphold their status. With this realignment there went an increasing emphasis upon economic protectionism and a modest degree of social-welfare legislation: just enough to hold the loyalty of a slight majority among the English (as distinct from Irish, Welsh, or Scottish) manual workers in industry and on the land, who by 1884 had all obtained the vote. On the other side of the political divide, the Liberal-Labor coalition drew much of its strength from the "Celtic fringe," but it also had a solid English following among the Nonconformist sects traditionally hostile to the Anglican Church. Liberalism thus remained influential among unionized workers, as well as among the lower middle class of farmers and shopkeepers, but there were awkward cross-currents:

> Sympathy for Toryism was reinforced not only by the social policy of Disraeli but also by the conflict of interest between the indigenous population and Irish immigrants, especially in industrial Lancashire. . . . Still, when it came to a choice between the existing parties, most of the better-off industrial workers and artisans, who alone were organized in trade unions and who therefore provided the articulate leadership of the working class, felt themselves to be more closely akin to the Liberal middle class, whose sober habits and dissenting religion they commonly shared. (Pelling, *The Origins of the Labour Party*, 6)

In the early 1880's recent recruits to socialism such as Hyndman (the descendant of a wealthy Protestant clan from Ulster and a businessman whose grandfather had amassed a fortune in the West Indies) made the distressing discovery that for every middle-class socialist who joined them they lost several working-class radicals. On March 14, 1883, Hyndman (who by then had managed to quarrel with Engels, but considered himself a follower of Marx, whose death occurred that very day) wrote to Henry George, the famous American author of *Progress and Poverty*: "The common English workmen are more or less embittered against the Irish and at times I feel despondent. But Socialist ideas are growing rapidly among the educated class" (Pelling, *ibid.*, 23). Henry George of course was no socialist, but his proposals for a tax on land, as outlined in his best-selling book published in 1879, provided a bridge across which growing numbers of middle-class intellectuals crossed over into socialist territory during those years. Some of them were former Liberals who had finally despaired of Gladstone and *laissez-faire.* Others, including Hyndman and his associate H. H. Champion (the son of a major-general), were disillusioned Tories. What drove them into the nascent socialist movement was quite simply loss of faith in economic liberalism and disgust with capitalism generally. This was the starting point. The problem for the socialists was how to effect a breakout from their tiny intellectual centers in London into the wider society whose leadership they meant to assume.

The rival groups were all constituted during this period: Hyndman's

Social Democratic Federation in 1884, the Fabian Society about the same time, the Socialist League of William Morris, Belfort Bax, Edward Aveling, Eleanor Marx, and others (patronized behind the scenes by Engels) a few months later. The Social Democratic Federation—soon to be wracked by splits—got off to a fairly hopeful start, as did its offshoot, the Socialist League. Both groups were nominally Marxist. They had acquired a notable convert in the person of William Morris, already a writer and artist of distinction and an honorary fellow of Exeter College, Oxford. Morris (who made no pretence of having read *Capital* but considered himself a Marxist all the same) had come to socialism by way of Ruskin, and he brought a number of like-minded followers with him. Others joined by way of the Land Reform Union of the early 1880's, itself a successor to the short-lived Land and Labour League founded by British members of the First International in 1869. From 1883 on, Hyndman's group (at first known as the Democratic Federation) preached socialism, while its concentration on practical problems such as housing and the eight-hour day brought it some working-class support. When in March 1884 the Federation organized a procession to the grave of Marx in Highgate cemetery on the first anniversary of his death, over a thousand people took part (according to Morris), with some two or three thousand onlookers present as well. This was a promising start, and the movement continued to grow, although plagued by internal dissensions and personal animosities—notably affecting the relationship between Hyndman, Morris, and the Avelings.

A few years later, a revival of militant unionism gave all the rival socialist groups the popular platform they had been looking for, but the Marxists were rather more effective than the Fabians in "permeating" the working-class milieu. There was thus a rebirth of radical laborism which became a factor in the formation early in 1893 of a (predominantly Scottish) organization with a quasi-socialist platform: the Independent Labour Party. This early predominance of the Scottish element is relevant to an understanding of how the British Labour Party came into being between 1900 and 1906, but we cannot deal with colorful figures such as James Keir Hardie (1856-1915) and his successor James Ramsay MacDonald (1866-1937), or with those working-class leaders—mostly centered in the London area—who received their political training in and through the S.D.F. and its Marxist or semi-anarchist rivals. Let it simply be stated that, while the Fabians proved effective in evangelizing the new middle class of professional men and women, the Marxists (or quasi-Marxists) were more successful in spreading their ideas among the leaders of the militant union movements in the London area and in England generally. At the same time the "Celtic fringe" of Scotland and Wales, with its Nonconformist tradition, drifted slowly from Liberalism to Laborism by way of the I.L.P. For these were the years when the Liberal Party began to lose its hold over the masses and the intellectuals alike. In the words of Gladstone's biographer, Philip Magnus:

> Many Radicals in Southern England had already been attracted to socialism. Many more, in the Midlands and elsewhere, had been drawn off by [Joseph] Chamberlain, who had broken finally with Gladstone, and those were later either absorbed, like Chamberlain, into the ranks of the Conservatives or recruited to the socialist creed. Gladstone's radicalism, therefore, became predominantly an expression of the centrifugal instincts of the "Celtic fringe" in Scotland, Wales, and Cornwall, where the masses vainly resisted for a time the centripetal tendencies of the age. The centripetal principle triumphed, and except on one occasion in 1906, after Gladstone's death, the Liberal Party never regained its hold upon England. As the years passed its light failed steadily; between 1918 and 1939 it ceased to be an effective political force and was pushed ever further into the extremities of the island, where the Atlantic Ocean breaks against Land's End, and moans in the Pentland Firth and Cardigan Bay. (*Gladstone: A Biography*, 395)

This being the background we may now inquire what the two principal British schools of socialist thought contributed to the formulation of a coherent body of doctrine: a topic which takes us back to the formative period of the 1880's. Marx had died in 1883, but Engels was there until 1895 to lend help and counsel to his followers. On the other side of the growing divide there stood the small but important Fabian Society. Let us pause to take a look at the founding members of this organization. Like the Positivists from whom they descended, they were a group of London-based intellectuals. Unlike their predecessors, they were socialists, but, although in some ways influenced by Marx as well as by Comte, they believed themselves to be in a peculiarly English tradition. What did this mean? The question is not altogether easy to answer, even if we take account of the fairly obvious fact that most of them were intellectual heirs of Bentham and Mill. They were not, that is to say, influenced by Hegel, but then neither were Hyndman and his friends. In fact, the only British Hegelians at this time were a group of Oxford philosophers who were idealists in metaphysics and Liberals or Conservatives in politics. The Hegelian philosopher T. H. Green did have some political influence during the 1880's, in that he induced a number of prominent Liberals (as well as the Christian Social intellectual Scott Holland) to make room in their thinking for state intervention, but there is no evidence that he influenced the middle-class socialists then joining the Fabians. If they read any philosopher, it was Mill or Comte. The most influential member of the group, Sidney Webb, took little interest in philosophy beyond a vague commitment to utilitarianism. Their ablest propagandist, Bernard Shaw, proposed an eclectic doctrine made up of badly digested fragments of Marx, Nietzsche, Ibsen, and Wagner. The Fabian Society was clearly not committed to either Marxism or anarchism, and it had no use for the romantic medievalism of Ruskin and William Morris. But what was its positive creed?

Perhaps the question is best answered by looking at the group's origins. It had come together at a time when socialism was only just beginning to revive in Britain, while in France, Germany, and elsewhere on the Continent it already possessed a following. When Kropotkin in 1881 visited England to lecture on socialism, he could hardly get an audience, and Marx's death two years later would have passed unnoticed had not the Paris correspondent of *The Times* filed a paragraph on his European reputation. Even some years later, when Hyndman's Federation, the Socialist League, and the Fabians had all enrolled a sizable following, there was a good deal of uncertainty where theoretical issues were concerned. William Morris, when asked by an earnest questioner, "Does Comrade Morris accept Marx's Theory of Value?" characteristically replied: "To speak frankly, I do not know what Marx's Theory of Value is, and I'm damned if I want to know" (Pelling, 31). The Fabians did know, or thought they knew, and they had concluded that in economics J. S. Mill and Stanley Jevons were more relevant for their purpose. But this particular issue arose *after* the group had come together on the basis of what it conceived to be a socialist philosophy.

How then did the future Fabians come to socialism in the first place? The answer is: by hearkening to the message of an itinerant prophet, the "wandering scholar" Thomas Davidson (1840-1900), who taught his followers to despise worldly riches. Possibly because he had spent much of his life in the United States, Davidson, a Scottish schoolmaster by origin, had become disenchanted with the gospel of wealth creation. The Fellowship of the New Life he founded in 1883 was an "ethical culture" society vaguely inspired by religious ideals, and its early meetings were taken up with debates about setting up a kind of Owenite community (in Bloomsbury or perhaps in Peru) whose members were to practice a "new life" based on love, wisdom, and unselfishness. There is a good account of the founder by his brother, J. Morrison Davidson, in his book *The Annals of Toil*, published in London in 1899, where the circumstances of the Fellowship's birth are succinctly stated:

> The Fabian Society was founded in London in 1883. Its virtual founder was my brother, Dr. Thomas Davidson of New York, author of the *Philosophy of Rosmini-Serbati, Aristotle and Ancient Educational Ideals,* the *Parthenon Frieze,* etc. He had just returned from Rome, where he had discussed affairs with His Holiness the Pope, and was in a frame of mind to regenerate mankind on lines which did not appear to me—who was then doing all I could to prevent the G.O.M. [Gladstone] from throttling Ireland—very promising. (McBriar, 1)

Dr. Thomas Davidson, then, was a classical scholar, philosopher, and linguist, with an urge to undertake the reformation of mankind along Rosminian lines, Antonio Rosmini-Serbati (1797-1855) having been the founder of an unorthodox Catholic religious order, the Brethren of Charity, which had the common misfortune of conflicting with the Jesuits and being condemned by Leo XIII in 1887. Davidson himself was a Protestant, and so were most of the early members of the sect, but their Protestantism was not of the familiar individualist kind. Individualism in fact was just what they could not stand. Mrs. Cole, in her *Story of Fabian Socialism,* makes light of these obscure beginnings. Davidson himself she describes as "a Scottish schoolmaster who had emigrated to America, and in that land of cranks and Utopians had developed a cloudy idealistic philosophy which demanded that its votaries should pledge themselves to live according to high ideals of love and brotherhood. . . . Most of what Davidson wrote is confused and rather nonsensical." Edward Pease with more justice calls him "a descendant of the Utopians of Brook Farm and the Phalanstery." At any rate his appearance in London in 1883 (hard on the heels of Henry George, whose visit to England in 1881-82 stirred up interest in social reform) acted as a catalyst in the formation of a group whose members had already broken with revealed faith under the influence of Darwin, Mill, George Eliot, and Comte. The "melancholy, long, withdrawing roar" of Arnold's "Dover Beach" (1867), marking the slow death of institutionalized religion, was plainly audible by the early 1880's to this generation of late Victorians. They were spiritually adrift and politically dissatisfied with the existing parties, schools, and sects. Henry George provided the rudiments of a social program. Davidson gave them a faith. There is perhaps something faintly ludicrous about these earnest seekers after truth, especially when one considers that the greatest thinker of the age had died in London a few months earlier (on March 14, 1883, to be precise) and that they were hardly aware of him. But one must be fair: *Capital* was not yet available in English, and to the early Fabians the name of Marx conveyed little beyond vague memories of the public uproar in 1871 over the Paris Commune. One of the difficulties all socialists in England then had was that people tended to associate the term "socialism" with memories of the French Revolution and everything that had flowed from it, down to the great disaster of the Commune. The First International had left few traces; German Social Democracy was not yet the powerful movement it was shortly to become; and to British intellectuals it appeared that Henry George, with his notions about a single tax levied on landowners, was more immediately relevant than Marx. In any event it was Henry George and Thomas Davidson, both visitors from the United States, who set this particular group of people in London thinking about the reformation of society.

To later Fabians, busy with municipal administration and eventually with solemn affairs of state, these cranky beginnings have always been a source of embarrassment, but it is simply a fact that the Society originated in a quasi-religious enterprise not untypical of the period. Davidson himself did not approve of socialism, and in consequence there was a split on January 4, 1884, when some of the original members withdrew and formed the Fabian Society, while the others continued under

Davidson's leadership, retaining the name of Fellowship of the New Life. The Fabian secessionists–Edward R. Pease, Frank Podmore, and Hubert Bland being the most important–had all attended the private gatherings convened by Davidson from September, 1883, on. Others present at this formative stage included Robert Owen's granddaughter, Miss Dale Owen; and H. H. Champion (a relative of the eccentric Tory-Radical David Urquhart), who later joined Hyndman and still later became the ancestor of a school of socialism destined to remain influential in Britain down to the 1940's, when it found a new embodiment in the person of George Orwell (1903-50). Edward Pease, for decades the indestructible Secretary of the Fabian Society and Sidney Webb's closest ally, was then a young man of twenty-six. A junior partner in a stock-exchange firm, he had undergone a spiritual conversion after reading Morris and determined to have done with Mammon. Hubert Bland, a journalist and failed businessman, was a Roman Catholic when he was not an atheist and a Tory when he was not a Marxist. Podmore, an Oxford graduate and Post Office clerk, believed in ghosts; after withdrawing from the Fabian Executive in 1888 he devoted the remainder of his life to psychic research. Shaw, who joined the Society in September, 1884, has left a characteristic account of the atmosphere at these early gatherings:

> They had one elderly retired workman. They had two psychical researchers, Edward Pease and Frank Podmore, for whom I slept in a haunted house in Clapham. There were Anarchists, led by Mrs. Wilson, who would not hear of anything Parliamentary. There were young ladies on the lookout for husbands, who left when they succeeded. There was Bland's very attractive wife Edith Nesbit, who wrote verses in the *Weekly Dispatch* for half a guinea a week, and upset all the meetings by making scenes and pretending to faint. She became famous as a writer of fairy tales. (In M. Cole, ed., *The Webbs and their Work* [1949], p. 7, quoted by Pelling, *op. cit.*, 35)

Shaw in this instructive passage makes no mention of the fact that among the sixteen people who assembled on October 24, 1883, at 17 Osnaburgh Street, Regents Park, to hear Davidson read a paper on the New Life there was Havelock Ellis, the psychologist. Among the others, Pease and Podmore had become acquainted while they were both waiting (vainly) for a ghost to appear in a supposedly haunted house at

Notting Hill. When the ghost failed to turn up, they spent the remainder of the night discussing Henry George and found themselves in agreement that something ought to be done about poverty, although they were not sure what. Both were present at the meeting on October 24 and joined the Fellowship on the occasion of its formal constitution on November 7, when it was resolved "that an association be formed whose ultimate aim shall be the reconstruction of Society in accordance with the highest moral possibilities." They retained this aim, but seceded two months later on the issue of socialism. The term "Fabian Society" appears to have been suggested by Podmore. It was a reference to the elderly Roman commander Fabius Cunctator, famous for his extreme caution in conducting military operations, especially when matched against Hannibal. Some of the earliest tracts of the Society bore a motto (composed by Podmore) which ran in part: "For the right moment you must wait, as Fabius did most patiently, when warring against Hannibal, though many censured his delays; but when the time comes you must strike hard, as Fabius did, or your waiting will be in vain, and fruitless." Closer acquaintance with Roman history might perhaps have induced Podmore to inquire where and when Fabius ever "struck hard": there is no record of such an occurrence. Malicious critics of Fabianism have been known to hint that there may have been something prophetic, or at least symbolic, in this misreading of history and that anyone who expects Fabians to "strike hard" for socialism or anything else is quite likely to have to wait until Doomsday. Be that as it may, the Society from the start was committed to taking the long view.

Sidney Webb, Sydney Olivier, Bernard Shaw, and Graham Wallas—who all joined between 1884 and 1886 and for many years formed the Society's effective leadership—had no patience with either Anarchism or Marxism (as that term was then interpreted by Hyndman and his associates). They and the majority of their associates, including Mrs. Besant, adhered to democratic procedures and orderly methods but had no objection to a certain degree of enlightened authoritarianism. Their fundamental assumption was that socialism would be introduced not through class conflict, but by way of democratic welfare legislation administered by the civil service, of which some of them were members. In maintaining this line, the Fabian Society was undoubtedly aided by its composition and by the practice of admitting new members through cooptation. The group was from the start almost exclusively composed of professional men and women. As Shaw put it retrospectively in 1892, "we were then middle-class all through." There was in fact only one working man among the founding members, an elderly retired housepainter named W. L. Phillips, and it is not recorded that he took a prominent part in elaborating the basic strategy. The others were teachers, journalists, civil servants, bank clerks, or people with independent incomes. A few union leaders did join in the 1890's, but there was never any questions of enrolling numerous members. The Society was elitist and determinedly so. It was proud to number among its members intellectual notabilities such as Graham Wallas (later a distinguished political scientist) and Annie Besant, who with Shaw did much to propagate its views, and in 1892 it acquired in Beatrice Potter (Mrs. Sidney Webb) a recruit from the class of industrial entrepreneurs who brought many of the virtues (and some of the limitations) of that important stratum into the organization. This is what Fabianism was really about: its purpose was to win the educated professional middle class over to socialism, although not everyone perceived this at the outset. Quite clearly it took some time before even the leaders grasped that their audience was restricted to one particular social stratum. Certainly a man like Pease, who had deliberately thrown up a business career to become a "worker with his own hands" as a cabinet maker, until the Society hired him as secretary at the princely salary of £100 per annum, could not be called a snob. It was simply, as he put it, that they thought it best to steer clear of "the more popular organisations" who required propagandists rather than theorists. Sidney Webb, a clerk in the Colonial Office until his marriage to Beatrice Potter freed him for other tasks, was not by nature fitted for popular agitation, but then few members of the group were. "We were thus," Pease writes, "in a position to welcome the formation of working-class Socialist societies, but it is certain that in the early days they would never have welcomed us" (*Op. cit.*, 61). To which it may be added that Beatrice Potter—a rich, spoiled, arrogant young woman with more beauty than brains—was determined to have as little as possible to do with the working class.

The decisive years were the early ones from 1884 to 1889. Everything that came thereafter, notably the rather over-publicized activities of the Webbs, was simply an application of the basic principles worked out during that period. In later years the Fabians presented themselves to the public as defenders of parliamentary democracy and "gradualism" against the Marxists, yet Hyndman's followers styled themselves Social Democrats, and William Morris abandoned the Socialist League in 1890 when it had been taken over by the Anarchists. Moreover, the first executive committee of the Fabian Society, elected at the end of 1884, contained an Anarchist (Mrs. Charlotte Wilson) as well as a Social Democrat (Frederick Keddell, who soon departed in the direction of Hyndman). The other three members were Pease, the archetypal Fabian "gradualist"; Bland, who had started his career as a Tory and who detested the Liberals to the point of refusing to have anything to do with them, even as temporary allies; and Shaw, who had not as yet made up his mind about political tactics but who was an instinctive elitist, as his subsequent adoption of Nietzschean doctrines (not to mention his later flirtation with Mussolini) was to show. Of the others who joined the Society in the two following years, Webb was a spiritual disciple of John Stuart Mill; Sydney Olivier believed in Comte; Mrs. Besant had previously worked with the prominent radical (i.e., anti-socialist) Charles Bradlaugh in promoting secularism and neo-Malthusianism (a polite circumlocution for birth control). It is quite impossible to distill anything specific out of this medley. In passing one may note that by the later 1890's Shaw had become totally cynical about democracy and convinced that the principal obstacle to the spread of socialism was "the stupidity of the working class" (McBriar, 84). William Clarke was an Emersonian, Hubert Bland eventually reverted to Roman Catholicism, and Mrs. Besant became a convert to Theosophy. What is one to make of all this?

There was nonetheless a distinctively Fabian theory of Socialism and, in particular, an economic doctrine whose core was a theory of exploitation. This took time to formulate, if only because Shaw had successively become an enthusiast for Henry George and Marx (after reading *Capital* in the French translation). The decisive moment occurred quite early, when Philip Wicksteed (a mathematical economist and Unitarian minister) persuaded Webb and Shaw that the labor theory of value was untenable. Wicksteed, a disciple of Stanley Jevons, put forward his criticism of Marx in the Socialist monthly *Today* in October, 1884, and then followed it up in a controversy with Shaw, who eventually persuaded himself that Wicksteed was right. This debate took place in the winter of 1884-85, and by February, 1885, Shaw had come round to the extent of urging the middle class to join the Socialist movement, so as to counteract the unfortunate influence of "a mob of desperate sufferers abandoned to the leadership of exasperated sentimentalists and fanatical theorists" (Pelling, 37). The affiliation of Webb, Olivier, and Wallas followed soon afterward. The authoritative history of the Society draws attention to the fact that the decision very nearly went the other way: "The most important time in the working out of a distinctively Fabian point of view was the period when meetings were held of the group which called itself the Hampstead Historic Club. This began as a Marxist reading circle at the house of Mrs. Charlotte Wilson early in 1885 and later met in other places, and finally at the Hampstead Public Library. . . . At the club, *Capital* was read out from the French translation, until the company fell to disputation," with F. Y. Edgeworth, the economist, and Sidney Webb defending Jevons and Mill respectively, while Shaw and Belfort Bax held forth on Marxian lines (McBriar, 30). When it is added that Mrs. Wilson was a disciple of Kropotkin and for some years edited the Anarchist journal *Freedom* one can easily see that there was no party line.

Nonetheless there was a crucially important theoretical point at issue. It has been stated with admirable clarity by McBriar, whose history of Fabian socialism is in a class by itself and wholly supersedes all previous discussions of the topic:

> Wicksteed's criticism raised the question whether the theory of surplus value was necessarily dependent upon the labour theory of value—a most serious problem for Socialists. The theory of surplus value was Marx's attempt to prove [that] even in the "very Eden of the innate Rights of Man"—the capitalist economists' state of perfect competition—the workers would be cheated of the full fruits of their labour by the capitalists. . . . Marx's economic theory is a rigorously worked out logical system. The labour theory of value and the theory of surplus value are used as a key in his analysis of the 'laws of motion' of capitalist society. . . . Wicksteed claimed that, by bringing forward an entirely different theory of the determinant of value, he had struck away the foundation of Marx's arguments and brought the whole edifice down in ruins. (*Op. cit.*, 31-32)

Now, whether the early Fabians preferred Marx or Mill as philosophers, they were bound to surrender the labor theory of value if they could no longer accept its classical Ricardian formulation. On the other hand, they had to hold on to *some* doctrine of "surplus value" if they were to show that capitalism was a system of exploitation. Hence they could not accept the marginal utility doctrine, as set out by Jevons and others. For marginal utility implied that under certain assumed conditions, "capital" and "labor" were being remunerated in proportion to the respective contributions they made to the production of wealth: where money is paid, equivalent goods or services have been rendered. Instead, they fell back upon a "theory of rent," which was independent of any kind of value theory

> ...in the sense that it could still stand whether one adopted a labour theory of value or a cost of production theory or a marginal utility theory. How far the Fabians realized this it is difficult to tell. Shaw probably did not; Webb probably, and Wallas almost certainly did. In Shaw's articles in *Fabian Essays*, the Jevonian theory of value and the Fabian theory of rent are both made part of the one story, whereas in Webb's various expositions of the theory of rent no value theory is specifically mentioned. (McBriar, 36)

Where Webb, Shaw, and Wallas agreed was in regarding their theory of rent as the centerpiece of Fabianism. It was the ark of their covenant, the "cornerstone of collectivist economy," in the later words of the Webbs, the foundation of their critique of capitalism and liberalism. For this reason, and because Fabianism eventually became the intellectual core of British Labourism and its various offsprings in the English-speaking world, the topic merits some consideration.

Unlike "value," which has a number of different meanings, as well as being rooted in philosophical considerations about labor, the notion of "rent" is fairly easy to grasp. In the form in which it had been developed by Ricardo and John Stuart Mill, and then vulgarized by Henry George, it appealed to the London Radical Clubs: that is, to the left wing of the Liberal Party which in 1885 had fought and won a parliamentary election on Joseph Chamberlain's so-called "unauthorized program." This included a slogan particularly attractive to the recently enfranchised farm laborers: Jesse Collings' demand for "Three Acres and a Cow," which held out the empty promise of landownership for all. "Next time," remarked a prominent Liberal by the name of Henry Labouchere, "we must have an urban cow." This of course was nonsense. An "urban cow" was just what the Liberals could never put forward, for whereas their radical left wing (Lloyd George's later following) was willing to threaten the great landowners with expropriation—not that anything was ever done about it—it would have been impossible to address even a verbal menace of this kind to the industrial manufacturers without alienating the solid core of Liberalism. "Three acres and a cow" for landless laborers was a respectable democratic slogan—it had the support of Frederic Harrison and other radicals who favored peasant ownership. Fabian Socialism was something else again. To put the matter in a nutshell, what the Fabians did was to propose an "urban cow" and then try to sell it to the Liberals: without success, of course, although Webb and Shaw (unlike Bland, who possessed more political sense) were naive enough to think they could "permeate" the Liberal Party and eventually take it over from within. The operation depended upon their ability to make democratic Liberals believe that Socialism represented the application to industry of the great Radical principle that unearned income was immoral. Ricardo and Mill had provided the theoretical foundation by arguing that the agricultural tenant was being exploited by the landlord. The Fabian doctrine of rent extended this conclusion to industry and then sought to show that *this* (rather than Marx's reasoning in *Capital*) was the true meaning of "surplus value." The theory was worked out in the Hampstead discussion circle between 1886 and 1888 by Webb, Shaw, Olivier, and Wallas; put forward by Webb in the *Quarterly Journal of Economics* for January, 1888; and given its popular form by Shaw in his contribution to the 1889 *Fabian Essays.* In introducing the 1920 reprint of the *Essays*, Sidney Webb wrote: "The part of the book that comes most triumphantly through the ordeal . . . is . . . the economic analysis. . . . Tested by a whole generation of further experience and criticism, I conclude that, in 1889, we knew our Political Economy, and that our Political Economy was sound." It was certainly the distinctive core of Fabianism as a body of doctrine. By comparison, everything else—from Shaw's brilliant journalism and play-writing to Beatrice Webb's rather unsuccessful intrigues with Liberal and Tory leaders—is relatively unimportant, at any rate from a theoretical standpoint.

Now what exactly did the Fabian literature on rent tell the reader? Shaw's exposition in the 1889 *Essays* is lively, albeit somewhat slapdash. After quoting Mill's statement that "the rent of land consists of the excess of its return above the return to the worst land in cultivation," and citing Alfred Marshall and Henry Sidgwick to the same effect, he introduces "the first disinherited son of Adam, the first Proletarian, one in whose seed all the generations of the earth shall yet be blest, but who is himself for the present foodless, homeless, shiftless, superfluous, and everything that turns a man into a tramp or a thrall": a fair description of those among Shaw's fellow-Irishmen who had been driven from their soil by the invading English, but not very relevant to the British industrial working class in 1889. From this somewhat arbitrary starting point the reader is taken at a brisk trot through a landscape marked by landlord-tenant relationship, differential rent, the tenant cultivator's need to sell his labor so as to feed his family, the principle of exchange value, and so on, until at last he arrives at the subject of wages in industry, the argument culminating in the demonstration that "shareholder and landlord live alike on the produce extracted from their property by the labor of the proletariat." Shaw had after all started out as a Marxist, and in a fashion he always remained faithful to the notion of surplus value. What he was after was a way of presenting this idea in such a way that the average radical liberal could grasp it:

> This, then, is the economic analysis which convicts Private Property of being unjust even from the beginning, and utterly impossible as a final solution of even the individualist aspect of the problem of adjusting the share of the worker in the distribution of wealth to the labor incurred by him in its production. . . . On Socialism the analysis of the economic action of Individualism bears as a discovery, in the private appropriation of land, of the source of those unjust privileges against which Socialism is aimed. (*Op. cit*., 22, 24)

Webb's exposition of the doctrine is rather more technical. It runs somewhat as follows:

1. The wages paid to the unskilled laborer employed on the worst soil, with the minimum of capital, and in the worst circumstances, will be the natural measure of the wages paid to all unskilled workers.

2. Assuming an unregulated growth in population, the minimum wage will equal the subsistence wage necessary to keep the unskilled worker and his family alive long enough to rear a new generation of unskilled laborers.

3. Higher productivity resulting from the application of capital and skilled labor, or from better soil, will yield a surplus which will in turn be divided up between various types of "rent." Such "rents" will arise in any circumstances where labor, land, ability, and capital vary in quantity and quality, but the distinctive feature of capitalist society is that the bulk of "rent" is appropriated by the owners of the means of production. Skilled and organized workers may get a proportion of the "rent of ability," but never the whole of it. Moreover, skill is related to education, which in turn is unequally possessed, the offspring of the wealthy classes getting more of it. Thus the return to the various factors of production (land, labor, capital, operative skill) is unfairly weighted against those who only have their labor to sell. Contrary to the assertion of the liberal economists (though quite in accordance with the marginal utility theory of value they profess), the various factors are *not* remunerated in proportion to the contribution they make to wealth (or value) creation: there is an "unearned increment" that goes to the owners of capital. In short, the capitalist is in the same position as the landlord: he is a monopolist *even in a state of perfect competition* (which is ceasing to exist for other reasons).

Fabian economics, then, was the application to capitalist industry of the Ricardian theory of rent with which radicals and labor leaders were already familiar. The landlord and the capitalist were shown to be in the same boat. For the benefit of those who argued that the capitalist (unlike the landowner) was an active agent of industrial production and moreover created capital by saving, the Fabians had a second string to their bow: the accumulation of capital was indeed necessary, but this did not justify the existence of a capitalist class, for saving could be done collectively by the community, instead of being left to private individuals (not to mention the fact that the rich did not inflict a great hardship upon themselves by saving some of their capital). As for the managerial function, it could and should be separated from that of the pure capitalist, but this had also been suggested by Marx in *Capital*, so there was no innovation here. The novelty—in so far as there was one—lay in a concept of "surplus" that did not depend on the labor theory of value.

Present-day historians and economists tend to think that the notion of rent is either politically neutral or relevant to liberal radicalism rather than to socialism. In any case it did not play much part in popular expositions of Fabianism, although its authors continued to be proud of it and regarded it as superior to Marx's version. To Marxists it has always appeared as a quaint attempt to bypass the analysis of capitalism as a dynamic system propelled forward by its own internal contradictions. It can hardly be thought an accident that the Fabians developed no theory of economic growth or that when confronted with the phenomenon of the trade cycle they did not know what to do about it—and consequently suffered a political catastrophe in 1931.

Most of the early members of the Society had previously been Radicals, that is to say, adherents of the left wing of the Liberal Party, which stood for universal suffrage, land reform, freedom for Ireland, anti-imperialism, and other democratic causes. Bland was the exception in that he was a former Tory who disliked both liberalism and democracy for being, in his words, "anti-national and vulgar." Since he had no use for liberalism and no belief in "permeation" as a political strategy, he was content to wait until there should be a broadly based socialist labor movement. The political struggle, in his opinion, was bound to become sharper. "There is a true cleavage being slowly driven through the body politic" (Pelling, 77). At the same time he had no patience with the "catastrophic" doctrines of the S.D.F. and the Socialist League, based as they were on mistaken analogies with the French Revolution and the Paris Commune. On the whole one may say that his political judgment was sounder than that of his colleagues—certainly better than that of the Webbs, who had a unique talent for backing the wrong horse in politics even in comparatively trivial matters, such as misjudging the personalities of the leading Conservative and Liberal politicians (M. Cole, 83). However, Bland represented a minority of one among the Fabian leaders. All the others believed in "permeation"—chiefly of the Liberals, although Mrs. Webb characteristically thought she could manipulate the Tories as well. In consequence they virtually ignored the growing labor movement, snubbed the most important union leaders, and made far less of a contribution to the eventual formation of the Labour Party than did the Social Democratic Federation, for all the eccentricities of its leader and his unfortunate tendency to envisage the socialist revolution in terms of popular riots, barricades, and Committees of Public Safety. As for their claim to have "broken the spell of Marxism in Britain," Hobsbawm and McBriar—writing from widely different standpoints—have reached the same conclusion: there was no such spell and consequently no chance of breaking it. In fact after Eleanor Marx-Aveling's suicide in 1898, there was no one in Britain who had any real understanding of Marxism, and since Anarchism had likewise petered out, the Fabians had the field to themselves.

What is rather more remarkable is their inability to make contact with those left-wing Liberals who were their natural allies: men like J. A. Hobson, the critic of imperialism whose economic writings anticipated some aspects of Keynesianism. When in 1894-95 the Webbs founded the London School of Economics, with funds over which they had exclusive control, Hobson was an obvious candidate for running it. The man they chose instead was a young Oxford don named W. A. S. Hewins, who had no use for either democracy or collectivism and who later became an ardent imperialist Tory and propagandist for Joseph Chamberlain's protectionist views. Nor was this episode an isolated aberration. The Webbs' attitude, as well as Shaw's and Bland's, during the Boer War (1899-1902), when they split the Society and issued an imperialist tract labelled *Fabianism and the Empire*, bore all the marks of a considered antidemocratic standpoint. Shaw was then in his Nietzschean phase—witness the "Revolutionist's Handbook" appended to *Man and Superman*—and his defense of British policy in South Africa represented *Realpolitik* of the crudest sort. He had already trailed his coat in public with a speech attacking "Gladstonian Liberalism" and claiming that a Fabian must necessarily be an imperialist. The Society had by then been abandoned by the more consistent anti-imperialists—some of them old Liberals, others former Marxists—and Shaw, with the approval of the Webbs and their supporters on the Executive, drafted a tract (in September, 1900) from which it will be sufficient to quote these phrases: "The problem before us is how the world can be ordered by Great Powers of practically international extent. . . . The partition of the greater part of the globe among such powers is, as a matter of fact that must be faced approvingly or deploringly, now only a question of time" (Pease, 135). Thus what purported to be a statement of fact was turned into a justification: because imperialism was a reality, all that Socialists could do was try to administer the system with the maximum of efficiency and the minimum of fuss. The tract goes on to declare, "The State which obstructs international civilisation will have to go, be it big or little." There follows a piece of sophistry about China, then in the throes of an anti-foreign rising (the Boxer rebellion):

"Without begging the question as to whether the Chinese civilization is a lower or higher one than ours, we have to face the fact that its effect is to prevent Europeans from trading in China, or from making railway and postal and telegraph routes across it for the convenience of the world in general." This was liberal imperialism at its purest and most outspoken. One may also call it applied Positivism, for Comte would certainly have approved. Marx would not have, though, and the left-wing Liberals typified by Hobson did not approve either—they took their moral guidance in these matters from J. S. Mill—whereas the Webbs and Shaw argued along Social Darwinist lines already made familiar by Herbert Spencer (Beatrice Webb's first teacher).

There was a certain perverse consistency about all this. The leaders of the Society believed themselves to be advancing the Socialist cause when they were being most anti-liberal (although paradoxically they also tried to "permeate" the Liberal Party). In the carefully chosen words of their latest and most erudite historian, "The Fabians stood at the parting of the ways, at the point where the modern attitude to the State diverged from the Liberal-Radical attitude of the nineteenth century" (McBriar, 73). To put it crudely, they were authoritarians. Their brand of socialism was of the sort that Lassalle and Rodbertus had at an earlier stage represented in Germany and for which the Comteans had prepared the ground in Britain. That is to say, their dislike of economic *laissez-faire* took the form of a wholesale rejection of liberalism (but not of Benthamism). What they were really after was the forcible reorganization of society by the state:

> It is interesting that the Webbs should have found their most congenial political associates for so long in the group of liberal imperialists who formed around that Bismarckian collectivist, R. B. Haldane. It is equally interesting that both the Webbs and Shaw should—partly in line with their debt to the economics of F. A. Walker, the American—have shown a marked preference for big, or even monopolist business over small and medium business, as being both more efficient, more long-sighted, capable of paying higher wages, and less committed to *laissez-faire*. (Hobsbawm, *Labouring Men*, 263)

The Webbs' uncritical enthusiasm for the Soviet Union and Stalinism in the 1930's plainly stemmed from the same authoritarian attitude, as did Shaw's brief flirtation with Italian Fascism. The leading Fabians were indeed "bureaucratic collectivists" before their time. Their version of socialism was nonliberal as well as non-Marxian, which is why it appealed to the rising stratum of administrators, technicians, and industrial managers who were beginning to develop doubts about economic *laissez-faire*. But was the case so very different with their rivals of the Social Democratic Federation? After all, Hyndman had entered politics by way of more or less successful business ventures in silver mining in California and Utah, and when he broke with the Tories in 1881 it was largely because he thought them incompetent to administer the British Empire. He was briefly what was then known as a "Tory Radical" and his interest in socialism was awakened not untypically by his friend George Meredith's novel *The Tragic Comedians*, which was based on Lassalle's private life (Tsuzuki, *Hyndman*, 31). Lassalle, he remarked approvingly, was "essentially a national Socialist, who wished, above all things, to raise the Fatherland to a high level of greatness and glory." The description fits Hyndman even after he had become a convert to Marxian economics, for he always remained a convinced imperialist, albeit critical of official brutality in India and elsewhere. *England for All*, his first and most successful publication (1881), carried the additional title *The Text-Book of Democracy*. But although it appealed to the working men of Britain and Ireland to unite in defense of their interests, it was really a prospectus for Tory democracy, with the doctrine of surplus value added as an afterthought (and without mentioning Marx's name: an omission Engels never forgot or forgave). In later years too Hyndman somehow managed to combine Marxian socialism with patriotism, even with imperialism. If the S.D.F. nonetheless became a nursery of labor leaders–unlike the Fabian Society–this is not to say that it was a revolutionary body even by the modest standards of Continental Social Democracy in that age. It was not, nor could it have been.

As for its founder, who remained active in politics until his death in 1921, we may take leave of him at the start of his career in 1880, struggling through the French translation of *Capital* while supervising his mining business among Utah's Latter Day Saints: queer company for a future believer in the dictatorship of the proletariat, but then it was an age when a romantic Tory might become a convert to socialism from sheer boredom with the prevailing liberal orthodoxy. "Below the surface of American politics are grave difficulties," he wrote from Utah to his friend John Morley, "and such a party as that which sprang up in favour of the rights of labour would have something to say for itself if organized aright and on sound principles." Morley, albeit a prominent Liberal and a close associate of Gladstone, duly published Hyndman's letter on March 1, 1881, in the *Fortnightly Review*, and by this somewhat circuitous route the message of Marx (whose acquaintance Hyndman had made a few months earlier) reached a select minority of the British reading public.

By the time a British edition of *Capital* appeared in 1887, Marx had left the scene, and Engels was supervising the growth of the Continental Socialist movement, while the handful of Marxist intellectuals in Britain were busy quarrelling among themselves. Both the Social Democratic Federation and the Socialist League gained some working-class followers, and Eleanor Marx-Aveling made influential converts among the labor leaders active in the London dock strike of 1889, itself soon followed by the "new unionism" of the unskilled workers and the first great May Day demonstrations. But at the theoretical level there was a fatal flaw. Hyndman could not, and Engels would not, rebut Wicksteed's Jevonian critique of Marx's value concept, and so the academics drifted away and eventually adopted the comforting notion that Marx was "all wrong about surplus value" and altogether out of date and not worth reading: a mental climate that survived the Russian Revolution and was terminated only by the depression of the 1930's. The field was thus left free for the Fabians, whose utilitarian philosophy was anyhow more congenial to the national temperament. In consequence no sizable body of opinion on the British Left adopted even a watered-down form of Marxism, for the evangelical Socialism of the I.L.P. stemmed from the secularized religiosity of English Dissenters and Scottish Calvinists, while Fabianism was deeply impregnated with the philosophy of Comte, the dull and derivative offspring of the French Enlightenment. Whether one applauds or regrets these circumstances, the historian is obliged to note that Marxism acquired a sizable following in Britain only after it had passed its peak as the theory of the Continental labor movement.

4. Marxism and Anarchism

The title of this section has been chosen in disregard of the fact that we shall in part be dealing not with pure anarchism but with its semi-Marxist offspring, the syndicalist movement. For chronological reasons, however, we are obliged to hark back to its parent, the movement founded in the 1870's by Bakunin and his associates who had left (or been expelled from) the First International in 1872. There is an additional complication: some of the libertarian socialists of the 1880's and 1890's were anarchocommunists, that is to say followers of both Kropotkin and Marx, who took their ethics from the former and their economics from the latter. It is not altogether easy to reduce them all to a common denominator, but they did share one trait: a pronounced bias against authority in general and the state—be it even a democracy—in particular.

So far as the political orientation of the British labor movement after 1900 is concerned, the competition between Marxism and Anarchism enters into the matter only in so far as it involved the Socialist organizations already mentioned. The share taken by these small competing London-based groups of intellectuals in the formation of a mass movement between 1900 and 1906 was, however, rather slight. The Labour Party's true forerunner was Keir Hardie's organization, the Independent Labour Party, whose leader (although himself a Socialist) publicly argued that the only possible basis for a distinctive political organization of labor was not socialism but quite simply laborism. To demand that the political arm of the Trades Union Congress—the Labour Representation Committee formally established in London on February 27, 1900—should be committed to socialism would, he argued, inevitably split it and wreck the whole enterprise (McBriar, 316). This was a realistic appraisal, and the Parliamentary Labour Party which came into being on this basis in 1906 (after a secret and rather shady electoral deal with the Liberals) managed to get along without a formal commitment to either liberalism or socialism until 1918, when its leaders—having quarrelled with Lloyd George—commissioned Sidney Webb to draft a socialist platform for the coming elections (Pelling, *A Short History of the Labour Party*, 22 ff.).

This sort of empiricism did not appeal to the more methodical Germans—not to mention the French—but the question has occasionally been asked why there was not an analogous development in America. Noted scholars, some of them Germans, have devoted weighty (in every sense) volumes to the question why socialism, or at any rate laborism, did not strike deeper roots in the United States (the Canadian development was rather different). In the same spirit, historians have wondered why Australia, which *did* acquire a Labor party on the British model, did *not* thereafter make the transition from laborism to socialism, its labor movement contenting itself with a welfare-state platform. These are important and fascinating topics, but anyone who tries to answer the question why something or other did *not* happen inevitably comes up against a difficulty: whatever hypothesis may be proposed, it is impossible to exclude some other and equally plausible explanation. It may even be that there is no particular riddle to be solved. Socialism went to sleep in Britain between 1850 and 1880 and then stirred once more for reasons that in retrospect seem fairly obvious—principally the disintegration of liberalism. On the other hand, socialism (no longer synonymous with Proudhonism or Blanquism, both of which lost ground after 1871 and eventually dwindled away) did not have to be reawakened in France following the debacle of the Commune because in a certain fundamental sense it had taken possession of the French working class ever since 1848. It became a force in Germany in the 1860's, as the middle class abandoned the democratic cause, leaving its defense to the Social Democrats: the latter in consequence inherited an older tradition of democratic radicalism and then injected a few half-baked socialist notions into it (the Lassallean movement and its "Marxist" counterpart, the Social Democratic Party of Liebknecht and Bebel). At the other end of Europe, a socialist movement arose in Spain and Italy during the 1880's, when anarchism had lost some of its early glamor and after it had become evident that industrial workers (as distinct from landless agricultural laborers in Sicily or Andalusia) were not disposed to smash machinery or to turn their backs upon the modern world. That is to say, the socialist movement was spreading outward from a particular geographical and cultural center in Western Europe. The concurrent failure of socialist parties or sects in the United States, in Latin America, or in Australia and New Zealand to capture the labor movement seems mysterious only if one assumes that socialism merely needs to be explained to an intelligent working man for him to be converted to it. In fact, it takes a deal of effort to persuade him to join a union, let alone a political party. And even if a labor party comes into being, it need not be socialist.

There is an obstinate confusion in the minds of social historians about the notion of class consciousness. Because socially defined groups have a corporate sense of identity, and on occasion display a willingness to fight for strictly economic aims, they are credited by some writers with "consciousness" in the Marxist sense, a term applicable only to a social stratum willing and able to undertake a radical reorganization of society and culture. Such a determination does not by any means arise spontaneously from the assertion of group interest. To take the most glaring example of all: the British working class, ever since its birth during the prolonged and painful crisis of the early industrial revolution, consistently displayed a profound sense of separateness from the other classes of society. But this consciousness was of the "corporate" variety. It assumed socialist forms of expression only after there had occurred a growing process of disillusionment with Disraelian Toryism and/or Gladstonian Liberalism, the crucial point being the 1914-18 war. Even so, the Social Democratic mass movement which then came into being under the auspices of the renovated Labour Party was socialist in name only. The great majority of the British (as of every other) working class was instinctively "laborist," in the sense of emphasizing its corporate separateness, rather than desiring to remodel society in its own image. The decisive factor was the absence, during the formative period, of a radical intelligentsia. Where no such stratum exists, the labor movement remains "reformist," pressing its sectional claims but failing to challenge the basic institutions of society. For varying historical and cultural reasons, France, Italy, and Spain produced such an intelligentsia, as did Russia, Poland, Austria-Hungary, and to a lesser degree Bismarckian Germany, whereas North America and Britain did not. Speaking generally, it is a waste of time to inquire why this or that country did not prove suitable soil or why its native socialist (or anarchist or communist) movement did not adapt to local circumstances. Historians of the Reformation have yet to agree on the reasons why Calvinism took hold in Scotland but not, on the whole, in England. There is a fairly obvious answer: namely that the English in the end rejected it because it had been taken up by the Scots, whom they detested for political and cultural reasons rooted in a long-standing national enmity. But this sort of explanation has rarely appealed to sociologists.

Once the uniqueness of every historical situation is perceived, one can begin to make sense of a phenomenon as puzzling at first sight as

Bakunin's role in helping to found an anarchist movement in Spain and Latin America. *Prima facie* no two countries seem to have less in common than nineteenth-century Spain and Russia. Politically their paths had never crossed; culturally they were poles apart. Few Russians ever bothered to read a Spanish author, with the exception of Cervantes. Conversely, Russian literature (enormously influential in Germany, where populism and anarchism never got off the ground) made little impact in Spain. In the religious sphere, Greek Orthodoxy, while fairly sympathetic to Lutheranism (and vice versa), was deeply antagonistic to Roman Catholicism. That ardent Slavophil and patriot Dostoyevsky hated the Roman Church with an intensity matched only by his loathing for the French Revolution and everything that had descended from it. Why, then, did Bakunin's message strike millions of Spaniards with the force of a revelation, whereas in Germany his writings barely stirred a yawn? Because Spain had an agrarian problem and a landless proletariat? But Spain, unlike Russia, possessed a genuine feudal tradition, while, on the other hand, there was never anything resembling Russian serfdom. The outlook of the Spanish *pueblo* differed profoundly from that of the Russian *mir*, and anyway Bakunin's doctrines failed to take hold in his own homeland. Once more one has to look at the particular circumstances: in this case Bakunin's ability to clothe his message in language borrowed from Proudhon, who *did* appeal to the Spanish mind—principally because his hatred of the state was expressed in language that every Spaniard could understand (Brenan, 131 ff.).

And there was something else. At the risk of puzzling those earnest souls who imagine that ideas (or "ideologies") grow out of the "social structure" in accordance with textbook rules that can be learned by heart, it has to be stated that history operates quite otherwise. What happens to people in a given milieu is in part at least determined by cultural sediments left behind by earlier experiences (or their absence). Spain and Russia had something negative in common: neither country had experienced the Reformation, nor had they really absorbed the Enlightenment. In consequence, Russians and Spaniards, while very different in other respects and indeed rather inclined to dislike each other, shared a distinctly medieval cast of mind. This mentality expressed itself in an attachment to the idea of a national community of true believers sharing the same moral values. Never having been converted to either Protestantism or liberalism, Russians and Spaniards alike were not disposed to divorce politics from ethics (or metaphysics) in the manner of most West Europeans (and North Americans). The Slavophil reaction to Western individualism had its counterpart in the furious resistance offered by Spaniards of both the extreme Right and Left to anything that threatened to disintegrate this aspect of the national tradition. The Spanish Anarchist, like the Russian Populist, conceived himself as being intimately involved in a social organism whose claims were not exclusively secular and materialist but spiritual and therefore "total." To put it crudely, if Catholicism did not work (or if the Church had become corrupt), then there had to be a replacement for it, and a substitute of this kind could not be just another political party: it had to be universalist and messianic. Furthermore–and this is the decisive point–*it had to be grounded in a total rejection of the modern world.*

Now it is arguable–it has indeed been argued by Communists since 1917 and by Socialists before this date–that Marx had made adequate concessions to this way of looking at the world. His Russian followers did not indeed idealize the *obshchina* in the Slavophil manner as the repository of timeless spiritual values, but Marx and Engels (albeit hesitantly) had held out hope that a socialist revolution might regenerate the village commune before it had been wholly dissolved by capitalism. It was just this element of their doctrine which, as we have seen, furnished a bridge from the mental universe of Herzen to that of Plekhanov. However, in the 1870's, when "libertarian" emissaries traveled through Southern Europe, denouncing Marx and proclaiming Bakunin the heir of Proudhon, few people in Spain had heard of these learned disputations about the village commune. To Spaniards, libertarian socialism signified the Paris Commune and the anti-state "federalism" of Proudhon. Marx was identified with German Social Democracy, born on Lutheran soil and equipped with a Hegelian philosophy derived from the secularized Protestantism of the German Enlightenment. Spain had for decades been undergoing a spiritual crisis ultimately induced by the failure of liberalism to establish itself in the void created by the loss of religious faith. German socialism sounded prosaic. It was only in the 1880's that Marx's followers were able to get a socialist movement under way in Spain: not untypically in "centralist" Madrid and among a "labor aristocracy" of printers and other skilled workers who had lost faith in anarchist utopias and were prepared to take their political model from that section of the French labor movement which had been converted to a somewhat doctrinaire version of Marxism.

The general reader who wants to inform himself about Spanish Anarchism can turn to Brenan's *The Spanish Labyrinth*; for the student in search of a historical and sociological analysis of the entire Spanish background since the Napoleonic era, there is Raymond Carr's monumental work, which *inter alia* has the singular merit of explaining once and for all why liberalism was a failure in Spain. Anarchism became a mass movement in only two European countries: Spain and Italy. Not accidentally, these were Roman Catholic societies. Likewise they were countries in which the great economic gear-change from an agrarian to an industrial order had begun (and then got stuck) under the auspices of a weak and ineffective liberal movement. In consequence, there was a tendency for agrarian radicalism to take on an anarchist coloration. One can also put it differently: the immemorial millennarianism of the poor, notably among the landless peasantry in southern Italy and southern Spain, ceased to be a Christian heresy and was transformed into a movement directed against the landowners and their protectors, the monarchy and the Catholic Church. The fanatical atheism of these Italian and Spanish anarchists is therefore no surprise. In our own century this particular situation has duplicated itself in Latin America. The agrarian roots of this kind of millennarianism have been traced by Hobsbawm in his collection of studies entitled *Primitive Rebels*, and the reader in search of source material on the subject can do no better than to consult the three authors just cited, in addition to James Joll's learned and sympathetic volume *The Anarchists.* The special merit of all these writings is that they bring out the religious character of anarchism as a doctrine and a morality suited to an uprooted peasantry which had lost its land and its traditional way of life and got nothing worth-while in return. When at long last an industrial labor movement developed in these countries, it shed the anarchist heritage and adopted socialist or syndicalist doctrines more or less in tune with the Marxist tenets already implanted in France, where the Republic had by the 1880's won general national acceptance—but had likewise disclosed its essentially bourgeois character.

The question *why* capitalism and liberalism were a failure in Spain (and to a lesser degree in Italy) has been debated at length by historians. Considering the unbroken predominance of the Catholic Church, its long-standing alliance with Spanish national pride and dislike of foreigners, and the weakness of the Spanish Enlightenment (never more than a pale shadow of its French original), it is no great surprise that liberalism did not win a decisive victory in Spain. Italy at least had the Risorgimento, which for a while effected a fusion of liberalism with nationalism, albeit only for the upper and middle classes. In Spain, patriotism worked against modernization, for the national rising against Napoleon in 1808-14 had been led by the clergy, while the aristocratic liberals by and large favored the French. Liberalism thus got off on the wrong foot. Marxian socialism, another offspring of the Enlightenment, encountered similar temperamental obstacles. Western modernity being suspect as such, Spanish Anarchism was thus not merely anti-capitalist but anti-industrial—at any rate until the rise of Anarchosyndicalism after 1900, when Bakunin's followers were reluctantly obliged to come to terms with urban life and the existence of an industrial working class. Even then they did their best to conserve a style of politics that predated the modern age. Not surprisingly they never obtained power. This, however, was not their aim, since they viewed politics as inherently immoral and corrupting. What is rather more remarkable is their ineffectiveness in the role they had chosen: that of a permanent opposition to Church and state. There never was a successful Anarchist-led peasant revolt, just as there never was a successful Anarchist-led workers' strike. Possibly for this reason the industrial workers, except for those in a few regions of Catalonia, in the end came to prefer the Socialists, even though by Anarchist standards they sounded a bit tame. Failure was somehow built into the fabric of Anarchism from the start. At the same time Bakunin and his followers quite clearly possessed an intuitive sympathy for the peculiar social and mental stresses affecting millions of Italian and Spanish peasants and laborers to whom reformist socialism made no great appeal. In part this was undoubtedly because Bakunin during his stay at Naples in 1865 had come to understand that the common people in southern Italy were wholly indifferent to the bourgeois-liberal regime recently established (under monarchist auspices) by Garibaldi and Cavour. In Spain this kind of alienation went even deeper. Among the upper classes it took the traditional form of cynicism, sham religiosity, and a quasi-Oriental mixture of indolence and corruption. With Bakunin's followers it assumed the guise of passionate hope and zeal for a social apocalypse. This had to be a total catastrophe: nothing less would serve, for the existing world was hopelessly corrupt. Some elements of this attitude were also to be found in France, but they were counterbalanced by the belief that, just as the bourgeoisie had won its freedom in 1789, so one day the proletariat would attain *its* goals. France after all was the country of a victorious revolution, Italy and Spain the scene of endless and hopeless revolts: an important difference.

In their own fashion Marx and Engels realized all this, which is why they evinced no great surprise when in the 1870's Bakunin ran away with most of the International's following in Spain and Italy. "It was the desperate poverty of Andalusia which most readily provided enthusiastic converts to the Bakuninist vision of a new society" (Carr, *Spain*, 327). As Marx and his followers saw it, time was on their side: it was only necessary to wait for these countries to become industrial, and Anarchism would fade out. At the same time they were conscious of the problem that would be created for their own party if the bourgeoisie persistently failed to get the industrial revolution under way. As Engels put it in a letter to the Italian Socialist leader Filippo Turati in 1894, Italy was among those European countries that (in a phrase made famous by Marx) were suffering not only from capitalism, but also from lack of capitalism. The Italian bourgeoisie, having gained political power in the wake of the national rising between 1860 and 1870, was not proving very good at developing modern industry. Moreover, the reigning Liberals had not done away with the remnants of feudalism and absolutism. Hence the persistence of a Republican movement among sections of the peasantry and lower middle class who clung to the Mazzinian tradition. In the 1890's, when Engels and Turati discussed this situation, the Socialist Party, based on the emerging industrial working class, was still very weak and unable to take the lead in the political struggle. What then was the likely outcome? Today we know the answer: what happened was that the Fascists—a radical nationalist movement of the intelligentsia—seized power in the 1920's and then tried (and failed) to modernize the country industrially without altering the political "superstructure." But in the 1890's Engels could not foresee this disastrous episode. On the whole he thought it likely that the growing dissatisfaction of the lower middle class and the peasantry would give the Republicans (including the neo-Jacobin followers of Mazzini) their chance. What was the proper line the Socialist Party should adopt in such a situation? That prescribed by the *Communist Manifesto*: the Socialists, he told Turati, must aid the democratic movement and help the Republicans to gain power, but not at the price of surrendering their own independence. The most dangerous moment, he thought, would come "after the common victory," when the Socialists might be offered a few seats in the new government. This temptation they must resist at all cost, if they did not wish to repeat the sad experience of Louis Blanc and Ledru-Rollin in 1848, who had become helpless prisoners of a bourgeois regime that used the first opportunity to let the army loose on the workers. "Ministerialism" in *this* sense was forbidden to Marxists: not because it meant exercising political power within a parliamentary framework (by the 1890's Engels was no longer a Communist), but because the Socialist Party must aim at political control. This became the standard Marxist attitude in the age of the Second International: notably in France, where a democratic Republic was already in being and participation in coalition governments dominated by the bourgeois Radicals had become a standing temptation. What distinguished Marxist Social Democrats from the Anarchists on the one hand, from the petty-bourgeois reformists on the other, was their insistence that the party of the working class must aim at the conquest of political power, within the context of democracy but not at the expense of socialism. Participation in parliamentary elections was a means of drawing the masses into political life, and parliamentary democracy possessed virtues of its own which no sensible Socialist denied; but the Socialist Party must never accept minority status within a government dominated by bourgeois formations. It sought a peaceful revolution, but a revolution all the same.

Now clearly a long-range strategy of this sort—which moreover presupposed that a bourgeois form of industrialization would temporarily prove successful—offered nothing in the immediate future to the poor peasants and day laborers in Italy or Andalusia who flocked to the Anarchist banner. Nor was it intended to. Marx and Engels recognized only one suitable vehicle for the propagation of socialism: an autonomous labor movement based on the industrial working class. It is arguable that this indifference to the peasantry represented a weakness in their strategy. Marx was not enamored of the Rousseauist side of early socialism, and ever since the Bonapartist triumph in France on the morrow of the 1848 upheaval he had plenty of justification for his distrust of agrarian movements. The future Napoleon III had been swept into the presidency of the Republic in December, 1848, by an avalanche of peasant votes, and Marx found it difficult to forgive the French peasants for what they had done, although he readily agreed that they had been provoked by the unbelievable folly of the bourgeois Republicans. "The symbol that expressed their entry into the revolutionary movement," he wrote in 1850, in the series of articles later published as *The Class Struggles in France*, "clumsily cunning, knavishly naive, doltishly sublime, a calculated superstition, a pathetic burlesque, a dazzlingly foolish anachronism, a world-historic piece of buffoonery, an undecipherable hieroglyph for the minds of the civilized—this symbol bore the unmistakable physiognomy of the class that represents barbarism in the midst of civilization." All very true, but not very helpful in countering Anarchist propaganda among peasants and laborers in the Italian and Spanish countryside. Socialism was, among other things, a civilizing movement, notably in a backward country such as Spain. A historian of the movement has noted that "the Socialist party set itself to raise the self-respect of the working classes" (Brenan, 218n.). It could not well have succeeded in this difficult task had it lowered itself to the level of the Anarchist mentality, which along with a certain puritanism and unworldliness always encompassed a good deal of easy tolerance for brigandage and other forms of violence: not to mention the burning of churches and the massacre of priests and monks.

The Anarchist movement is an important one, but by now its relevance for the student of European Socialism is strictly historical, for as a mass phenomenon it has faded out, even in the country of its origin, where for a while it assembled hundreds of thousands of followers. Anyone curious to discover how and why Bakunin's Neapolitan emissary Giuseppe Fanelli was successful, late in 1868, in evangelizing Spanish working men in Madrid and Barcelona has ample source material at his disposal. If his patience lasts, he can even wade through the authoritative history of the sect, Max Nettlau's *Bakunin y la Internacional en España*. He will then discover something odd and significant: namely that while Fanelli was spreading Bakunin's version of Proudhon's gospel among the proletariat, a bourgeois-reformist variety of the same creed was simultaneously being preached to the middle class by the Federalist leader Pi y Margall, who later took command of the short-lived Spanish Republic in 1873. After what has been said about Proudhon's legacy, it is perhaps unnecessary to add that the experiment was as complete and disastrous a failure as the Paris Commune of 1871, although fortunately less destructive of human lives. The brief tragicomedy was largely due to Pi y Margall's obstinate adherence to Proudhon's "federal" creed which made effective government impossible, but the Bakuninist wing of the International also had its share of responsibility for the debacle. Not that it possessed a powerful organization: in 1871 it could not even meet its mailing expenses. But its bloodcurdling propaganda frightened the middle class just sufficiently to undermine the Republican strategy of an alliance with the workers, which might have turned Spain into a functioning democracy (Carr, 326 ff.). It was a foretaste of the greater debacle of 1931-39, also principally due to the Anarchists, who first did their best to wreck parliamentary government, then helped to provoke the outbreak of civil war in 1936 by murdering the political leaders of the Right, and finally displayed their usual incompetence when it came to fighting, as distinct from the massacre of civilians, in which they excelled (just like their Fascist opponents, who incidentally borrowed most of their slogans, as well as the color of their banner, from their Anarchist competitors). All told, Bakunin's disciples remained true to the legacy of their master. Ruin and disaster followed them wherever they went, and the working class had to suffer the consequences.

When one turns from this bloodstained tale of woe to the Syndicalist movement, which in the 1890's arose from the wreckage left behind by Bakunin and his progeny, one immediately notices an important difference. Syndicalism was rooted in the industrial working class. Moreover, it grew up in France and Belgium and took shape in the age of the Second International. This meant that the Syndicalists did not have to bother about Bakunin's personal vendetta against Marx, whom in his writings and letters he pictured as the head of an international Jewish conspiracy. This crapulous rubbish (like Bakunin's mania for founding secret societies blindly obedient to his despotic command) became and remained part of the treasured legacy inherited by the Black International, as the organization spawned by Bakunin's followers in 1881 came to be called (to distinguish it from the Red International of Socialism). These aspects of Bakuninism have proved a standing embarrassment to Anarchist historians. The more respectable among them have long felt obliged to concede that men like Elisée Reclus or Peter Kropotkin, who inherited part of the "libertarian" legacy, were baffled by Bakunin's peculiar mixture of anti-authoritarian philosophy *in abstracto* and dictatorial, indeed despotic, practice *in concreto*. It was hardly possible, after all, to ignore his celebrated letter of February 7, 1870, in which he demanded from his followers absolute submission to his personal authority. Nor could one disregard what he had to say about the "invisible dictatorship" that his secret organization would have to exercise to keep the revolution on the right path (Drachkovitch, ed., 71). But if his friends and admirers could not deny the evidence, they could do the next best thing–namely, minimize it. In any case, these fantasies were destined to bear fruit in senseless acts of terrorism that did nothing to advance the cause of labor's emancipation. And when they did so, the more civilized Anarchists–by then for the most part won over to Kropotkin's genuine libertarianism–were duly horrified and would have nothing to do with the practical application of Bakunin's peculiar doctrines.

West European Syndicalists drew on other sources even when, as in Spain, they went to the length of describing themselves as anarchosyndicalists, in deference to tradition. Spain being what it was, anarchosyndicalism assumed a quasi-religious cast absent from the doctrine of its French founders. There was likewise a marked difference on the issue of armed violence.

While from the 1890's the French union movement committed itself to the theory and practice of political strikes, few labor leaders accepted the cult of violence preached by the amateur philosopher Georges Sorel (1847-1922) in his numerous writings, among which *La Décomposition du Marxisme* (1906) and *Réflexions sur la violence* (1908) are the best known. Sorel, a retired civil engineer and an instinctive Proudhonist who in the 1890's rather half-heartedly adopted Marx's historical materialism, developed an eclectic doctrine of his own, in part derived from the then fashionable philosophy of Henri Bergson (1859-1941) but more particularly marked by a Nietzschean faith in the regenerative power of violence. When grafted upon the idea of the general strike–which he did not invent but inherited from the radical labor leaders of the period–Sorel's revolutionary credo amounted to this: bourgeois society, already in decay, could and should be overthrown by the unleashing of violence. Parliament was a sham, and the reformist Socialists were traitors to the working class. While ready enough to accept the latter proposition, the Syndicalists favored the general strike precisely because it promised to bring about a social transformation with a minimum loss of human life. Matters were different in Spain, where Sorel's doctrines intoxicated both the Anarcho-syndicalists and their Fascist rivals. "In the Civil War the two branches of his descendants met, and sordid firing squads and bloodstained cemetery walls then showed exactly what was to be got out of Sorelian ethics" (Brenan, 171).

It seems reasonable to describe French Syndicalism (*syndicat* is simply the French term for what in the English-speaking world is known as a trade union) as a synthesis of Proudhonism and Marxism. The fusion was brought about in the 1890's by Fernand Pelloutier (1867-1901), a young idealist who died of comsumption at the early age of 34, leaving behind an indelible memory that inspired two generations of French working men and their leaders. Before striking out on his own, Pelloutier had been a follower of Jules Guesde (1845-1922), the leader of the Marxist wing within the French Socialist movement. Among Pelloutier's principal associates and heirs, Victor Griffuelhes (1874-1923) had gone through the Blanquist school, while Émile Pouget (1860-1932) and Paul Delesalle were Anarchists. What brought them all together was contempt for parliamentarism on the one hand and dissatisfaction with Guesde's rather primitive and doctrinaire version of Marxism on the other. As early as 1888, a federation of unions established two years earlier at Lyon had passed a resolution declaring that the labor movement must be autonomous (i.e., not controlled by any political party) and that "only the general strike, that is to say the complete cessation of all labor, or the revolution, can lead the workers toward their emancipation." The somewhat ambiguous phrasing of this passage enabled Guesde's followers to claim that they all meant the same thing by "revolution," but by 1894 the Marxists had quarrelled with the Syndicalists, as the believers in the general strike now came to be called. Moreover, Pelloutier and his friends had in the meantime established a new organizational model, the Bourses du Travail. These had come into existence in 1887 alongside the regular unions (*syndicats*), the difference between the two being that the Bourses had a local basis and that workers of all trades could belong to them. When in 1895 Pelloutier became secretary-general of the Fédération des Bourses du Travail, Syndicalism acquired both a doctrine and an organizational armature. But the decisive moment in the history of the movement had occurred three years earlier, in 1892. In February of that year fourteen Bourses du Travail federated at Saint Étienne and at the same time declared their independence from all political parties. In September, meeting in a joint assembly held at Tours, they adopted a resolution proclaiming their faith in the general strike as the instrument of proletarian revolution. Two years later, in September, 1894, the Nantes congress of the Fédération des syndicats et groupes coopératifs followed suit with a similar statement, drafted by Pelloutier and presented to the congress by a young lawyer named Aristide Briand (1862-1932)–in later years destined to become a dissident Socialist, still later Prime Minister or Foreign Minister in various governments of the Third Republic which, whatever their other accomplishments, certainly never did anything to help the proletarian revolution forward.

For practical purposes Syndicalism meant workers' control. The movement had grown up spontaneously, was international, and possessed a sizable following in countries other than France and Belgium, where it was strongest because of the continuing influence of Proudhon's doctrines. In its classical version, as spelled out by Pelloutier and his disciples, the existing centralized political system was to be replaced–either gradually or as the result of a revolutionary crisis culminating in a general strike–by a federalized order based on local organizations of producers. Industry in each locality would be run by the syndicats, and the latter would send delegates to the local Bourse du Travail which would act as coordinating center. Over larger areas, responsibility would be shared between the Bourses and the unions, brought together in a general labor federation. The principal French trade-union federation, the Confédération Générale du Travail (C.G.T.), did in fact adopt syndicalism as its ideological guideline down to 1914. Elsewhere the movement was less broadly based, but it was not negligible. Its offshoots in Italy and Spain gradually managed to overcome the tradition of "pure" anarchism: the anarchism of the village poor and the semi-criminal urban *lumpenproletariat*.

Meanwhile, its American counterpart, the Industrial Workers of the World, inspired similar efforts in Britain and Australia. American syndicalism, or industrial unionism, had grown out of the struggle between the conservative craft unions of the American Federation of Labor and the new immigrants who turned for political direction to the Socialist Labor Party of Daniel de Leon (1852-1914). A British branch of the movement (bearing the same title) was founded in 1903 by the Irish labor leader James Connolly with the help of Glasgow socialists who had read de Leon. The British S.L.P.'s influence remained largely confined to Scotland, but it was not unimportant. From 1910 onward the veteran labor leader Tom Mann introduced French and American ideas of workers' control into Britain through his journal, *The Industrial Sydicalist*, and from 1912 onward a Guild Socialist movement (mainly composed of dissident Fabians and other intellectuals) put forward a watered-down version of syndicalist ideas, while discarding the notion that manual workers alone could and should administer industry unaided.

Guild Socialism asserted that the government of industry must embrace all those concerned with production, including the managerial and professional elements. This was a sensible qualification of the original syndicalist conception, while at the same time it corrected the orthodox Fabian emphasis on state ownership and bureaucratic management. The theoretical case in favor of Guild Socialism as set out by G. D. H. Cole in *The World of Labour* (1913) rested upon a conflation of modified syndicalism with an older tradition inherited from Ruskin and Morris. The centerpiece was the notion that collectivism, whether of the Marxian or Fabian variety, would give too much power to the state, an argument also developed by the Guild Socialist S. G. Hobson, who had become disillusioned with Fabianism, in various writings between 1910 and 1914. There was in those years an undercurrent of corporatist thinking in Britain among political and legal theorists such as Frederic Maitland, Ernest Barker, A. D. Lindsay, and others, by no means all of them Socialists. The general trend was in the direction of suggesting that collective groups within society, standing between the individual and the state, should be regarded as having real wills and personalities, since they were logically and historically prior to the state and not created by it. This approach was shared by the genuine medievalists (for the most part Roman Catholics or High Anglicans, who in Britain generally tended toward romantic Toryism but on occasion also displayed socialist sympathies). In France, where the Catholic and medievalist tradition was deeply entrenched, the political Right welcomed arguments of this kind in its struggle against Jacobinism. For the same reason, the French Syndicalist movement, being profoundly hostile to the Church, generally disdained this kind of support. Nonetheless, some of the more nationalist leaders on the fringe of Syndicalism between 1908 and 1914 established contact in a discussion club, appropriately named *Cercle Proudhon*, with followers of the royalist *Action française*, thereby giving birth to a forerunner of the ideological frenzy of the 1930's. These meetings occurred under the patronage of Sorel, who by then had abandoned Marxism for a private confection of his own.

At the political level, the train of events set in motion by the pioneers was marked by a number of important dates: 1896, when the C.G.T. adopted the principle of the general strike; 1902, when Victor Griffuelhes became secretary-general of the C.G.T.; and 1906, when during a brief stay in Berlin (occasioned by growing alarm over the possibility of a Franco-German war) he discovered that the German unions controlled by the Social Democrats were not prepared to join their French comrades in simultaneous demonstrations against their respective governments, the excuse being that they were too busy holding public meetings in support of the Russian revolutionary movement of 1905-6, which had recently been defeated. This disillusioning experience (a foretaste of 1914) was followed in the autumn of that year by the adoption of the Charte d'Amiens. In this document, the C.G.T. affirmed its independence of the French Socialist Party, which had recently been constituted by a fusion of various competing political currents. In passing one may note that the idea of "direct action" had been taken over by the French unions from the American labor movement of the 1880's–specifically from the Knights of Labor, who had called for strike action as a means of obtaining the eight-hour day. This novel method of winning concessions from the employers made a deep impression upon French workers' leaders like Pouget, and when he and others moved from Anarchism to Syndicalism, they introduced it into the C.G.T., where it became the favorite weapon of the French workers' movement.

It is perhaps unnecessary to observe that there was no corresponding development in Germany. In fact the German Social Democrats could not even be induced to stop work on May 1, 1890, when all their European comrades (including the Austrians, who lived under a very similar political regime) did so. In Germany, both the party and the unions it controlled found reasons for contenting themselves instead with public meetings on the first Sunday in May (Braunthal, I, 246-48). This lamentable episode was revelatory of a state of mind profoundly ingrained in the German labor movement from the very start. It had nothing whatever to do with the "opportunism," or "reformism" of a "labor aristocracy" (all Socialist and Syndicalist movements were drawn from this stratum) but was quite simply due to the absence of any kind of revolutionary tradition: an inheritance from the German middle class. Liberalism had already manifested a strikingly similar outlook between 1848 and 1871, when the German Spiessbürger (or Staatsbürger) displayed himself in all his glory.

The issue of May Day demonstrations was to have important consequences and thus deserves a brief airing. The American practice of strikes to secure the eight-hour day was appropriate to an environment where the struggle on the industrial front was traditionally pursued with considerable vigor, even in the absence of long-range political aims. Thus, no socialist program was involved or required when in December, 1888, the American Trade Union Congress, meeting at St. Louis, decided to organize mass demonstrations for the eight-hour day throughout the United States on May 1 the following year. When the inaugural congress of the Second International met in Paris on July 14, 1889–the centenary of the fall of the Bastille–it was natural that the subject of May Day demonstrations should be ventilated. Although not on the agenda, a resolution calling on the workers to display their solidarity "simultaneously in all countries on a given day" was introduced by a French delegate and hurriedly carried without debate shortly before the conference closed. There is reason to believe that many of the delegates who voted for the motion did not foresee what they were letting themselves in for. The United States and France were republican democracies with a revolutionary tradition that had automatically been inherited by their respective labor movements, even though the American unions were predominantly nonsocialist. Britain, Germany, and Scandinavia were in a different category, being constitutional monarchies without experience of recent revolutions. At the other extreme, Russia occasioned no problem, since it possessed a plethora of revolutionaries but as yet no legal labor movement. Austria-Hungary did have one, and a Social Democratic Party had recently been formed (in 1888). The French resolved to celebrate the first of May in 1890 with a general strike, while the Germans and the British decided to hold public meetings on the first *Sunday* in May, and the Socialist parties of most other countries compromised by holding meetings on the evening of May 1.

This was not in accordance with the resolution of the International, but, given the torpid spirit of the British and the Germans, it was the next best thing.

In the event, work stopped on May 1, 1890, in 138 French cities and in a few mining areas. In Milan, Turin, and other Italian centers the workers marched through the streets in serried formation. Demonstrations also took place in Britain, Belgium, Sweden, Portugal, Catalonia, and (illegally) Warsaw and Lodz. The London demonstration on Sunday, May 4, 1890, was peaceful but brought out crowds estimated at over 100,000, much to Engels' delight. Throughout Austria-Hungary the army was called out to cope with what the authorities feared might be the start of a general rising, and in the following year the stoppage of work on May 1 was countered by the employers in Bohemia, Carinthia, and elsewhere with a general lockout.

In contrast to the Austrians, with whom otherwise they had much in common and whose general outlook they shared, the German Social Democrats confined themselves to public meetings on Sunday, May 4, declined to sanction work stoppages, and in 1891 (under pressure from the Austrian Socialist leaders) only compromised to the extent of changing the date of public meetings to the evening of May 1. Having just recovered from twelve years of enforced semi-legality, they were determined not to risk a showdown with the authorities, although (or because) Bismarck had recently been dismissed and the repressive 1878 laws directed against Socialist agitation had not been renewed. They did not want to court trouble, and nothing could move them. As for the notion of a revolutionary general strike to transform society, it never entered their heads.

In consequence, the German Socialists—like the British, who indeed had the excuse of being in a much weaker position numerically—ignored the resolution of the Brussels Congress of the International in 1891, which pledged all parties to celebrate May Day on the first day of the month, by demonstrations and strikes as well: "The day of demonstrations is to be a day on which work ceases, in so far as this is not rendered impossible by conditions in the various countries." For the Germans this last phrase became a permanent escape clause. Conditions, they claimed, made it impossible either to strike or to demonstrate. When the Zürich Congress of the International in 1893 pledged the various parties to at least "attempt" strikes on May 1, the worthy August Bebel, speaking for the S.P.D., sagely observed that any such attempt in Germany would "bring about, as nowhere else in the world, a head-on collision with the *bourgeoisie* and the government," a calamity to be avoided at all cost. "If we want such a struggle, we should prefer to choose our own time," he added (Braunthal, I, 249). For some reason no suitable occasion was ever discovered, not even in 1905-7 when enthusiasm over the first Russian Revolution ran high in Germany and the radicals in the S.P.D. urged political strikes as a means of securing universal suffrage in Prussia: a perfectly legitimate course of action which had nothing to do with revolution in the socialist sense, and for which there would have been moral support among middle-class democrats. However, the party leadership, solidly backed by the unions, successfully evaded this challenge to all its traditions, and that was the last pre-1914 Germany heard of the idea of using the strike as a political weapon (Schorske, 36 ff.).

To say, then, that Germany never developed a Syndicalist movement is not just to state the obvious: that there was no room in German society for anarchism, except as a romantic daydream of interest to expressionist poets, futurist painters and their models, plus a few eccentric philosophers and pedagogues. Syndicalism was indeed cradled in France, but its appeal was much wider; moreover, the original impetus had come from North America, so the whole phenomenon could not be dismissed as a peculiarity suitable only to the Latin temperament. It is true that the French, in their customary fashion, were rather doctrinaire about the wonder-working powers of the general strike. Those American, British, Irish, and Australian labor leaders who in 1910-14 worked out something like a theory and practice of Syndicalism did not seriously think in terms of capturing political power. Rather, they were concerned to give an extra dimension to the industrial struggle, at a time when in their respective countries there was little or nothing to be got out of legislative politics. The French, being the inheritors of a revolutionary tradition, naturally went a good deal further. The 1906 Charter of Amiens, already referred to, was the work of militants like Griffuelhes, Delesalle, and Pouget, who had worked with Pelloutier until his untimely death in 1901. The doctrines they inherited from him were certainly revolutionary, combining as they did the ancient Proudhonist vision of workers' self-government with the Marxist notion of class struggle. The strategy to which the C.G.T. had by then committed itself was described by Delesalle somewhat as follows:

1. A general strike by individual unions, comparable to maneuvers.
2. Cessation of work everywhere on a given day, comparable to general maneuvers.
3. A general and complete stoppage, which places the proletariat in a state of open war with capitalist society.
4. General strike–revolution.

The distinction between the third and fourth stages is difficult to grasp. A few Syndicalists may have toyed with the notion of escalating the movement to the point of an armed seizure of political power; but this was never stated, and under the existing regime in France, with the bulk of the working class firmly committed to republican democracy, it would have been insanity to pursue such tactics. (Matters were different in Spain, where violence was endemic and where the army had throughout the nineteenth century been repeatedly drawn into insurrectionary movements. Moreover, Spain still possessed what no other West European country had retained: a potentially revolutionary peasantry.) What the French Syndicalists really had in mind was explained by their leaders at an Anarchosyndicalist congress held at Amsterdam in 1907 and attended by, among others, the veteran Errico Malatesta, Bakunin's associate and (as one of the French put it) "the last representative of the old insurrectionary anarchism" (Joll, *The Anarchists*, 203). Most of the younger delegates were Syndicalists, that is to say labor leaders and semi-Marxists. Where they differed from the Social Democrats of their age, who of course were also Marxists or quasi-Marxists, was in placing their faith in the unions rather than in the political party. Amédée Dunois and Pierre Monatte, two youthful union organizers who represented the French at this meeting, put it very clearly: "The workers' union (*syndicat*) is not just an instrument of combat, it is the living germ of the future society, and the society of the future will be what we have made of the *syndicat*. . . . Syndicalism does not waste time promising the workers a paradise on earth, it calls on them to conquer it and assures them that their action will never be wholly in vain." To which Malatesta, speaking for the older tradition, replied that the general strike was "pure utopia": either it would fail, or it would turn into an armed insurrection, in which case "victory will go to the strongest." Without armed violence there could be no successful revolution. This was also Sorel's view, which is why he never had any real influence on the labor leaders who ran the C.G.T. These men, from Griffuelhes to Jouhaux and Merrheim, neither knew nor cared about him. So far as they were concerned, their ultimate aims had been stated, once and for all, by Fernand Pelloutier: a martyr to their cause, as well as the first theorist of the movement. Sorel arrived late on the scene, and the notion that he pioneered the Syndicalist doctrine is a fantasy. Where he scored was in furnishing a philosophy for both anarchist and proto-fascist intellectuals on the eve of 1914: an undercurrent of violence already perceptible in art and literature before European civilization committed suicide on the battlefields of World War I.

5. The Second International: 1889-1914

On the threshold of this section something like a brief review of the troops seems to be called for: if only because thereafter we shall see them engaged in a series of maneuvers terminating in the catastrophe of 1914, when the International failed in its purpose and died without honor. To say this is not to attribute faults or failings to anyone in particular: it is simply to record the verdict of history. The Second International had been founded in 1889 with one overriding political aim: to promote a reconciliation between the French and German working classes in particular and between France and Germany in general. When in 1914 its two principal units–the German and French Socialist parties–lined up with their respective nations, then engaged in mutual slaughter, it was plain to all that the International had not accomplished what was generally understood to be its main purpose. It had not prevented war or even preserved its own unity. This simple fact has been overlaid in the course of time by the dramatic circumstances stemming from the Russian Revolution of 1917 and the Communist split of 1919, when the Third International came into being; but in 1889 no one expected such a cataclysm. What thinking people did fear was precisely what was to occur: that the European governments would launch a great war and that the two leading Continental nations would once more find themselves on opposing sides, as they had in 1870-71. Socialists were not alone in predicting this outcome. Fear of it was so widespread in Europe as to be well-nigh universal, and the Socialist International was not the only body whose pretensions were shown up as hollow in 1914. It shared this fate with all sorts of liberal and pacifist organizations, not to mention the churches. But Socialism was relatively novel, and its aims were expressed in the language of supranationalism. Consequently, when in 1914 the house of cards collapsed, Socialist internationalism appeared discredited. This depressing conclusion was drawn not simply because the working-class movement had been unable to prevent the outbreak of war, but because Frenchmen and Germans found themselves on opposing sides and because their respective Socialist parties succumbed to nationalism.

This view of the matter–while familiar to European historians and above all to historians of the Second International–is not very widely shared outside Europe, where people are understandably vague about what exactly happened during this quarter century. It is therefore worth emphasizing at the outset that in what follows we shall be dealing with the affairs of the Old Continent. The Second International was primarily a European organization, although its congresses regularly featured a substantial North American contingent and a few delegates from Latin America and Japan. Moreover, its cornerstone was a carefully cemented Franco-German alliance, whereas the First International (whose American offshoot quietly expired at Philadelphia in 1876) had been primarily an Anglo-French affair. It was wrecked by the Paris Commune, which temporarily destroyed the French movement, scared the British union leaders out of their feeble wits, and demoralized the remainder, so that they fell prey to the destructive intrigues and quarrels started by Bakunin and his followers. The Second International, having been founded in the hope of promoting amity between the two main Continental nations, lasted just as long as there was peace between France and Germany. To say this is not to overlook the fact that there was a Russo-German antagonism as well as a Franco-German one. But–and this is crucial–the long-standing political rivalry among the three Eastern empires–Germany, Austria-Hungary, and Tsarist Russia–did not engage national loyalties to the same degree as did the conflicts between France, England, Italy, and Germany. To put it crudely, the Second International might have survived a war between Russia and Germany over the Austrian succession; it could not survive a war between France and Germany, unless the French and German Socialists proved able to resist the nationalist tide. When in 1914 they failed to do so, the International had signed its death warrant.

To understand why this was so, it is necessary to go back to the inaugural meeting held in Paris in July, 1889. Strictly speaking there were two meetings organized respectively by the French and German Marxists and by their "Possibilist" (that is, reformist) rivals. To make confusion worse confounded, the Possibilists under Paul Brousse were allied for tactical reasons with Hyndman's Social Democratic group in London, whereas the Marxist Parti Ouvrier Français of Jules Guesde and Paul Lafargue had enrolled the Blanquist Comité Révolutionnaire Central in support of its endeavors to convene an international congress in Paris to mark the centenary of the French Revolution (Braunthal, I, 196 ff.; Tsuzuki, *Eleanor Marx*, 187 ff.; Joll, *The Second International*, 30 ff.). After various attempts by the Germans to bridge the gap between the rival French groups, Brousse and his friends were left to their fate—partly because Eduard Bernstein (then Engels' principal assistant) had denounced them publicly as "Ministerial Socialists." In fact the issue was a good deal more complicated. Brousse was committed to the defense of the Republic (bourgeois though it was) against the reactionary nationalist movement led by General Boulanger, and to this end had entered into an alliance with the bourgeois Radicals. On the other hand, some Blanquists flirted with Boulangism, while the Guesdists (despite Engels' repeated warnings) affected to stay neutral in the matter. It was a dress rehearsal for the Dreyfus Affair a decade later, when rival factions re-enacted a similar confrontation: the consistent democrats coming out for the defense of the Republic (Jaurès), the self-styled Marxists (principally Guesde, who on this occasion was not supported by Paul Lafargue) averring that only the class struggle mattered.

In 1889 these internal French dissensions resulted in the holding of two rival meetings in Paris: both convened for July 14. The French and German Marxists and their allies met in the Salle Petrelle, while their rivals convened in the rue de Lancry. Outside the world of organized socialism, few people took note of these gatherings. The Possibilist Congress was briefly reported in the London *Times*, the Marxist gathering barely mentioned at all. There was a good deal of confusion, especially since Anarchist delegates tried to gain access to both meetings, and some of the other delegates seem to have wandered to and fro, attending now one gathering, now the other. In the end, the conference at the Salle Petrelle turned out to be the inaugural session of the Second International, while the rival congress had no further sequel.

This outcome was largely determined by the fact that the German

Social Democrats (urged on by Engels) abandoned the attempt to mediate between the French factions and settled down in the Salle Petrelle. Altogether, there were 81 German delegates, in addition to 221 French ones: the latter including the Blanquist leader Édouard Vaillant, a veteran of the Paris Commune who in 1872 had sided with Marx against Bakunin (and deplored, as noted before, the transfer of the First International's General Council to New York). Despite their alliance with Marx, the Blanquists, as inheritors of the Jacobin tradition, were ardent patriots rather than internationalists in the Marxist sense, and they had been bitter-enders during the war of 1870-71: their willingness to work with German Social Democrats was a crucial factor in making it possible for the International to get under way. The Marxists under Guesde, Lafargue, and Charles Longuet (the latter two being Marx's sons-in-law) still trailed numerically behind the Blanquists, at any rate in Paris. There was also a French Anarchist group at the Salle Petrelle, led by Sébastien Faure and apparently reconciled to the idea of working with Blanquist and Marxist "centralists." Britain, Holland, Belgium, the Scandinavian countries, Italy, Spain, Russia, the United States, Argentina, and various other countries were likewise represented: the British by twenty-two delegates, including Keir Hardie (for the Scottish miners); John Burns (then a well-known union leader, later to become a singularly reactionary and inept Minister in the Liberal government of 1906-14); William Morris; and Eleanor Marx-Aveling. Hyndman, with his usual talent for backing the wrong horse, had gone to the rival meeting at the rue de Lancry. Belgium had fourteen representatives, including the veteran César de Paepe, a former Proudhonist and a leading figure in the First International. Italy was represented by twelve delegates, including two veterans of the First International and the Anarchist Saverio Merlino (Anarchists were formally barred from Socialist congresses only in 1896). From Austria there came a delegation of eleven, led by Victor Adler, for the next thirty years the irremovable leader of one of the strongest Socialist parties in Europe. Spain had one delegate–Pablo Iglesias, the founder of its Socialist Party. Russia had two–Peter Lavrov and Plekhanov. Their presence had considerable symbolic value, but everyone knew that only the French and the Germans really mattered, and the Germans were beginning to matter more than the French.

This, indeed, is the key to the whole story of the subsequent twenty-five years. Germany was becoming the most powerful industrial country in Europe, its labor movement was swelling in numbers, and the German Social Democrats automatically became the leading party in the International, especially since their organizational and parliamentary strength continued to grow, so that before long they overtopped all others numerically. Moreover they had the advantage of being formally committed to Marxism, as interpreted by Karl Kautsky (1854-1938), and of being the homeland of Marx and Engels, now recognized by Socialists the world over as the foremost thinkers of the movement. Marx had always viewed the politics of his native land with a good deal of detachment, and he held no very high opinion of Wilhelm Liebknecht, the veteran leader of the unified Social Democratic Party born from the fusion of the Liebknecht-Bebel group with the surviving Lassalleans. But Marx's private opinion of the S.P.D. was not generally known, he himself had left the scene in 1883, and Engels entertained high hopes for the party he had helped to found. He had been its grand strategist, from its early beginnings in 1865–when Liebknecht and Bebel came together in Saxony–to his death in 1895, and it was his firm conviction that "scientific socialism" would prove its worth in Central Europe. Germany then held the commanding position in Europe, and the imperial regime of William II seemed to have been invented for the express purpose of alienating the working class from the state, so that a democratic revolution appeared not only probable but inevitable. The mere fact that the Prussian (though not the all-German) franchise virtually excluded the working class from the vote was an adequate guarantee of trouble in the not too distant future. A peaceful democratization of the German Empire was impossible, for reasons that anyone could grasp who took the trouble to consider what would happen to the aristocracy if it ever lost political control of the state it had founded. In this respect Prussia-Germany–as Marx and Engels countless times explained to their followers–resembled Austria-Hungary, even Tsarist Russia, rather than the West European countries. This was just why the German, Austrian, and Russian Social Democrats had all gone Marxist: whatever might be said about the chances of peaceful socialization in France, England, Holland, or North America, the three Eastern empires were fated to pass through the turmoil of popular revolution–as indeed they did in 1917-18.

At the same time, however, Engels and his German followers entertained rather optimistic notions about the importance of their party's electoral following. This was considerable though not overwhelming (by 1912 it amounted to over 30 percent), and in any case the Reichstag had no real power, so that it mattered little how many Social Democratic deputies were elected. Then there was the curious business of the May Day demonstrations, to which reference has already been made. The philistine spirit in which the German Social Democrats debated this issue angered even the Austrian Victor Adler, who was not an extreme radical. Engels intervened personally at one stage to urge greater audacity on Bebel, but without success. In Germany, May Day remained an occasion for evening meetings, and there were even attempts by the stodgier trade-union leaders to adopt the amiable British habit of celebrating the occasion with a sort of large-scale picnic on the first Sunday in May. The truth is that the German Socialists had no stomach for a showdown with the government, and their attitude "meant the end of May Day as an effective demonstration of international solidarity. . . . A great symbolic gesture faded away when the practical difficulties were explored and when the realism of the German Party was brought to bear on them" (Joll, *The Second International*, 54). For "realism" read "philistinism"–a trait the German Social Democrats had inherited from their middle-class predecessors of 1848. An International based on a party of this kind was not likely to survive its first serious test.

In 1889 these undercurrents were concealed by the revolutionary façade of the Paris Congress, at which the French Marxists and Blanquists set the tone. France indeed remained important, and eventually it even acquired a unified Socialist Party alongside a Syndicalist union movement. The party as finally constituted in 1905 was fairly evenly split between Guesdists and Jaurèsists, but even the latter–although rather eclectic in their doctrine–were far more radical and indeed revolutionary in temper than the German Socialists: with the exception of a small and quite unrepresentative faction led by Rosa Luxemburg (1871-1919), which had a following in Berlin and Saxony and among the Polish workers in Silesia. At all the congresses of the International after 1889 the German delegation represented the conservative element, a circumstance veiled by the Marxist language in which its leaders expressed their refusal to sanction Socialist participation in bourgeois governments. This was not possible in Germany, and the S.P.D. consequently could afford to adopt an intransigent attitude when the matter was put to the vote at the Amsterdam Congress in August, 1904, exactly one decade before the International's collapse. On that occasion August Bebel, Kautsky, and the other German leaders sided with Guesde against Jaurès, who during the Dreyfus upheaval in 1898-1902 had sanctioned the entry of his friend Millerand into a coalition government to defend the Republic. Jaurès was duly rebuked, but he more than got his own back when in his speech he characterized the German party as a colossus with clay feet. "Behind the inflexibility of theoretical formulas with which your excellent Comrade Kautsky will supply you until the end of his days, you conceal . . . your inability to act," he told Bebel (Joll, *The Second International*, 103). The issue of "ministerialism"–superficially entangled with the question of "revision" of Marx's doctrine, as suggested by Eduard Bernstein (1850-1932) from 1898 on and opposed by Karl Kautsky and the "Austro-Marxists" around Adler–had very little to do with it. Participation in democratically elected parliamentary governments was not an issue in Germany and Austria-Hungary, which in those days possessed elected parliaments, but no real democracy. On the other hand, it was quite possible to be both a "reformist" (in the democratic sense) and a Marxist, as indeed became obvious after 1918, when the Russian Revolution introduced an entirely different set of issues. Social Democrats were by no means obliged to favor revolutionary violence in all circumstances: after all, they had in 1872 parted company with the Anarchists precisely on this issue, and in 1896 the London Congress of the International formally barred Anarchist participants. What Marxist orthodoxy in the age of the Second International implied was something quite different: the primary obligation of Socialists was to the class struggle. What they did about the parliamentary politics of their respective countries was a secondary matter. Their real business was to organize the working class and lead it forward in what was assumed to be a war of movement against bourgeois society.

It is in this sense, and in this sense only, that the victory of the Salle Petrelle meeting over that in the rue de Lancry in 1889 possessed historic significance (Drachkovitch, ed., 96). What happened on that occasion was that Socialists from a number of countries committed themselves to the Marxist ideas of internationalism and the class struggle. It is well to remember that at the Salle Petrelle the French had 221 delegates out of a total of some 400 and that the French contingent included Vaillant and his Blanquists with whose help Marx had in 1872 beaten off Bakunin's attack. The Guesdists were not yet as important as they were to become a decade later, when their version of Marxism gained mass support among the proletariat. In 1889 Paris was still a Blanquist stronghold for the same reason that it had repeatedly throughout the nineteenth century been the scene of revolutionary risings, culminating in the colossal disaster of the 1871 Commune: its working class had inherited the Jacobin tradition of armed insurrection. When Marxism took the place of Blanquism among the French, this antiquated outlook was solemnly abjured–if only because Jules Guesde and his associates found their strongest support among the miners and textile workers in the bleak new industrial areas of the Nord and Pas de Calais departments, who had not inherited Parisian memories or Blanquist illusions about armed violence. In this sense Marxism was an innovation. It signified that henceforth the class struggle was to be waged on the industrial front, and it was just this feature of the doctrine that made it acceptable to the Syndicalists. Nonetheless, the fact that the International had been founded in Paris–and on the centenary of the Great Revolution at that–lent a distinctly Jacobin tone to its first proclamations. The delegates who left the Salle Petrelle had implicitly sanctioned not merely the economic analysis of *Capital*, but also the political doctrine of the *Communist Manifesto*: society was split into warring classes, and the class struggle was fated to issue in a more or less violent political conflict. To the French, the Italians, the Spaniards, the Poles, and the Russians, this made obvious sense–whence their readiness to call themselves Marxists. To the Germans and the Austro-Hungarians it made sense too, on the understanding that the political struggle was to be waged peacefully and that the immediate aim was the attainment of democracy. To most of the British delegates, talk of class struggle sounded rather outlandish, unless they were en route to becoming Syndicalists. The same applies to the Americans. The men who founded the I.W.W. in Chicago in 1905 were ready to employ the vocabulary of Marxism, but they were in fact Anarchosyndicalists, which is why in the end they broke not only with the Socialist Party of Eugene Debs and Victor Berger, but also with the Socialist Labor Party of Daniel de Leon, whose rather rigid theorizing represented a peculiar fusion of doctrinaire Marxism and intransigent "laborism" (Bell, 32 ff., 66 ff.).

If, then, one inquires just what the Second International stood for during the quarter century of its existence, there is no clear answer. The British and French organizations which (under prodding from Engels) had laid the groundwork for the original meeting in 1889, were numerically weak, and most of the British were barely socialist, let alone Marxist. The Germans and Austrians, on the other hand, who increasingly represented the geographical and political center of gravity, were divided among themselves, and even the Marxists among them–that is to say, the followers of Engels, Kautsky, and Adler–were not disposed to sanction either Syndicalism or the Latin tradition of armed insurrection. As for the Russians, the Poles, and the other East Europeans (in so far as they were not integrated into the Austro-Hungarian contingent), their influence at first was small. They could always be relied upon to vote for radical resolutions, but few people expected them to shake the earth–at any rate until 1905, when the first Russian tremor made itself felt (Braunthal I, 298 ff.).

The repercussions of this upheaval on the internal situation in Germany have already been referred to in connection with the strike controversy, but it may be useful to take a closer look at some of the political implications. Wilhelminian Germany, from the constitutional viewpoint, was situated somewhere midway between Tsarist Russia and late Victorian or Edwardian Britain. It had a parliament, but the parliament had no real power–certainly less than the House of Commons, though even the latter down to 1914 could still be effectively blocked by the House of Lords. The empire Bismarck had put together in 1871 was governed by a "hegemonial" elite made up of two distinct strata: a military caste with roots in the landed gentry and a rapidly expanding big-business element with vague national-liberal traditions and growing imperialist appetites. The political center of gravity lay not in the Reichstag, but in Prussia, which did not possess a democratic franchise. Hence when the Russian revolution of 1905 placed the political "mass strike" on the agenda, the question was whether the radicals in the S.P.D. would commit the cautious party leadership to a struggle for democracy fought by industrial means. The issue had nothing whatever to do with socialism:

> The problem was essentially whether the German workers could destroy, by legal means, the supremacy of the Junkers which had

> been maintained over many centuries, making use of the strength of Prussia, her monarchs, armies, bureaucracy, law courts and *bourgeoisie*. The centre of Junker power lay in the methods by which Prussia was ruled, and particularly in the three-tier election system on which the entire regime in Germany rested. As long as the Junkers maintained this centre of privilege, there were strict limits to the development of German democracy and working-class power. (Braunthal I, 300)

The destruction of this peculiar political complex would have turned Germany into a (bourgeois) democracy, which was precisely what Engels, Liebknecht, Bebel, and Kautsky regarded as the proximate political goal.

It is thus all the more significant that when the issue presented itself in the clearest possible manner in 1905, the party leadership, under pressure from the radical wing, first toyed with the idea of a political general strike to secure a democratic franchise in Prussia, then drifted away from it, and finally buried it: and this although by 1913 the proposal was backed not only by authentic revolutionaries like Rosa Luxemburg and her friends, but by reformists who saw no other way of turning Prussia into a democracy. The reason for this surrender to passivity is simple enough: the trade-union leaders would have nothing to do with the idea of a political strike. By giving in to their obstruction, the party of Bebel and Kautsky surrendered its political birthright, and it did so long before the outbreak of war in 1914. "Revisionism" had nothing whatever to do with it. The unions had obtained control of the party, and the union bureaucracy was solidly committed to avoidance of political conflict.

This is the place to say a few words about the men who first built up, and then led to ruin and disaster, the greatest Socialist party in Europe. Wilhelm Liebknecht (1826-1900), a direct descendant of Martin Luther, came from a long line of Protestant clergymen, academics, and civil servants. A democrat since his student days and a participant in the 1848 uprising, he spent thirteen years in London as a member of the Marx circle, returned to Germany in 1862, quarrelled with Lassalle's followers in Berlin, and eventually established himself in Leipzig (Saxony), where he won the young labor organizer August Bebel (1840-1913) for the Social Democratic cause. Elected to the

North German parliament on a democratic platform, the two men abstained on the vote for war credits in 1870 (unlike the Lassalleans), went on opposing Bismarck's militarist and annexationist policies, were prosecuted for their resistance to a war of conquest against the French Republic, went to prison, and duly became heroes to their followers (Roth, 49 ff.). Their Socialism (so far as it existed) was of a variety that need not have alarmed anyone, and indeed the unified party they led from 1875 on was joined by numerous middle-class democrats who had despaired of the Liberal opposition. On the other hand, they were quite serious about democracy, and Liebknecht at least was never reconciled to the existence of Prussia or to the Bismarckian unification of Germany. Bebel, who succeeded him, was at once closer to the actual labor movement and more remote from the traditions of the First International, in which he had not taken an active part. Both men, for all their professions of Marxist orthodoxy, always remained within the ideological realm of democratic radicalism, as did their party as a whole (a few leftwingers excepted). The notion that German Social Democracy, at any stage of its career, represented a threat to bourgeois society is a fantasy which no competent historian has found it possible to take seriously (Schorske, *passim*; Roth, 212 ff.). The real issue was whether the S.P.D. could democratize Prussia-Germany before the ruling caste, with its pan-German nationalist following, plunged Europe into the great war whose coming Marx had predicted since 1871, when Bismarck annexed Alsace-Lorraine, thereby driving the French Republic into the arms of Tsarist Russia. On the outcome of this race between European war and German democratization everything depended, for only a democratic Germany could have restored Alsace-Lorraine to France and thus removed a basic cause of tension. The failure of the S.P.D. to gain effective power thus determined the fate of the Second International. When in 1914 the French and German labor movements not only failed to preserve the European peace, but voted for war credits and participated in the general orgy of nationalism, the International fell to pieces.

Anyone familiar with the world of European Socialism in general, and German Social Democracy in particular, could have predicted this outcome, and a great many people did. To do them justice, Engels' German followers had been proclaiming ever since 1891—when it first became obvious that Russia and France were about to conclude a military alliance against Germany—that they would, if necessary, fight in defense of their fatherland against "Russian barbarism." By implication this also meant that they would, if necessary, fight the French Republic, an attitude for which they could claim the authority of Engels. This did not entitle them to underwrite an imperialist war of conquest, but then most of them would have been sincerely shocked had such an aim been imputed to them in 1914. As they saw it, they were simply doing their patriotic duty. The same, needless to say, applies to the French and the Belgians, who had the excuse that in 1914 they were actually being invaded. As for the British, Hyndman, who was not merely a patriot but a convinced defender of the Empire, had for years prepared his followers for the likelihood of war with Germany (Tsuzuki, *Hyndman*, 198 ff.). The Fabians did not share his pro-French bias (a legacy from the Positivists, who since 1870 had consistently opposed the traditional Germanophil orientation of the British ruling class). Some of them might even have been termed pro-German, but they had by 1914 become the allies of the governing Liberal Party of Asquith, Haldane, Grey, and Lloyd George, whom they supplied with some notions about economic planning and managerialism generally. In the circumstances their ostensible neutrality on the issue of war amounted to a tacit admission that a military showdown with Germany was inevitable and perhaps even desirable in the interest of democracy. Even so, a few Fabians in 1914 took a neutralist line, while others condoned the German invasion of Belgium as a disagreeable necessity imposed upon the Germans by the wickedness of their Russian and French opponents (McBriar, 140).

Within a movement so constituted, Marxism functioned as an integrative ideology, not as a theory of action. It was invoked to explain why the labor movement had to lead a separate existence within bourgeois society. In the words of a later historian, "Marxism now served, above all else, to enable the proletariat to differentiate itself ideologically from the middle class. In other words—to secure for itself an independent class existence within capitalist society" (Rosenberg, *A History of Bolshevism*, 18 ff.). The paradoxical result was to establish a nominally socialist subculture within the official aristocratic-bourgeois civilization. Marxism thus equipped the workers' movement with an ideology that was both a defensive armature and a "false consciousness." The ideology immunized the workers to conservative or liberal ideas and to that extent articulated a kind of corporate political awareness. At the same time it enabled the movement to settle down within the existing system. In this respect German Socialism was not peculiar, for the same phenomenon could be observed in Britain, where Social Democracy was a mere sect. Its adherents constituted an elite of the working class, took pride in their understanding of economics, and for the rest relied upon what they termed the "laws of history" to usher in the new society. This passivity went with a pronounced class consciousness of a nonrevolutionary kind. "The tradition was not so much revolutionary as intransigent: militant, firmly based on the class struggle, but quite unable to envisage (as an Irishman like Connolly could) the problems of revolt or the taking of power, for which there was no precedent within living memory in Britain" (Hobsbawm, *Labouring Men*, 236). The German and Austrian movements were differently oriented, in that they had inherited the legacy of 1848. This did not make them revolutionary in any serious sense, but it did mean that they had to envisage circumstances in which they might have to exercise political power. Thus when in 1918 the German Empire and the Dual Monarchy collapsed under the strain of military defeat, their Social Democratic parties were able to step into the breach: the passive inheritors of a debacle, not the active promoters of revolution.

But we have run ahead of our main theme: the war of 1914, which wrecked the Second International, also destroyed something else—the precarious balance between "reformist" and "revolutionary" strands within the European labor movement. The tension was necessarily greatest in those areas where a democratic revolution had not yet occurred: Germany, Austria-Hungary, and Russia. One can also put it differently: reformism was strongest where liberal democracy was firmly established, while radicalism possessed a mass following where the labor movement was confronted with authoritarian regimes. On the other hand, the controversy about the "revision" of Marxist theory, over which so much ink was spilled after 1900, had only a marginal connection with the subsequent political line-up. When the crash came in 1914, orthodox Marxists like Plekhanov, Hyndman, and Guesde found themselves among the "patriots," while the arch-revisionist Eduard Bernstein, being a good liberal democrat, refused to support his party's pro-war stand, and Karl Liebknecht—a Kantian, not a Marxist, in philosophy—became a leader of the extreme Left.

Jean Jaurès–the most celebrated "opportunist" of them all–had gone on hoping against hope that peace might be preserved. No one will ever know what he might have said and done in August, 1914, for he was murdered by a nationalist fanatic on July 31, 1914, having just returned to Paris from the last fateful session of the International's Bureau at the Maison du Peuple in Brussels.

> All the main representatives of the European movement were there: Jaurès, Guesde, Longuet, Adler, Vandervelde, Kautsky, Haase, Rosa Luxemburg, Keir Hardie, Bruce Glasier, Axelrod, Morgari, Angelica Balabanov, Grimm, and many others. They spoke for millions. But they had little confidence in their ability to prevent the threatened war by direct mass action. Though Keir Hardie referred briefly to the possibility of a general strike, it played no other part in the conference discussions. (Braunthal I, 351)

The International had been powerless to avert war, but it could still summon up thousands for a peace demonstration. Vandervelde, Haase, Hardie, and Jaurès spoke from the platform on the theme of "war against war," and for Jaurès at least it was the last time.

Then the curtain fell, and, when it rose again, the old pre-1914 Europe lay in ruins, and the unity of the Socialist movement along with it. Those familiar with the spirit of its two principal national components had no excuse for surprise at this outcome, for the Germans had long made it clear that they would fight in defense of their country, while in France only a handful of anarchosyndicalists stood out against the Jacobin patriotism of Guesde and Jaurès alike. In the Europe of 1914, nationalism was still the most powerful of emotions. There is a case for saying that the Socialist leaders ought to have resisted the avalanche of madness then let loose, but it is as well to recognize that they could have done so only by severing themselves from their followers, at any rate temporarily. Being for the most part democrats and patriots, they were unfitted for such a role. It is absurd to speak of "treason." The failure was existential, not moral. And it was final. When democratic socialism rose from the ashes in 1919, it no longer laid claim to a world-transforming mission, having become reconciled to the claims of patriotism and the nation-state. Those who still believed in a revolutionary International of the proletariat had to turn elsewhere.

9 Social Democracy and Communism: 1918-68

1. War and Revolution

The 1914-18 war is one of the great watersheds in history, for it inaugurated both the decline of Europe as the world's power center and the disintegration of liberal democracy as the political form of Western civilization. While the full extent of this change became manifest only after the 1939-45 war, the earlier shock was in some respects more severe, since it terminated a lengthy period of relative peace, social stability, and faith in evolutionary progress. In relation to the labor movement one major casualty was the belief that the working class could restrain the European governments from going to war with each other. So far from this being the case, the torrent of hatred that engulfed all the belligerents had the effect of transforming most of the existing Socialist parties into pillars of their respective national societies. On the other hand, significant minorities of the intelligentsia and the working class were radicalized by the patriotic slaughter and became profoundly alienated from the liberal-democratic tradition. Before 1914 such sentiments had been confined to Anarchosyndicalists; after 1919, they found an embodiment in the Communist International founded in Moscow at the beginning of that year. The war did not (as is sometimes said) destroy the unity of the international workers' movement, for the pre-1914 Social Democratic orthodoxy already had to contend with the Syndicalist current. But it opened a new cleavage by identifying revolutionary socialism with the Bolshevik regime which in 1917-18 emerged from the turmoil of the Russian Revolution. At the same time, reformist Social Democracy grew stronger in numbers and influence, at any rate in Western and Central Europe. The war had made all governments conscious of the importance of securing the loyalty of organized labor; Socialist parties and trade unions had forced their way into the front rank; and their progress was speeded by the military defeat and political disintegration of the three Eastern empires, whose mutual hostility had provoked the outbreak of war in 1914. In so far as the 1919 settlement was a belated triumph of liberal democracy—represented at the Paris peace conference in the persons of Woodrow Wilson, David Lloyd George, and Georges Clemenceau—the labor movement in the West profited indirectly by having the democratic part of its program written into the constitutional fabric of the new international order crowned by the League of Nations.

From the Socialist standpoint, however, this outcome had been purchased at too high a price. Not only had the war been enormously destructive, it laid bare the political weakness of organized labor when confronted with the elemental force of nationalism. When on August 4, 1914, the strongest section of the International, the German Social Democratic Party, acting through its parliamentary representatives in the Reichstag of imperial Germany, voted unanimously for war credits, internationalism was shown up as a myth. The celebrated vote was in itself merely the outward expression of a state of mind which followed inexorably from the party's evolution during the preceding decade, but the shock was nonetheless very great. It was deeply felt not only by revolutionary East European Marxists such as Lenin, Trotsky, Martov, and Rosa Luxemburg, but also by moderate Socialists in Britain, the United States, France, Italy, Holland, and Belgium, who had counted on the S.P.D. to restrain German militarism or at least not to support it. For obvious reasons the resulting reaction was strongest in France and Belgium, but pacifist Socialists in neutral areas such as Holland, Switzerland, and Scandinavia likewise felt let down, to put it mildly. It is arguable that the French and Belgian Socialists were in no position to cast stones, since they too had lent their support to the cause of national unity by joining what in France was termed the "sacred union" in defense of the homeland. But they had the excuse of reacting to an armed invasion, however culpable their own governments had been in promoting the disaster. France, moreover, was a democratic Republic, whereas the German Empire was an anachronism even from a liberal standpoint. To this the German Social Democrats might (and did) reply that the French Republic had become the ally of Tsarist Russia, and that anyway every country had the right to defend its national existence. Ever since it had become obvious in 1907 that Germany would have to fight a war on two fronts, the S.P.D. had been formally committed to the slogan "In the hour of danger we shall not leave the Fatherland in the lurch" (Schorske, 285). However, the speed with which the bulk of the German labor movement realigned itself in support of the war effort disclosed a state of mind which had hitherto escaped close scrutiny. Neither the party nor the unions seriously contemplated any alternative which might have invited governmental repression. A wave of patriotic sentiment had engulfed the entire country, and the deeply rooted Russophobia of the German working class did the rest.

That Germany was nonetheless a rather special case became evident in the spring of 1917 when, in the midst of war, the pacifist and internationalist minority of the S.P.D. split off from the main body and established an organization of its own, the Independent Socialist Party (U.S.P.D.), with a platform that might be called radical-democratic: peace, no annexations, national self-determination, open diplomacy, general disarmament, and a return to old-style internationalism. This was in part a response to the February Revolution in Russia which had removed the Tsarist regime; in part it reflected the shock of America's entry into the war and the influence of Wilsonian liberalism. Most of the Independents–whose leadership included both Karl Kautsky and his old opponent Eduard Bernstein–were pacifist in sentiment. The party, as constituted at Easter, 1917, comprised both the old center-left and the ultra-left Spartacist group of Karl Liebknecht and Rosa Luxemburg, who maintained that the war could only be ended by a proletarian revolution. The pacifists outnumbered the Spartacists and were in turn outnumbered by the main body of the S.P.D., as the postwar elections in 1919 and 1920 were to show. Nonetheless the U.S.P.D. played a crucial role in promoting the great wave of strikes in 1917-18 which hastened the collapse of German military resistance and the fall of the monarchy in October-November, 1918. In the months that followed, the party narrowly missed its chance of pushing the democratic reorganization of Germany through to a conclusion. Had it triumphed, as under more resolute leadership it might have done, the country would still have been far from socialism, but the Republic would have evolved into a genuine democracy, the old army and bureaucracy would have been destroyed instead of being preserved, and the Prussian landowners would have been dispossessed. In short, Germany would at last have undergone a genuine bourgeois-democratic revolution. This never happened, and the history of the Weimar Republic is largely the record of a steady slide toward nationalism, militarism, and authoritarianism, culminating in 1933 in the alliance between the conservative forces, symbolized by Hindenburg and the Reichswehr, and a plebeian movement assembled under the demagogic banner of National Socialism.

Since we cannot deal with political history in detail, it must be sufficient to note these consequences of the 1914-18 upheaval. The crucial period opened in 1917 when Russia passed through revolution, leading in November of that year to the establishment of the Bolshevik regime—thinly disguised as the rule of "soviets" (workers' and peasants' councils), which in theory were supposed to exercise authority but in fact were controlled by Lenin's party, which, after March, 1918, shed the appellation "Social Democratic" and styled itself Communist. We shall have to glance briefly at this phenomenon, but before doing so it may be useful to introduce a few observations on the topic of political democracy and its relation to the labor movement.

It has already been shown that the Social Democratic tradition was rooted in a frame of mind derived from the 1848 Revolution. Even after 1864, when modern socialism came into being, it was assumed by Marx and his followers that Continental Europe (Britain was viewed as a special case) would have to undergo a political upheaval. The assumption was made not—as his critics kept repeating—because Marx had remained the man of 1848 and the *Manifesto*, but because democracy was still a revolutionary cause in Central and Eastern Europe, as well as in Italy and Spain. Democracy could either be liberal (based on peasants and the lower middle class) or socialist (based on the workers). The Social Democrats in principle aimed at a workers' democracy: at any rate those among them who had acquired the habit of calling themselves Marxists. In practice most of them were quite happy with the prospect of liberal democracy, if only they could get it—peacefully or otherwise. Given a steady advance of industrialization, they felt confident that the electorate would eventually vote them into office. Where parliamentary democracy already existed or was being introduced gradually and peacefully—e.g., in Britain, Holland, Scandinavia, and Switzerland—it was possible to base this kind of strategy on straightforward and quite sensible political calculations. In these areas the half century from 1914 to 1964 did in fact witness a gradual transition from liberal to social democratic predominance in politics and from economic *laissez-faire* to the mixed economy and the welfare state. The two world wars simply hastened the process. There was no violent break in continuity. The adoption of a Fabian platform by the British Labour Party in 1918 did not occur because the unions had been won over to the cause of revolution: all it signified was that, the liberal radical tradition being finally exhausted, reformist socialism had arisen to fill the vacuum.

The picture was different in Southern Europe, where industry was as yet undeveloped and the urban working class did not constitute a majority but where it could be argued that labor might win over the poorer strata of the peasantry. The same argument was applicable to East European countries such as Poland, Rumania, and other economically backward states established or enlarged after 1918. These areas, for obvious geographical reasons, experienced the full blast of the Russian Revolution and were thus especially prone to political extremism of the Communist or Fascist variety, the more so since—with the important exception of Czechoslovakia—they possessed neither a democratic tradition nor a significant middle class. Lastly there was Germany: a country of 60-70 million people in the heart of Europe, highly industrialized, and still a contender for European hegemony. The monarchy had fallen in November, 1918, and the Republic was a hopeless failure from the start. For all these reasons, Germany after 1918 became a political storm center. It was the principal arena in which the conflict between East and West was fought out, hence also the scene of the sharpest contest between Social Democracy and Communism. And because German Social Democracy had once nominally, and to some extent actually, been the party of Marx and Engels, its internal strains and stresses translated themselves into rival interpretations of their doctrines.

On its political side this heritage was as ambiguous as the German situation itself. Germany before 1914 was neither a liberal democracy nor a conservative autocracy. Neither was it a ramshackle multinational empire like Austria-Hungary, which for decades had been nearing the point of collapse, the government in Vienna having failed to keep the mutinous nationalities under control. Unlike Russia and Austria-Hungary, imperial Germany was both a modern industrial country and a nation-state. Unlike France, Britain, and the United States, it was not governed on liberal democratic lines, although it did have a semblance of constitutional rule. This political structure was bound to collapse under the stress of a major military defeat: a circumstance foreseen by Engels who steadfastly maintained that German Social Democracy was the predestined heir of the imperial regime. It was plain to him that the monarchy could neither reform itself nor cope with the exigencies of the great European war whose advent he predicted in the 1890's: war would come and would bring revolution in its train. All this accounts in part for the curious mixture of fatalism and self-confidence with which German Socialists during those years contemplated the future. Since the more intelligent among them felt certain that the Wilhelminian regime was steering the country straight to catastrophe, they could assume the role of an intransigent opposition, while at the same time reserving the right to defend the national soil if called upon to do so. In this perspective there was no conflict between democracy and patriotism. In consequence those German Social Democrats who in 1914-18 supported the war effort preserved a perfectly good conscience and never understood what their radical left-wing opponents or their foreign critics were talking about. For the rest, the Russian Revolution and, especially, the terrorist character of the Bolshevik regime confirmed them in their deeply ingrained conviction that democracy–by which they meant parliamentary government–was the only sensible form of rule for a civilized country.

There was, however, a problem which, in common with most other democrats of the age, they had not seriously considered. While constantly engaged in debating the prospects of (peaceful or violent) political change in pre-1914 Germany, they systematically shied away from considering the issues involved in the actual exercise of power at the national level. It was somehow taken for granted even by the more radical among them that the growing numerical strength of the industrial working class would result in a redistribution of political power such that the transition to some form of socialist democracy would occur by a kind of automatism. A theorist like Karl Kautsky, who was quite convinced that Germany and Austria would have to pass through a democratic revolution in order to get rid of the remnants of monarchical absolutism, saw no problem once the principle of majority rule had been secured. In rejecting the Leninist model (for Russia as well as for Germany, be it noted), he committed himself to the "orthodox" interpretation of Marxism worked out between 1890 and 1914 by Engels, Plekhanov, and himself, plus his "Austro-Marxist" pupils: socialism was to be attained by way of democracy. Socialist democracy in this sense presupposed a high degree of industrial development and the maintenance of all the traditional liberties inherited from the past. The fact that earlier revolutions had gone through a dictatorial phase was explained away. The coming takeover was going to have the industrial working class behind it and would therefore be different. By the time the working class formed a majority of the electorate, the economy (for reasons explained by Marx in *Capital*) would be ripe for socialization. In brief, the strategy of the political struggle was deduced from sociological considerations. Germany being the most highly industrialized country in Continental Europe, it followed from this reasoning that it stood the best chance of witnessing a peaceful changeover to democratic socialism, once the imperial regime, with its autocratic military armature, had been got rid of–peacefully or otherwise.

In the light of what actually occurred during the half century following World War I, it is evident that this reasoning was faulty. Germany and Austria-Hungary did indeed in 1918-19 pass through a democratic revolution, and to that extent the pre-1914 Marxist prospectus turned out to be realistic. But the Russian development was unforeseen, and in Central Europe the attainment of republican democracy in 1918 did not usher in the promised peaceful transition to socialism. Instead it inaugurated a political upheaval leading straight to the advent of fascism, the collapse of the labor movement, and a second round in the pan-German attempt to attain European hegemony. When this had been beaten off in 1945–at a cost of some 40 million dead and the virtual destruction of European civilization–the Continent had been partitioned along an East-West axis, with the Soviet Union transformed from a revolutionary volcano into an expansionist military power in permanent conflict with the Western world. In short, the Social Democratic model turned out to be applicable only to those areas of Europe where liberal democracy was firmly entrenched; in these regions Social Democracy became politically effective to the extent that it provided the ideology for a labor movement profoundly integrated into a new type of industrial society. This society, if not exactly bourgeois any longer, was still predominantly capitalist. Thus democracy appeared to function only in so far as it was not socialist, while socialism (on the Russian model) had been established in regions of Europe that were not democratic. Something had gone wrong with the orthodox prospectus worked out before 1914-18. What was it?

In the first place it seems plain that all concerned had underrated the catastrophic effect of modern war on European society and its political institutions. The 1914-18 war did not merely destroy the three Eastern empires (four if one includes Ottoman Turkey, which, however, did not form part of Europe), it shattered the established framework of private and public life and prepared the way for the totalitarian movements of the 1920's and 1930's. The traditional acceptance of constitutional rule was discredited in the eyes of a middle class ruined by war and inflation; armed violence was introduced into domestic politics; and the notion of class conflict—hitherto employed mainly for sociological purposes—was given a new and sinister meaning: it came to be regarded as a convenient shorthand for the expropriation, even the physical liquidation, of social strata that stood in the way of a total reorganization of society.

This kind of thinking was quite unprecedented and could not be accommodated within the traditional categories inherited from the democratic revolution, including those that underlay the notion of "proletarian dictatorship." Such a dictatorship had been envisaged, by Marx and the more radical among his followers, as a brief emergency operation to prepare the ground for the rapid introduction of genuine democracy. The totalitarian state-party, with its capacity for remolding society by a controlled "revolution from above," was something quite new. It had originally come into being as a result of the manner in which Bolshevism evolved under Lenin's leadership in a Russia torn and wrecked by civil war, and it was then copied by the various Fascist movements. In its Stalinist form it later became the instrument of forced-draft industrialization, with workers and peasants subjected by a privileged bureaucracy to all the horrors of the "primitive accumulation" Marx had described in *Capital*. None of this had been foreseen, least of all by Lenin's followers who in 1917 committed themselves to the notion that by proclaiming a proletarian revolution in Russia they would hasten its advent in Germany. When this did not occur they were thrown back on their own resources, and in due course the Russian Communist Party was launched upon the task of industrializing an enormous country at breakneck speed and without democratic restraints or popular consultation. Socialism in Russia thus became a substitute for capitalism, and eventually an excuse for restoring the sort of police despotism familiar to Russians from centures of Tsarist rule. The whole phenomenon, while explicable in terms of Russia's political heritage, was quite incompatible with the aims and beliefs of the labor movement, and the worship of state ownership to which it gave rise had only the remotest connection with the Marxist tradition, to which Communists were obliged to appeal as a matter of self-justification. The Bolsheviks perhaps had no option, short of surrendering power altogether, but the Stalinist "collectivization" of the peasantry in the 1930's–and its sequel, the great terror of 1934-38–finally wrecked Lenin's party and replaced it by something quite different: an organization of the ruling bureaucracy, held together by fear of the dictator and the secret police. Even when the worst features of the system were dismantled, the country remained subject to the uncontrolled rule of a political apparatus that had fused with the state bureaucracy. This peculiar system was then exported abroad and eventually became the model for the satellite regimes established under the military protectorate of the Soviet Union.

While this gigantic transformation was under way in Russia and subsequently in those parts of Eastern Europe that were taken over by the Soviet Union and in effect incorporated in the Soviet empire, the democratic labor movement in Western Europe and North America traveled in the opposite direction: toward integration within the established society and a marked antagonism to the Russian model and everything connected with it. In between these two great poles of attraction, Central European Social Democracy for some decades tried to adhere to the tradition established before 1914, but finally had to confess defeat. There appeared to be no way of bringing about that alliance of workers, peasants, and the lower middle class which was needed to give a socialist movement the mass basis for a genuine transformation of society. Social Democratic governments in Germany and Austria after 1918 found themselves reduced to the role of political caretakers, and by 1939 they had been swept off the field. Not only had there been no advance toward socialism: democracy itself had been destroyed by reactionary mass movements inflamed by nationalist and racist passions. The Social Democratic parties proved unable to stem this tide, and their defeat became the curtain-raiser for World War II, which in turn led to the partition of Germany and the subordination of the various European states and nations to the control of the Soviet Union and the United States.

While these familiar facts need only the briefest recapitulation, something must be said about their significance for the theory and practice of socialism. The Central European catastrophe in particular holds important lessons for anyone who reflects upon the circumstance that Germany's labor movement had been founded in the wake of an aborted democratic revolution.

Social Democratic theorizing, as it developed in Germany and Austria between 1848 and 1918, was realistic in as much as it centered upon the need to democratize the authoritarian structures that had been left intact after 1848. It was inadequate in that it deduced political conclusions from what its theorists took to be the Marxian doctrine of class conflict. This doctrine incorporated a highly original analysis applicable to long-run changes in the economic and social foundations of the political order. It thus provided an important tool for historians and sociologists concerned with the evolution of society since the sixteenth century, but it was useless as a guide to short-term political action. The analysis of bourgeois society to which the bulk of Marx's work had been devoted issued in the recognition that this society was bound to undergo a transformation in the direction of socialism. It would do so for reasons inherent in the automatism of the economic order, and the latter's evolution in due course would bring about a corresponding transformation of the political and cultural "superstructure." Marx had intended all this as a theory of long-run changes in the social order. The prevalent Social Democratic interpretation of his work had the effect of treating politics as a mere appendage of economics. It assumed that the labor movement, by virtue of its position within society, would gradually take over the sphere of political decision-making, that is to say the state. When this failed to occur, the conclusion was drawn that the electorate needed additional information concerning the superiority of socialism over capitalism. In reality the question was whether the labor movement was fit to govern. The reply is that it was not. Social Democracy's inability to defend constitutional freedom against Fascism and to maintain full employment during the world economic crisis of the 1930's discredited it as well as the liberal parties and forces with whom the labor movement normally cooperated. Socialist doctrine habitually confused economics with politics, sociological analysis with political action, propaganda for a new social order with the government of the state.

> This confusion was shown most clearly at the last party congress of German Social Democracy before 1933, the Party Congress at Leipzig in 1931, when the question "capitalism or socialism" was discussed, in a situation in which the very existence of democracy was at stake. There was, in the period from 1918 to 1933, an abysmal gulf between the social-reformist achievements and the political weakness of the labor movement. (Neumann, 263)

The triumph of German National Socialism in 1933 was rendered possible by the concurrent failure of Social Democracy. The record of the German Communist Party (K.P.D.) does not enter into consideration, because that party—whatever else may be thought of it—did not in 1933 possess the means of seizing political power. It represented only a minority of the working class (mostly the unemployed), had no significant following in the countryside, and could count on no sympathy within the professions, the universities, or the state apparatus. There never was a choice between National Socialism and Communism before 1933, just as there had been none in Italy when Mussolini's Fascists seized power in 1922. The only real question was whether or not democracy would survive. If it did not, the Communist movement would be smashed along with its Social Democratic rival. The fact that the German Communists did not realize this (any more than the Italian Communists had a decade earlier) is of no theoretical significance, although it tells one something about their mental make-up. The relevant point is that Fascism triumphed in both cases because democracy was discredited, and it was discredited because Social Democracy after 1918 had not made use of its opportunities. "Social Democratic politics of 1918 corresponds to the politics of Louis Blanc" (Neumann, 262).

Reformist labor legislation was substituted for a thorough transformation of the state. Communism and Fascism were both oriented toward the capture of political power. Social Democracy was not. In consequence it lost the battle in the decisive areas of Europe. If it survived elsewhere (notably in Britain and Scandinavia), it did so because the crisis of society was less acute in these regions and the traditional conservative-liberal ruling elites remained in control or left the government to the Social Democrats, as in Sweden, where they were lucky enough to preside over an expanding economy. Even so, the debacle of the British Labour government in 1931 was on such a scale that it took World War II, and Labour's participation in the Churchill government of national defense, to re-establish the party's credentials with the electorate.

These brief remarks are intended to establish a perspective against which to assess the record of Social Democracy and Communism in Europe after 1914 or, if one prefers it, after 1917. It is no great matter whether one takes 1914 or 1918 as the starting point, but for convenience one may treat the half century from 1914 to 1964 as a transitional age during which the democratic labor movement in Western Europe effected its entry upon the political scene, culminating in the peaceful establishment of Labor governments and mixed economies in Britain, Scandinavia, and a few fringe areas. If one prefers to reckon forward from the Russian Revolution, one may say that the period from 1917 to 1967 witnessed the transformation of Russian Communism from a revolutionary movement into the conservative "establishment" of an industrial and military super-power, with control firmly lodged in a political machine representing a new privileged stratum. These tremendous changes were mediated by the two world wars, which altered not only the political map but also the basic character of European society beyond all recognition. Wars and revolutions being the "locomotives of history," their interaction during this half century had the effect of a gigantic speed-up, so that political and intellectual trends only dimly visible before 1914-18 assumed quite new dimensions. In what follows we shall consider the impact of the Russian Revolution and its offspring, the Communist movement, before reverting to the consideration of topics more closely related to the theory and practice of democratic socialism.

2. Leninism and the Third International

"The crisis of Socialism was engendered by the collapse of an illusion—the illusion that the International could prevent the outbreak of a European war" (Braunthal II, 4). The crisis of Communism, one might say, was engendered by the collapse of faith in the world revolutionary mission of the European proletariat. When in August, 1939, the Soviet government concluded an alliance, imperfectly disguised as a nonaggression pact, with the Third Reich, Communists the world over suffered a shock comparable in depth with the effect produced a quarter century earlier by the capitulation of the German Social Democrats. Internationalism had been sacrificed on the altar of *Realpolitik*, for the only defense offered by the Stalinist regime and its apologists in 1939 was that the interests of the Soviet Union took precedence over all other considerations. For practical purposes the Third International, founded in Moscow in 1919, died there twenty years later, even though the official death certificate was published only in 1943 (by which time the Soviet Union had been invaded by the Germans, and the Soviet government had come to rely for its survival on traditional Russian patriotism). The effective life of the Third International thus covered a span of twenty years—the interval of so-called peace in Europe, better described as an armistice between the first and second European wars. It had been founded on the morrow of the 1914-18 war in the firm expectation that the Russian Revolution would touch off a general European upheaval. When the latter failed to materialize, the Third International was doomed, although Communism was not. The movement continued to survive and to receive both formal and informal directives from Moscow, but there was no longer an authentic International alongside the Russian Communist Party: merely a loose congeries of satellite organizations whose leaders were occasionally assembled in Moscow to have their separate activities properly coordinated.

Considered in this perspective, the half century after the founding of the Second International in 1889 neatly divides into two periods of equal length separated by the outbreak of war in 1914, when Social Democracy collapsed. Or did it? After all, its national components continued to exist, and some of them even grew stronger. Perhaps one ought to say that what ended in August, 1914, was a particular kind of faith in internationalism. A corresponding phenomenon occurred in August, 1939, this time on a larger scale and with different results, for the Third International centered upon a state (the Soviet Union) and an organization (the Russian Communist Party) which were supposed to embody the Leninist version of Marxism. Again, just as the various Socialist parties had picked themselves up after 1914, dusted themselves off, and gone on as though nothing had happened, so the Communist parties after 1939 tried to make themselves and others believe that nothing fundamental had changed. In reality they knew quite well by then that their existence depended on the survival of the Soviet Union and that the further spread of Stalinism was a function of armed Russian expansion into Eastern Europe. This was something quite different from the Leninist faith in 1919 that the European working class (above all, the German working class) would follow the Russian example, seize power, and establish some form of socialism. By 1939 it was plain that the Russian Revolution could be exported only in the wake of military conquest, much as the legacy of the French Revolution had been spread abroad by the armies of Napoleon. This simple truth was never publicly proclaimed, but it underlay the long-term strategy of the Stalinist regime and its satellite parties, while the Trotskyist sect, self-styled the Fourth International, went on repeating the Leninist slogans of 1919.

The time scale proper to this topic does not conform to the conventional account, which begins with the Russian Revolution in 1917 and for convenience employs 1967 as the terminal date. There is no harm in adopting either perspective, as long as one keeps in mind the distinction between Bolshevism as a Russian phenomenon and Communism as a world movement. The two were after all not altogether identical. The Leninist faction of the old prewar Russian Social Democratic movement (since 1903 informally known as the Bolshevik group) seized power in Petrograd late in 1917 and established what was officially styled the Soviet regime. In due course it became the core of the Third, or Communist, International formally proclaimed on March 2, 1919, when the foundation meeting assembled in the Kremlin under Lenin's chairmanship (Braunthal, II, 162). Without the Russian Revolution—to be exact, without the Bolshevik seizure of power in November, 1917, eight months after the fall of Tsarism and the proclamation of a democratic Republic—there would have been no communist movement. At most there might have been—there doubtless would have been—a split within the old Socialist movement which had disintegrated in 1914. There would then have come into existence, alongside the Social Democratic majority organizations led by the British Labour Party and the German S.P.D., a rival formation of all those left-wing opposition groups which in 1914 had refused to sanction the patriotic line officialized by the dominant wing. But an International of *this* kind, although Marxist, would not have been Communist in the Russian sense. The proof is that when these left-wing Socialists did actually come together in the Vienna Conference of February, 1921, all they managed to achieve was the establishment of an informal working union whose proclaimed purpose was to try "to organize the International of the future" (Braunthal II, 233). The participants, mostly pacifists and left-wingers who had resisted the official line in 1914-18, included representatives of the exiled Mensheviks. They were all denounced in the most violent language by Lenin, and although for a time they had a considerable following in Western Europe, they never succeeded in dislodging either the Communists or the reformist Social Democrats. After a brief interval the whole enterprise was abandoned and the old International reconstituted (at Hamburg, in May, 1923) as a union of all Socialist parties not affiliated to the Communist International (Braunthal II, 264).

If for a moment we ignore the fortunes of the Western labor movement and fix our attention upon the origins of the Third International, we are confronted with the significance of the Russian Revolution and Leninism—a theme that relates back to our earlier chapter on the rise of Russian socialism between 1840 and 1880. It has been shown that this movement arose in response to problems peculiar to Tsarist Russia: notably the agrarian question, the dispute over the future of the village commune, and the role of the radical intelligentsia in a country where there was as yet no significant workers' movement. Some of these features had parallels in Italy and Spain, also in Rumania, Yugoslavia, Poland, Hungary, and Bulgaria. In the main, though, the Russian development was unique, and Bolshevism remained a distinctly national phenomenon. This was recognized by Polish Marxists such as Rosa Luxemburg and her associates, who on some occasions before 1914 cooperated with Lenin. There was no common denominator, for the simple reason that Lenin had revived the central core of the Populist inheritance, in the "Jacobin" interpretation given to it by Tkachev. Although a Marxist—in his own estimation the most orthodox of Marxists—he was from the start temperamentally out of tune with the political strategy developed between 1880 and 1900 by Plekhanov. His organizational model, systematically worked out from 1902 onward, was centralist and dictatorial: not merely for the usual conspiratorial reasons (which anyhow ceased to be operative after 1905, when Russia obtained a parliamentary constitution, with legal political parties and a free press) but because Lenin held that a revolutionary seizure of power could not be effected by a purely sectional labor movement or by a spontaneous rising of the 1848 type. There had to be effective centralized leadership by a political elite sealed off from the mass movement: an organization of "professional revolutionaries," as they came to be called. This was quite in accordance with the ancient doctrines of the Russian "Jacobins." In some respects, indeed, Lenin's guiding principles went back to Chernyshevsky. They were not, however, in accordance with Social Democratic teaching, and Lenin at no time of his career was what might be termed an orthodox Social Democrat (Haimson, 92 ff.).

Vladimir Ilyich Ulyanov (1870-1924), better known as Lenin, was the heir of Chernyshevsky, Dobrolyubov, and all those intelligentsia radicals of the 1860's who, in a phrase occasionally employed by their spiritual descendants, were determined to "swim against the stream of history." Chernyshevsky's novel *Chto Delat?* (*What Is To Be Done?*) was already Lenin's bible before he came across Marx, and it remained the single most important factor in determining his intellectual and moral values (Valentinov, 63-68). It is a commonplace that the event which launched the young Ulyanov on his revolutionary career was the execution of his elder brother for conspiring against the life of the Tsar. Alexander Ulyanov went to the scaffold on May 8, 1887, following the discovery of an amateurish terrorist plot, and it took Vladimir thirty years to avenge him. These biographical details enter into our theme only in so far as they help one to grasp the logic that led from Lenin's impassioned study of Chernyshevsky in 1887 to the publication in 1902 of his own *Chto Delat?*—the work in which he set out his political and organizational creed. The doctrine advanced in this seminal piece of writing was superficially patterned on the existing Social Democratic model but diverged from it at the decisive point: the political party was to be rigorously independent of the "spontaneous" workers' movement, condemned as it was by its nature (according to Lenin) to the perpetuation of a merely corporatist or trade-unionist form of class consciousness. Socialism transcended the narrow class horizon of the labor movement; hence the historic aims of the proletariat could not be entrusted to leaders who contented themselves with expressing the sectional economic aims of the working class. For practical purposes this meant that the party had to be made up of "professionals" drawn from the intelligentsia. Needless to say, this was never stated in so many words. It is not even certain that Lenin realized what he was doing when around 1903-4 he constructed an organization whose ideological purity was guaranteed by the circumstance that its self-appointed leaders were *not* controlled by a membership which in any case was largely made up of students and *déclassé* members of the landed gentry. Be that as it may, Bolshevism came into being on the eve of the 1905 upheaval as a political grouping which was nominally Social Democratic and in actual fact Blanquist or Jacobinical. Its luckless opponents, the Mensheviks, took some time to grasp what Lenin was up to, and when they finally realized that he was not a Social Democrat at all, it was too late (Haimson, 183 ff.).

Bolshevism and Menshevism parted company at the Second Congress of the (illegal and conspiratorial) Russian Social Democratic movement, held abroad in July-August, 1903. "In the curious setting of a London socialist church" (Haimson, 174), having been expelled from Brussels by the Belgian authorities in response to protests from the Tsarist government, the conferees resumed their sessions on August 11 and in due course split over Lenin's draft proposals concerning the rules of party membership. The Menshevik standpoint was adequately formulated by Julius Martov (Iulii Osipovich Tsederbaum, 1873-1923) when he declared, "In our eyes, the labor party is not limited to an organization of professional revolutionaries. It consists of them, plus the entire combination of the active leading elements of the proletariat" (*Ibid.*, 176). Lenin would have none of this, and the schism followed, with Trotsky joining Martov, while Plekhanov sided with Lenin. Thereafter the Menshevik group (the term literally signifies "minority") was led by Martov, Axelrod, and Trotsky, all three of them Jews, as were most of their articulate adherents. With the exception of a Georgian group in the Caucasus which formed itself somewhat later, Menshevism thereafter came to represent a current within the Jewish intelligentsia, plus a "labor aristocracy" of the better educated and unionized skilled working men in Russia's two capital cities, who favored a democratic organization on the European pattern and in general tended toward the Social Democratic model.

It is somehow typical of the suicidal spirit which from the start presided over this ill-starred faction that its leaders permitted their Bolshevik opponents to fasten the damaging term "minorityites" upon them. In 1904 they secured the reluctant adherence of Plekhanov, but even this did not save them. Plekhanov quite correctly pointed out that Lenin's political and organizational doctrine was in flat contradiction to everything Marx and Engels had said on the subject (Haimson, 193). This was true enough, but not wholly relevant: after all, the real question was whether the German model was suitable for Russia. Moreover, Plekhanov fell into the then customary error of interpreting Marx's historical materialism to signify that economic necessity would somehow by an automatic process carry the working class to power. We have already seen that this fatalistic creed became the ruin of German Social Democracy. Lenin did not hesitate to reject it, but he had some trouble with the formulation of his own standpoint. It was one thing to say that the revolutionary intelligentsia had hitherto spread radical ideas among the people: neither Plekhanov nor anyone else denied it. It was quite another matter to affirm as a point of principle that the labor movement would *never* rise to a level of political maturity such that it could dispense with a "vanguard" of "professional revolutionaries." Yet this was precisely what Lenin asserted, although he did not always express himself with complete clarity on the subject. His terminological obscurities enabled him and his group to go on operating within the broader Russian and international Social Democratic movement, while his opponents vainly tried to persuade the leaders of the Second International that the Bolsheviks were not really democratic socialists at all. Moreover, from time to time the two factions cooperated and indeed held joint congresses. In consequence, when the split was made irrevocable in 1912-14, it left Lenin's group in the stronger position. "The Russian 'Gironde,' led by Martov, missed its opportunity to crush the Russian 'Montagne' and its Robespierre. From that point the initiative passed into the hands of Lenin" (Getzler, 132).

A personal factor entered into the matter: Lenin and Martov had in 1895 jointly organized an illegal Marxist organization in Petersburg; they had both been deported to Siberia thereafter; and in 1900-1901, once safely abroad, they joined Plekhanov and others in founding the periodical *Iskra* as an organ of revolutionary socialism. From 1900 to 1903 Martov, like Lenin, devoted considerable energy to the struggle against the consistent reformists in the Russian socialist movement, whose platform could accurately be described as "trade-unionist," in that it did not center on the political overthrow of the autocracy. In the process, Martov committed himself to attitudes not easily distinguishable from Lenin's, in that he too insisted on the absolute paramountcy of politics. Hence the split of 1903 placed him in the awkward position of having affirmed the need for political revolution, while refusing to accept Lenin's leadership, his organizational model, and his consistent advocacy of armed violence. Martov would have nothing to do with "revisionists" and "reformists," whereas he repeatedly showed himself ready to cooperate with the Bolsheviks and to envisage a formal reunion with them. In consequence, the final split in 1912, when Lenin proclaimed his own group "the party" and broke off relations with Menshevik left-wingers who had previously worked with him, found Martov in no position to offer serious resistance.

Bolshevism possessed a strategic advantage that its rivals could not match: its very primitivism appealed to the masses of the newly formed Russian factory proletariat, whereas the Mensheviks could make an impact only on a thin stratum of Europeanized workers. It is noteworthy that by 1913 the Bolsheviks had won control of the Metal Workers Union in Petersburg, so that even before the outbreak of war in 1914 the Mensheviks had in fact lost the fight. Martov at that time still drew some comfort from the discovery that in Bolshevik strongholds such as Moscow and the Urals their intellectual leadership was weak and that many leading Bolsheviks (Bogdanov, Lunacharsky, Pokrovsky, and others) had for various reasons parted company with Lenin. He could not well foresee that after 1917 most of them would return to the fold or that Trotsky, his principal ally in these factional quarrels from 1904 to 1914, would go over to the Bolsheviks in the summer of 1917, just in time to be put in charge of the October uprising (the date relates to the old calendar). As Martov saw the situation on the eve of war's outbreak in 1914, all that had then remained of the Bolshevik leadership was

> . . . a handful of people literally without names, or with names that had an unsavoury ring, a group which belonged rather to the intellec-

> tual *Lumpenproletariat* than to the intelligentsia. Having taken the baton into their hands, they turned corporals, carrying the name of one intellectual—Lenin—as their ideological banner. If by taking the baton they could turn corporal, this means that in the Bolshevik section of the proletariat there was a demand for such a baton and for such corporals. (Getzler, 137)

Most of the Russian proletariat, "romantic, primitive and rebellious," yearned for revolution and eventually got it. These masses of people, only recently uprooted from their villages and still at a primitive level of consciousness, hungered and thirsted for the sort of leadership the Bolsheviks offered. Had the Europeanization of Russia continued for a few more decades, this stage would have passed and a Social Democratic form of Marxism might have gained the mass following it lacked in 1917. But it was not to be. The Tsarist autocracy, by plunging into war in 1914, committed suicide and dragged the country with it. When Lenin arrived at the Finland station in April, 1917, he was able to arouse mass emotions of the sort Bakunin had once vainly hoped for: not only the desire for an immediate end to the war, but a raging determination to smash the existing state and society, plant the red flag on the Winter Palace, and proclaim the dictatorship of workers and peasants. Still, it all depended on one man being present at the right moment. Without Lenin there would have been no October Revolution; as to that the historians have left us in no doubt. For even the oldest and stoutest Bolsheviks in 1917 were not prepared for the sort of platform Lenin brought back from his long European exile. The Tsarist regime had fallen, and most of them were ready to work within the framework of a democratic republic, elections and all, while awaiting their opportunity. It was Lenin who determined upon the immediate seizure of power, and he did so at least in part because he gambled on the coming revolution in Germany. Hence in 1917 he did what in 1905 he had declared to be impossible: he came out for the full "maximum" program.

The events of 1917 have been described countless times and cannot be recapitulated here. From our chosen angle what matters is the brief period between the fall of the Tsarist regime in March and the Bolshevik seizure of power in November (October according to the ancient pre-revolutionary calendar). During this interval it looked for a moment as though European Social Democracy might be able to assert itself as a peace-making force. The chosen venue was Stockholm, where a conference was to take place representing all member parties of the Socialist International (including those officially "at war" with one another) for the purpose of putting pressure on the belligerents to make peace. For a brief while, Stockholm became the symbol of the longing for peace felt by the workers in the principal European countries. A leading German Social Democrat wrote years later: "The thought of Stockholm hovered over the trenches like some new star of Bethlehem. . . . For three months the thoughts of all the millions in the armies were concentrated on the discussions of the labour representatives." The conference had been proposed by the "neutrals" but was eventually backed by the British Labour Party, the French and Italian Socialist parties, and numerous other labor organizations throughout the world. It was vetoed by the Allied governments. It was also regarded with disfavor by Lenin, who did not want the war to end by a compromise peace, but through revolution. What followed is best described by the historian of the Socialist International:

> Lenin was the architect of the October Revolution; Trotsky was its brilliant chief of staff. Their accomplices were the statesmen of the imperialist Western powers. By frustrating the convening of the Stockholm Conference they had played straight into Lenin's hands. For he had also wanted to frustrate it. . . . The breakdown of the Stockholm Conference also created the most favorable psychological climate for Lenin's *coup d'état.* To the masses Stockholm had symbolized their hopes for an end to the war. . . . The Bolshevik conquest of the Moscow and St. Petersburg Soviets in the election of September 1917 enabled Lenin to overcome the desperate resistance within his own party against the idea of an armed rising. And it was only the control over the St. Petersburg Soviet which gave Trotsky the military instrument necessary to carry through the *coup d'état.* (Braunthal II, 91-92)

In Communist parlance, the soviets became a substitute for elected parliaments and the instrument of proletarian dictatorship. In actual fact they were from the start controlled and manipulated by whatever political party gained the upper hand within them. They had been thrown up by the revolutionary wave, spontaneous creations of a mass movement which chose this organizational form. But they never held political power, and the notion of a "soviet government," in the sense of a direct representation of the workers and peasants, was a myth.

The subsequent fortunes of Communism as an international movement were basically determined by the fact that the German working class was not revolutionary in temper, nor was there a revolutionary "vanguard" in the Bolshevik sense, that is to say an organization capable of seizing political control even in the absence of immediate mass support. The Third International thus got under way with a perspective that turned out to be wholly mistaken. By the time the delegates assembled in Moscow, the Spartacist rising in Berlin had been crushed, the handful of German Communists had been driven underground, and the leaders of the newly founded party–above all Karl Liebknecht and Rosa Luxemburg–had been murdered. This disaster was not the temporary setback it appeared to be at the time. It signified that there was not in Germany a "revolutionary situation" at all. There never would be, for reasons that were plain to Luxemburg before her untimely death, if not to Lenin and Trotsky: the great majority of the German working class was willing to give the Social Democrats a chance, and the peasants were for the most part conservative and hostile even to democracy, to say nothing of socialism, the very notion of which they abominated. To say that the Bolsheviks misjudged the German situation is an understatement. In their eyes the apparent passivity of the working class was simply and solely due to the cowardice and treachery of the Social Democrats. Given resolute leadership, the masses could be set in motion. This never occurred, nor could it have happened, even though a Communist mass party did eventually come into being. Years were to pass before it began to dawn on Communist theorists that in an advanced industrial country there just was no popular sentiment for the sort of revolution that had swept across Russia in 1917.

This discovery still left room for one more illusion: that the crisis of capitalism, once it took the form of mass unemployment, would radicalize the whole of society. This became the esoteric faith of the Comintern theorists in the later 1920's. When matters were put to the test between 1930 and 1933, it turned out that the Communists had a substantial following only among the unemployed, while the unionized workers who still had jobs clung to their Social Democratic faith. The middle class, the peasantry, and large numbers of the intelligentsia attached themselves to a demagogue who spoke the familiar language of nationalism, populism, and pseudo-socialist rant against "Jewish financiers." This phenomenon of "National Socialism" mobilized plebeian sentiments which had been dormant in Central Europe since the failure of 1848. To that extent it was a parody of the democratic revolution, with the significant difference that its ideology was from the start anti-Western and anti-liberal. Secondly, "National Socialism," while at no time anticapitalist, was sufficiently indifferent to *laissez-faire* to permit public works, state intervention, and deficit financing on a scale adequate to mop up the millions of unemployed whom the Weimar Republic had left to starve (and for whom the S.P.D. and the trade unions it controlled had done nothing). Fascism thus appeared as an alternative to liberalism and Marxism alike, and this circumstance gave it considerable appeal for a time: here—so it seemed—was a solution of the economic problem which guaranteed full employment while leaving private property intact. That the phenomenon was made possible only by rearmament was another matter. Between 1933 and 1939, when Germany went to war, National Socialism won a mass following, including the bulk of the working class. This discovery spelled the end of Leninism and Trotskyism alike, for Trotsky had taken over from Lenin the belief that the German working class was potentially revolutionary. By 1929, however (Trotsky having been expelled from Russia), the C.P.S.U. had already recovered from its brief flirtation with world-transforming utopianism. Under the leadership of J. V. Stalin (1879-1953), it was about to take the plunge into the "second revolution" which would transform the Soviet Union into a major industrial power.

In the light of what actually occurred in the half century leading up to 1939, it is worth pondering Plekhanov's confident announcement, at the foundation congress of the Socialist International in Paris in 1889, that the coming Russian revolution "will succeed as a workers' revolution or it will not succeed at all" (Schapiro, *The Communist Party of the Soviet Union*, 19). His listeners must have felt reasonably certain that he was talking about the distant future—as, indeed, he himself seems to have thought, for he can hardly have foreseen that one of his own pupils would go back on his teachings and revert to the Jacobinism of the 1860's. Nonetheless this is just what happened. In retrospect one may say that while Bolshevism was an accident in the sense that it needed Lenin to produce it, the failure of Social Democratic strategy in its orthodox form was not. Tsarist Russia simply was not the sort of country where a party of this type could come to power, although under different circumstances it might have grown into a mass movement. The specific character of Bolshevism was determined by the Populist inheritance: that is to say, by Lenin's determination to effect a seizure of political power by a *coup d'état* and then to ignite the fires latent in Russia's unsolved peasant problem. For obvious reasons there could be no repetition of this experience on West European soil, which is why the Communist International was condemned to failure from the day of its birth. It was too "Russian" to suit the Germans, let alone the other Europeans; on the other hand, it was too "European" to make much of a dent in Asia, Africa, or Latin America. These realities disclosed themselves gradually and painfully. During the interval between 1919 and 1939 the International provided millions of people with a myth: faith in a proletarian revolution triumphant in Russia and destined to become global.

It has become a commonplace to say that the myth was shattered by the reality of Stalinism: the term signifying not merely the horrors of despotic collectivization of peasant farming in 1929-32, the institution of slave-labor camps for millions, and the bloody purges of the later 1930's, but also the growing cynicism of the regime, culminating in the Stalin-Hitler pact of 1939, the partition of Poland, and the systematic prostitution of the Communist International in the interest of expanding the power of the Soviet Union. There is no occasion to quarrel with these judgments, which are only too well founded. However, something needs to be said about the fortunes of Communism as a doctrine after Lenin had left the scene in January, 1924. The subsequent internal struggles within the Communist Party of the Soviet Union are commonly discussed in terms of a personal duel between Stalin and Trotsky, whereas in reality Stalin and his faction occupied an intermediate position between a Trotskyist "left wing" and a "right wing" led by N. Bukharin (1888-1938) and others who stood for a compromise with the peasantry, a slow tempo of industrialization, peaceful relations with the West, and democratization at home. Stalin's triumph over these opponents, and the consequent decision to embark upon forced-draft industrialization and a permanent reign of terror, has often been described.

In our context it is relevant to inquire what Leninism, Stalinism, Trotskyism, and Bukharinism signified internationally for the world Communist movement.

Toward the end of his active life, in 1922-23, Lenin had come to view the Russian Revolution as a link in a chain of global upheavals which in the long run would shatter Western capitalism and its political expression, imperialism. The wars and revolutions inherent in the decay of the system would establish an unbreakable alliance between the Asian peasant and the European or American city-worker. This was the long-term perspective to which all factions adhered after Lenin's death. It left room for differences over strategy and tactics, above all the question whether the defense of the Soviet Union should in all circumstances take precedence over the interests of the Communist International. By answering this question in the negative, Leon Trotsky (1879-1940) inevitably cut himself off from the majority of the Party (to say nothing of Russian popular sentiment) and thus ensured his downfall, already consummated by 1930, a decade before his own physical liquidation at the hands of a Stalinist assassin. Trotskyism was largely a repeat performance of the suicidal tactics which a generation earlier had led to the collapse of Menshevism. The Bukharinist faction, which stood for peace abroad and gradual democratization at home, suffered from a different kind of weakness. Unlike the Trotskyist opposition, it was thoroughly "Russian" and quite commonsensical as to the chances of a proletarian revolution in Germany, which it rightly judged to be nil. Its weakness lay in a failure to follow through with its own logic. This would have required the liquidation of the terrorist dictatorship and the institution of a more or less democratic regime giving proper weight to the peasantry. Such a course would have been popular with the majority of the working class, but not with the party membership which thirsted for full-blooded communism. In the long run it probably would have paid off economically. It was, however, incompatible with the decision taken by the real controllers—the political bureaucracy at the center of the state apparatus—in the late 1920's, which was to turn the Soviet Union into a great industrial and military power able to meet the "imperialists" on equal terms.

By adopting this course of action, which was urged upon him by the planners, the managers of heavy industry, the military leaders, and the secret police, and then sticking to it at the cost of millions of lives,

Stalin ensured the triumph of his faction and the acceptance of his own personal despotism (Nettl, *The Soviet Achievement*, 115 ff.). Stalinism, then, was the outcome of a uniquely terrible situation: a country already devastated by years of civil war, an inert peasantry and working class, a tradition of bureaucratic despotism, and the rule of a terrorist party apparatus able and willing to enforce its authority by the deliberate slaughter of millions in labor camps and man-made famines. No one will ever know the precise human cost of Stalin's "iron age" (setting aside the military losses in 1941-45); but 20 million dead seems a reasonable estimate, if one includes the millions of Ukrainian peasants deliberately left to starve in 1932-33 "to teach them a lesson." In principle the regime might have adopted Bukharin's policy of social peace and cooperation with the peasantry–and perhaps would have done so had Lenin lived a few years longer. But the mere fact that so much depended on the accident of one man's presence points up the dangers inherent in despotism.

The International was thus sacrificed to the short-range political aims of a regime which became ever more closely identified with the interests of the Soviet Union and, specifically, of its new ruling stratum. Having been amalgamated with the state apparatus, the Party was inevitably bureaucratized, and this circumstance facilitated the eventual triumph of the Stalinist faction, whose inner core rested on the terrorist apparatus of the secret police. The Trotskyist opposition, which after Trotsky's expulsion from the Party (1927) and from the territory of the Soviet Union (1929) reconstituted itself on an international basis, never acquired an important following and in the end dwindled away into an unimportant sect with a small following among the intelligentsia. While Stalinism came to represent the reality of the Soviet regime, Trotskyism stood for the utopian side of Communism: belief in an imminent world revolution. These rival positions found their embodiment in the personalities of Lenin's two principal heirs after his death in 1924. In this sense, they may be described as different aspects of Leninism, but they were likewise caricatures of Lenin's own theory and practice, which was a good deal more flexible and in the end perhaps closer to Bukharin's moderate standpoint. Neither Stalin nor Trotsky ever managed to establish the sort of practical and theoretical equilibrium that was the secret of Lenin's success. Stalin identified himself totally with the interests of the Soviet state, Trotsky with the revolutionary aims imputed to the world proletariat. The resulting murderous cleavage, which rent the Communist movement and caused torrents of blood to be spilled by the victorious Stalinist faction, concealed a theoretical difference no less profound, and in the long run of greater importance, than the political and personal hatreds that animated the participants and for years monopolized the foreground of events.

In his empirical fashion—for he lacked any sort of theoretical capacity and indeed can hardly be thought to have understood what he was doing—Stalin had stumbled on a major discovery. He had come to realize that a revolutionary party in control of the state could under modern conditions undertake a radical reorganization of the "economic infrastructure." Once in possession of political power, the party—provided it was animated by the necessary ruthlessness—could employ the state apparatus for the purpose of effecting a social revolution from above. This was a discovery of great importance. It was also a complete innovation. The French Revolution had witnessed nothing of the sort. On the contrary, the Robespierrist experiment had failed precisely because in those days it was *not* possible for men in control of the political sphere to stand society on its head. When the more romantic Jacobin terrorists tried something of the sort, they were promptly got rid of by their colleagues, and in the end Napoleon confirmed the bourgeoisie in all its property rights, even though he paid no attention to its political and ideological claims.

Now Trotsky—like Martov and the Mensheviks before him—had always assumed that the Russian Revolution was basically subject to the same sort of fatality that had dogged its French precursor. In the then prevailing fashion, he interpreted Marxism to mean that the "political superstructure" would reflect the automatism of the class struggle, which in turn was rooted in the production relations of the economic order. This after all was what historical materialism was supposed to be about. It never seems to have occurred to him—any more than to Plekhanov, Martov, or Axelrod, who had already broken with Lenin on this issue—that the Marxian analysis was applicable only to bourgeois society, specifically to the process of the bourgeois revolution. What Marx would have thought of the matter it is impossible to say, since he was never confronted with the phenomenon of a society that no longer rested on market relations and the automatism of economically determined class conflict. Lenin (as we have seen) already possessed a clear awareness that the orthodox approach to the political seizure of power was inadequate. But since he thought of the coming Russian revolution as a "bourgeois" one–in the sense that the Tsarist autocracy would fall because it was being undermined by an economic process–he had no need to revise his basic assumptions. Nor did Stalin do so. He merely behaved as though the possession of power was adequate to his purpose, as indeed it was. In the mid-1930's it began to dawn on him and his closest associates that the European working class was not revolutionary. Being concerned primarily with the interests of the Soviet Union, this did not bother him–it merely induced him to take an increasingly cynical view of the international Communist movement. As for Trotsky, he went on analyzing political conflicts (including his own conflict with what he called "the Soviet bureaucracy") in sociological terms, evidently blind to the fact that sociology by its nature could never clarify a purely political issue. One may say that he regarded the political sphere–the state–as a neutral arena of class conflict. It never occurred to him or his followers that the modern state might have an autonomy of its own and that a party in control of it could make nonsense of all the "laws" of economics. To that extent Trotsky, for all his revolutionary fervor, remained a Menshevik, whereas the Stalinists drew the logical conclusion from Lenin's approach by treating the Communist Party as the infallible representation of the General Will: a self-activating force able to make a revolution, if necessary *against* the working class!

The Fascist seizure of power in Italy after 1922 had already brought into question some of the principles with which Socialists and Communists in those days still approached the political problem: that is to say, the problem of power. Mussolini, a former Socialist converted to nationalism in the course of World War I, formed his party out of officers, students, white-collar workers, and the unemployed; equipped it with a pseudo-socialist ideology in large part inherited from the prewar Syndicalists; and then launched it against the organized working class. His capture of power was facilitated by the ruling Liberals, who were split among themselves and in the end decided to take him into partnership to ward off a wholly imaginary Communist danger. Moreover, Fascism had the tacit consent of the monarchy (which controlled the army) and the Vatican, though not of the Catholic peasant masses, whose party, the Popolari, was destroyed by Mussolini with the active connivance of the Church hierarchy. In consequence of all this, it became a Communist dogma that Fascism was a purely reactionary phenomenon born from the confusion and despair of the petty bourgeoisie, and Mussolini himself the paid servant of the financial oligarchy. In actual fact, the Fascist movement was pseudo-revolutionary, and its ideology, a weird attempt to combine socialism with imperialism, was part of a general European current. Its intellectual antecedents in part went back to Sorel, whose followers had already worked out some elements of the Fascist ideology before 1914. Its popular appeal was due to the exploitation of nationalism, a sentiment it took Moscow a long time to understand. A serious analysis of the whole phenomenon became possible only after the Communists had got over their primitive economic determinism and their habit of treating politics as a "reflex" of the class struggle. In the later 1940's the Italian Communist Party evolved a more sophisticated approach by drawing on the theoretical legacy of its co-founder, Antonio Gramsci (1891-1937). But during the decisive years of the anti-Fascist struggle in Europe, from 1933 to 1939, the Communist International remained the prisoner of its inadequate doctrines (Cammett, *passim*; Tarrow, 96 ff.).

To sum up: the Third International was founded in the expectation of a proletarian revolution in the industrially advanced countries of Central and Western Europe, an event destined never to take place. When no such upheaval occurred, the Communist parties inevitably became mere appendages of the Soviet regime. For the rest they spent most of their time and energy denouncing their Socialist rivals. When in the 1930's the depression and the spread of mass unemployment stimulated the growth of radical movements, there was some increase in the size of the Communist following, but it was the Fascists who reaped the major benefit. This was in part owing to their ability to exploit nationalist sentiments, the despair of a ruined middle class, and the connivance of the state apparatus. But the crucial factor was the resolve of the Fascist leaders to center all their efforts on the political and ideological spheres, while ignoring economics and the class struggle. To put it crudely, they were solely concerned with the seizure of power. They too had a "vanguard" concept, but they intended the ruling elite to be classless, whereas Leninism laid it down that the Communist Party must represent the working class, a term so defined as to exclude practically everyone who was not a manual laborer. It was only after Stalin had destroyed Lenin's party in the purges of 1934-38 that totalitarian Communism became a serious rival of totalitarian Fascism.

For the essence of the new post-Leninist doctrine was just this: the recognition that the party did *not* represent the working class. This fact, however, could not be publicly proclaimed, whence the peculiar mental and moral climate of Stalinism, with its esoteric truths for the elect and its lies for the masses. Stalinism and Fascism were thus able from about 1939 onward to compete on equal terms because they shared a common faith in the omnipotence of the state—concretely, of the totalitarian apparatus in control of the politico-ideological sphere. In the end the Stalinists, being more systematic, proved able to beat the Fascists at their own game (largely by copying their methods). By then the Third International was dead and so was the faith in a revolutionary mission of the proletariat. What took its place was a mortal conflict between two rival movements which shared a common conviction: the certainty that elites in possession of power could reorganize society, by force, from above. In this sense Stalinism and Fascism were both "technocratic" as well as totalitarian, for the residual differences between them, although important, did not inhibit them from recognizing that it had become possible to do away with democracy and the labor movement. By the 1940's, then, Communism had ceased to represent the working class, while Fascism had escaped from bourgeois control. Liberal democracy crumbled, and on its ruins the two great totalitarian movements enacted the dreadful spectacle of a European civil war.

3. Laborism and Democracy

The Socialist-Communist split had occurred during the decade following the outbreak of war in 1914. It was formalized and rendered permanent in 1924, when a revived Socialist International confronted a world Communist movement centered on Moscow: two rival Internationals, as there had been after the split of 1872 which divided Socialists from Anarchists. This time the struggle was global and it encompassed entire continents. In a certain fundamental sense Lenin had come to occupy the vacant throne of Bakunin; but there was an important difference. Bakunin had been the opponent of Marx, whereas Lenin spoke in his name and denounced Social Democracy as a reformist perversion of the true doctrine. Superficially the conflict was over rival interpretations of Marxism, for the majority of German, Austrian, French, Italian, and Spanish Socialists considered themselves Marxists. In actual fact the split had been brought about by the Bolshevik seizure of power and the establishment of a regime which repudiated the heritage of bourgeois democracy, including political freedom and the rule of law. Western Socialism was henceforth defined by its commitment to democratic principles, which the Communists dismissed as no longer valid. "Communism," then, was not synonymous with Marxism. In so far as it embodied the theory and practice of the Russian Revolution, it signified "Marxism-Leninism" and was so understood by all concerned. Was Democratic Socialism therefore to be identified with "orthodox" Marxism as against Lenin's heresies? There were those who took this view–notably Kautsky's pupils, the Austro-Marxists–but it was far from being universally shared. For growing numbers of Socialists, a pragmatic attachment to the labor movement's aims, plus defense of democracy against all comers, became the yardstick of fidelity to the Social Democratic tradition.

The resulting practical problems, largely related to the running of a planned economy under conditions of political freedom and democratic control, will be briefly considered in the final chapter. Here we can only summarize that part of the story which comes under the heading of political history. For practical purposes the decisive areas, from the standpoint of anyone concerned with the fortunes of democratic Socialism during this period, were Germany, Austria, Czechoslovakia, France, Italy, Great Britain, Belgium, Holland, Switzerland, and Scandinavia. Their fortunes varied considerably. The French Socialist Party split at Tours in December, 1920, when a majority of the delegates joined the Third International, taking about two-thirds of the membership with them (Wohl, 114 ff.). Italian Socialism was crushed by the Fascist dictatorship, which after 1925 became fully totalitarian and systematically banned all rival political organizations. Elsewhere less ground was lost because not much had been won in the first place. Spanish Socialism played an important role in establishing the short-lived Republic in 1931, but a few years later it became one of the principal casualties of the civil war. The Latin American parties–for the most part offshoots from the West European stem and sustained by immigrants from Italy and Spain—hardly counted, save in Chile and Argentina. In the United States, the Socialist movement had reached its peak on the eve of 1914, declining thereafter in part because it was not sufficiently "nativist" to withstand successive waves of governmental repression and patriotic resentment, directed first (in 1917) against pacifist or pro-German Social Democrats and later against Communist sympathizers with the Russian Revolution who were mostly immigrants from Eastern Europe (Bell, 96 ff.). The Japanese movement was suppressed by a military dictatorship after 1931 and became genuinely important, in numbers anyway, only after Japan's defeat in 1945 and the establishment of a parliamentary constitution.

In Europe the two crucial areas were Germany and Great Britain. After what has been said about German Social Democracy's record, it should occasion no surprise that Central Europe proved to be a disaster area: by 1934 German and Austrian Socialism had been destroyed. The relevant section in Braunthal's authoritative history of the International (II, 347 ff.) is duly labelled "The Catastrophe," and the chapter devoted to the Weimar Republic bears the grim caption "The Death Struggle of German Socialism." In contrast, the preceding chapter is headlined "Victory and Defeat in Britain." A corresponding account of Social Democracy's steady progress in Scandinavia since about 1920 would be an undiluted success story, but this circumstance points to a rather awkward conclusion: reformist socialism worked best in small civilized countries where democracy was not an issue, class tensions were not very acute, and military problems hardly impinged upon the life of the average citizen. Even so, progress might be slowed by linguistic and national conflicts, as in Belgium, or by religious divisions, as in Holland, where even after 1945 the ancient cleavage between Catholics and Protestants absorbed much of the country's political energy. Here too the "ideological superstructure" presented obstacles which were a good deal more stubborn than old-fashioned labor leaders had supposed. The antipodes provided a similar example: a powerful Labor Party had come into existence in Australia before 1914, and its leaders more than once formed governments based on parliamentary majorities. But the party was not socialist; its motive force was largely derived from the ancient antagonism dividing a predominantly Irish Catholic working class from an English Protestant business community; and it displayed a regrettable tendency to split over relatively trivial issues.

For that matter, the British Labour Party was temporarily ruined by a more serious split in 1931, after having suffered the mortification of seeing the minority government of Ramsay MacDonald in 1929-31 shipwrecked when unable to cope with mass unemployment.

There is, however, a different way of looking at the matter. If one considers the situation in Western Europe a century after the founding of the First International in 1864, one cannot fail to see that most of the aims set out by the pioneers of the democratic labor movement at the peak of the Victorian era had been achieved or were close to fulfillment. In 1964, Social Democracy provided the governmental majority party in Great Britain and throughout most of Scandinavia; it had become a cooperating or competing partner–sometimes the stronger partner–of the Christian Democrats (representing respectable conservatism) in West Germany, Austria, Holland, Belgium, and Switzerland, joining in the administration of those countries or forming the official opposition. It still had powerful support in France, although since 1936 it had lagged numerically behind the Communists, and it participated in the government of Italy. On the other hand, Democratic Socialism had irretrievably lost the positions it once held in Eastern Europe, where its survivors had been forcibly amalgamated with the ruling Communist parties after the Soviet occupation of the area in 1945-48.

Geographically and culturally as well as politically, then, Social Democracy had come to be identified with one particular area of the world: Western Europe. Its short-term and long-term aims were predicated upon assumptions that made sense only in industrialized countries with a solid democratic tradition. There were differences between wholesale nationalizers and advocates of a mixed economy with a large private sector, but whether they stood for socialization in the traditional sense or had accommodated themselves to welfare-state policies and the mixed economy, all took for granted a certain social and cultural milieu characteristic of Western Europe and, outside Europe, to be found in Canada, Australia, New Zealand, and perhaps Japan. This still left room for differences between Social Democrats in the narrow sense, who were content with reformist labor and welfare policies, and authentic Socialists who aimed at something qualitatively different from capitalism. These arguments were relevant to countries such as Britain, France, Germany, Austria, Italy, or Sweden; they had small import either for the poorer southern regions of Europe (Spain, Portugal, Greece) or for backward areas on the threshold of modernization. Outside Europe there was only one major country with an important Socialist party, and significantly it was Japan, now rapidly becoming a major industrial power. Yet Japan's astonishing transformation was taking place under conservative-liberal auspices, with the Socialists seemingly condemned to the role of a permanent opposition, albeit a numerically powerful one. Elsewhere, notably in India, "socialism" had by 1969 become either the creed of an intelligentsia with no significant mass following or the ideological label attached to parties which in fact were nationalist, drawing their electoral support from the peasantry and their financial backing from the emerging class of industrial entrepreneurs. In different forms, suitably adapted to the Buddhist tradition or the Islamic mentality, a similar situation prevailed temporarily in Burma, Indonesia, and Egypt. In all these areas, "socialism" became the ideology of the ruling political elites. In practice, these elites, whether military or civilian, governed dictatorially and attempted to industrialize and modernize the societies under their control along state-capitalist lines. The sole exception to this rule, Israel, was an industrial country largely peopled by European immigrants who had built up a genuine labor movement. Where no such movement existed, radical parties or sects had to seek a clientele among army officers, government clerks, students, and the unemployed. Not surprisingly, these strata tended in a fascist direction. Mussolini's abortive experiment in Italy had sprung up in a situation where the ruling liberal oligarchy had come to rely on a reformist labor bureaucracy to keep it in office at the expense of the peasantry and the swelling army of urban unemployed. Where this sort of situation duplicated itself, as it did in parts of Latin America, democratic socialism was thrown on the defensive or even blotted out altogether.

Put schematically, the Socialist movement since the 1930's had to fight on two fronts: against the Third International, which tried to universalize the Bolshevik experience; and against conservative or liberal parties which continued to defend private ownership (including peasant ownership), free enterprise in a market economy, and the cultural values of a propertied or salaried middle class. This last-mentioned qualification is important for two reasons. First, the new salariat was middle class in its habits without being bourgeois in the economic sense of the term, since for the most part it owned no property. Hence its principal concern was to ensure "full employment," meaning job security for itself and its descendants. Secondly, the numerical weakening of the old middle class of farmers, shopkeepers, and small entrepreneurs steadily undermined the electoral basis of the conservative or liberal parties. The economic process thus assembled some of the preconditions for a peaceful take-over by way of majority rule. This perspective had since 1864 been the foundation of democratic socialism. Hence when the British Labour Party in 1918 adopted a socialist platform (drafted by Sidney Webb in person), what had once been called Marxism became the strategic guideline of Fabian practice in the world's oldest and most mature industrial country–a country, moreover, in which parliamentary institutions were solidly based and a "Scandinavian" type of development seemed probable. The Labour Party came close to winning a parliamentary majority in 1929, suffered defeat (through its own ineptitude in government between 1929 and 1931) two years later, obtained a genuine majority for the first time in 1945, was once more driven into opposition in 1951, and recovered parliamentary control in 1964-66 under conditions where anything beyond a very modest type of reformism was ruled out by Britain's precarious external-trade position and her resultant dependence on foreign creditors. These ups and downs, however disappointing and inglorious, in sum amounted to a confirmation of the soundness of the original Fabian strategy. But the record also showed that in an ancient European country with a heavy dependence on foreign trade and a backlog of antiquated industries in urgent need of modernization, a Labour government could not socialize the economy with the full support even of the working class (of which one-third consistently voted Conservative), let alone the salaried middle class. Moreover, the growing strength of trade unionism and political reformism bore fruit only after the imperial burden had been shed. Social Democracy thus showed itself able to govern more or less effectively only under conditions where economic, social, and cultural problems took precedence over all others, and where democracy was not seriously threatened.

On the other hand, the Socialist-led Popular Front government in France between 1936 and 1938 was a complete failure. It could neither ensure full employment, nor prevent the flight of capital, nor yet conduct a successful foreign policy. Its helpless passivity (to employ no stronger term) in the face of the Fascist assault on the Spanish Republic in 1936-39 discredited it in the eyes of those surviving heirs of the Jacobin tradition who for a moment had thought that socialism might save the Republic. What in the end saved it, after the military debacle of 1940, was a national resistance movement in which the Socialists played an honorable (but not a decisive) part. The Italian record between 1920 and 1945 was broadly similar, save that Fascism triumphed earlier and was only got rid of after defeat in war. And in Spain, where the Republic was crushed out of existence by military rebellion, clerical hostility, Anarchist and Fascist lunacy, Stalinist treachery, and foreign intervention–the Socialist Party was too weak (possibly also too civilized) to triumph over this combination of destructive forces.

If German and Austrian Social Democracy after 1918, while nominally Marxist, became in effect reformist, there was no comparable issue after 1945, when the Allied victory in World War II ensured the more or less regular functioning of democratic institutions on the truncated territory of the German Federal Republic and in Austria. In these areas the Social Democrats duly abandoned the remaining vestiges of their past, although the Austrian party at least retained the goal of a socialized economy, with a public sector large enough to set standards for the remainder. The West German S.P.D. by contrast had by 1960 been officially converted to economic liberalism and, at the close of 1969, seemed destined to govern in partnership with the survivors of middle-class liberalism, after having proved its trustworthiness in a coalition with the Christian Democrats. The Party's evolution since the war has often been described as an emancipation from Marxism. In actual fact its leadership after 1945 centered on the idiosyncratic personality of Kurt Schumacher (1895-1952), a Lassallean who had spent the Hitler era in various prisons and concentration camps, and during those grim years formed the conviction that what had ruined the S.P.D. after 1918 was a lack of national backbone and excessive willingness to fulfill the terms of the 1919 Versailles treaty. In consequence, he set himself the task of uniting democratic socialism with German patriotism, while at the same time he proclaimed that capitalism was finished. This turned out to be a misconception. So far from being dead, German capitalism after 1950 flourished like the green bay tree. But what really undid Schumacher's strategy of turning the S.P.D. into a great national-democratic movement was Germany's partition and the constitution of the Bonn government in 1949 on a predominantly Roman Catholic foundation, while East Germany was lopped off and transformed into a Russian satellite under Communist management. It did the S.P.D. little good with the voters that Schumacher placed national reunion in the forefront, accused the Adenauer regime of connivance with those in the West who wished to keep Germany divided, and denounced the Catholic Church as "the fifth occupying power." His death in 1952 brought the abortive national-democratic experiment to a close, and his successors—led by the former Communist Herbert Wehner—in the Godesberg program of 1959 abandoned nationalism and socialism alike. Instead they committed the party to a vaguely humanist and democratic outlook quite compatible with Christian ethics. For the rest, social harmony was affirmed not merely in practice but in principle, and even nationalization of key industries no longer figured among the party's aims. Schumacher, true to his Lassallean ancestry, had held that a democracy, to be effective, must be socialist and based on the working class. His heirs abandoned both his philosophy and his politics. If the reward they reaped was modest, it could at least be argued that the S.P.D. had become an effective governing force.

The British development after 1945 differed markedly from the German, if only because Great Britain counted officially among the victors in World War II and the Labour Party had established its credibility with the voters by participating in the government from 1940 to 1945. Thereafter, tenure of power between 1945 and 1951 initiated a debate over the relevance of nationalization for Britain's ailing economy. The decision to place key industries and services—principally coal mining, electric power, and public transport—under state ownership could be defended on pragmatic grounds and was consequently not challenged when the Tories recovered control in 1951. For the rest, the emphasis was on hard work and rationing of essential consumer goods, as befitted an administration struggling with postwar shortages. Much of the credit for the government's success in imposing unpopular choices went to its principal administrator, Stafford Cripps, an austere figure who neither smoked nor drank and was rumored to live on watercress grown off the blotting-paper on his desk. After his death in 1950 he became the inspiration of the "revisionist" faction led by Hugh Gaitskell (1906-63), a group of modernizers who tried to dispense with the party's traditional cloth-cap image so as to make it more attractive to technicians and professional people. On the whole they were successful, although the sudden death of their leader in 1963 for a time concealed the full extent of their achievement.

Labour's return to office in 1964 was preceded by a lengthy wrangle over socialization, which ended in an all-around stalemate. And the dispute became associated with the question of giving the party a new image more attractive to the salaried and professional middle class, although in strict logic these issues had nothing to do with each other. From the resulting cleavage between the factions respectively led by Gaitskell and Aneurin Bevan (1897-1960) there emerged in 1963-64 a compromise solution personified by the opportunistic leadership of Harold Wilson, a "technocrat" who spoke the language of socialism while in practice following a line of conduct hardly distinguishable from American liberalism of the variety represented by Professor J. K. Galbraith and the "New Frontier" of the 1961-63 Kennedy administration. Labour's effective guiding light after the disaster of the MacDonald government in 1931, and more especially after the electoral victory in 1945, had been the liberalism of J. M Keynes, although the party leaders from habit spoke the language of traditional working-class socialism.

In principle, the same situation applied to all West European countries after 1945, but the mutation from a genuinely bourgeois to a partly centralized economy proceeded at an uneven pace, and the strains it set up were aggravated by purely national problems. Italy after 1945 witnessed an industrial boom and the departure of millions of peasants for the towns, where they created a housing problem but also helped to sustain a rapid growth in the new industrial sector. In this respect the Italian situation was similar to the Japanese. France had undergone extensive nationalization of basic industries immediately after the war, under the direction of a coalition government running from the Gaullists to the Communists. This semi-socialist trend was continued under the Fourth Republic (1946-58) and its Gaullist successor by the official adoption of central planning. In consequence, all French governments assumed an increasingly "technocratic" character, in that control of the economy was vested in the central political bureaucracy and the planners. The Socialist Party should have been well placed to exploit this development, but it lost public support owing to its political ineptitude and saw its share of the electorate shrink between 1945 and 1969 from 24 to 12 per cent. While the party's political outlook increasingly reflected the growing importance of the technical intelligentsia, its leadership bungled the task of refashioning the theoretical content of its program. Similar weaknesses were observable in Italy. Generally speaking, French and Italian Socialism, in competition with numerically stronger Communist parties, retained the phraseology of class conflict but in practice became more attractive to salaried white-collar and professional employees than to industrial workers, who for the most part preferred the familiar Communist emphasis on the unique worth of the industrial proletariat. This kind of language implied that value creation was the sole prerogative of the manual workers, all other classes of society being parasites riding on the backs of the "toilers." Aside from being theoretical nonsense (and without foundation in Marx's mature writings, popular notions to the contrary notwithstanding), this bias tended to isolate the Communists from salaried and professional people, not to mention scientists and technicians in industry. It therefore ensured the continued survival of reformist socialism as a counter-attraction, but it also laid the technical and managerial stratum open to new temptations emanating from the political Right. In principle there was no reason why Socialists (or Communists for that matter, once they had got rid of the Stalinist incubus) should not have made an appeal to these new strata. But the Socialist parties, here as elsewhere, had taken shape in the nineteenth century, when the term "labor" signified manual labor and the most urgent order of the day was to protect trade unions from employers and hostile governments. It was not easy to grasp the fact that the newer forms of technology had created an army of brain workers who could not be reached by slogans once addressed to the proletariat. It was even more difficult to incorporate the technicians within the older unions alongside the manual workers, who continued to regard themselves as the only trustworthy basis of a labor movement. These problems were not insoluble, but they raised awkward theoretical and practical questions concerning the relation of the intelligentsia to the working class properly so described.

The political cleavage occasioned by the Russian Revolution and its Stalinist aftermath superimposed itself upon this situation and added to the confusion. The Western labor movement would in any case have been plunged into a crisis by differing reactions to World War I, the depression of the 1930's, and the rise of Fascism. The Communist split added an extra dimension, and matters were not eased by the sectarian quarrels among Stalinists, Trotskyists, and (from about 1960 on) Maoists who had discovered a new model in China, supposedly applicable not only to the pre-industrial "third world" of backward areas, but to advanced countries as well. In the face of all these distractions it is perhaps remarkable that something like a Socialist movement continued to survive at all. No doubt it did so because there was in fact no other option for its adherents, whether workers or intellectuals. Soviet Communism had become identified with the East European police state: so much so that after the Hungarian blood-bath of 1956 and later with the invasion of Czechoslovakia in 1968, even some of the more alert West European Communists began to edge away from the once admired Stalinist model. Social Democracy might be boring, but at least it was familiar and held no menace to freedom and decency.

It thus continued to enjoy mass support, on the tacit understanding that it would act as a reformist agency in defense of labor's interests against the steady encroachment of industrial technology and state control. Socialization was to proceed slowly (if at all) and only on condition that a majority of the voters was prepared to sanction it. For reasons already explained, this latter qualification became easier to fulfill once it was realized that growing numbers of salary-earners were prepared to tolerate or even welcome a measure of socialism, in the name of economic planning, job security, and full employment.

In principle, a legal guarantee of work for all—that most ancient of socialist slogans—might become a transition to the stage of guaranteed tenure, already operative in the civil service and the universities, and applicable to industry as well, notably if the economy became state-controlled. The general trend in all the old industrial countries toward stability and away from the perpetual insecurity associated with the free market responded to deep-seated human cravings. But it presupposed an advanced stage of capital formation, a reasonable rate of economic growth, industrial discipline, and general political maturity. It was clearly impractical to prescribe a regime of this kind as the solution for the problems of newly industrialized countries, where production had perforce to take precedence over all other considerations. Once more democratic socialism disclosed itself as a theory and practice appropriate to the privileged areas of the world. Beyond these regions, with their painfully accumulated capital equipment and their relatively stable political institutions, the ancient dream of combining equality and liberty assumed a distinctly utopian look. And even this assessment took no account of the anarchosyndicalist wave that rolled across Europe in 1968, producing a general strike in France and a semblance of worker-student cooperation in other industrial countries as well: proof positive (if any was needed) that the forces set in motion by the industrial revolution had not yet found an adequate political and cultural framework. What students–largely drawn from the new middle class of salaried and professional people–rebelled against clearly had no direct connection with the traditional aims of the labor movement, even though it might be argued that the "alienation" they experienced was an aspect of exploitation. For an oppositional intelligentsia had likewise begun to make its appearance in Eastern Europe, where capitalism was not an issue. Setting aside the horrors of Stalinism, which by the late 1960's had anyhow been partly eliminated, what students and workers in the nominally socialist countries of the Soviet bloc (plus Yugoslavia) revolted against were the bureaucratic and authoritarian structures implanted after 1945. But if the movement was directed against corporate capitalism in the West, and against state socialism in the East, then it could not be subsumed under terms left over from the bourgeois era, when "exploitation" (in the Marxian sense) signified the appropriation of surplus value by individual capitalists. It would then be necessary to conclude that the common factor was the emergence, east and west of the political frontier splitting the Continent, of a new type of society for which only the term "technocratic" had so far been found suitable. In this sense, the classical confrontation between socialism and liberalism had by the late 1960's taken on a somewhat antiquated appearance.

What is perhaps less obvious, but worth stating, is that the Communist parties in advanced industrial countries have not escaped from the general rule (one might almost call it a truism) that has presided over the destinies of the labor movement from the time it took shape in Western Europe in the 1830's: that it is the "aristocracy of labor" which is the most militant and politically conscious stratum of the working class and the prime vehicle of socialist (or communist) activities. For France–with Italy the only Western European country to possess a Communist mass movement–there are authenticated figures showing that at the eighteenth congress of the P.C.F. in 1967, out of 409 working-class delegates, 349 were qualified professionals and only 60 general laborers (Kriegel, 62). Nor could it be otherwise: every class is led by its professionally trained elite. The circumstance would hardly be worth noting were it not in such glaring contradiction with the Leninist ideology which the Communist movement has sought to conserve, in the teeth of its own official statistics about the social composition of its membership! As every Marxist knows, no socialist force worth mentioning has ever emerged from the lower depths of society. In backward pre-industrial countries the rural unemployed constitute an important reservoir for movements which may as easily be led in a fascist as in an anarchist or communist direction; but that is a different issue altogether. When one speaks of Socialism and/or Communism in the West, one speaks of movements sustained by the "aristocracy of labor": just as Syndicalism in its heyday was the faith of an elite of skilled craftsmen, not of a slum proletariat. The latter obstinately voted for the Tories and their counterparts elsewhere. There is no correlation between pauperism and socialism, or between revolution and despair. To assert the contrary is to fly in the face of all the sociological evidence we possess. For that matter, the records of classical antiquity show with sufficient clarity that there has never been such a thing as a successful slave revolt.

4. The Third World

It should be evident from the foregoing that "democratic socialism" is not definable in simple geographical terms, albeit in Europe the east-west split consequent upon World War II created a state of affairs where after 1948 a military and political frontier separated the countries of the Soviet bloc from regions where political democracy survived. The basic division cut across the Soviet-American antagonism, for the so-called free world of North Atlantic phraseology included Spain, Portugal, and Greece, where democratic liberties had been suppressed by authoritarian regimes of the Right. Conversely, the Yugoslav Communist regime after 1948 was no less Leninist in its ideology for being independent of Moscow. When in 1968 a brief attempt was made by the leadership of the Czechoslovak Communist Party to introduce both inner-party and intra-party democracy, the experiment was promptly suppressed by armed Russian intervention. In practice, therefore, democratic socialism remained a forbidden heresy in Eastern Europe, although it might be argued that under favorable conditions (e.g., in Czechoslovakia, where the Communist Party was solidly rooted in the labor movement and possessed genuine popular support) socialism and democracy were in principle compatible.

Beyond Europe, the term "democratic socialism" does not have an easily definable meaning. On the one hand, it may legitimately be applied to Socialist parties operating within a pluralist political system such as that possessed by India, Japan, or Israel, whatever the degree of industrial development. On the other hand, it is clearly applicable to democratic labor movements in countries such as Canada and Australia which are already fully industrial and have reached the stage of welfare-state legislation. In principle this would also be true of the United States, except that there happens not to be a sizable social-democratic, let alone socialist, movement in North America outside Canada. The Latin American republics for the most part resemble southern Asia rather than their northern neighbor, although this is not true of Argentina and Chile. Finally, there is Cuba. A country whose economy has been effectively socialized cannot well be excluded on the grounds that it does not possess democratic institutions of the Western type. Socialism is not identical with democracy, although ideally the two are compatible. Cuba, then, must count as a socialist dictatorship, and so of course must China.

The importance of these distinctions lies in the fact that they enable one to discriminate between genuinely socialist regimes which have been imposed dictatorially and pseudo-socialist movements or governments whose real character is quite unrelated to their public rhetoric. Socialism having become fashionable among the political and intellectual elites of newly independent countries, it is by no means uncommon for the nascent bourgeoisie of a backward country to strut about in borrowed socialist clothes. Nationalists anxious to exclude foreign competition, or governments rightly concerned to impose protective tariffs so as to give their home industries a chance to grow, may in all good faith imagine themselves to be following a socialist line of policy, when all they are doing is to facilitate the emergence of capitalism. For this reason it is perfectly legitimate to inquire into the credentials of nationalist movements in the countries conventionally grouped together under the label "third world." This classification was originally devised to signify nonmembership of either the Sino-Soviet bloc or the Western camp grouped around the United States. To economists and cultural anthropologists it connotes all the pre-industrial civilizations, whatever their shifting political alignments. In this sense, China forms part of the "third world," and so does India, whereas Japan does not. If one wants to avoid confusion, one had better apply one particular set of criteria and then stick to it. The conventional Marxist criterion is social relations. Now it is plain that the social structure of pre-industrial countries does not lend itself to class analysis, since for Marxists the phenomenon of class is tied up with the emergence of a market economy. Under state despotism–where the state owns the means of production and an irremovable bureaucracy owns the state, as in ancient China and possibly in modern China too–there are no classes in the Marxian sense, although there are different social strata: principally a peasantry to perform the necessary physical labor and a bureaucracy to supervise it and run the administration. These strata are symbiotically related, but they do not engage in class conflict, the latter being a phenomenon peculiar to bourgeois society and moreover dependent on a state of affairs where "politics" and "economics" can be clearly distinguished from each other and where economically rooted interest groups (classes) struggle for control of the political sphere. No such distinction exists in backward countries, for the good and sufficient reason that a society must (1) possess a market economy, with labor transformed into a salable commodity and (2) have gone through the industrial revolution, before it can be said to possess "classes" in the Marxian sense. In their absence, radical movements, especially when directed against outside (imperialist) control, will appeal to the unity of the tribe, the folk, the nation, or the race, in the struggle against (native or foreign) oppressors. The ruling ideology will emphasize anti-imperialism rather than anticapitalism, and one will get variations on the ancient populist theme of capitalism being a foreign importation, subversive of the home-grown solidarity of the extended family, the village, the clan, the community of religious believers, or whatever happens to take the ideologist's fancy. Basically the pre-industrial countries are so structured as to give their intelligentsia an opportunity to lead the peasant masses, with whom it shares the national-popular ideology that comes naturally to them. The outcome may be a primitive caricature of European Fascism, as in Sukarno's Indonesia, Nasser's Egypt, or the Ghana of Nkrumah; a regime modelled on French Bonapartism, as in Kemalist Turkey between 1918 and 1938; or a regression from Leninism to populism, as in Maoist China (Harris, 188).

The term "regression" seems appropriate because of the typically populist confusion between "the people" and the proletariat. In the populist ideology (which is eternally the same under every sky and in every clime) "the people" is seen as a body of virtuous toilers confronted by a handful of native or foreign exploiters whom it is the Party's (or the Leader's) duty to expel or repulse, so that the nation may accomplish its destiny. Thus nationalism is equated with socialism, the community is seen as essentially classless, and the ruling elite appears as the historical incorporation of the General Will, even though it may never go to the trouble of actually consulting the people under its control as to their real desires. Maoism, Castroism, and "African Socialism" constitute different variants of this peculiar ideology. The differences are important, but the intellectual content is in every case pretty much the same. As for the effectiveness of this creed, an ideology that promises people both the defense of their (tribal or national) traditions and painless economic growth under conditions of social equality and justice for all will never lack an audience.

The term "democratic socialism" has a definable meaning in our context only when applied to areas with political institutions that allow their inhabitants a choice between competing political models. Where no such choice exists–in other words, where democracy has been stamped out or not permitted to grow and where the labor movement is state-controlled–it may still be legitimate to speak of "socialism" (if the means of production have been placed under public control), but one cannot well speak of democratic socialism. Conversely, where agrarian populism permits free expression of opinion and the formation of rival political groups–as in India–one may speak of democracy, but it is meaningless to invoke the vocabulary of socialism merely because the ruling political elite from time to time indulges in the habit of extolling the benefits of greater equality. One can have democracy without socialism, and vice versa. Whether the two can be effectively combined is the prime question of our age. It is not a question that can reasonably be posed in pre-industrial societies engaged in a national struggle against foreign enemies. Nationalist movements are classless by definition. The popular appeal of Maoism and Castroism rests upon the fact that they are able to mobilize sentiments deeply rooted in every agrarian community. If one looks for ideological antecedents, they are to be found not in Marx, but in Rousseau's doctrine of the General Will asserting itself (with the help of all-wise and all-powerful leaders or legislators) against the intrigues of faction and the corrupting influence of material comfort and social privilege. "Communism" is thus equated with puritanical austerity and patriotism, while the term "bourgeois" loses its class connotations and comes to stand for attachment to the fleshpots of Egypt. It would doubtless come as a surprise to these zealots to learn that their way of looking at the world is not merely pre-Marxist, but quite specifically Jacobinical: Rousseauist and Robespierrist to be exact. It is the necessary accompaniment of every radical national revolution in a retarded country. From a pragmatic viewpoint there is much to be said for this kind of regime, especially if it does not become corrupt, as it did in Ghana and Indonesia. In a poor country it ensures a modicum of sustenance for all, does away with scandalous contrasts between luxury and poverty, and limits (if it does not eliminate entirely) the sordid habits associated with a "kleptocracy" where politics (dressed up in "socialist" clothing) becomes a means of enriching a parasitic caste of demagogues and office-holders. Given the choice between such a state of affairs and the regimentation of Castroism, or even Maoism, what starving peasant would not choose the latter?

This does not, however, establish any genuine connection between socialism and revolutionary nationalism. At the same time, it is well to bear in mind that a "regression from Leninism to populism" could not have occurred if the Bolshevik movement had not from the day of its birth been mired in populist thought forms. The infantile parody of Lenin's thought known as Maoism could only be institutionalized on Chinese soil: that is, in a peasant society torn by civil war and confronted by the evident failure of a rival nationalist movement (the Kuomintang) to do for China what Bolshevism had done for Russia: get rid of the foreigner and transform the country into a modern industrialized power. But the Leninist roots of Maoism are still perceptible, even though Lenin's heritage had already been grossly perverted and barbarized by Stalin. These roots were ultimately derived from one particular element in the populist tradition: the belief in the key role of the radical intelligentsia. All Mao Tse-tung had to do was to substitute the peasantry for the industrial working class as the "mass basis" of his movement, and the new creed had an adequate (for China) formulation. It was also quite appropriate to the actual circumstances, at least in its earlier stages and before Mao had succumbed to the common disease of all-powerful and uncontrolled political leaders: personal despotism and belief in his own infallibility.

What Maoism asserted, and what Castroism echoed in a somewhat different vocabulary adapted to the heritage of Latin American nationalism, was the *identity* of socialism with revolutionary nationalism. If only the people could be led in the right direction and the party purged of the "handful of traitors in high places" whose ghostly presence has haunted every populist since Robespierre first denounced them as corrupters of the Revolution and enemies of the General Will, all would be well. Socialism, meaning an egalitarian community, could be built by the united and selfless labor of the toiling masses, guided by an omniscient and infallible leadership which incorporated the long-term aims of the nation, watched over its safety, and for good measure possessed the key to the riddle of history and the meaning of the universe. For all its Taoist overtones and its almost childlike simplicity–Chinese philosophy, having got stuck at the pre-Socratic stage, has never been a school of critical or dialectical thinking in the Western sense–the Maoist model still bears the imprint of its Leninist origin (Schram, *passim*). Compared to Stalinism, which in principle extolled the proletariat, Maoism is more consistent and less burdened with insincerity: the People are led by a Party which embodies the General Will. Its endless appeals to moral virtue are both nationalist and typically Rousseauist. All that is then left of Marxism is a class-struggle vocabulary absurdly inappropriate to the actual situation. Appeals to the virtuous toilers over the heads of the sinful bureaucracy emanate from a leadership whose authority is based on control of the army: itself made up of peasants whose loyalty during the civil war ensured the Communist victory over the Kuomintang, the latter representing the landed gentry. It is the classic pattern of every radical democratic revolution, even though the leaders are sincere in imagining themselves to be Communists and to stand in the succession of Marx and Lenin. The inevitable outcome is direct military rule, the army having from the start been the vanguard of the revolution. Castroism may be regarded as a Latin American variant of this faith, except that it relies more heavily on Jacobin rhetoric, as befits a movement descended from the French Revolution and operating in a predominant Catholic culture.

Now it may be held that radical nationalism is quite compatible with socialism, at any rate in backward pre-industrial societies whose leaders are free to make a choice between the capitalist and the socialist form of industrialization. This after all was the original rationale of Russian Populism, and some such belief has subtended all forms of Communism since 1917. It is arguable that even if the insanities of Maoism had been avoided, it would still have been necessary to enforce the most rigid austerity and conformism, in order to scrape together the capital for industrialization. In the absence of foreign aid, an economic surplus had to be accumulated in agriculture and then drained off to feed the urban working class. For practical purposes this is what "Communism" has come to mean in any retarded country. The alternative—capitalist industrialization on the Japanese model—requires special circumstances and is perhaps no longer feasible for political reasons.

The only remaining question, then, is how much should be squeezed out of the peasantry and by what means. If the regime is genuinely committed to some form of socialism, the surplus will at least not be wasted on frivolous outlays—the importation of useless consumer goods or the construction of spectacular public buildings. Socialism will then quite simply serve the aim of economic growth and will be employed by the political elite as the ideological justification for nation-building and modernization in general. The farcical misuse of socialist phraseology by political clowns and demagogues such as Nasser, Nkrumah, and Sukarno does not in itself constitute an argument against this line of reasoning. The general principle was spelled out two decades ago by a distinguished economist of West Indian origin, Professor Arthur Lewis, in a study produced for the Fabian Society. In this influential piece of writing, the readers were offered a definition of socialism in terms proper to advanced and backward countries alike. "Socialism and nationalisation of property are now commonly identified, but this is as great an error as the identification of socialism and the extended state. Socialism is not, in the first instance, about property any more than it is about the state. Socialism is about equality. A passion for equality is the one thing that links all socialists; on all others they are divided" (Lewis, 10).

The trouble with this argument is that it turns socialism into an aspiration quite unconnected with the historic aims of the labor movement. If the term is defined so loosely as to be synonymous with egalitarianism, then any kind of radical movement may claim to be socialist, irrespective of its social and intellectual make-up. The spokesmen of such a movement may then also assert that in the interest of equality (or for some other reason) freedom must be curtailed. As an emergency operation under primitive conditions, a dictatorship may pass muster, notably if the only available alternative is the Indian or Brazilian pattern: inadequate or unevenly distributed economic development under the direction of private entrepreneurs, plus systematic squandering of public resources by a swollen caste of bureaucrats and their hangers-on. Given the almost insoluble population problem of the third world, and the steadily widening gulf between the industrialized countries and the remainder, one can hardly blame revolutionaries in Latin America, Southeast Asia, and Africa for aiming at dictatorial short-cuts. The usual justification for this approach is the inevitable slowness, muddle, and corruption of the ordinary democratic process. But the real obstacle to progress is the numerical weight of peasant electorates. This is not a problem that can be solved by better education. However ignorant they may be, peasants are quite capable of grasping the point that the funds for modernization have to be pumped out of the villages into urban areas. They will therefore be opposed to measures calculated to promote capital accumulation, and this will be the case whether or not the regime is professedly socialist.

The real problem of every nationalist elite in a backward country is how to get around this stubborn peasant resistance. If it is not to be done in Stalinist fashion—that is, by herding the masses into collectives and shipping all opposition elements off to labor camps—it has to be done by some other means: bribery, electoral trickery, appeals to national sentiment, or the straightforward imposition of military rule. If the governing stratum is able and willing to enforce rigid austerity upon itself and the whole of society, so much the better. But even if socialism is defined to signify "equality of income" (Lewis, 30), there remains the awkward fact that industrialization by itself tends to bring about new social alignments, notably the emergence of a technical intelligentsia which in the fullness of time will rebel against enforced equality and the imposition of standards proper to a primitive peasantry. To say that democratic socialism in the Western sense is impossible under such circumstances is merely to state the obvious.

But this is no reason to despair, nor does it constitute an argument for allowing the gulf between advanced and backward countries to become even wider. If "uneven development" is inevitable, societies which have already accumulated a surplus of capital and technological skill are under an obligation to help the others. In the language of conventional morality, appeals of this sort are commonly addressed to disembodied entities supposedly anchored in the individual conscience. In reality, the need to assist one's neighbors is rooted in the fact that the destinies of all are interlinked. A world in which a few wealthy and powerful empires permanently exploit the poorer countries, while systematically inhibiting their progress, is theoretically conceivable; but such a world would be unsafe for all, as well as being morally repulsive. The case for socialism on a universal scale is best stated by making the commonsensical assumption that the pacification of the globe is in the interest of all its inhabitants.

10 Contemporary Problems of Socialism

1. History and Theory

At the close of the last chapter mention was made of the difficulties that arise if the term "socialism" is divorced from the significations it has traditionally possessed for the labor movement. In the present concluding section a brief critical summary will serve as a launching-pad for a short and circular space-flight into the theoretical sphere.

For a start let us take a look at some of the general notions about historical progress which socialists share with liberals, and with the secularist (or humanist) tradition in general. Here a qualification is in order. In the course of our survey we have come across some distinguished representatives of what may be called Christian socialism: a current of thought whose British, Dutch, Swiss, and Scandinavian representatives have done much to ease the transition from older to newer forms of democracy in those fortunate lands. Space permitting, one might draw up a list of distinguished thinkers who have combined religious faith with lifelong commitment to some form of socialism. Among theologians, Karl Barth, Paul Tillich, and Reinhold Niebuhr are familiar names in Western Europe and North America. An equivalent array on the political side is inevitably less impressive in terms of intellect. Still, a portrait gallery that includes R. H. Tawney, Norman Thomas, Stafford Cripps, Kurt Schumacher, and Ernst Reuter is not easily matched for political courage and moral earnestness. All concerned belong to the Protestant tradition and to the Anglo-American or Germanic cultures. This is not necessarily a reflection upon the Latin Catholic world: it merely so happens that whereas Roman Catholics have regarded Christian democracy as respectable since the 1890's, they have only very recently accorded Christian socialists a grudging toleration. Historically, socialism in France, Belgium, Ireland, Italy, Spain, and the Luso-Hispanic cultures of Latin America has until quite recently been associated with militant atheism. This state of affairs may change, but for the time being it rules out the inclusion of Roman Catholics of any eminence among the roll-call of thinkers whom for convenience one may style Christian socialists.

Much the same applies to the various non-Christian faiths. Socialists of Jewish origin, to adopt an awkward circumlocution, have generally tended to be either Spinozists or Marxists. In either case they were inevitably regarded as radical secularists by their former co-religionists. Where Islamic and Buddhist civilizations prevail, a picture similar to the Latin American appears: that is to say, socialism is generally associated with secularism. What is occasionally described as Islamic socialism or Buddhist socialism usually turns out on inspection to be yet another variant of medievalism: religion (one is told) is the cure for social ills. Alternatively it is affirmed that the culture in question has no need of Western importations because it is intrinsically healthy, egalitarian, and free from class conflict. To anyone familiar with nineteenth-century European conservatism, this kind of talk can only sound like the hollowest of echoes. Pre-industrial civilizations typically react to the birth-pangs of modernity by asserting their indifference to the problems of the "decadent West." If they have conserved a few remnants of primitive egalitarianism in the form of common ownership of the soil or some vestiges of tribal ethics, they may actually be in possession of a valuable heritage, but this circumstance by itself does not render them immune to the tensions that go with modernization. However, illusions of this sort are notoriously incurable. We shall no doubt hear a great deal more about "African socialism," "Arab socialism," "Indonesian socialism," and of course "Hindu socialism" before all these sacred cows are despatched to their final resting place.

Bearing in mind these qualifications one may say that the socialist movement inherited the basic assumptions of humanism in the age of the French Revolution. This is another way of stating that, when the early socialists were confronted with the new world of industrialism, they accepted technology and science, though not bourgeois society and the individualist ethic that went with it. From the liberal viewpoint this attitude amounted to wanting to have one's cake and eat it. From the conservative or Christian socialist angle the situation looked somewhat different. Christian socialism in the end amalgamated with social-democratic laborism. Conservatives of the romantic variety sympathized with complaints against individualism, but not with the socialist faith in a better future based on science and industry. Their own preference was for a return to the past or, if that was impossible, for the creation of a new hierarchical order with a paternalistic state in control of a docile church-going population. The agrarian utopia found a lasting monument in the writings of Tolstoy and the politics of Gandhi, the proto-fascist dream its poetic embodiment in the weird fantasies of William Butler Yeats and his spiritual progeny. Neither had any relevance for the socialist movement, although in fairness one must register the survival of romantic medievalism in Guild Socialism, not to mention the various forms of anarchism. These of course were protest movements, not authoritarian attempts to harness the new forces let loose by technology to the elitist rule of self-appointed supermen. In the end, what separates the fascist from the anarchist is not a different analysis of society–for both are in agreement as to the facts of the case–but a difference in purpose. Anarchism rejects the modern world. Fascism seeks to dominate it for the purpose of eternalizing the rule of a privileged caste or race supposedly threatened by an upsurge of inferior breeds. Both are pathological reactions, and for the rest they may be said to feed on each other: occasionally–as in the case of Spain–with consequences dire to contemplate.

Before turning to the politics and economics of socialism, it will be convenient to clarify a subject on which a good deal of nonsense has been written: some of it by Marxists, the remainder by their positivist critics. The topic bears the general label "historical necessity"; alternatively it is described as the search for historical "laws of motion." Belief or disbelief in the existence of such laws is held to constitute a major issue in dispute between socialists and liberals, or between dogmatists and empiricists, or yet again between the ancients and the moderns. It has even been asserted that until the quarrel over "historicism" has been settled, there is no point in arguing about anything else—a notion that makes an immediate appeal to the academic mind.

A point to be noted in this connection is that when political theorists disagree about history they are not carrying on a debate over the use of language, but over occurrences that actually do take place in the real world of men. This is sometimes overlooked by people who imagine that the first order of business is to clear up conceptual muddles. In some areas this may actually be the case. Suppose two philosophy students are having an argument about that ancient puzzle, the nature of physical objects. Here is a table. Is it "really" a piece of solid wood or rather a set of invisible atomic particles? Common sense will reply "Both, of course." The two descriptions do not exclude each other: they relate to different levels of perception or to different "language games." It is all a matter of perspective. There is no sense in asking which of the two descriptions is truer than the other, although there may be a logical problem of settling their relative status in the hierarchy of concepts.

Now disputes over history or politics are not like that at all. In the first place they commonly have a practical purpose: the concepts are intended to serve as guides to action. Secondly, they inescapably involve value judgments as to the final purpose of life or the ultimate standards of morality. This is so even if the participants are unaware of it. To take a fairly obvious instance: when biological notions about supposedly inferior peoples or races are employed to advocate or legitimate their oppression or extermination, what we have is not just a political program (for convenience let us employ short-hand and call it racism) but a world-view that denies the essential unity of mankind. Such a standpoint may be made explicit by a writer, as in the case of Carlyle or Nietzsche, or it may simply be taken for granted by people too unlettered to bother about general ideas. In either case the connection between theory and practice will eventually be brought home to the participants by conflicts arising from incompatible views of the world. Such conflicts need not involve bloodshed, but in the majority of cases they will tend to do so, and even if there is no clash of values, there will be differing perspectives. In the nineteenth century it was commonly assumed by conservatives and radicals alike that the great issue of democracy could in the end be settled only by force. In France, for historical reasons, this approach was extended to the new phenomenon of class conflict between bourgeoisie and proletariat, albeit not all socialists took such a pessimistic view. Similarly, in our own age, Lenin's followers affirmed that capitalism as a world system entailed imperialism, that is to say, the subjection of the backward countries by a handful of hegemonial powers, themselves engaged in endless warfare. Later still this doctrine was modified to make room for the Maoist notion that socialist systems too could become imperialist, and that the "real" issue dividing the world lay between the advanced countries (including the U.S.S.R.) and the great mass of mankind still struggling to overcome the handicaps imposed by history and geography. In at least some of these cases the truth of the basic propositions is not demonstrable by argument, save to those who are already predisposed to believe them. This state of affairs is intended when one speaks of incompatible "ideologies" filling the air with their rival claims. The difference between an "idea" and an "ideology" in this sense is quite simply the difference between a proposition that can be debated on theoretical grounds and a belief which may or may not possess a rational core but which for those who hold it has become a faith that cannot be argued out of existence. The faith may be harmless, as with astrologers and flat-earthers, or dangerous, as in the case of the racial myths associated with the Third Reich of German National Socialism. In either case it is not amenable to rational disproof.

Now the awkwardness, for anyone concerned with social action, is that our working concepts are always embedded in some kind of philosophical perspective. In the course of this brief study we have repeatedly come across instances of conservative, liberal, and socialist writers offering quite different and incompatible interpretations of notions such as progress, welfare, justice, freedom, etc. If these differences were merely the reflex of class or party standpoints–in other words, if they were simply rationalizations–there would be no point in pursuing the topic. One might content oneself with the observation that different people will see the same situation differently. This is obviously true, but too trivial to be of assistance. After all, any mode of reasoning that aspires to the status of a theory must aim at generality. Even if it takes off from what is admittedly a partisan standpoint, it cannot limit itself to mere assertion. At a minimum it must spell out a few propositions which, in principle anyhow, can be grasped by anyone capable of rational thought. In the case of political movements, these propositions will normally have some bearing upon the understanding of what is called history.

For anyone within the socialist tradition, the trouble here stems from the misuse of historical concepts to certify the alleged "inevitability" of this, that, or the other: usually the coming triumph of something called "communism," which on inspection turns out to be a state of affairs quite different from anything that the early communists intended by this term. If one inquires further into the matter, one soon discovers (1) that Lenin was a voluntarist who believed in "swimming against the stream of history"; (2) that the genuine determinists in the Russian revolutionary movement were the Mensheviks, plus a few eccentric Bolsheviks such as Bukharin; (3) that Stalinists and Maoists (like their Fascist rivals) were and are even more extreme voluntarists than Lenin; (4) that in their case the endless talk about "inevitability" has degenerated into a ritual cant quite unrelated to their actual political practice; (5) that the neo-Marxist "revisionists" in Eastern and Western Europe have quietly abandoned Lenin and returned to Marx; and (6) that most of Marx's liberal critics have mistaken him for an orthodox Hegelian. In consequence, solemn treatises are written to the end of demonstrating that there is no such thing as historical inevitability or that one cannot look to metaphysics for guidance or that the future can only be conjectured, not predicted. Thus one may find empiricist philosophers busily at work demolishing what they conceive to be Hegelianism and/or Marxism as a "historicist" aberration. "Historicism," as defined by these authors (e.g., Karl Popper, in his widely read and influential *Poverty of Historicism*) represents "an approach to the social sciences which assumes that *historical prediction* is their principal aim, and that this aim is attainable by discovering the 'rhythms' or the 'patterns', the 'laws' or the 'trends' that underlie the evolution of history" (*Op. cit*., 3). When one tries to correct these and other misapprehensions by pointing out that Hegel never tried to predict anything and, indeed, regarded prediction as impossible, that anyway Marx was not an orthodox Hegelian, and that faith in inevitability is not the same as belief in coherence, one discovers that one is wasting one's time: the empiricist has either not read or not understood the writings he is criticizing and is attacking a straw man of his own invention. He does not even understand that genuine "historicists" (meaning people who think they *know* where history is going) may feel certain about the *goal* without having any clear idea of how to get there (Leff, 78 ff.).

In brief, the entire quarrel is about nothing. For even if it were the case that "historicism" has misled its adherents into resigning themselves fatalistically to the historical process (in reality it has typically had the effect of stimulating them into frenzied activities which otherwise they would not have undertaken), this would not be a good reason for abandoning the attempt to understand what history is about. One can do this without attempting prediction, and indeed historians typically discern the logic of history *after* the event. It is useful to be reminded that political forecasts are necessarily speculative. Sociological analysis, too, cannot employ the model of the physical sciences, if only because the time scales are different; not only may the structure of society alter while it is being studied by the theorist, it may also be consciously remolded, in which case of course the theory has to be revised. For example, the statement that the industrial working class is the only possible basis of a socialist movement may have to be modified or altered if technological change brings about a situation where "work" no longer signifies "expenditure of physical energy." It may then be necessary to redefine the concept of "work" or "labor" so as to make room for the application of science, in other words, for a compound of physical and mental input (a probability foreseen by Marx in 1858). But whatever the refinements, an approach that has nothing to say about the manner in which societies change in historical time is not likely to be of interest either to historians or to sociologists. If by "historicism" is meant not the scarecrow encountered in contemporary liberal writings (for the empiricists are, one and all, political liberals) but the search for significant patterns of societal evolution, then not only is such an approach perfectly licit, it is essential to the understanding of the world we live in.

There exists, in short, a genuine theory of the political process and even of the historical process. In saying this, one must be careful not to overstep the boundary separating the natural sciences from the understanding of history, the latter term signifying all that men have wrought. Science in the positivist sense studies an external environment which is "given" and unalterable, whereas history is made by men and its understanding thus involves an effort at self-comprehension. The agent of history, in the last resort, is man himself—with the obvious proviso that this species-being is not fixed and unchanging, but a self-activating entity whose characteristic traits are modified in and through the process whereby society refashions itself. This conception of history goes back to Vico, was introduced in eighteenth-century Germany by J. G. Herder, was later systematized by Hegel and then adopted by Marx, who fused it with the naturalism of the French materialists. It is not a determinist doctrine. To say that "man makes himself" is to acknowledge that he is capable of modifying what the ancients called his "nature." Were it otherwise, then what is called development would merely be the unfolding of a pre-existing and unalterable human essence. This notion has a respectable ancestry, going back to Aristotle and recurring in certain variants of German idealism, but it is incompatible with historical materialism.

There is, however, an awkwardness that must be squarely faced. Socialists in the Marxist tradition have inherited those elements of Hegel's thought which Marx, tacitly or explicitly, built into the fabric of his own theorizing. While this does not commit them to determinism, or to the ontological system of "dialectical materialism" worked out by Engels after the death of Marx, it does entail the acceptance of Hegel's peculiar synthesis of rationalism and realism concerning the realm of politics and ethics. Anyone who has read Hegel's *Philosophy of Right* knows that its author was very much in the Enlightenment tradition. For proof one need only consider a passage such as the following:

> While it might seem a bitter jest to stifle all animus against tyranny by asserting that the oppressed find their consolation in religion, it still must not be forgotten that religion may take a form leading to the harshest bondage in the fetters of superstition and man's degraded subservience to animals. (The Egyptians and the Hindus, for example, revere animals as beings higher than themselves.) This phenomenon may at least make it evident that we ought not to speak of religion at all in general terms and that we really need a power to protect us from it in some of its forms and to espouse against them the rights of reason and self-consciousness. (*Op. cit.*, para. 270)

Students familiar with Marx will recognize an unmistakable echo of these observations in some of his asides on Indian culture in 1853. This is an aspect of Marxism which need not give liberals any trouble. Matters change when one turns to Hegel's doctrine of the state and its place in history. It is arguable that a pronouncement such as "If states disagree and their particular wills cannot be harmonized, the matter can only be settled by war" (*Op. cit*., para. 334) is merely descriptive, not prescriptive, and does not commit one to anything. But Hegel goes further than that. In his chapter on sovereignty (paras. 321 *et seq*.), one cannot fail to see that he regards a people's willingness to put its physical existence at risk as the test of its ability to exist as a sovereign nation. Hence the notorious passage where war is exalted as "the state of affairs which deals in earnest with the vanity of temporal goods and concerns" (*Op. cit*., para. 324). Hence the statement "Peoples unwilling or afraid to tolerate sovereignty at home have been subjugated from abroad." What Hegel is saying here and elsewhere is that a state attains sovereignty only in so far as its citizens are prepared to lay down their lives for it. His ideal was the ancient *polis* in general and Athens in particular; but this does not deprive his utterances of a certain flavor which liberals have generally not found to their liking.

Now it has to be said plainly that on this issue the Marxist is obliged to take Hegel's view of the matter. Historically, no independent state or nation has ever come into existence otherwise than by war or the threat of war, either against an imperial oppressor or against neighbors threatening its existence. Liberals are able to ignore this awkward fact only because theirs is an individualist philosophy which typically comes into being within a pacified and civilized community after an era of wars and revolutions has ended and violence, domestic or foreign, has been solemnly abjured. A nation may be so powerful that it can close its eyes to the material preconditions of its own hegemony. This was the case of Great Britain in the mid-nineteenth century, when liberalism (not accidentally) found its classical formulation in the works of J. S. Mill. Alternatively, it may have become so weak as to choose neutrality and pacifism as a permanent way of life, in which case it can preserve its independence only by the grace of others. In either case, its citizens will be tempted to ignore the actual condition of the world, and its ideologists will do their best to promote faith in international law as a guarantee of peace, forgetting that laws have to be enforced and that (in Hobbes' well-known phrase) "covenants, without the sword, are but words and of no strength to secure a man at all."

If this is what is meant when it is said that Marx inherited Hegel's disillusioned view of politics, then there is no occasion to dispute the statement; indeed, one may add that Marx extended this manner of reasoning to the relationship between oppressor and oppressed within a national community. It does not follow that such a relationship can be altered only by violence. What *does* follow is that the issue of political power cannot be eluded. A class, like a nation, proves its readiness to play a "historic" role by securing sovereign control over its own destiny. If–like the German middle class in 1848 or the German working class in 1918–it fails this test, it thereby discloses its incapacity for the exercise of political power. Likewise, a nation may not only lose its independence, it may actually commit suicide and be finished *as a nation*, though not as a collection of individuals. If these truths had not been forgotten or ignored by so many liberals and socialists brought up on the optimistic philosophy of the later nineteenth century, it is conceivable that the world might have been spared at least some of the disasters it has endured during the past half century.

On the positive side, one may note that a community is able to transcend its limitations by incorporating within its self-awareness the universal ideas (or "values") of religion or humanist philosophy. From the German Reformation of the sixteenth century to the French Revolution of the eighteenth, a succession of historic turning-points altered the consciousness of the Western world and, *inter alia*, furnished a suitable theme for the philosophy of history. The particular case of the French Revolution is of special significance for our theme, for it was by way of this bloody deluge that the universal ideas of the Enlightenment entered the collective inheritance of Europe. The lesson was not lost upon Hegel, who witnessed the event, and it accounts for a certain stoical resignation in his later utterances. But it did not make him a worshipper of force, nor did it blind him to the essential unity of mankind. What his heirs, including Marx, inferred from this world-shaking experience was rather the gloomy certainty that progress was likely to be painful. It was just this which distinguished them from the utopians.

2. Class and Social Change

In earlier chapters of this study concerned with the origins of class conflict in nineteenth-century Europe, we have seen that one could speak of an interdependence between market relations and social antagonism. The industrial revolution under bourgeois control transformed society in such a way as to convert the ancient "orders" or "estates" into "classes" held together solely by economic ties. It took some time before thinking people grasped what had occurred, but by the 1850's they had become used both to the new situation and to the language that went with it. This vocabulary replaced the term "estate" (*état, Stand*) by that of "class" (save in the United States where the existence of classes was and is officially denied). For the most part, liberals and socialists agreed as to the facts of the case, even if they differed in their interpretation. Liberalism generally tended to credit the middle class with a set of virtues proper to the efficient functioning of the new industrial-capitalist order; socialism performed a similar service for the working class, with the difference that its spokesmen distinguished between industrialism as such and its bourgeois-entrepreneurial form, of which they disapproved. In principle there was agreement that classes existed, and that they were rooted in economics. The phenomenon was likewise recognized (and deplored) by agrarian conservatives who advocated a return to a corporative organization of society, with each "estate" assuming fixed duties and responsibilities of a noneconomic kind. The conventional liberal reply to this was that such a solution presupposed a static order, whereas modern society was dynamic.

On this latter point liberals and socialists likewise concurred. But what sort of dynamic was it that kept capitalism going, and what was to be expected in the more distant future from the uncontrolled operation of the system? On this topic the disputants no longer spoke the same language. Liberalism assumed a self-regulating market economy directed by private entrepreneurs. Socialism demanded public intervention, in some cases total state ownership or control. Marx added a further refinement: he demonstrated that capitalism was undermining its own social foundations by doing away with small-scale private property. On this point at least he could not be controverted by statistical evidence. In the middle of the nineteenth century, the social base of bourgeois democracy was sufficiently broad. In the United States, to cite a favorable example, some 80 per cent of the population (excluding slaves) owned the means of production with which they worked. Whether they were farmers, traders, craftsmen, or manufacturers, these people possessed "a stake in the country." Hence their problems could be discussed in the time-honored language of the Founding Fathers. A century later, approximately the same proportion consisted of wage- or salary-earners. Their living standards as consumers had risen beyond all comparison with earlier ages, but their social status no longer corresponded to the assumptions of Jacksonian democracy. In consequence even economists who credited capitalism with a capacity for limitless *economic* progress reluctantly concluded that in the long run it was not viable as a *social* system. This pessimistic forecast had nothing whatever to do with any kind of economic stagnation thesis of the sort rendered popular by Keynes and some of his followers in the 1930's. It rested solely on sociological considerations, chief among them the gradual extinction of the private entrepreneur as the mainspring of the self-regulating market economy (Schumpeter, *Capitalism, Socialism, and Democracy,* 131 ff.; see also Sievers, 26 ff.).

In principle this development should have been gratifying to socialists, whether Marxists or Fabians, since it undercut the assumptions so long and tenaciously held by their opponents. In practice it confronted them with a set of new and unexpected difficulties: (1) the actual transformation of unregulated into planned and regulated capitalism; (2) the problem posed by a new kind of social stratification based on differences of status and education; and (3) the unsolved theoretical problem of relating physical and mental labor to each other.

We have seen that in the nineteenth century liberals and socialists, if they were honest, agreed as to the reality of class conflict. They also agreed that classes were definable in economic terms, unlike the old estates, membership of which was hereditary, corporate, fixed by tradition, and a matter of legal and social status. On the liberal side, the new concept of class was implicit in Smith and became explicit with Ricardo. Among socialists, Marx introduced a new historical and moral perspective by relating the phenomenon of class to the dissolution of the feudal order, wherein the quality of being a nobleman or a commoner had been inseparable from the personality of the individual. In an early work, the *German Ideology* (1845-46) he already had made a point later expanded in *Capital*: "The division between the personal and the class individual, the accidental nature of the conditions of life for the individual, appears only with the emergence of the class, which is itself a product of the bourgeoisie. This accidental character is only engendered and developed by competition and the struggle of individuals among themselves" (*Op. cit.*, 95). Classes make their appearance *pari passu* with the rise of a social order in which individuals are free, in the sense that they are no longer marked for life by an inherited status which they cannot shake off. This freedom has a positive aspect for the possessing class, a negative one for the proletarians, because "the condition of their existence, labor, and with it all the conditions governing modern society, have become something accidental, something over which they, as separate individuals, have no control, and over which no *social* organization can give them control" (*Ibid.*, 96). In current parlance we may say that classes are an aspect of the market-centered society that emerged in eighteenth-century England. The irony lay in the fact that the automatism of the self-regulating market first dissolved the estates and then replaced them by classes, while the active or passive agents of the process imagined themselves to be wholly free and independent–at least, if they were of a class which owned its means of production. If they lost control of them, the illusory nature of their freedom was forcibly brought home to them, and they were obliged to see themselves as possessing a collective existence and a common aim: the abolition of class society.

This was the heart of the Marxian argument. Is it still valid? Let us set aside the cruder forms of popular Marxism, as instanced by the notion that the economic interest of the possessing class finds an automatic reflex in the political operations of the "power elite." On this interpretation, the "capitalist state" (a term not employed by Marx) functions as the instrument of the "ruling class," "the capitalists," "the corporations," or "big business" and occasionally goes to war at their behest for the purpose of acquiring new markets. There exists a liberal version of this populist, or *kindergarten*, form of economic determinism. Its spokesmen suffer from similar delusions. Typically they assert that "selfish interests"–monopolists, trade unionists, and protection-minded farmers–are joined in an unholy conspiracy to wreck the beneficial automatism of the self-regulating market by imposing protective tariffs, guaranteed wages, and social-welfare legislation, instead of letting the price mechanism work in accordance with its logic. There is no profit in pursuing these rival brands of nonsense. Even in its more sophisticated form, the idea that sectional class interests invariably translate themselves into irresistible political pressures does not have much to commend it. Situations of this kind are rare, and when they do occur it is usually in the context of a social system which has temporarily lost its political steering mechanism. The famous scene in the French National Assembly on the night of August 4, 1789, when the nobility solemnly renounced its (largely worthless) seignorial rights, was clearly inspired by fear of peasant risings which had grown alarmingly for some months; but it was also due to a temporary collapse of political authority at the center, and in any case historical research has shown that by then the issue of "feudalism" had become fictitious, many bourgeois being landowners and vice versa, so that class lines were blurred and no one could say exactly who stood to benefit. If panic measures adopted under such circumstances are conceived as a model of what is meant by social change, then it is plain that constellations of this sort will not occur very often.

The real question, then, is whether we can go on assuming that class interest and class conflict will operate as they did when there was a purely market-centered society; and the answer must be that we need a different model. Some of our present difficulties are due to the fact that the classical approach in the nineteenth century provided no more than a rough-and-ready way of describing what was actually going on. Other problems stem from recent changes in the structure of society. There exists a kind of conceptual shorthand, common to liberals and socialists alike, which has become a source of serious misjudgments when applied to political reality. Its intellectual roots go back to the great economists who were the first to analyze the operation of a fully developed market economy: Smith, Ricardo, John Stuart Mill, and Marx. The common factor is the belief that long-run changes in the social order are normally mediated by short-run class interests. Given a society of the early capitalist type this assumption is fairly realistic, although it has to be borne in mind that the interrelation of class interest and national (or societal) interest is dialectical. "The fate of classes is much more often determined by the needs of society than the fate of society is determined by the needs of classes" (Polanyi, 152). Even in a market-centered society, important sectional interests that run counter to national or state interests—the state existing primarily for the purpose of safeguarding the sovereignty of the nation; in other words, its independence from other nations—may quite simply be disregarded.

Conversely, there may arise temporary or permanent alliances which are politically effective just because they are *not* sectional. A "political bloc" (to employ Gramsci's terminology) may be formed not only by a ruling class of great landowners and captains of industry (as in Wilhelminian Germany) but likewise by an alliance of entrepreneurs and farmers (as in the Republican Party during and after the American Civil War) or by industrialists and workers (as in pre-Fascist Italy, where the ruling liberal oligarchy took the unions into partnership, so as to impose a policy of tariff protection plus welfare legislation) (Gramsci, 37). This kind of situation is analyzable in class terms only if one bears in mind that sectional pressures may be ignored in the interest of promoting some overriding political goal essential to the continued existence of the whole society. In the case of nineteenth-century continental Europe, the prime goal was national unification plus tariff protection to aid the growth of industry, so as to survive in the competition with foreign rivals. Interests that got in the way were bought off, or sacrificed, or simply ignored. If the political process ran into insurmountable obstacles the result might be civil war and social disintegration (as in Spain) or imperialism and national catastrophe (as in Italy and Germany after 1914). In either case the outcome was mediated by intellectual currents that eventually transmitted political aims and sentiments—socialist, or nationalist, or both—to the masses. In Germany, nationalism provided the necessary unifying sentiment, until it was discredited by two lost wars and the monstrosities of the Third Reich. In Italy, Mussolini's movement arose as a more or less conscious perversion of socialism and syndicalism, the precondition of its temporary success being the antecedent collapse of liberalism and the inability of the Socialists to come forward as a *national* force with a solution for the country's problems. The consequence of this twofold failure was an explosion of frenzied nationalism.

> The phenomenon of emigration gives rise to the conception of the "proletarian nation" . . . the Libyan war [of 1911] appears to whole strata of intellectuals as the beginning of the offensive of the "great proletarian nation" against the capitalistic and plutocratic world. A

whole group of syndicalists passed over to nationalism; in fact the Nationalist Party was originally constituted by former syndicalist intellectuals. . . . When Mussolini left *Avanti* and the Socialist Party he was surrounded by this cohort of syndicalists and southernists." (Gramsci, 38-39)

Not all Marxists were capable of such intellectual insight. If they did not content themselves with the platitudes of reformism, they tried to copy the October Revolution. (Gramsci himself mistook the latter for a proletarian seizure of power.) The concept of the "historical bloc" or class alliance exercising an ideological and practical hegemony by virtue of its ability to tackle the nation's problems is an important contribution to political theory. Whether it is compatible with belief in the hegemonial role of the proletariat is another matter. At any rate Antonio Gramsci (1891-1937) may be said to have provided the Communist movement in Western Europe with a theory of class conflict that was an improvement on the Leninist model.

The crucial point here is the recognition that control of the political "superstructure" is the key to the reorganization of society. In his own fashion Lenin had perceived this quite early—whence his determination to break with the Mensheviks and all other representatives of "economism"—but Russia could never offer a suitable model for the remainder of Europe, not even for Eastern Europe. Gramsci, writing in and for a Western country, proposed an interpretation of Leninism that made it palatable to the intelligentsia: socialism must set itself to solve the tasks left unsolved by liberalism. In particular, it must promote the "cultural unification of mankind." This sort of language, an inheritance from the long tradition of Italian humanism, established a bridge across which liberal intellectuals could move into the Marxist camp while maintaining that degree of spiritual continuity without which no civilized existence is possible. As a disciple of Benedetto Croce (a liberal influenced by the Hegelian idealist tradition), Gramsci possessed a lively awareness of what is involved in reconstructing a society's cultural heritage. What he called *egemonia* (hegemony) was something quite different from the Jacobin-Blanquist notion of an emergency dictatorship to suppress the "class enemy." He thought in terms of creating a new cultural consensus around a "historical bloc" furnished by the working class and "its" intellectuals. Some of this was an inheritance from pre-

1914 Syndicalism, specifically from Sorel in his earlier quasi-Marxist and pre-nationalist phase. It had its counterpart in the thinking of the Guild Socialists, save that their successors in Britain were less likely than Gramsci to mistake the Russian Revolution for a proletarian seizure of power. Absolved as he was by his personal circumstances (he spent the last eleven years of his life in prison) from the necessity of confronting the reality of Soviet totalitarianism, Gramsci was free to work out a body of doctrine that could serve as a theoretical guideline after Fascism and Stalinism had both vacated the scene. The value of his legacy is considerable–not least in the light it throws upon the pathetic imitations of European Fascism currently prevalent in Latin America, Southeast Asia, and the Middle East. It is plain enough that any authentic Socialist movement in those parts will have to nourish itself on Gramsci's work if it aspires to the spiritual *egemonia* that a new political order requires for its permanence. The question of Gramsci's relevance for Socialist movements in advanced industrial societies is rather more difficult to answer. His admirers have a way of overlooking the awkward circumstance that he was struggling with the problems of a country in the throes of modernization: an ancient Mediterranean country, moreover, whose Catholic culture was falling to pieces and which had never experienced the Reformation. There is a further difficulty: Gramsci had seen through the Fascist system of make-believe, but he died before the significance of Stalinist totalitarianism became apparent even to Communists.

A philosophical training in the Hegelian tradition is useful in establishing a perspective upon history that transcends the narrow context of politics. Gramsci was fond of comparing Socialism to the Enlightenment or to the Reformation. In consequence it did not greatly matter to him that there was not as yet much to show in the way of intellectual refinement, notably in the domain of philosophy. After all (as he used to point out), it had taken German Protestantism three centuries to evolve from the crudities of Luther to the metaphysical splendors of Hegel. As an argument in the life-long dispute Gramsci carried on with Croce and his pupils, this was effective enough. Meanwhile, however, there were urgent problems pressing for solution, chief among them the role of the party as the embodied consciousness of the working class. For Gramsci, socialism was not something external to the "spontaneous" labor movement, as it was for Lenin. Rather it was the conscious articulation of what was dimly felt by the working masses. Socialist intellectuals, organically related to the class from which they stemmed, represented the *autocoscienza critica* of their class, the creators of its consciousness. This was a notable divergence from the Leninist model; but then Gramsci had come to Communism from Syndicalism; hence he retained his faith in the ability of the working class to produce an intellectual elite of its own, ultimately a new world-view dimly foreshadowed in Marxism. Cultural "hegemony" in this perspective entailed a new philosophy of life, accorded universal acceptance because its truth was demonstrable. All this may account for the fact that Italian Communism in the post-Stalin era cast itself in the role of a humanist movement representing the heritage of the Renaissance and the liberal Risorgimento. It does not supply an adequate answer to the problems posed by the Stalinist epoch, for to treat Stalinism simply as a response to Russian backwardness is plainly an evasion. The Stalinist regime had carried through a consciously controlled "revolution from above"–in a horrifying fashion, but in the end successfully, even though in the process every shred of "proletarian democracy" was sacrificed. Had he lived long enough to witness the outcome, Gramsci would presumably have had to conclude, as his Italian pupils have reluctantly done in substance, that socialism must be democratic if it is not to become indistinguishable from Fascism. His theoretical legacy was sufficiently ample to permit an unavowed return to the classical Marxian position: the liberal heritage must be preserved, not surrendered in the name of expediency. But what is possible in Western Europe may be impracticable elsewhere, notably in countries lacking any kind of democratic tradition and under pressure to modernize at breakneck speed, in the teeth of worker-and-peasant resistance. The political elites in charge of a revolutionary dictatorship may then be driven to the conclusion that enlightenment has to be imposed by force even if the more retrograde strata do not want it. This after all had been the "Jacobin" view, and Gramsci had some sympathy with Jacobinism. There is no unequivocal moral to be drawn from all this, save that Communists and democratic Socialists can both read Gramsci with profit, so long as they do not expect to find political recipes applicable to their very different problems.

While Gramsci did not live long enough to witness the fusion of Bolshevism with Fascism in the fully developed Stalinist system around

1940, his experience of Mussolini's regime supplied him with a key to the new phenomenon of totalitarianism. This is a term which must be employed with some caution, having been largely emptied of its operational meaning by writers eager to discredit anything they happen to dislike, from the French Revolution onward. What the term signifies is the forcible reconstruction of the social order by a single-party regime in effective control of the political superstructure. This is quite different from the imposition of authoritarian rule by a conservative oligarchy determined to keep things as they are—the sort of aim that some intellectuals have traditionally imbibed by way of Plato's notorious idealization of Sparta in the *Republic*. A totalitarian regime is dynamic, or else it does not deserve this particular label. The confusion stems from the intellectual orientation known as elitism. The concept of the political elite is of Italian origin, and not accidentally it was put forward by Gaetano Mosca (1858-1941) and Vilfredo Pareto (1848-1923) in a place and at a time when liberalism was coming under fire from left and right. The centerpiece of the doctrine was an analysis of politics as an autonomous realm: not (as Marx was supposed to have thought) a mere reflex of social conflict. Politics was about control of the state, and political leadership was invariably exercised by elites made up of individuals endowed with superior talents for governing inferiors. This was so whether the system was nominally democratic or not, from which it followed that democracy was a myth if taken to mean popular self-rule. As for the classless society of Marxian socialism, it was utopian by definition.

Anyone familiar with Italian history will have no trouble picking out the Machiavellian roots of this doctrine, but then much of Gramsci's political thinking too revolved around the problematic fortunes of the Italian city-state and its failure in the later stages of the Renaissance. A case can thus be made for the proposition that in the 1890's, when Mosca and Pareto developed their elitist doctrine, while Antonio Labriola expounded Marxism and Benedetto Croce acclimatized Hegelianism, Italian political thinkers played variations upon a single theme. This is not to say that all they wrote was equally significant. Mosca's theory of the ruling class (first sketched out in 1884 and then elaborated in 1896) was poor stuff, and Gramsci had no trouble disposing of it. "Mosca's so-called 'political class' is nothing but the intellectual section of the ruling group" (Meisel, 315). Pareto's *Trattato* of 1916, for all its impressive bulk, proved wholly sterile, and the worthy Robert Michels, with his ponderous analysis of German Social Democracy, made more of an impression upon his Italian readers than upon Germans who knew the topic at first hand. But for all their essential provincialism, these authors (like Sorel, who made extensive use of them) gave an impetus to what may be called the sociology of politics. If they had no solutions to offer, at least they asked some relevant questions.

Instead of going into the merits or demerits of elite theory, let us simply note a few historical circumstances. (1) The doctrine, as outlined by Mosca in 1896 and revised by Michels and Pareto around 1910, was both anti-liberal and anti-Marxist; it thus made an appeal to conservative nationalists, but also to disappointed Syndicalists, some of whom after 1918 came to swell the Fascist ranks. (2) Fascism, though originally conceived on Italian soil and put into practice by Mussolini, developed in an international context. In particular, it found favor in Latin America, where it provided both the ruling oligarchies and the more nationalist elements among the military and the intellectuals with an ideological equipment of sorts. (3) It evoked a Marxist response from Gramsci, who had been impressed by the collapse of Italian Liberalism and the helplessness of the labor movement (Socialist and Communist alike) when confronted with the Fascist onslaught. (4) For all its claims to represent a "totalitarian" regime, Italian Fascism was in fact hobbled by its original compromise with the monarchy and the Church, but for which it could not have come to power. Of the various Fascist regimes, only the German after 1933 came close to being genuinely totalitarian, to the degree that it became independent of the conservative elements in state and society with which it had originally allied itself. Stalinism by contrast was fully totalitarian, the Revolution having pulverized all the existing institutions of society and concentrated political authority within the leadership of the Communist Party. The Stalinist regime was thus able after 1929 to effect a "revolution from above" by expropriating the peasantry, re-introducing a form of state serfdom, and imposing a degree of labor discipline unparalleled in any other country on the road to full-scale industrialization. This latter feature induced its Trotskyist or Bukharinist critics to describe the regime as "bureaucratic," the implication being that a new ruling class had arisen (or an old one been restored) in the state bureaucracy which collectively owned or managed the nationalized means of production. The trouble with this analysis was that it presupposed the traditional distinction between an autonomous economy and its political superstructure, whereas the originality of Stalinism (and to a lesser degree of Fascism) lay in the fact that it had done away with this difference. The issue was posed in 1957, when it became briefly possible to discuss such topics in Eastern Europe, by a distinguished Polish sociologist in the following terms:

> When the conceptual system and problems of bourgeois sociology were being formulated, when the ideas of Marx and Engels were being developed into a great and cohesive doctrine, the social consequences of the second technical revolution . . . which were to transform the social life of the twentieth century were not yet known. . . . A social system based on the nationalization of the means of production was also unknown. No one could yet have had any experience of the kind of planning which was over a great part of the globe to embrace in a centralized system almost the entire economy, including the production of the so-called "cultural values," and to take over the direction of the labour force, the large-scale distribution of privileges and discriminations, and the conscious shaping of the social structure. . . .
>
> In situations where changes of social structure are to a greater or lesser degree governed by the decision of the political authorities, we are a long way from social classes as interpreted by Marx, Ward, Veblen, or Weber, from classes conceived of as groups determined by their relations to the means of production or, as others would say, by their relations to the market (Ossowski, 2-3, 184).

Classes, in other words, are a phenomenon peculiar to bourgeois society. That this conclusion was drawn in the 1950's by a Polish author fully conversant both with Leninist theory and with Stalinist reality certainly enhances its interest. The disintegration of class society is plainly related to the phenomenon of totalitarianism. If the "political authorities" can permanently alter the social structure, the one-party state acquires its own dynamic and becomes the conscious instrument of reconstruction. The ruling political caste, unhampered by any organized opposition, can then impose its will in a manner inconceivable under conditions where "state" and "society" are related to each other in such a way that the former appears as the "executive organ" of the latter. It is perhaps worth emphasizing that the "Machiavellian" tradition associated with Mosca and Pareto was quite innocent of these discoveries: it was solely concerned with the manipulation of power. These conservative writers were critical of parliamentary democracy as an ineffective system of government, but they never foresaw (let alone advocated) the forcible reconstruction of the entire socio-economic "base" in accordance with decisions emanating from the "superstructure." Neither, for that matter, did those democratic socialists who took their line from Marx or from Engels and his successors. As for the Fabians, they were indeed suspected, as we have seen, of favoring the rule of an enlightened bureaucracy which would stifle individual enterprise. But a glance at their literature, or that of their Marxist and Guild Socialist critics, shows that a Fabian regime was simply intended to *administer* a country already collectivized by the impersonal pressure of economic forces. Such a society would presumably be stable, if not stagnant, and in any case governed on democratic lines, with plenty of built-in checks and balances. The totalitarian phenomenon arose under exceptional circumstances on the semi-civilized borderlands of Europe and was then catapulted into political space by the rival Communist and Fascist movements. Its coming was unforeseen, if not perhaps wholly unforeseeable.

What is the relevance of this "bureaucratic collectivism" (if that is what one wants to call it) to the so-called "new class" of managers or administrators? First of all, what is called managerialism obviously relates to *all* types of advanced industrial society: whether capitalist or socialist, democratic or authoritarian, pluralist or one-party, Western or Eastern. In other words, being a global phenomenon associated with what may be termed bureaucratization, it cannot be pressed into service for purposes of argument in a controversy between liberals and socialists, or between democrats and authoritarians. If there is a "new class" in the sense of a social stratum spontaneously generated by the scientific and industrial production process, then its emergence is not dependent on specific political arrangements. *Is* there such a class? It may seem mere logic-chopping, but if one adheres to the notion that "classes" are characteristic of a market-centered economy, then it makes no sense to say that a "new class" has come into being under conditions where the market economy is giving way to centralized planning (which need not be totalitarian). At most one might speak of a new directing stratum. However, economists of the Keynesian persuasion are fond of the term, possibly because it fills the gap left in the older type of sociology by the reluctance of its founders to employ the term "class," for fear of being mistaken for socialists. Thus one now finds it stated that "A New Class has emerged in affluent America and it will grow. . . . The passport to this class is education. In the final analysis, the growth of the New Class, for whom labor is pleasurable, is the true index of progress" (Sievers [summarizing Galbraith], 69). It is not clear whether this is more than a new way of stating that there has been a numerical growth of the intelligentsia, or the salariat in general. Professor J. K. Galbraith in the 1960's had come to see the New Class as the pace-setter of what in the 1950's he was pleased to describe as the "affluent society":

> We have barely noticed that the leisure class has been replaced by another and much larger class to which work has none of the older connotation of pain, fatigue, or other mental or physical discomfort. We have failed to appreciate the emergence of this New Class, as it may be simply called, largely as the result of one of the oldest and most effective obfuscations in the field of social science. This is the effort to assert that all work–physical, mental, artistic, or managerial–is essentially the same. (*The Affluent Society, 264-65*)

A decade later, the key term was no longer "affluence" but "technostructure." The basic argument, however, remained substantially the same (*The New Industrial State*, 86 ff.).

All this appears to have only a very tenuous connection with the familiar assertion that a New Class has risen to power in the collectivized societies of the U.S.S.R. and Eastern Europe. Whether accurate or not, such a statement affirms something quite specific: that ownership and/or control of the collectivized means of production is vested in an irremovable bureaucracy which monopolizes both political and economic power, employing the Communist Party as its chosen instrument. A ruling stratum of this kind, if equipped with powers to perpetuate itself, would resemble the ancient nobility rather than the bourgeoisie, for it would combine military, political, economic, social, and cultural functions–something the European middle class never managed to do on a national scale, although arguably it attained this goal in the city-states of northern Italy, Flanders, Holland, and Switzerland during a period ranging from the fourteenth to the sixteenth century. If a stratum of *this* sort is in process of formation somewhere, it is extremely unlikely that its existence will become apparent to itself, let alone to outsiders, at an early stage. A new class, like a new culture, does not sprout overnight. There clearly is something in the notion that the functional separation of physical from mental labor may contain the germ of a new division along class lines. If this process should turn out to be irreversible, it would become necessary to conclude that the goal of a classless society is utopian, in so far as it assumes that the division of labor can be overcome. But whether or not this is actually the case remains to be seen. In any event it has no bearing on the exercise of power. Class analysis deals with long-run processes, not with transitory political and ideological phenomena.

The current fashion in sociology, however, has made it impossible to discuss the one without bringing in the other. If the term "ruling class" is employed to describe the political elite of any given society, the discussion will revolve around the sort of topic rendered familiar in sociological literature by the work of Weber, Schumpeter, Parsons, and Pareto. If the argument concerns the polarization of social classes in *bourgeois* society, one had better stick to the Marxian apparatus, which is expressly designed to deal with this particular subject. If one intends to investigate the twentieth-century phenomenon of totalitarianism, it is useful to bear in mind what Ossowski has to say about the built-in limitations of liberal and Marxian theorizing alike. Alternatively one may confine the debate to the theme of workers' control in industry, in which case one is bound to stay within the socialist terminology, and one will then be brought back to the issues already at stake in the controversies started before and after 1914 by the Webbs, Bernard Shaw, William Morris, Tawney, Cole, and their associates. The purpose of the exercise in the present chapter is not to "solve" this particular problem, but to sort out the conceptual tool-kit required.

Let us now apply the historical perspective. In its origins, socialism in Western Europe grew out of the nascent workers' movement in Britain and France around 1830: specifically the "labor aristocracy" of skilled and unionized workers. The movement had some trouble emancipating itself from its agrarian-populist ancestry, which connected it with a more ancient democratic tradition. In its further development it acquired a political consciousness during the struggle for the attainment of what were then accurately defined as class aims. At the same time it attracted the sympathy and support of theorists stemming from the intellectual elite of the middle class. Lenin and his followers later interpreted this circumstance to mean that the labor movement, left to itself, could not spontaneously rise above a "trade unionist" level, from which it followed that a socialist consciousness had to be introduced into it "from without" by radical intellectuals. This was indeed the case in Russia. But elsewhere the intellectuals largely generalized what was inherent in the workers' spontaneous rebellion against their condition of life under capitalism. Recognition of this fact was central to the Syndicalist movement from which a number of Communists stemmed: Gramsci being foremost among a generation of labor leaders who mistook the Russian Revolution for a proletarian seizure of power. In fact, it was nothing of the kind, nor could it have been. Russian Socialism was the creation of the gentry–a stratum already prominent before the belated rise of an ineffective bourgeoisie which missed its chance in 1917. Lenin was the last and greatest of those *déclassé* intellectuals who for a century had given form and content to the Populist doctrine that Russia could and should "skip" the capitalist stage. He was right in asserting that this doctrine had to be imported into the workers' movement, but the conclusion he drew–that "the party" must be composed of "professional revolutionaries"–was irrelevant to the conditions under which Communist movements arose after 1919 in Central and Western Europe. A purely Russian notion, it was unacceptable even to Polish Marxists such as Rosa Luxemburg, and doubly unacceptable to labor leaders shaped by the Syndicalist tradition. The latter, however, had in the meantime developed a different kind of elitism–based on the notion that only a minority of class-conscious workers were capable of rising to an adequate awareness of their historic task. In consequence it was possible for theorists like Gramsci to regard themselves as Leninists. The misunderstanding latent in this situation became apparent only after the Soviet bureaucracy had visibly cut its connection with the workers' movement. The delayed shock of this discovery accounts for the disarray of the Communist parties in all those advanced industrial countries in which the labor movement has outgrown the primitive rebelliousness normally associated with the impact of early capitalism. Conversely, the Russian model, having been propounded in a retarded country by revolutionaries stemming from the gentry, continues to have an emotional and intellectual appeal for radical intellectuals similarly situated, notably in Latin America and Southeast Asia.

What does all this have to do with the concept of a "new class" or with Paretian notions about the "circulation of elites"? Nothing whatever, save in so far as a certain amount of elitist theorizing is inevitable in a situation where a socialist tradition has come into being before the emergence of an authentic labor movement. Russia was such a country, and there were analogous tendencies in Spain, which is why Bakunin's anarchist version of gentry socialism went down well with Spaniards who had no use for bourgeois democracy. It also made an appeal to the *lumpenproletariat* of Naples (but not to the labor aristocracy of Milan and Turin, from which Gramsci's party has drawn its strength for the past half century). It is true that the Italian Communist Party, unlike its Socialist predecessor, has made an effort to reach the peasantry, having been warned by the Fascist experience not to neglect the rural areas for the sake of mere urban labor reformism. But it has done so on the basis of mental attitudes formed in the industrial centers. In other words, it has throughout its career been Leninist only in so far as it has aimed at total power and the one-party state, and in its latest transmutation it has effectively abandoned this aim, thereby reverting to its origins. To no one's great surprise, the lead given in the West European country where Communism is numerically strongest has begun to affect the remainder of the Communist movement in Europe. In the measure in which these parties rediscover their Marxian inheritance, they are inevitably obliged to revise the Leninist construction they had placed upon it.

3. Beyond Capitalism

It seems fitting to conclude this survey with a few observations on the economics of socialism: not as a contribution to the analysis of technical problems, but so as to remove a few misconceptions. There is no purpose in pretending that the historian can do more than register recent developments in what has increasingly become a matter for specialists. Oskar Lange's and F. M. Taylor's slim volume, first published in 1938 and several times reprinted since then, lists a number of writings published in the 1930's on the topic of resources allocation under central planning. Since then the trickle has broadened into a stream to which Lange himself made a notable contribution in 1959-63 with a severely professional analysis of economic theorizing along strictly Marxist lines, an analysis that had behind it the authority of a distinguished theorist then still in charge of socialist planning in his native Poland. Anyone curious to know what a Marxist economist had to say in the late 1950's and early 1960's about the problems and prospects of capitalism (and about the historical approach customarily associated with German authors such as Werner Sombart and Max Weber) is advised to consult him. Even if he or she gets nothing more out of it than the shock of finding Weber's celebrated analysis of the Reformation treated as a piece of Hegelian idealist philosophizing (*Political Economy*, 268) the experience will have been worth while. There is never any harm in subjecting one's conventional assumptions to the test of a hostile judgment that has behind it the weight of solid learning and practical experience. Lange had no use whatever for non-Marxian economics, whether "subjectivist" or "historical," to employ his terminology. He knew all about mathematical programming and made lavish use of it but saw no reason to depart from the basic assumptions Marx had extracted from the classics of political economy. From his standpoint the empirical approach which dispensed with "abstract" concepts and the utilitarian or marginalist doctrine represented two parallel aberrations: the historical school did away with theorizing altogether, while the marginalists replaced the sociological realism of the classics by a crude psychologism. Classical political economy had to do with wealth-creation, and in its Marxian version with historically determined relations of production. Marginalism—the doctrine associated with Jevons, Walras, Pareto, Marshall, and Menger—focussed on the behavior of individuals in a social framework that was implicitly taken for granted. From being an analysis of the structure of socio-economic relations, "political economy becomes the study of the relation of man to the objects satisfying his needs, to the goods the possession of which causes pleasure or constitutes wealth" (Lange, 234). Man's behavior is supposed to conform to the principle of maximizing an entity known as "utility"; hence economics, in its origins an exercise associated with the rise of the market economy, becomes the study of one particular aspect of an invariant human nature. The end result is to transform economics into a "logic of choice," the external framework of which is the relationship between ends and scarce means. Sociology is dissolved into psychology. It escapes this fate in the school of Weber and his descendants only at the cost of helping to transform economic *theory* into economic *history*. The attentive reader of Lange's learned diatribe discovers before long that these criticisms are *not* directed against Joseph Schumpeter. But then Schumpeter was a conservative pessimist who detested socialism but held its coming to be inevitable. As for Keynes, it is common knowledge that he reverted to macro-economics, notably the study of topics such as unemployment and the trade cycle. To that extent his pupils and the neo-Marxists are in the position of rival armies engaged in a contest for possession of the same piece of ground (Robinson, *Economic Philosophy*).

Lest it be supposed that these brief remarks are intended to do justice to a topic which has now occupied some of the best minds in the learned world for over a century, let us move to shallower and safer waters. It may seem a trifle odd to say, "To the right of the Marxists are the socialists" (Heilbroner, 291), but it is certainly the case that some distinguished economists have made out a theoretical case for socialism without troubling about Marx. It is true that they have generally done so by reviving the ethical critique of capitalism associated with Robert Owen or with William Morris and his progeny. That is to say, they have stressed the distinction between "production for profit" and "production for use." Now in a sense all production is for use: if marketable commodities possessed no use value, they could not be sold and no one could make a profit out of them. This is the standard apology for capitalism or private enterprise, whichever term one prefers. Even the mightiest corporation has to produce what it can sell, and it can only sell what other people need (or think they need because they have been told so, which admittedly makes a large difference). In this sense, production for profit is automatically converted into production for use by the operation of the market. There exists a rather simple-minded version of anticapitalism which condemns the whole performance on the grounds that it is motivated by the self-interest of the producers. But this is plain foolishness. Self-interest is not necessarily anti-social, and if it could be shown that the "invisible hand" of the price mechanism transmutes individual selfishness into activities tending to promote the public good, the system would be immune to criticism on ordinary moral grounds. It would then still be open to socialists or anarchists to prefer a different arrangement, but they could not well assert that capitalism is harmful to the public interest, or that a better mechanism can be designed to satisfy the material needs of society. This, however, is just what socialists do affirm, and their reasons for holding this view have to be backed by arguments that take account of their opponents' case.

Setting aside the Marxian thesis concerning the exploitation of labor —a concept that depends on general propositions about labor and value unacceptable to non-Marxian economists—the minimal case for socialism as an economic system boils down to the proposition that public planning is socially superior to an unregulated market economy of the capitalist type. To avoid misunderstanding, let it be clear that "capitalism" signifies control over the means of production by individual or corporate owners of capital who are obliged to make a profit if they want to stay in business and must therefore place economic calculation foremost among their concerns. Further, we have to make the assumption that rational allocation of consumer goods by the operation of a price (or market) mechanism is possible even under central planning. There are economists who dispute this, and clearly if they are right the *economic* case for socialism collapses. People who have already got used to a market economy (i.e., an economy in which goods are supplied on demand) are unlikely to prefer an arrangement whereby the satisfaction of needs is dependent on the whims of an uncontrolled bureaucracy. There is a case for saying that in a genuinely free and equal society production would be solely controlled by demand. Theoretically such a state of affairs is envisioned as a goal both by communists and by the most extreme *laissez-faire* liberals. It is therefore quite pointless to argue about it. The division of opinion on this particular issue has to do with the question whether capitalism does or does not approximate to a state of affairs where the consumer is sovereign, in the sense of having a reasonable expectation that his demands will be satisfied. Let it also be clear that the dispute between liberals and socialists on this topic is quite unrelated to what one thinks of the wage relationship. Even if all capitalist property is confiscated by the state, this does not remove the wage relation, since people will have to go on working and be paid in accordance with their performance. There is some confusion on this point, which is why it seems best to deal first with the market mechanism before moving on to the question of social ownership.

Socialists are at a minimum committed to economic planning that goes counter to the operation of an economy in which private firms predominate and profits are distributed among shareholders and managers. A system of this kind necessarily perpetuates the class division between a wealthy minority and a propertyless majority. A capitalist economy, moreover, can only respond to "effective demand" backed by actual purchasing power. It operates for the benefit of paying customers only and does not recognize the existence of other people. In consequence it normally fails to satisfy basic material needs except in a roundabout way that is not to everyone's taste. To put it crudely, the logic of the system entails the production of luxury goods for the few, rather than the provision of food, clothing, and decent housing for the many. This is not due to the bad will or imbecility of those in control: it follows logically from the operation of the market. In an egalitarian community this would not happen, since all customers would have approximately the same purchasing power, but bourgeois society is not egalitarian. The result is that social inequalities are constantly reproduced and even rendered more acute, even though society grows richer and there is some rise in real incomes. The built-in automatism is such that those who start off with material advantages (including advantages in skill, training, and education) secure a disproportionate share of the social product. "The price mechanism rewards people according to the scarcity of the resources (labour and property) that they possess, but it does not itself contain any mechanism for equalising the distribution of scarcities. For justice in distribution we clearly have to summon the forces of the state" (Lewis, 12).

Taken by itself this is a democratic rather than a socialist line of reasoning. The distinction is important, and its neglect leads to some confusion. The systematic correction of built-in social inequalities by appropriate public action is an aspect of what has come to be known as the welfare state. In its usual formulation the "welfare-state" doctrine leaves the wage relationship unaltered. Under optimal conditions, Social Democratic governments based on parliamentary majorities are able to make the welfare state a reality, the classic case being the Scandinavian countries. Under somewhat less favorable circumstances, as in post-1945 Britain, they can still correct the worst inequalities resulting from the unrestricted operation of a capitalist price system. The obvious means to this end are taxation of the rich and the expansion of the public sector (education, health, and housing). However important and beneficial, such arrangements fall short of socialism inasmuch as they do not alter the status of wage- and salary-earners, not even if key industries and public services are nationalized or municipalized. The wage relationship is rooted in the fact that wage- and salary-earners do not own the means of production, i.e., the instruments of labor. If they owned them, they would still have to work, but the profits would no longer go to the owners of capital. Anything that falls short of abolishing the wage relation has no claim to being described as socialism, although it may be a station on the way thereto.

It is sometimes argued that under continuous full employment the status of wage earners loses its degrading character, since employers have to bid for labor in circumstances where the workers (unionized or not) are in a position to dictate terms. But such conditions have never existed anywhere, save for brief and exceptional periods (generally during a war), and even if they were somehow rendered permanent by appropriate monetary management, this would not alter the fact that the profits of the enterprise would still go to the shareholders, who also benefit automatically from the steady march of technical progress. It follows that Socialists (as distinct from Social Democrats) cannot regard full employment and the welfare state as their ultimate goal. Equally they cannot be satisfied with a kind of central planning that vests all authority in the government, notably if the latter is not democratically controlled. Full employment and central planning existed under Hitler and Stalin, the latter having also done away with private ownership in the means of production. But only Fascists and/or Stalinists were satisfied with the resulting state of affairs. Even setting aside the monstrosities associated with these two regimes, the kind of central planning that vests all control in a political bureaucracy is unlikely to be efficient, and it is certain to be destructive of freedom. If liberal *laissez-fairists* had no other competition to face, they could save themselves the trouble of trying to prove that capitalism will in due course make everyone rich and happy. People who have once seen a Stalinist or Fascist regime at work will go to great lengths to avoid having one imposed on them. They will even put up with slumps and unemployment, so long as there is a reasonable chance of getting back to normal. A certain minimal degree of economic planning is after all attainable even under modern corporate capitalism, and the social injustice that goes with the system is preferable to being shot or sent to a labor camp, or at best made to queue endlessly for a capricious supply of inferior goods and services. If socialism were to become permanently identified with the kind of life imposed after 1945 on Eastern Europe, few sane people would want it.

To balance the account it has to be added that while Communists tend to confuse socialism with state ownership, Social Democrats are in the habit of equating it with labor reformism and welfare policies. Both attitudes reflect short-term political options that may be inevitable, given the circumstances, but cannot serve as a suitable definition of traditional socialist aims. These aims may be unattainable, in which case democratic socialism will have to be written off, but it is just as well to be clear as to the meaning of what one is arguing about. The term "socialism" was originally coined for the purpose of designating a society in which the producers own their tools. Since under modern industrial conditions this cannot be done individually (the common error of liberals and anarchists is to believe that private ownership can be restored, whereas in fact it cannot, setting aside consumer goods which by definition are not "instruments of production"), the only reasonable description of socialism is one that centers on common or social ownership. The distinction between state property and social ownership ought to be obvious: the former vests effective control in a political bureaucracy, the latter does not. If one feels in need of a summary definition, that offered by Dickinson in 1939 still seems the best:

> Socialism is an economic organization of society in which the material means of production are owned by the whole community and operated by organs representative of and responsible to the community according to a general economic plan, all members of the community being entitled to benefit from the results of such socialized planned production on the basis of equal rights. (Cited by Smith, 113)

The objection that such a community might be so poor "that life within it might be well-nigh intolerable" (*Ibid.*) is valid in principle, but for practical purposes it has always been assumed that one is talking about an advanced industrial society, not about a return to primitive conditions. It is of course open to individuals to settle for monastic poverty if that is what they want, in which case comparisons with wealthier communities are unlikely to bother them.

If one adopts Dickinson's formulation as a yardstick, one necessarily parts company with Schumpeter, for whom socialism is defined as "an institutional pattern in which the control over means of production and over production itself is vested with a central authority" (*Capitalism, Socialism, and Democracy*, 167). By this standard Pharaonic Egypt and Stalin's Russia were both socialist societies. Schumpeter expressly excludes "guild socialism, syndicalism and other types" (*Ibid.*, 168) on the grounds that "Centralist Socialism seems to me to hold the field so clearly that it would be waste of space to consider other forms." His distinguished contemporary Oskar Lange, viewing the scene some years later from the opposite political pole, agreed substantially that socialism signified state control and central planning. Although he spoke of "social ownership of the principal means of production" (*Political Economy*, 81), he was silent on the difference between state ownership and common ownership. In practice this amounted to equating nationalization with socialization–inevitable in post-1945 Poland and the remainder of Soviet-controlled Eastern Europe, but misleading from the standpoint of socialist theory. The consequent tensions were duly illustrated by the events in Czechoslovakia where the reformers were treated as a potential threat by the Soviet autocracy and its East European satellites because they tried to convert bureaucratic dictation into genuine social control. In practice this meant introducing a measure of democracy in the shape of works councils, so as to counterbalance the hitherto unchecked power of the political bureaucracy in charge of the central planning apparatus. The latter being the mainspring of the state-socialist systems introduced throughout Eastern Europe after 1945, it is hardly surprising that the Czechoslovak experiment in 1968 was dubbed "revisionist," as the rather more successful Yugoslav model had already been stigmatized years earlier.

For all its inadequacy when measured by socialist standards, electorates (if they are consulted) generally prefer modern, controlled, or "post-Keynesian" capitalism to both state ownership on the Soviet model and the *laissez-faire* system which periodically restores its equilibrium by way of gigantic crises and the wholesale waste of human and material resources through mass unemployment. Keynes had no social vision extending beyond the England of his day, but he did have an answer to the problem of unemployment. When accused of wanting to set the unemployed to work digging holes and filling them up again, he pointed out correctly that even if they were paid for doing nothing else, they would spend their wages on food and other necessities, thereby increasing the sum of real incomes. Keynesian economics are morally neutral and can be employed in the service of capitalism, socialism, or anything else. Keynes had the candor to admit this; witness his celebrated argument that socially wasteful investments may be economically useful:

> Ancient Egypt was doubly fortunate, and doubtless owed to this its fabled wealth, in that it possessed *two* activities, namely pyramid-building as well as the search for precious metals, the fruits of which, since they could not serve the needs of man by being consumed, did not stale with abundance. The Middle Ages built cathedrals and sang dirges. Two pyramids, two masses for the dead, are twice as good as one; but not so two railways from London to York. (*General Theory of Employment, Interest and Money*, 131)

This elegant cynicism (a notable feature of the Bloomsbury set and its culture, of which Keynes was the most distinguished ornament) was merely frosting on the cake of economic reasoning. The argument itself was convincing enough, and once it had sunk in the practice of digging holes in the ground (largely for military purposes) was employed whenever growth rates threatened to slacken, or unemployment rose above a level judged politically tolerable. The incidental benefits of the new system were considerable, even taking into account the unsolved problem of inflation. But there was nothing socialist about the motor propelling the machinery. It was still the old competitive nexus based on the investor's profit expectations. The chief difference was that the state now undertook to make up for inadequate investment on the part of capital-owners.

State socialism may be regarded as a perversion of authentic social ownership. State capitalism differs from it principally in that it retains private ownership of the means of production: typically in the form of corporate monopoly. Unlike private capitalism it acts systematically to promote employment, if necessary through the wholesale waste of public funds on armaments and other unproductive forms of expenditure which (unlike public housing) have the advantage of not competing with the private sector.

It avoids the waste of the free market, and it does not permit invest-

> ments to be misplaced in the stage of development or to become obsolete in the stage of saturation. It can direct investments toward ventures which create new demands–Keynes's "pyramids," Tugan-Baranovsky's tower of equipment, a huge defense establishment, or a "New Frontier"–and it may even balance inefficient production units against overproductive units. (Pachter, in Howe, ed., *The Radical Papers,* 41-42)

Although wasteful, the system is superior to "free" capitalism in that its built-in stabilizers enable it to even out the fluctuations of the trade cycle. Like state socialism it works best if there is little or no democratic control, although the formalities of constitutional rule may be preserved. Unlike state socialism it is burdened with the irrationality of having to conceal its planning apparatus behind a phraseology inherited from the age of "pure" market-economy capitalism. It also operates against the public interest by making the great monopolies the final arbiters of the key decisions which are invariably taken behind closed doors. Moreover, for all the rhetoric in which it is typically enveloped, the system functions most effectively if there is a moderate degree of unemployment, so as not to give undue bargaining power to the unions. Alternatively it may take the strongest unions into partnership, at the cost of steady wage-price inflation, the effects of which are mostly felt by the elderly, the unemployed, the unskilled, and the nonunionized sections of the salariat. This is what modern neo-liberalism amounts to in practice, which is why its social achievements rarely match up to the enthusiastic verbiage of its sponsors.

If one abstracts from the rather hollow phrase-mongering that surrounds it, the neo-liberal system is a capitalist economy which retains the market mechanism but employs the "countervailing powers" of state intervention to ensure a rate of growth substantially higher than the normal expansion achieved under a "free" system in which the propertied class retains full control over the economy and the government. Ideally the adoption of the "new economics," by permitting a relatively rapid rate of growth and near-full employment, also makes possible a steady expansion of the social services. In practice this goal is usually sacrificed to other aims, unless political pressures become sufficiently strong to secure some diversion of resources to public sectors such as health and housing. Under Social Democratic rule the balance of power shifts from the side of private enterprise and corporate management to organized labor. This is the justification for describing an economy of this type as "laborist," even though the ownership of the means of production remains wholly or predominantly private. Much of the verbal confusion surrounding the British and Scandinavian variants of this system is due to the habit of equating laborism with socialism. What actually happens under Social Democratic management is a more or less steady expansion of welfare-state services designed to equalize the distribution of incomes. This process may, but need not, be accompanied by the nationalization of a significant sector of the economy.

Conversely, both nationalization and the expansion of social services may occur where Social Democratic control is lacking: witness the record of France and Italy since 1945. The same applies to central planning, which has indeed come to play a more important role in France than in Britain: the main impetus behind it being the long-established Saint-Simonian tradition of the French political and bureaucratic elites. This bias became important in an environment where state intervention to speed economic growth had been rendered respectable by the failure of classical liberalism, the rise of the war-time Resistance movements, and the temporary break-through achieved by the labor movement in 1945. Contrary to popular misconceptions, Keynesian theorizing had nothing whatever to do with it. Neither has it accounted for the superior performance of the French economy, compared to the British, since about 1950. It would be truer to say that the French were favored both by their national tradition and by the fact of not having to bother about the "new economics" (Shonfield, 80 ff.). The upshot has been to place centralized economic planning in the forefront of public debate in France, Italy, Britain, Holland, and Austria, where Communist or Social Democratic pressures were strong. Yet no one would describe the resulting pattern as socialist, save in so far as there has been a growth in the importance of central planning. The system in some respects now departs from the classical model of a society in which state intervention occurs only to facilitate the maximizing of private profit. The government, by enlarging the public sector, may set itself noneconomic goals such as the equalizing of incomes, the financing of public health and housing, or the provision of cultural amenities. But in all essentials the economy still operates in accordance with market criteria, and it does so in the public sector no less than in the private. Budgets must be balanced, investments must be planned in accordance with profit expectations, and human needs for the most part are still satisfied in relation to the "effective demand" of paying customers. In a socialist economy, welfare services would be equally available to all at zero prices, the wage relation would gradually disappear, and claims arising from capital or property would not enter into the reckoning at all. Whatever falls short of such an arrangement is not socialism, even though it may be socially progressive in the sense of substituting social for economic (profit-and-loss) criteria (Pachter, in Howe, *Op. cit.*, 48 ff.).

What has been said so far relates to production and to the social relations arising from the production process. This is the "classical" approach, common to liberals and Marxists alike. Historically, it is the outcome of a situation in which wealth-creation takes precedence over all other considerations, as it must do in a scarcity economy. Today this is still the case in most developed countries (let alone the undeveloped ones), which is why the topic of economic growth tends to be debated in terms of competing capitalist and socialist models. It is also the reason why "Communism" of the Russian variety has become a misnomer for a system of state-enforced capital accumulation. In economically backward countries, capital creation and the efficient utilization of labor are overwhelmingly the most important issues. Even in a fairly advanced industrial society such as Japan it would be eccentric to discuss socialist aims without reference to economic scarcity. The same, more or less, applies to most European countries and to the Americas, North and South. But in a theoretical excursion we are not obliged to confine ourselves to what is politically relevant. We can abstract from short-term considerations and inquire what a socialist economy would look like under conditions where the production process is taken for granted. We assume then that the economy, or the greater part of it, is socialized, i.e., that the principal means of production are publicly owned. On these assumptions, which are of course quite arbitrary, how does socialism work as a system of distribution?

If a socialist system of distribution is defined as one in which consumption is divorced from capital, so that all citizens have an equal claim upon the provision of goods and services, irrespective of property ownership, then clearly no such system is in existence in any industrially advanced country. It is sometimes alleged that such an arrangement corresponds to the higher stage of socialism (described as "communism" by Marx in 1875) when society will have become sufficiently wealthy to permit everyone to draw upon the common pool according to his needs. But a moment's consideration will show that even at the lower stage, where people still have to be paid in accordance with their labor, it is possible to provide a number of basic services on the principle of equal distribution to all, irrespective of ownership or social status or personal merit. Even the most fanatical *laissez-fairist* will grant that criminal justice can and must be so dispensed, and he may also make a grudging acknowledgment to that effect in regard to public transport, sanitation, or the post office. That this is in fact practicable, without throwing any undue strain on the public sector, is taken for granted not only in Europe, but also in Canada, Australia, and New Zealand. If it appears problematic in the United States, the explanation has to do with the political system, not with lack of resources. When it comes to matters such as education, public and private claims may indeed conflict, in that freedom of choice may be endangered by uniformity arising from demands for equal access to all types of learning. Genuine equality is in fact possible only in a homogeneous community where cultural standards do not conflict so violently as to render social intercourse intolerable. This is among the reasons why relatively small and stable countries such as Denmark and Sweden have been pace-setters in education and in the equal provision of social services generally. But the relatively smooth and peaceful integration of hundreds of thousands of immigrants in contemporary Britain, France, and Holland can serve as proof that—up to a point determined by public sentiment—a democracy is capable of digesting an influx of newcomers without having to establish "separate but equal" treatment. If economic conflict as a source of political antagonism is ruled out, as on our assumption it would be, the residual cultural tensions in such a society need not and doubtless will not fall to zero; but they can be held down to a tolerable level.

Let us now consider why even under relatively favorable external conditions—e.g., in Western Europe since the end of World War II—progress in the direction of socialism has been slower than was originally expected. The main reasons can be summarized under two heads: continuing economic scarcity, with the resulting pressure to place rational economic calculations first; and the reluctance of the electorate (including a majority of the industrial working class) to press on more rapidly toward genuine social equality.

As to the first, it needs no great effort of the imagination to conceive a state of affairs where noneconomic considerations have become paramount because all reasonable economic demands have been met or are in process of being satisfied. Unfortunately, such a state of things is not yet sufficiently general, even in the richest and most civilized countries, to remove the topic of economic growth from the agenda. And nothing less will do. Unless and until a majority of the electorate in a democratically governed country is prepared to do without a continuous rise in living standards (as conventionally interpreted) economic considerations will take precedence over social and cultural claims. In such an atmosphere the expansion of welfare services out of taxation is all that can be done by governments dependent on public opinion. Genuine equality—the distribution of the "national dividend" according to criteria of need alone—cannot be attempted if the result is likely to be a significant decline in economic efficiency, a slowing down of growth, loss of export markets to foreign competitors, and a consequent fall in living standards and in the funds available for private and public consumption. For of course international trade enters into the matter. How should it not? If the balance of external trade acts as an economic pace-setter, any decline in relative efficiency will promptly make itself felt in the form of stagnation, unemployment, and other disagreeable consequences. The smaller and more highly specialized a country, the more likely it is to suffer from fluctuations in world trade, unless it manages to keep ahead of its competitors. Success in this field is always uncertain, some countries benefiting from temporary advantages at the expense of others. If we stay with Western Europe after 1945, the outstanding success story along neo-liberal lines has been the expansion of West Germany's external trade, a performance paradoxically helped along by military defeat and the resultant ban on heavy and wasteful arms expenditure. That similar results can be obtained under Social Democratic government is attested to by the case of Sweden, once more a combination of good luck and good management, aided by specialization in the newer industries. One might also cite the corresponding examples of Austria, Denmark, Holland, and Switzerland, where the labor movement has contented itself with being a partner in a rapidly expanding capitalist economy, wage rates rising on an average no faster than output per head, so that prices have been kept relatively stable. Under less favorable circumstances, e.g. in Britain, wages have risen appreciably faster than productivity, thus driving prices up more rapidly than among some of Britain's main competitors. Apart from the inevitable damage to the country's share of world trade (not to mention the stability of its currency), the result has been to associate laborism with inflationary price rises from which people living on fixed incomes are notoriously the chief sufferers. In the political vocabulary of the welfare state, laborism is equated with socialism, so that socialist theory is made to take the blame for the typically capitalist behavior of employers and unions alike. The appropriate moral was drawn in 1966 by an eminent British economist who combined socialist convictions with long-standing adherence to the Keynesian school:

> The proposition that, in an industrial economy, the level of money-wage rates governs the level of prices was an essential element in the analysis of Keynes' *General Theory of Employment, Interest and Money*, published in 1936. The part of his argument which concerned the need for government policy to maintain "a high and stable level of employment" was accepted into the canon of received orthodoxy in this country even before the end of the war in 1945, but the part which concerned wages and prices was resisted much longer. It was easy to predict that if we stumbled into near-full employment with institutions and attitudes unchanged, the balance of power in wage-bargaining would tip in favour of the workers, so that a vicious spiral of wages and prices would become chronic. Yet it took about fifteen years of experience for the point to really sink home. (Robinson, *Economics: An Awkward Corner, 19*)

It seems probable that the British economy had by the 1960's reached an "awkward corner" for historic reasons quite unconnected with the current behavior of employers and unions, but this does not invalidate the theoretical part of the argument: in a capitalist economy, whether or not administered by a Labor government, the attainment of even relatively modest welfare-state goals depends on growth rates which in turn depend, in part at least, on competitiveness in the world market. International trade takes place predominantly among industrially advanced countries and only marginally between them and the "underdeveloped," which is why the loss of their colonies did no economic harm to the West European countries, or to Japan, which was likewise stripped of its colonial possessions in 1945. Since the industrially developed countries outside the Soviet bloc are for the most part governed democratically and since their electorates are predominantly salaried, any advance toward socialization hinges upon the willingness of the labor movement to back long-term planning at the expense of short-range economic gains.

This applies with particular force if reformist rather than socially conservative parties are in political control. It also applies to the hypothetical case of a completely socialized economy. In such an economy the quarrel would be over the distribution of the social dividend as between the state and the producers, with politics resolving themselves into a tug between the central planning bureaucracy and the more or less autonomous works councils representing all those engaged in the production and distribution of goods and services. Needless to say, none of this has any relevance to the backward countries, with their rising populations and stagnant incomes per head, or to the Soviet orbit, where socialism performs the historic function normally associated with the earlier stages of capital accumulation. We are solely concerned with regions which have passed beyond this phase and have become sufficiently rich and productive for something like equality to be attainable. There is no point in debating the question whether wealth should in all circumstances be equitably divided, even if the result is economic stagnation (as it certainly would be in any poor country lacking the necessary capital equipment). Nor is there any need to waste time and energy over frivolities such as the demand that the "consumer society" be abolished. This kind of talk commonly issues from people who do not have to work for a living. The crisis through which the contemporary socialist movement is passing has not been brought about by the corruption of the working class through excessive rise in money incomes or the desire to possess consumer goods. It is due to the unresolved cleavage between short-term and long-term aspirations, the socialist parties having failed to reconcile their ultimate aims with the pressures arising from the normal political process in a democracy where wage-earners have become a majority of the electorate. The gap between socialist rhetoric and laborist performance measures the difficulty of making social equality relevant to people overwhelmingly concerned with simple economic issues: specifically, guaranteed full employment and a steady rise in living standards.

When one says that even in the most highly industrialized countries of the Western world the transition from a "mixed" to a socialist economy still lacks adequate popular support, one is not just saying something about the power of conservative ideology or the relative failure of Social Democratic (or for that matter Communist) parties to expand beyond their traditional base in the industrial working class. One is also saying something about the inherent conflict between two quite different and possibly irreconcilable goals: economic growth and social equality. The former *may* occur under capitalism or socialism alike, but a socialized economy devoted to the aim of keeping up with the fastest growth rates achieved in the capitalist world must give preference to economic rationality at the expense of other considerations. Conversely, if a democracy is to opt voluntarily for a greater degree of social equality than even the best managed capitalist system can permit, the voters may by the same token have to opt for a slowdown in economic growth. A conscious choice to this effect is conceivable, but not very likely in the short run. At their present political and cultural level even the most advanced democracies are unlikely to forego the advantages accruing from rapid technological change, higher productivity, rising money wages–and the inequality that goes with it. If a socialist society is defined as one in which the wage relation has been abolished, the producers placed in control of their tools, and the cleavage between physical and mental labor overcome through an all-round development of the human personality, we are still far from the attainment of such goals.

The inner logic of the production process does indeed favor socialization, inasmuch as the "post-industrial" development of automation gives rise to a new hierarchy of functions no longer measurable by the cruder standards of an earlier epoch. Social conflict assumes new forms, the steady growth of monopoly and the expansion of a bureaucratically controlled public sector driving the private entrepreneur out of business and producing novel confrontations dimly foreshadowed by the strikes and factory occupations of recent years. If theoretical development does not lag too far behind, socialism as a movement may transcend its class origins and come to represent the aspirations of the intelligentsia, as well as those of a working class itself in process of acquiring new skills and higher levels of education and awareness. These hopeful factors must be weighed against the inherent problem of making equality rhyme with the requirements of a culture shaped by the recent speed-up in the rate of technological change. The goal of a classless and conflict-free society is not easily reconciled with the drive toward ever higher levels of economic performance in a competitive world, most of which is still desperately poor. The prospects of socialism in the classical sense are brightest where economic pressures are negligible and people can envisage an egalitarian way of life on the basis of social ownership of the means of production. In this sense the preconditions of a socialist order do not at present exist anywhere. Much of the world is still going through the early phases of the industrial revolution, while the advanced countries are taken up with the attainment of higher living standards. Socialists will find plenty to occupy them during the coming decades, if only because liberalism has disintegrated both as a philosophy and as a way of managing the political system. But if they are honest they will not pretend that the kind of society they would like to see is inscribed in the logic of the immediate future.

Selected Bibliography

1. General and Historical

BERLIN, I., *Karl Marx: His Life and Environment* (London-New York-Toronto: Oxford University Press, 1948, 1963)

BLOOM, S. F., *The World of Nations* (New York: Columbia University Press, 1941)

CARR, E. H., *The Romantic Exiles* (Boston: Beacon Press, 1961; London: Penguin Books, 1968)

———, *Studies in Revolution* (New York: Grosset & Dunlap, 1964)

CARR, R., *Spain 1808-1939* (Oxford: Clarendon Press, 1966; New York: Oxford University Press, 1966)

CARSTEN, F. L., *The Rise of Fascism* (London: B. T. Batsford, 1967; Berkeley, Calif.: University of California Press, 1967)

COLLINS, H., and ABRAMSKY, CH., *Karl Marx and the British Labour Movement* (London: Macmillan, 1965; New York: St. Martin's Press, 1965)

DROZ, J., *Europe Between Revolutions: 1815-1848* (London: Collins, 1967; New York: Harper & Row, 1968)

FOOTMAN, D., *The Primrose Path: A Life of Ferdinand Lassalle* (London: The Cresset Press, 1946)

——, *Red Prelude: A Life of A. I. Zhelyabov* (London: The Cresset Press, 1944, 1968)

GRAY, A., *The Socialist Tradition* (London: Longmans, Green, 1963; New York: Harper & Row, 1968)

GURVITCH, G., *Proudhon. Sa vie, son oeuvre* (Paris: Presses Universitaires, 1965)

HARRISON, R., *Before the Socialists: Studies in Labour and Politics 1861-1881* (London: Routledge & Kegan Paul, 1965; Toronto: University of Toronto Press, 1965)

HERZEN, A., *From the Other Shore* and *The Russian People and Socialism* (London: Weidenfeld & Nicolson, 1956)

——, *My Past and Thoughts,* 6 vols. (London: Chatto & Windus, 1924); rev. ed., 4 vols., with Preface by ISAIAH BERLIN (London: Chatto & Windus, 1968; New York: Knopf, 1968)

——, *Selected Philosophical Works* (Moscow: Foreign Languages Publishing House, 1956)

HOBSBAWM, E. J., *Industry and Empire* (London: Weidenfeld & Nicolson, 1968; New York: Pantheon, 1968)

——, *Labouring Men: Studies in the History of Labour* (London: Weidenfeld & Nicolson, 1964; New York: Basic Books, 1965)

——, *Primitive Rebels* (Manchester: University Press, 1959; New York: Praeger, 1963)

HOROWITZ, I. L., *Radicalism and the Revolt Against Reason* (London: Routledge & Kegan Paul, 1961; Urbana, Ill.: University of Illinois Press, 1968)

JACKSON, J. HAMPDEN, *Marx, Proudhon and European Socialism* (New York: Macmillan, 1962; London: English Universities Press, 1964)

JELLINEK, F., *The Paris Commune of 1871* (New York: Grosset & Dunlap, 1965)

JOLL, J., *The Anarchists* (Boston-Toronto: Little, Brown, 1964)

——, *The Second International 1889-1914* (London: Weidenfeld & Nicolson, 1955; New York: Harper & Row, 1965)

KENDALL, W., *The Revolutionary Movement in Britain 1900-21* (London: Weidenfeld & Nicolson, 1969)

LEFRANC, G., *Jaurès et le socialisme des intellectuels* (Paris: Aubier-Montaigne, 1968)

LIGOU, D., *Histoire du socialisme en France 1871-1961* (Paris: Presses Universitaires, 1962)

MAITRON, J., *Histoire du mouvement anarchiste en France (1880-1914)*, 2d rev. ed. (Paris: Société Universitaire d'Editions et de Librairie, 1955)

MALIA, M., *Alexander Herzen and the Birth of Russian Socialism* (Cambridge, Mass.: Harvard University Press, 1961)

MANUEL, F. E., *The Prophets of Paris* (New York: Harper & Row, 1965)

MEHRING, F., *Karl Marx: The Story of His Life* (London: Allen & Unwin, 1951; Ann Arbor, Mich.: University of Michigan Press, 1962)

NETTL, J. P., *Rosa Luxemburg* (London-New York-Toronto: Oxford University Press, 1966)

NICOLAEVSKY, B. and MAENCHEN-HELFEN, O., *Karl Marx: Man and Fighter* (London: Methuen, 1936)

NOLTE, E., *Three Faces of Fascism* (New York-Chicago-San Francisco: Holt Rinehart & Winston, 1966)

PLAMENATZ, J., *The Revolutionary Movement in France 1815-71* (London-New York-Toronto: Longmans, Green, 1952)

POLANYI, K., *The Great Transformation* (Boston: Beacon Press, 1957)

PROUDHON, P. J., *Justice et Liberté,* ed. JACQUES MUGLIONI (Paris: Presses Universitaires, 1962)

———, *Oeuvres choisies,* ed. JEAN BANCAL (Paris: Gallimard, 1967)

ROSENBERG, A., *Democracy and Socialism* (Boston: Beacon Press, 1965)

———, *A History of Bolshevism* (London: Oxford University Press, 1934; New York: Russell & Russell, 1934)

SOREL, G., *Reflections on Violence,* new edn. (Glencoe, Ill: Free Press, 1950)

SPITZER, A. B., *The Revolutionary Theories of Louis Auguste Blanqui* (New York: Columbia University Press, 1957)

TALMON, J. L., *The Origins of Totalitarian Democracy* (London: Secker & Warburg, 1952; New York: Praeger, 1961)

———, *Political Messianism: The Romantic Phase* (London: Secker & Warburg, 1960; New York: Praeger, 1961)

THOMPSON, E. P., *The Making of the English Working Class* (London: Victor Gollancz, 1964; New York: Pantheon, 1964)

TSUZUKI, C., *H. M. Hyndman and British Socialism* (New York-London: Oxford University Press, 1961)

———, *The Life of Eleanor Marx 1855-1898: A Socialist Tragedy* (Oxford: Clarendon Press, 1967; New York: Oxford University Press, 1967)

WILLARD, C., *Les Guesdistes: Le mouvement socialiste en France (1893-1905)* (Paris: Editions Sociales, 1965)

WILLIAMS, R., *Culture and Society 1780-1950* (London: Penguin Books, 1961)

———, *The Long Revolution* (London: Chatto & Windus, 1961; Penguin Books, 1965)

WOODCOCK, G., *Anarchism* (Cleveland, Ohio: World, 1962; London: Penguin Books, 1963)

2. Theoretical

ADAMS, H. P., *Karl Marx in his Earlier Writings* (New York: Russell & Russell, 1940; London: Frank Cass, 1965)

AVINERI, S., ed., *Karl Marx on Colonialism and Modernization: His Dispatches and Other Writings on China, India, Mexico, the Middle East and North Africa* (New York: Doubleday, 1968)

———, *The Social and Political Thought of Karl Marx* (New York-Cambridge, England: Cambridge University Press, 1968)

BORKENAU, F., *Pareto* (London: Chapman & Hall, 1936)

BOTTOMORE, T. B., *Elites and Society* (London: C. A. Watts, 1964; New York: Basic Books, 1965)

———, *Karl Marx—Early Writings* (London-New York-Toronto: McGraw-Hill, 1964)

BOTTOMORE, T. B., and RUBEL, M., eds., *Karl Marx—Selected Writings in Sociology and Social Philosophy* (London-New York-Toronto: McGraw-Hill, 1964)

CARRÈRE D'ENCAUSSE, H., and SCHRAM, S., *Marxism and Asia* (London: Allen Lane, 1969)

CAUTE, D., ed., *Essential Writings of Karl Marx* (London: Panther Books, 1967; New York: Macmillan, 1968)

DOBB, M., *Papers on Capitalism, Development and Planning* (London: Routledge & Kegan Paul, 1967)

DUNN, J., *The Political Thought of John Locke* (Cambridge, England: Cambridge University Press, 1969)

FREEDMAN, R., ed., *Marx on Economics* (New York: Harcourt, 1961; London: Penguin Books, 1962)

GALBRAITH, J. K., *The Affluent Society* (London: Hamish Hamilton, 1958; Boston: Houghton Mifflin, 1958)

———, *The New Industrial State* (London: Hamish Hamilton, 1967; Boston: Houghton Mifflin, 1967)

HARRIS, N., *Beliefs in Society: The Problem of Ideology* (London: C. A. Watts, 1968; New York: International Publications Service, 1968)

HEILBRONER, R. L., *The Worldly Philosophers* (New York: Simon & Schuster, 1953, 1961)

HENDERSON, W. O., ed., *Engels—Selected Writings* (Baltimore, Md.-London, Penguin Books, 1967)

HOOK, S., *From Hegel to Marx,* 2d ed. (Ann Arbor, Mich.: University of Michigan Press, 1962)

HOWE, I., ed., *The Radical Papers* (New York: Doubleday, 1966)

JORDAN, Z. A., *The Evolution of Dialectical Materialism* (New York: St. Martin's Press, 1967)

KAMENKA, E., *The Ethical Foundations of Marxism* (London: Routledge & Kegan Paul, 1962; New York: Praeger, 1962)

KORSCH, K., *Karl Marx* (New York: Russell & Russell, 1963)

LANGE, O., *Political Economy, Vol. I, General Problems* (New York: Macmillan, 1963)

LANGE, O., and TAYLOR, F. M., *On the Economic Theory of Socialism* (New York-Toronto-London: McGraw-Hill, 1964)

LEFF, G., *The Tyranny of Concepts* (London: Merlin Press, 1961)

LEWIS, W. A., *The Principles of Economic Planning* (London: Dennis Dobson, 1949)

LICHTHEIM, G., *Marxism: An Historical and Critical Study,* 2d ed. (New York: Praeger, 1965; London: Routledge & Kegan Paul, 1967)

LUXEMBURG, R., *The Accumulation of Capital,* with an Introduction by JOAN ROBINSON (London: Routledge & Kegan Paul, 1951; New York: Monthly Review Press, 1964)

MACINTYRE, A., *A Short History of Ethics* (New York: Macmillan, 1966)

MACRAE, D. G., *Ideology and Society* (London-Melbourne-Toronto: Heinemann, 1961; Glencoe, Ill.: Free Press, 1961)

MANNING, D. J., *The Mind of Jeremy Bentham* (London: Longmans, Green, 1968; New York: Barnes & Noble, 1968)

MARX, K., *Capital*, Vol. I (London: Allen & Unwin, 1946). A reprint of the English translation first published in London in 1887.

———, *The German Ideology* (London: Lawrence & Wishart, 1965)

———, *Pre-Capitalist Economic Formations* (London: Lawrence & Wishart, 1964)

MARX, K., and ENGELS, F., *Selected Correspondence* (London: Lawrence & Wishart, 1965)

———, *Selected Works,* in one volume (London: Lawrence & Wishart, 1968)

MEEK, R. L., *Economics and Ideology. And Other Essays* (London: Chapman & Hall, 1967; New York: Barnes & Noble, 1967)

———, *Studies in the Labour Theory of Value* (London: Lawrence & Wishart, 1956)

MEISEL, J. H., *The Myth of the Ruling Class: Gaetano Mosca and the "Elite"* (Ann Arbor, Mich.: University of Michigan Press, 1958, 1962)

MOORE, S., *The Critique of Capitalist Democracy* (New York: Paine-Whitman, 1957)

———, *Three Tactics. The Background in Marx* (New York: Monthly Review Press, 1963)

MYRDAL, G., *Beyond the Welfare State* (New Haven, Conn.: Yale University Press, 1960)

NEUMANN, F., *The Democratic and the Authoritarian State,* ed. and with a Preface by H. MARCUSE (Glencoe, Ill.: Free Press, 1957)

OSSOWSKI, S., *Class Structure in the Social Consciousness* (London: Routledge & Kegan Paul, 1963; Glencoe, Ill.: Free Press, 1963)

ROBINSON, J., *Economic Philosophy* (London: Watts, 1962; Penguin Books, 1966; Chicago: Aldine, 1962)

———, *Economics: An Awkward Corner* (London: Allen & Unwin, 1966; New York: Pantheon, 1968)

———, *An Essay on Marxian Economics,* 2d ed. (New York: St. Martin's Press, 1966)

RUNCIMAN, W. G., *Social Science and Political Theory* (New York-Cambridge, England: Cambridge University Press, 1963)

SCHUMPETER, E. B., ed., *Ten Great Economists: From Marx to Keynes* (New York: Oxford University Press, 1965)

SCHUMPETER, J., *Capitalism, Socialism, and Democracy* (London: Allen & Unwin, 1950; New York: Harper, 1950)

———, *History of Economic Analysis* (New York: Oxford University Press, 1954)

SIEVERS, A. M., *Revolution, Evolution, and the Economic Order* (Englewood Cliffs, N.J.: Prentice-Hall, 1962)

SMITH, H., *The Economics of Socialism Reconsidered* (London-New York-Toronto: Oxford University Press, 1962)

SWEEZY, P., *The Theory of Capitalist Development: Principles of Marxian Political Economy* (New York: Oxford University Press, 1942; London: Dennis Dobson, 1946, 1949)

ZEITLIN, I. M., *Marxism: A Re-Examination* (Princeton, N.J.: Van Nostrand, 1967)

3. Western Socialism

ANDERSON, P., and BLACKBURN, R., *Towards Socialism* (London: New Left Review, 1965; Ithaca, N.Y.: Cornell University Press, 1966)

BALOGH, T., *The Economics of Poverty* (London: Weidenfeld & Nicolson, 1966; New York: Macmillan, 1967)

BARRATT BROWN, M., *After Imperialism* (London: Heinemann, 1963)

BEER, M., *A History of British Socialism,* 2 vols. (London: Allen & Unwin, 1953; New York: Humanities Press, 1953)

BELL, D., *Marxian Socialism in the United States* (Princeton, N.J.: Princeton University Press, 1967)

———, *Work and Its Discontents* (Boston: Beacon Press, 1956)

BERNSTEIN, E., *Evolutionary Socialism* (New York: Schocken Books, 1961)

BRAUNTHAL, J., *History of the International,* Vol. I: 1864-1914; Vol. II: 1914-1943 (London: Thomas Nelson & Sons, 1966, 1967; New York: Praeger, 1967)

BRENAN, G., *The Spanish Labyrinth* (New York-Cambridge, England: Cambridge University Press, 1967)

BRIGGS, A., ed., *Chartist Studies* (London: Macmillan, 1959; New York: St. Martin's Press, 1960)

———, *Victorian People* (London: Odhams Press, 1954; Penguin Books, 1965; Chicago: University of Chicago Press, 1955)

COLE, G. D. H., *Essays in Social Theory* (London: Oldbourne Book Co., 1962)

COLE, G. D. H., and FILSON, A. W., *British Working Class Movements. Select Documents 1789-1875* (London: Macmillan, 1965; New York: St. Martin's Press, 1965)

COLE, M., *The Story of Fabian Socialism* (London: Heinemann, 1961; Mercury Books, 1963; Stanford, Calif.: Stanford University Press, 1961; New York: Science Editions, 1964)

CROSLAND, C. A. R., *The Future of Socialism* (London: Cape, 1956; New York: Macmillan, 1957)

DICKINSON, H. D., *The Economics of Socialism* (London: Oxford University Press, 1939)

Documents of the First International. 1864-1866 (London: Lawrence & Wishart, 1964)

DODGE, P., *Beyond Marxism: The Faith and Works of Hendrik de Man* (The Hague: Martinus Nijhoff, 1966)

DROZ, J., *Le Socialisme démocratique 1864-1960* (Paris: Armand Colin, 1966)

Fabian Society, *Fabian Essays 1889* (London: Allen & Unwin, 1950)

GAY, P., *The Dilemma of Democratic Socialism* (New York: Columbia University Press, 1952)

GLASS, S. T., *The Responsible Society. The Ideas of the English Guild Socialists* (London: Longmans, Green, 1966; New York: Barnes & Noble, 1966)

LANDAUER, C., *European Socialism: A History of Ideas and Movements,* 2 vols. (Berkeley and Los Angeles: University of California Press, 1959)

LIEBKNECHT, W., *Briefwechsel mit Karl Marx und Friedrich Engels* (The Hague: Mouton & Co., 1963)

MCBRIAR, A. M., *Fabian Socialism and English Politics 1884-1918* (New York-Cambridge, England: Cambridge University Press, 1962, 1966)

MORRIS, W., *Selected Writings*, ed. ASA BRIGGS (London: Penguin Books, 1962)

PEASE, E. R., *The History of the Fabian Society,* 3d ed. (London: Frank Cass, 1963; New York: Barnes & Noble, 1963)

PELLING, H., *America and the British Left: From Bright to Bevan* (London: Adam and Charles Black, 1956; New York: New York University Press, 1957)

———, *The Challenge of Socialism* (London: Adam and Charles Black, 1954; New York: Barnes & Noble, 1954)

———, *The Origins of the Labour Party 1880-1900* (Oxford: Clarendon Press, 1965, 1966; New York: Oxford University Press, 1965)

———, *A Short History of the Labour Party* (London: Macmillan, 1961; New York: St. Martin's Press, 1961)

PERROT, M., and KRIEGEL, A., *Le Socialisme français et le pouvoir* (Paris: Etudes et Documentation Internationale, 1966)

PHILIP, A., *Les Socialistes* (Paris: Editions du Seuil, 1967)
ROTH, G., *The Social Democrats in Imperial Germany* (Totawa, N.J.: Bedminster Press, 1963)
SCHORSKE, C. E., *German Social Democracy 1905-1917* (Cambridge, Mass.: Harvard University Press, 1955; New York: Science Editions, 1965)
SEMMEL, B., *Imperialism and Social Reform* (London: Allen & Unwin, 1960; New York: Hillary House, 1960)
SHONFIELD, A., *Modern Capitalism* (London-New York-Toronto: Oxford University Press, 1965)
STRACHEY, J., *Contemporary Capitalism* (London: Victor Gollancz, 1956; New York: Random House, 1956)
——, *The End of Empire* (London: Victor Gollancz, 1959; New York: Praeger, 1964)
TAWNEY, R. H., *The Acquisitive Society* (New York: Harcourt, Brace, 1946; London: Collins, 1961)
——, *The Radical Tradition* (London: Allen & Unwin, 1964; Pelican Books, 1966; New York: Pantheon, 1964)
WORSLEY, P., *The Third World* (Chicago: University of Chicago Press, 1964)

4. Communism

AVRICH, P., *The Russian Anarchists* (Princeton, N.J.: Princeton University Press, 1967)
BAKUNIN, M., *Gesammelte Werke*, 3 vols. (Berlin: 1921-24)
——, *Oeuvres*, 6 vols. (Paris: 1895-1913)
BALABANOFF, A., *Impressions of Lenin* (Ann Arbor, Mich.: University of Michigan Press, 1964)
BARON, S., *Plekhanov: The Father of Russian Marxism* (Stanford, Calif.: Stanford University Press, 1963)
BERDYAEV, N., *The Origin of Russian Communism* (Ann Arbor, Mich.: University of Michigan Press, 1960, 1964)
BLACKSTOCK, P. W., and HOSELITZ, B. F., eds., *Karl Marx and Friedrich Engels: The Russian Menace to Europe* (London: Allen & Unwin, 1953)

BORKENAU, F., *The Communist International* (London: Faber & Faber, 1938)

———, *The Spanish Cockpit* (London: Faber & Faber, 1937; Ann Arbor, Mich.: University of Michigan Press, 1963)

BROIDO, E., *Memoirs of a Revolutionary* (London-New York-Toronto: Oxford University Press, 1967)

BRZEZINSKI, Z. K., *The Soviet Bloc: Unity and Conflict* (New York: Praeger, 1961)

BUKHARIN, N., *The ABC of Communism* (Ann Arbor, Mich.: University of Michigan Press, 1966)

CAMMETT, J. M., *Antonio Gramsci and the Origins of Italian Communism* (Stanford, Calif.: Stanford University Press, 1967)

CHERNYSHEVSKY, N. G., *Selected Philosophical Essays* (Moscow: Foreign Languages Publishing House, 1953)

CONQUEST, R., *The Great Terror: Stalin's Purge of the Thirties* (London: Macmillan, 1968; New York: Macmillan, 1969)

DEUTSCHER, I., *Stalin: A Political Biography* (London-New York-Toronto: Oxford University Press, 1949, 1967)

———, *The Unfinished Revolution: Russia 1917-1967* (New York: Oxford University Press, 1967)

DJILAS, M., *Conversations with Stalin* (London: Rupert Hart-Davis, 1962; New York: Harcourt, Brace & World, 1962)

———, *The New Class* (London: Thames & Hudson, 1957; New York: Praeger, 1957)

DRACHKOVITCH, M., ed., *The Revolutionary Internationals, 1864-1943* (Stanford, Calif.: Stanford University Press, 1966)

DRAPER, TH., *American Communism and Soviet Russia* (New York: Viking, 1960)

———, *The Roots of American Communism* (New York: Viking, 1957)

GETZLER, I., *Martov: A Political Biography of a Russian Social Democrat* (Cambridge, England: Cambridge University Press, 1967)

GRAMSCI, A., *The Modern Prince and Other Writings* (New York: International Publishers, 1959; London: Lawrence & Wishart, 1967)

HAIMSON, L. H., *The Russian Marxists and the Origins of Bolshevism* (Cambridge, Mass.: Harvard University Press, 1955)

HUDSON, G., *Fifty Years of Communism* (London: C. A. Watts, 1968; New York: Basic Books, 1968)

KEEP, J. L. H., *The Rise of Social Democracy in Russia* (Oxford: Clarendon Press, 1963; New York: Oxford University Press, 1963)

KINDERSLEY, R., *The First Russian Revisionists: A Study of "Legal Marxism" in Russia* (Oxford: Clarendon Press, 1962; New York: Oxford University Press, 1962)

KLATT, W., ed., *The Chinese Model* (Hong Kong: University Press, 1965)

KRIEGEL, A., *Les Communistes français* (Paris: Editions du Seuil, 1968)

LABEDZ, L., ed., *Revisionism: Essays in the History of Marxist Ideas* (New York: Praeger, 1962)

LAMPERT, E., *Sons Against Fathers. Studies in Russian Radicalism and Revolution* (Oxford: Clarendon Press, 1965; New York: Oxford University Press, 1965)

LENIN, V. I., *Selected Works,* 3 vols. (Moscow: Progress Publishers, 1967)

MAO TSE-TUNG, *Selected Readings* (Peking: Foreign Languages Press, 1967)

MARCUSE, H., *Soviet Marxism* (New York: Columbia University Press, 1958)

MAYNARD, J., *The Russian Peasant And Other Studies* (London: VICTOR GOLLANCZ, 1942; New York: Macmillan, 1962)

NETTL, J. P., *The Soviet Achievement* (London: Thames & Hudson, 1967; New York: Harcourt, Brace & World, 1968)

NORTH, R. C., *Moscow and Chinese Communists* (Stanford, Calif.: Stanford University Press, 1953, 1963, 1965)

NOVE, A., *An Economic History of the U.S.S.R.* (London: Allen Lane, 1969)

PLEKHANOV, G., *Selected Philosophical Works* (Moscow: Foreign Languages Publishing House, n.d.; London: Lawrence & Wishart, 1961)

SCHAPIRO, L., *The Communist Party of the Soviet Union* (London: Eyre & Spottiswoode, 1960; New York: Random House, 1960)

———, ed., *Lenin: The Man, The Theoretician, The Leader* (New York: Praeger, 1967)

———, ed., *The U.S.S.R. and the Future* (New York: Praeger, 1963)

SCHRAM, S., *Mao Tse-tung* (London: Penguin Books, 1967; New York: Simon & Schuster, 1967)

———, *The Political Thought of Mao Tse-tung* (New York: Praeger, 1963)

SETON-WATSON, H., *The Russian Empire, 1801-1917* (Oxford: Clarendon Press, 1967; New York: Oxford University Press, 1967)

STALIN, J., *Problems of Leninism* (Moscow: Foreign Languages Publishing House, 1947)

SUKHANOV, N. N., *The Russian Revolution 1917* (London-New York-Toronto: Oxford University Press, 1955)

TARROW, S. G., *Peasant Communism in Southern Italy* (New Haven: Yale University Press, 1967)

THOMAS, H., *The Spanish Civil War* (New York: Harper & Row, 1963)

TROTSKY, L., *Basic Writings,* I. HOWE, ed. (New York: Random House, 1963)

———, *The History of the Russian Revolution* (Ann Arbor, Mich.: University of Michigan Press, 1957, 1960)

———, *My Life* (New York: Grosset & Dunlap, 1960)

———, *Stalin* (New York Harper, 1941; 2d ed., London: McGibbon & Kee, 1968)

ULAM, A. B., *Expansion and Coexistence: The History of Soviet Foreign Policy 1917-1967* (New York: Praeger, 1968)

VALENTINOV, N., *Encounters with Lenin* (London-New York-Toronto: Oxford University Press, 1968)

VELIZ, C., ed., *The Politics of Conformity in Latin America* (London-New York-Toronto: Oxford University Press, 1967)

VENTURI, F., *Roots of Revolution* (London: Weidenfeld & Nicolson, 1960; New York: Knopf, 1960)

WALICKI, A., *The Controversy over Capitalism: Studies in the Social Philosophy of the Russian Populists* (Oxford: Clarendon Press, 1969)

WEBER, H., ed., *Der deutsche Kommunismus. Dokumente* (Berlin-Cologne: Kiepenheuer & Witsch, 1963, 1964)

WOHL, R., *French Communism in the Making. 1914-1924* (Stanford, Calif.: Stanford University Press, 1966)

WOLFE, B., *Three Who Made a Revolution: A Biographical History* (New York: Dial Press, 1948, 1964)

Index

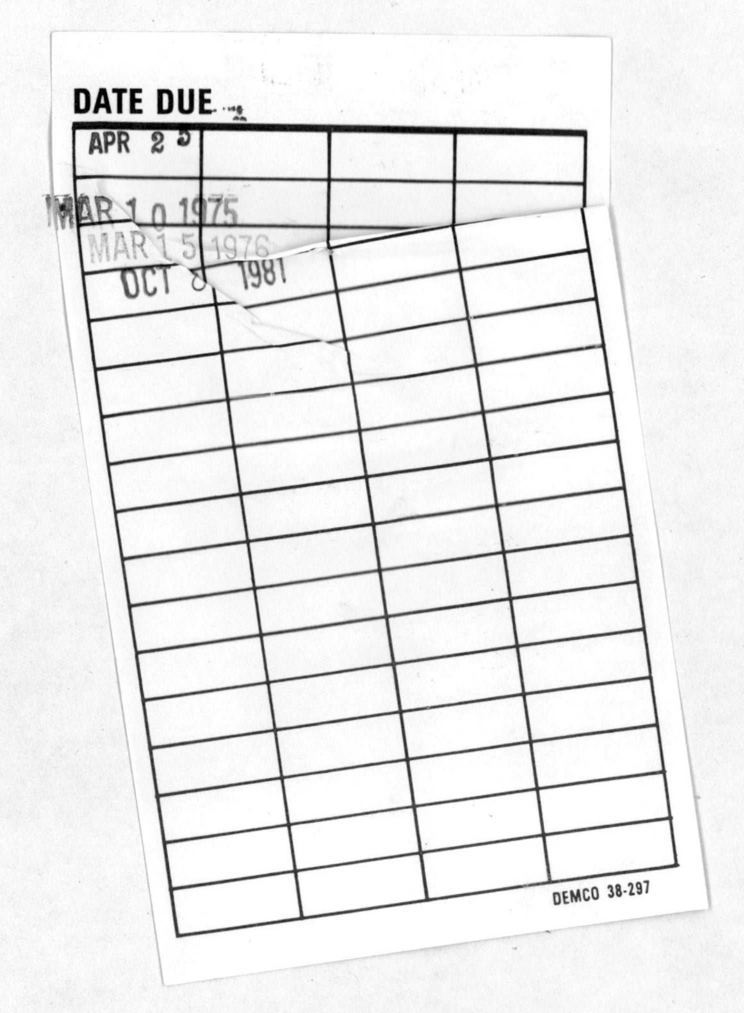
DATE DUE
APR 2 5
MAR 1 0 1975
MAR 1 5 1976
OCT 8 1981
DEMCO 38-297